Introduction to Financial Compliance:

Consumer Financial Services Regulation

Contributing Author,

Morgan Clemons

DURY CONSULTING

www.duryconsulting.com

PREFACE

This text is intended for those with an interest in consumer financial services regulation and the representation of traditional and non-traditional financial services providers.

This text provides historical context for the current state of consumer financial services regulation and policy. In addition to a variety of cases and inclusion of regulations, the regulatory powers of the Consumer Financial Protection Bureau are considered. The text also includes discussion questions and sample consumer complaints throughout to help engage the reader in both policy and real-world context.

While consumer financial services regulations apply to a variety of transactions, services, and products, this text focuses on consumer financial services related to extending credit. More specifically, this text focuses on consumer financial services regulations with provisions applicable to closed-end credit. The text is not exhaustive and is intended to be supplemented by articles and other sources. The text is progressive; each chapter is intended to build on the previous chapters. Part I provides introductory material, including a discussion of the history of financial services, different types of financial institutions, and different types of financial services. In addition, Part I introduces themes interwoven throughout the text to consider periodically whether regulations are meeting intended objectives as well as to evaluate public policy considerations. Part II provides introductory material concerning the state of financial services regulation following the 2008 financial crisis, namely the role of the Consumer Financial Protection Bureau and its rulemaking, supervision and enforcement powers. The introductory information in Parts I and II is essential to understanding terms and references in later Parts that focus on specific laws and regulations.

Parts III-VIII focus on federal consumer laws and rules. The discussion of the laws and rules is in no way exhaustive of all permissible consumer protections. In fact, the laws and rules referenced may be reduced and intentionally edited to avoid very special circumstances or nuances to the law. The text is intended to serve as an introduction to financial services compliance. As such, limitations, exceptions, and unique provisions may be precluded from inclusion unless relevant to the basic discussion.

Each Part is organized into three chapters. The "Law and Rules" chapters provide a roadmap for the current laws and rules that serve to protect consumers. The Laws and Rules chapters also provide some historical context for the laws and rules and, where appropriate, public policy considerations. The Laws and Rules chapters create a starting point for basic understanding of consumer protection scenarios contemplated by the laws, describes the laws in detail, and focuses on a discussion of express laws and implementing regulations intended to clarify the laws. The Enforcement chapters detail the administrative enforcement and civil liability actions that are available to regulators and to individual consumers for students to glean a clear understanding of potential consequences of violations. The enforcement chapters do not reference class actions nor attorneys' fees. Class actions are beyond the scope of the introductory text and may require additional discussion. However, some cases included within the text reference class actions. In addition, the Enforcement chapters delineate what the law or rule permits regarding the powers but also encourages building a connection to the Consumer Financial Protection Bureau's general enforcement powers as expressed in Part II. Finally, the Interpretation chapters include specific case law interpreting select aspects of the laws and rules. The Interpretation chapters are intended to highlight sources of contention frequently recurring in the laws or rules, illustrate common challenges, and represent the current state of consumer financial services regulation.

The text has recurring themes including, the "Five Ws." Students should conclude each of Parts III-VIII with a clear understanding of (1) who is regulated under the law and corresponding rules/regulations, (2) who is protected under the law and corresponding rules/regulations, (3) what is the protection, (4) when is the protection applicable, and (5) why does the protection exist. Students should develop the capacity to articulate what type of law or rule is at issue and to what extent the law or rule serves its intended purpose. In order to assist the students with applying the laws and rules in context and better grasping concepts, the text concludes with "practice problems." The practice problems permit students to apply the laws and rules to a specified set of facts. Students should be able (1) to identify existing relevant facts, (2) to identify facts unknown or needed for a specified outcome, and (3) to analyze the "test" established for each law or rule.

About the Author

Morgan Clemons is an attorney in Atlanta, Georgia experienced in representing financial institutions with their regulatory compliance matters. She has experience working with start-up online lenders, money service businesses, community banks, and mortgage companies. She focuses her practice on representing financial institutions on matters related to consumer protection issues, including advising institutions in connection with supervisory examinations, investigations, and enforcement actions related to the Fair Debt Collection Practices Act, the Fair Credit Reporting Act, the Equal Credit Opportunity Act, the Secure and Fair Enforcement for Mortgage Licensing Act, Truth in Lending Act, and Regulation P, which governs the treatment of nonpublic personal information about consumers by financial institutions. She is experienced in reviewing examination findings and negotiating administrative action settlements for national lenders and money service businesses.

She has experience drafting and filing no action letters and requests for interpretive guidance on behalf of payments companies, advising mortgage companies and marketplace lenders on licensing as well as ongoing reporting and record-keeping requirements, and assisting retail banks with compliance issues.

She has drafted language implementing key changes to money service business laws to update terms and account for emerging business models. She has served on national committees as a subject matter expert and has been consulted for expert testimony in connection with litigation preparation.

Ms. Clemons has published articles in journals and industry publications. Prior to representing financial institutions in private practice, Ms. Clemons worked for a state regulatory agency. She is an adjunct professor at Emory University School of Law. Ms. Clemons is a graduate of Duke University School of Law.

This page intentionally left blank.

Table of Contents

TABLE OF FIGURES

I. FINANCIAL SERVICES

A. HISTORY

The United States has had long-lasting conflicts among different factions' views on money, banking, and regulations. Amidst opposition, including from statesman Thomas Jefferson, the first national bank was established in 1791. Thereafter, the bank essentially "expired" as its charter was not renewed in 1811. During this time individual state banks were also established in the new country. These state banks printed their own, individual currency. As a result, "money" was not standardized but rather redeemable potentially only by the issuing bank.

The second national bank was established in 1816. The second bank ended in 1836. During this time national and state banks co-existed, but the ability of financial institutions to print their own monies proved challenging in historical context, especially considering the factions of those in favor of a national bank and those against a national bank.

Following the closing of the second national bank, various financial panics and bank "runs" occurred. During this time, if depositors placed funds within a bank and learned, by whatever means, that the deposits were in jeopardy, the depositors had reason to withdraw their funds. At this time, with a large number of depositors demanding withdrawal of their funds, this may cause a bank to close if the bank is unable to return funds to depositors on demand. In order to meet the obligation of returning funds to depositors, a depository institution may, essentially, sell assets at a discount to access cash to provide to depositors demanding return of funds. However, once more depositors learn, by whatever means, that the bank is in financial trouble and/or is selling assets at a discount, these bank actions may cause remaining depositors to have less confidence in their access to their deposits. As a result of this diminished confidence, these remaining depositors may also demand return of their deposits. If the bank is not able to meet the continued demands for return of deposits, this may have caused the bank to fail, and any remaining depositors will have lost remaining funds.

The National Banking Act created a national currency and "required national banks to hold reserves—i.e. a percentage of high quality, liquid assets that can be sold to pay off customer deposits if they are redeemed."[1] Further, the Federal Reserve Act came about in 1914. As described above, at times of panics and bank runs, banks had limited opportunity to respond timely to demands for deposits. For example, a bank may have made sound financial decisions but was experiencing liquidity issues—a need for access to cash.

---

[1] MICHAEL S. BARR, HOWELL E. JACKSON, & MARGARET E. TAHYAR, FINANCIAL REGULATION: LAW AND POLICY 40 (Robert C. Clark et al. eds., 1st ed. 2016).

1A How could the bank meet depositor demand for access to cash?

With the creation of the Federal Reserve, the Federal Reserve could serve as a lender to banks and could increase the money supply by putting more money into circulation.

The Banking Act of 1933 established the Federal Deposit Insurance Corporation ("FDIC"). The FDIC helped to restore depositor confidence to help reduce dramatically bank runs. The FDIC insured, up to a certain amount, the deposits of consumers held by participating banks. In other words, if the bank failed or otherwise experienced trouble, a depositor could have confidence that his or her deposits would be redeemable up to the insured amount.

These evolving regulatory changes are easily related to money, policy, the economy, and the U.S. financial system. Specifically, these changes were primarily at the institution level rather than direct changes to the relationship between consumers and financial services or products. What themes can be discerned concerning the development of *consumer* financial services specifically? In other words, thus far, pre-World War II financial services reforms have been referenced. How have consumer financial services evolved post-World War II? Andrea Ryan, Gunnar Trumbull, and Peter Tufano explain in the article, *A Brief Postwar History of U.S. Consumer Finance*, that:

> An examination of consumer decisions, changes in regulation, and business practices identifies four major themes that characterized the consumer-finance sector: innovation that increased the choices available to consumers; enhanced access in the form of consumers' broadening participation in financial activities; do-it-yourself consumer finance, which both allowed and forced consumers to take greater responsibility for their own financial lives; and a resultant increase in household risk taking.[2]

Post-World War II, there occurred an expansion in consumer financial services available as well as an increasing push toward consumer access and choice. Specifically,

> [C]onsumers were not only allowed to make financial choices, but were also frequently forced to make financial choices. Through revolving credit and new flexible forms of mortgages, consumers could fashion their own repayment plans. Rather than just hold cash in banks, they could choose from a variety of money-market mutual funds. Rather than work with a full-service broker, they could use online discount brokerages to trade stocks and bonds at will. Rather than getting a fixed pension, workers were allowed— and were mostly required—to make their own retirement decisions as part of tax- exempt, personal retirement funds. Rather than sit on previously illiquid assets, like

---

[2] Andrea Ryan, Gunnar Trumbull, & Peter Tufano, *A Brief Postwar History of U.S. Consumer Finance*, 85 Bus. Hist. Rev. 459, 461 (2011).

pensions and houses, individuals could monetize these holdings by borrowing against retirement funds or home equity.[3]

As a result of this increased access to financial services and autonomy in decision-making, various concerns began to develop related to fairness, duties, equality, and outcomes. Some questions were posed, that remain unanswered definitively today and serve as the dividing line between warring factions in the modern U.S. tasked with consumer protection, freedom of choice, and economic stability: Are consumers well-suited to access and to make financial services decisions? Is consumer decision-making rational and/or beneficial to the consumer?

In 2010, the Dodd-Frank Wall Street Reform and Consumer Protection Act (hereinafter "the Dodd-Frank Act" or "Dodd-Frank") was signed into law by President Barack Obama, following the 2008 financial crisis. The Dodd-Frank Act established the Consumer Financial Protection Bureau (hereinafter "CFPB"), a bureau with the mandate of consumer financial protection, as the name suggests. Part ID: Types of Regulation, and Part II: The Consumer Financial Protection Bureau, discuss the CFPB, including the extent to which its authority is unlike any other regulatory body.

It may perhaps be discernable that the passage of the National Banking Act, the Federal Reserve Act, the creation of the Federal Deposit Insurance Corporation, and the passage of Dodd-Frank (and corresponding creation of the CFPB) followed different types of financial crises. This legislation/regulation can perhaps be described as reactive rather than proactive in historical context. Roberta Romano, Sterling Professor of Law at Yale Law School and Director of the Yale Law School Center for the Study of Corporate Law, argues that "emergency financial legislation is inherently ill-suited for addressing crises, given information difficulties. The politics of financial crises requires acting before sufficient information can be developed on what might be the wisest course of action, and thereby provides an opportunity for well-positioned political actors opportunistically to advance an agenda that is tangential to the crisis at hand and may well be inapposite given the best available data."[4] These periods of regulation could also perhaps be viewed as a means, both direct and indirect, to protect consumers and/or the financial system as a whole.

Financial system stability and consumer protection can be closely related.[5] For example, the National Banking Act's creation of a national currency and reserve requirement perhaps enhanced financial

---

[3] *Id.* at 462.

[4] Romano, Roberta, *Further Assessment of the Iron Law of Financial Regulation: A Postscript to Regulating in the Dark* 9-10 (European Corporate Governance Inst. (ECGI) - Law Working Paper No. 273/2014; Yale Law & Econ. Research Paper No. 515, 2014), *available at* https://ssrn.com/abstract=2517853.

[5] *See* Philip R. Lane, Governor, Cent. Bank of Ir., Speech at University College Cork: The Role of Financial Regulation in Protecting Consumers (Feb. 23, 2017)("A fundamental protection for consumers lies in ensuring that the financial system is stable and the firms that operate within it are financially safe and sound."); *see also* Stephen Lumpkin, *Consumer Protection and Financial Innovation: A Few Basic Propositions*, 2010 OECD J.: FIN. MARKET TRENDS 117, 125 ("Maintaining the stability of the financial system depends in some large measure on preserving confidence. Episodes of widespread financial distress have often been sparked by a contagious loss of confidence in the integrity of major institutions or the system as a whole. A second, but closely related objective is to protect

stability but also made it less likely that *individual* depositors (consumers) would be unable to redeem their cash. The creation of the Federal Reserve permitted banks to have a lender or other means of obtaining cash during periods of liquidity challenges—a benefit to the bank. However, this ability to have a lender of last resort helped to buttress the banking system. The FDIC helped to create additional confidence in the banking system to prevent bank runs. These efforts reduced depositors' loss of funds. However, these efforts may be more appropriately described as indirect consumer protection efforts at the national/federal level.[6] Ultimately, these laws and rules are based on a few common rationales, as described by David Llewellyn, Emeritus Professor of Money and Banking at the Loughborough University School of Business and Economics: (1) the need for consumer confidence, (2) government seeking to create a "safety net," for example in the case of the Federal Reserve serving as the "lender of last resort" and the creation of the FDIC for deposit insurance, and (3) "consumer demand for regulation in order to gain a degree of assurance and lower transaction costs."[7] It is important to return to the question of what occurred in consumer financial services between post-World War II and the Dodd-Frank Act CFPB creation.

Direct consumer protection laws and regulations in financial services and products were more clearly established in the 1960s and 1970s.[8] Prior to the creation of federal laws in the 1960s and 1970s, most consumer financial services protections were at the state level, namely through (1) tort laws, (2) usury laws, and (3) product restrictions.[9] For the purposes of this text, we will focus on some of the federal laws and regulations that came about during this period, including but not limited to, the Equal Credit Opportunity Act of 1974, the Truth in Lending Act of 1968, and the Fair Credit Reporting Act of 1970.

Demonstration of the fragility of the financial system is not a novel occurrence. Further, corrective regulation and deregulation are recurring incidences rather than original themes. However, attempting to place the fragility of the financial system in the context of expanding or constricting consumer protections is a constantly developing war cry. At the risk of oversimplifying political, historical, and economic considerations, the two warring factions may be described, with a high degree of generality, as those who were in favor of a strong national government in contrast to statesmen in favor of strong state governments. This dichotomy continued as a mainstay within U.S. financial services as differences between the agricultural United States (primarily Southern states) and the commercial United States (primarily Northern states). This conflict is marked more recently with the pitting of "Wall Street" against so-called "Main Street" following the financial crisis of 2008. There remains indication of ongoing conflict between economists, behavioralists, politicians, and those in between, regarding financial services regulation.

---

consumers. Absent some form of assurance that their rights will be fully protected, consumers will not have confidence in the financial services system and the products and services it provides.").

[6] *See* Adam Levitin, *The Consumer Financial Protection Bureau: An Introduction*, 32 REV. OF BANKING & FIN. L. 321, 325 (2013).

[7] *See* David Llewellyn, *The Economic Rationale for Financial Regulation*, FSA Occasional Paper (Apr. 1999) at 9-10.

[8] *See* Barr, *supra* note 1, at 51.

[9] *See* Levitin, *supra* note 6, at 323.

B. TYPES OF FINANCIAL INSTITUTIONS

There are various types of financial institutions that provide services to consumers. When a layperson considers a financial institution, most individuals think of a bank. A bank may be distinguished from many different financial institutions types because a bank is what is known as a "**depository**" institution; in other words, a bank accepts deposits. Besides banks, credit unions are also depository institutions. A bank traditionally provides many types of financial services to consumers. These different financial services have now been shifted to different institution types. Review Part IC: Types of Financial Services, for more information on the type of financial services provided by financial institutions.

Banks are typically "organized" in two ways: a bank is (1) chartered by the state or is (2) a national bank. Banks are regulated by the Office of the Comptroller of the Currency, the Federal Reserve, the Federal Deposit Insurance Corporation, and individual state banking regulators. At the federal level, the Office of the Comptroller of the Currency has oversight with respect to banks that are organized via national charter. At the federal level, the Federal Reserve Bank has oversight over state-chartered member banks and bank holding companies. Such state-chartered, member banks may also be regulated by their individual state banking regulator. Recall from Part IA, that the Federal Reserve serves as a lender of last resort to these member banks. The Federal Deposit Insurance Corporation has oversight over state-chartered banks that are *not* members of the Federal Reserve System. Recall from Part IA that the Federal Deposit Insurance Corporation insures depositors' funds up to a certain amount, which yields a sense of confidence from the consumer-depositor. These state-chartered banks may also be regulated by their individual state banking regulator. Finally, while this text does not discuss credit unions in detail, the National Credit Union Administration has oversight with respect to federally-chartered credit unions.

Prior to the creation of the Consumer Financial Protection Bureau, many agencies/regulators tasked with regulating depository institutions were primarily focused on what is known as the **"safety and soundness"** of depository institutions. The safety and soundness concept relates to the health of the depository institution—the depository institution's solvency. Recall from Part IA, that bank troubles may have stemmed from a lack of liquidity. In other words, during a panic or "bank run," a bank was not able to meet its *short-term* obligations, namely redeemed deposits. Safety and soundness, on the other hand, refers, in a general sense, to the bank's financial condition, namely its ability or inability to meet *long-term* obligations, among other considerations.[10]

---

[10] "Safety and soundness" is based on the CAMELS System, namely: (1) the quality and adequacy of the bank's Capital, (2) the quality of a bank's Assets, (3) the capability of the board of directors and Management, (4) the quantity, sustainability, and trend of the bank's Earnings; (5) the adequacy of the bank's Liquidity position; and (6) the bank's Sensitivity to market risk. *See* St. Louis Fed., https://www.stlouisfed.org/bank-supervision/supervision-and-regulation/safety-soundness-supervision (last visited Dec. 8, 2018).

Safety and soundness was primarily handled by the **prudential regulators**.[11] Safety and soundness as a regulatory objective likely makes sense in historical context. For example, in *Financial Regulation: Why, How and Where Now?*, the authors explain that "the case for prudential (rather than systemic) regulation and supervision is that consumers are not in a position to judge the safety and soundness of financial institutions . . . [and protection is needed for] those who finance the safety net or compensation scheme . . ."[12] Individual consumers do not have sufficient information about bank decision-making to exercise oversight to protect themselves. Recall from Part IA, that the Federal Reserve and Federal Deposit Insurance Corporation are responsible for financing the "safety net" i.e. by serving as the lender of last resort and providing deposit insurance, respectively. Therefore, it is logical that the Federal Reserve Board and Federal Deposit Insurance Corporation would be interested in the safety and soundness of the safety net provided. However, "safety and soundness" as an objective, arguably, failed to meet other important oversight interests, namely consumer protection. It is possible that the financial institution's interests in remaining operable and ensuring solvency do not align with the interests of the consumers the financial institution serves.[13] Similarly, a regulator focused on safety and soundness could consider consumer protection a secondary goal.[14] Regulatory objectives are discussed in more detail in Part ID. The Consumer Financial Protection Bureau's primary regulatory objective is consumer protection rather than safety and soundness. A goal in its creation was to take the consumer protection regulatory powers spread over various prudential regulators and house these consumer protection regulatory powers within one agency.

Other financial institutions, which do not accept deposits, are known as **nondepository** institutions. Prior to the Dodd-Frank Act and the creation of the Consumer Financial Protection Bureau, nondepository institutions were not heavily restricted by federal supervision. Supervision, the CFPB, and its powers will be discussed in more detail in Part II. Nondepository institutions were often licensed and supervised by individual states. As a result, in contrast to banks and other depository institutions that may be chartered at the state or national level, nondepository institutions are organized and registered in the individual states in which the nondepository institution conducts its business. Because nondepository institutions do not accept consumer deposits, nondepository institutions' source of capital/ongoing funding is different from depository institutions. Nondepository institutions must rely

---

[11] Prudential regulators are the federal banking agencies for insured depositories and the National Credit Union Administration for insured credit unions. *See* 12 U.S.C. § 5481(24) (Fastcase 2018). Prudential regulators include the Office of the Comptroller of the Currency for national banks, the Federal Deposit Insurance Corporation for state-chartered, insured banks who are not members of the Federal Reserve, and the Board of Governors of the Federal Reserve System for state-chartered member banks and bank holding companies. *See* 12 U.S. C. § 1813(q) (Fastcase 2018); *see also* 12 U.S. C. § 5301(10) (Fastcase 2018).

[12] CHARLES GOODHART, PHILIPP HARTMAN, DAVID LLEWELLYN, LILIANA ROJAS-SUÀREZ, & STEVEN WEISBROD, FINANCIAL REGULATION: WHY, HOW, AND WHERE NOW? 5 (1998).

[13] *See* Stephen Lumpkin, *Consumer Protection and Financial Innovation: A Few Basic Propositions*, 2010 OECD J.: FIN. MARKET TRENDS 117, 126.; *see also* Levitin, *supra* note 6, at 330-31 ("The safety-and-soundness mission conflicted with the consumer mission. Safety-and-soundness ultimately means profitability. Only profitable financial institutions can be safe-and-sound.").

[14] *See* Levitin, *supra* note 6, at 330 ("Because consumer protection was everyone's responsibility, it became no one's responsibility, and regulatory accountability and performance suffered.").

on investment, usually in the form of debt—money the institution borrows. In contrast to state-chartered banks that were regulated by the state-chartering governmental agency and at the federal level by either the Federal Reserve or the Federal Insurance Deposit Corporation, discussed *supra*, nondepository institutions had no federal supervising body concerning oversight for consumer financial services protection. In some respects, this is logical. For example, because nondepositories did not accept deposits, and neither the Federal Reserve nor the Federal Deposit Insurance Corporation was providing a "safety net," no "prudential regulator" supervised such entities. At least for the time being, states were more equipped to regulate state-licensed entities, including with respect to the services and products offered by such entities, the authority to conduct business, and the impact to consumers. There was little regard to the "safety and soundness" of such nondepository institutions considering no entanglement with consumer deposits nor, theoretically, risk to the financial system that required the "safety net."

Nondepository institutions can include consumer finance companies, auto finance companies, money service businesses, and mortgage companies, for example. A consumer finance company typically offers consumer loans—loans for personal, family or household purposes. An auto finance company offers loans to finance the purchase of automobiles. A money service business transfers or converts money and can usually include, money transfer companies, bill pay companies, check-cashing companies, and currency exchange companies. This text will not discuss money service business regulations in detail. A mortgage company may serve as a lender, a broker, and/or a servicer of mortgage loans. A lender, broker, or servicer is responsible for different stages of the loan transaction and will be discussed in more detail later in the text. Consumer loans, auto loans, and mortgage loans are also defined in Part IC: Types of Financial Services.

In the context of this text, a financial institution is generally an institution engaging in activities that are considered to be financial in nature, as defined by the Bank Holding Company Act of 1956.[15] These activities will be discussed in more detail in the next chapter.

---

[15] *See* 12 U.S.C. § 1843(k)(4) (Fastcase 2018).

C. TYPES OF FINANCIAL SERVICES

Financial product or service is defined in 12 U.S.C. § 5481(15). **How does 12 U.S.C. § 5481(15) define a financial product or service?** Recall how "activities that are financial in nature" are defined by the Bank Holding Company Act of 1956. Compare the definition of financial product or service in 12 U.S.C. § 5481(15), found in the Dodd-Frank Wall Street Reform and Consumer Protection Act, with the definition of "activities that are financial in nature" in the Bank Holding Company Act.

A financial institution may offer products and services to businesses and/or may offer products and services to consumers. This text focuses on products and services financial institutions provide to **consumers**. Read 12 U.S.C. § 5481(4), Definitions. **How is consumer defined?** A consumer is an individual—a natural person. A corporate entity is not a consumer. Consumer financial services typically fall within five primary categories:

1. Moving funds between consumers and other actors (payments)
2. Moving funds forward in time (saving and investing)
3. Moving funds backward in time (borrowing and credit)
4. Managing risk (insurance)
5. Providing information and advice about these decisions[16]

This text is not exhaustive but will instead consider a narrower scope of consumer financial products and services, the federal laws and rules that apply to certain products and services, and regulators tasked with oversight concerning the consumer financial products and services. A financial institution may offer various services to consumers including accepting deposits, extending **credit**, and offering money or payment services such as money transfer and/or bill pay.

This text will focus on borrowing and credit. A financial institution may offer **loans** or extend **credit**. Credit is "the right granted by a creditor to a debtor to defer payment of debt."[17] A financial institution may extend **open-end** credit, or a financial institution may extend **closed-end** credit. Open-end credit is typically the right to defer payment of funds repeatedly advanced up to a specified amount.[18] With open-end credit, the consumer may continue to borrow until the set amount is depleted, resulting in ongoing transactions. Closed-end credit, in contrast, amounts to one transaction. The transaction concludes with the last payment after a specified term. The consumer receives the right to defer payment on one lump sum amount borrowed at one time.

A **loan** is a promise to repay funds advanced. The repayment amount, usually in monthly installments, is typically composed of principal and interest. The principal is the amount advanced, and the interest is

---

[16] RYAN ET AL., *supra* note 2, at 463.

[17] 15 U.S.C. § 1602(f) (Fastcase 2018).

[18] *See* 12 C.F.R. § 1026.2(a)(20) (Fastcase 2018).

the amount the lender charges for the cost of advancing funds. Interest rates may vary by lender or by loan type but are typically regulated by state law. In other words, the amount of interest that a lender may charge may be limited by state "usury" law. Under state usury law, the state passes a law that determines that X percent interest rate is criminal; rates above the usury cap are excessive, unethical and not permissible. If a financial institution offers loans, these loans may further fall into additional categories. For example, a financial institution may offer an **unsecured** loan or a **secured** loan. A secured loan is a loan in which the lender has a security interest in the borrower's property as collateral for repayment of the loan.[19] If the borrower does not repay the loan or otherwise violates the terms of the loan agreement, the lender may take possession of the borrower's property. An unsecured loan is a loan in which the lender does not have a security interest in the borrower's property.

A financial institution may offer (1) a personal loan, (2) a payday loan, (3) an auto loan; (4) a student loan; or (5) a mortgage loan, among other loan types. A **personal loan** is, typically, an unsecured consumer loan for personal, family or household purposes.

A **payday loan** is a short-term loan of a small amount to be repaid at the borrower's next payday. Because the **maturity date**, or date by which the entire loan (including principal and interest) should be repaid, may be associated with the borrower's next payday, the loan advance presupposes that the borrower is employed. Therefore, it is not uncommon for employment verification to be a part of the loan application and approval process. When the consumer obtains the loan, the consumer may execute a check to the lender or give the lender permission to debit the consumer's bank account, if the consumer does not repay the loan. As a result, the lender has a security interest in the borrower's future earnings if the loan remains unpaid. Payday loans are typically associated with high rates of interest and have been greatly restricted or prohibited in some states.

An **auto loan** is a loan to finance the purchase of an automobile, with a security interest in the automobile if the borrower defaults. An auto loan is an example of a loan secured by personal property. A **student loan** is a loan to finance the cost of education. Personal property is typically movable items of value owned. For example a loan with a security interest in a boat would be considered a loan with an interest in movable property: the boat. A **mortgage loan** is the promise to repay funds advanced for real estate. Many laws and rules include special provisions for mortgage loans, in particular for refinances of existing mortgage loans and for home equity loans. This text will focus on mortgage loans tied to the purchase of real estate. A financial institution may offer a **residential mortgage loan** or a **commercial mortgage loan**. A **residential mortgage loan** is a mortgage loan related to real property intended to be used as a residence. Examples of a residential mortgage loan include financing the purchase of a primary residence, a vacation home, or a residential investment property. A **commercial mortgage loan**, however, is a mortgage loan related to real property intended to be used for commercial purposes. A mortgage loan is an example of a loan secured by real property. Real property is owned land and improvements to the land, such as structures.

---

[19] *See* 12 C.F.R. § 1026.2(a)(25).

A loan, most commonly mortgage loans, may involve multiple stages over the life of the loan. Each of these stages could be performed by one financial service institution or spread among multiple financial service institution. Consider Figure 1C on the next page, and keep Figure 1C in mind as you continue to learn more about loans, financial service providers, and applicable laws and rules.

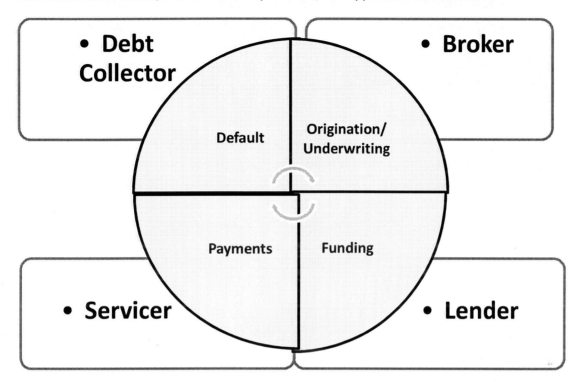

Figure 1C

In Figure 1C above, the loan transaction begins with **origination/underwriting** in the top right quadrant. Origination and underwriting may be considered the first stage in the loan transaction process. Origination and underwriting typically include, taking a loan application and applying a set of pre-determined factors to consider when making a credit decision. At this stage, a decision is made regarding whether to extend credit. This stage in the loan transaction process may be conducted by a financial services provider known as a **broker**. Once a decision has been made regarding whether to extend credit to the applicant-borrower, if the credit extension has been approved, the applicant borrower must receive the proceeds from the loan. However, how is the loan funded? Where does the money that the borrower-applicant receives come from?

Moving clockwise in Figure 1C, it is notable that, typically, the loan is funded by the **lender**. The lender is the "**creditor**." In other words, the lender has offered a loan, and the borrower-applicant is obligated to repay the lender. The term "creditor" is more clearly defined under various consumer financial services laws and rules. Who serves as the creditor is extremely important in the application of the consumer financial services laws and rules. The applicant-borrower is obligated to repay the lender-creditor at the time of contracting with the lender-creditor for payment and the extension of credit. Once the lender-creditor extends credit, this right to repayment is an asset for the lender-creditor; money is owed to the lender-creditor. A lender that utilizes the process described above, i.e. the lender funds the loan and has no contact with the consumer, but rather relies on other financial institutions, including brokers, to take loan applications, is called a wholesale lender. The broker will need to use the underwriting criteria of the wholesale lender to determine whether the loan has been approved. In addition, some lenders, referred to as warehouse lenders, lend money to other lenders to make loans. Warehouse lenders also have no consumer contact. The lenders who receive funding from warehouse lenders, however, may make their own underwriting decisions. In this case, the lenders receiving the funding are the creditors. Lenders are not required to use a separate broker. In many instances, the lender may perform origination and underwriting activities as well as fund the loan all within the same entity.

At this point the lender-creditor has at least two "rights": (1) ownership of the loan/the right to enforce repayment on the loan and (2) the right to collect payment on the loan and/or perform other administrative duties related to the loan. The first right shall be referred to as "ownership," and the second right shall be referred to as "servicing." The entity that holds the right to enforce repayment is the creditor. Return to Figure 1C. The entity that holds the right to collect payment is the **servicer**. Either of the aforementioned "rights" may be held, purchased, assigned, sold, etc. Ownership rights typically mean that the loan is held on the balance sheet of the entity with the right. Servicing rights do **not** definitively mean that the loan is held on the balance sheet of the entity with the right.

Once the funds/loan proceeds have been provided to the applicant-borrower, the applicant-borrower is the "**debtor**" and is responsible for repaying the entity that holds the right to repayment—the creditor. After funding, the lender-creditor has several options:

(1) The lender-creditor can maintain the existing rights of ownership and servicing. The lender-creditor can keep the loan on its balance sheet and perform servicing for the life of the loan. In this case, the lender would remain the creditor and the servicer.

(2) Alternatively, the lender-creditor may sell one or both rights. If the lender-creditor sells both rights to one party, the loan will be owned and serviced by that third party. This person will become the creditor and the servicer.

(3) If the lender-creditor sells the loan but retains servicing rights, the loan no longer appears on the lender's balance sheet as an asset as the lender no longer owns the loan. The lender will continue to collect payments. Instead of collecting payments for itself, however, the lender is collecting payments for the third party who now owns the loan, usually for a fee. The third party is now, arguably, the "creditor," even though this third party did not originate nor fund the loan initially.

(4) The lender could retain the ownership rights of the loan but assign the servicing rights. In other words, the lender retains the right to receive payments and the benefit of the loan as an (ideally performing) asset on the lender's balance sheet but utilizes a third-party servicer to service the loan. The arrangement by which the owner of the loan uses a **servicer** for servicing can be more

efficient. In some cases, the entity that owns servicing rights may also contract with a third party to perform these duties. This third party is referred to as a subservicer.

Even if the lender-creditor retains ownership and servicing upon funding the loan, the lender-creditor is not beholden to this decision. The lender-creditor may perhaps decide to sell, assign, etc. these rights later. In addition, a financial institution that is properly licensed and authorized to engage in such activity may even purchase rights from others. Some lenders originate and fund loans with the intention of selling the loans to investors. These lenders are called correspondent lenders. Other lenders originate and fund loans with the intention of keeping the loans, rather than selling any rights. These lenders, who retain the loans on their financial statements, are referred to as portfolio lenders.

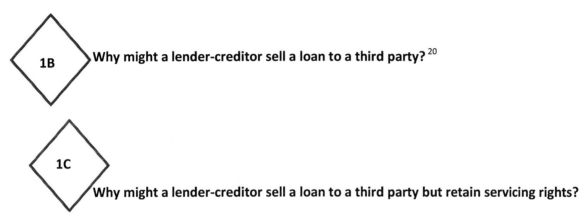

1B Why might a lender-creditor sell a loan to a third party?[20]

1C Why might a lender-creditor sell a loan to a third party but retain servicing rights?

Much can happen over the life of a loan, which, in the case of residential mortgages, may include a repayment term of thirty years. Over the course of thirty years, for example, the applicant-borrower may experience changes that make loan repayment difficult. Failure to submit timely payments on a debt obligation is known as **default**. Default may never happen during the life of the loan. However, if default does occur, this may create an important regulatory shift by invoking additional consumer protections. There are additional laws and rules that may be applicable to financial institutions engaged in collecting defaulted debts. These laws and rules will be explored in more detail later in the text. Return to Figure 1C. This stage in the loan transaction, if it occurs, may be referred to as **debt collection**.

As mentioned, a financial institution that is properly licensed or authorized to do so, may perform origination, funding, servicing, and debt collection. This is known as performing activities "inhouse." Increasingly, however, these different activities are spread across multiple entities for economies of scale. In other words, some companies focus entirely on limited activities in the loan transaction process. Some companies focus on origination and broker loans. These companies may work to match

---

[20] *See* Hynes, Richard M. and Posner, Eric A., *Law and Economics of Consumer Finance* 26 (Univ. Chi. Law & Econ., Olin Working Paper No. 117, 2001), *available at* https://ssrn.com/abstract=261109 ("The division of labor between seller and third-party creditor clearly has advantages. Each party can specialize in developing expertise in its own market.").

borrowers with different lenders who will fund the loans. These companies are profitable because of the services they provide to consumers and to lenders who do not have the expense associated with finding borrowers, reviewing loan applications, and other elements of the initial loan transaction. Other companies focus solely on servicing activities. Servicers are adept at compliance with the laws and rules related to servicing. These companies are profitable because of the service they provide, for a fee, to those who hold ownership rights. Still further, some companies focus solely on debt collection. These companies do not originate, fund, nor engage in general servicing activities, but rather, focus solely on collection of payment on debts in default.

1D — **How might a creditor, funding loans originated by a broker, determine which loans to purchase and/or reduce its risk of purchasing nonperforming loan assets?**

Lending, broker, servicing, and debt collection are all types of financial services. As previously discussed, these services may occur "inhouse" or be spread across different entities. Return to Part 1B. Lending, brokering, servicing, and debt collection as separate services may similarly be referred to as different financial institution types, namely, lenders, brokers, servicers, and debt collectors.

How is <u>credit</u> defined?

How is <u>open-end</u> credit defined? What is an example of open-end credit?

How is <u>closed-end</u> credit defined? What is an example of closed-end credit?

How is <u>loan</u> defined?

How is an <u>unsecured</u> loan defined?

How is a <u>secured</u> loan defined?

1E — **Is a student loan a secured or an unsecured loan?**

D. REGULATORY POLICY

There are different methods by which to regulate financial institutions. The United States has a dual governing system at both the federal and state level, and the regulation of financial institutions is no different. Recall the discussion of banks in Part IB. Some financial institutions are regulated by states, and some financial institutions are regulated at the federal level. Even still there are different ways to regulate financial institutions and different causes for concern.

ENTITY/SERVICE/OBJECTIVE REGULATORY METHODS

For example, a financial institution may be regulated by (1) entity, by (2) service, or by (3) objective. To regulate by entity would be to regulate by institution type. During the first half of the twentieth century, much financial services regulation was based on regulating by entity/institution type. The Office of the Comptroller of the Currency regulated national banks. State banking regulators regulated state-chartered banks. The National Credit Union Administration regulated federal credit unions. There are clear benefits to regulating by institution type. First, a regulator who is responsible for regulating banks alone, for example, can have a birds-eye view of what is happening in banking. In addition, a regulator who has oversight over banks may also get a clear picture of an individual bank's business activities as whole. This micro and macro view can be beneficial to recognizing and predicting systemic issues and financial stability.

However, there are some challenges to regulating by **entity**. For example, a national bank may offer many different types of financial services as discussed in Parts IB and IC. Similarly, a credit union or state-chartered bank may provide many of the same services that a national bank provides. As a result, a regulator regulating a bank, would have to be aware of the laws and rules that apply to all the services the bank provides. A bank regulator would need to be aware of lending laws and rules, of payments laws and rules, of insurance laws and rules, and of deposit laws and rules, for example. Similarly, a credit union regulator would need to be aware of the laws and rules that apply to all the services the credit union provides; namely, a credit union regulator would need to be aware of lending laws and rules, of payments laws and rules, of insurance laws and rules, and of deposit laws and rules, for example. This regulatory method could prove burdensome to the regulator and require that the regulator narrow its oversight to focus on particular laws and rules. It is challenging to be aware of, manage, and enforce the body of laws that may apply to a bank. In addition, regulating by entity/institution type inherently creates additional distinctions among institution types. One might consider the current state of U.S. financial regulation as regulating by entity. As stated above, the Office of the Comptroller of the Currency regulated national banks. State banking regulators regulated state-chartered banks. The National Credit Union Administration regulated federal credit unions.

1F If national banks, state-chartered banks, and credit unions are all offering the same or similar services, should these institutions be regulated differently? Why or Why Not?

Some posit that financial institutions' regulatory agencies should instead be organized to regulate different services rather than different financial institution types. In other words, instead of having a regulator that functions to regulate banks, a regulator exists for each service that a financial institution offers. So, for example, a mortgage company offers mortgage loans only. Through regulating by service, a regulator would exist solely to regulate institutions that offer mortgage loans. For the mortgage loan company, the mortgage loan company would have one regulator.

Regulating by **service** has some benefits. First, regulating by service can create expertise among the regulators and allow the regulator to be equipped better to understand services and products. In contrast to regulating by institution-type, where the regulator may have to narrow its focus, regulating by service allows for concentrated understanding.

However, there are obvious challenges to regulating by service. First, regulating by service may prove burdensome to financial institutions that offer many services. For example, a bank may have a regulator for every service the bank offers, including for example, a mortgage regulator, an insurance regulator, a payments regulator, and a securities regulator. The burden is created because the bank may be subject to government "intrusion" more frequently and at a higher cost than an institution that offers a more limited number of products or services. It is arguable whether this burden should be considered when weighed against the benefits that an institution that offers diverse products and services may experience.

One might also consider the current state of U.S. financial regulation as regulating by **objective**. There are a variety of potential objectives to financial services regulation. The most common objectives are (1) safety and soundness of the financial institution (discussed *supra*), (2) law enforcement/prevention of terrorism, (3) systemic stability, and (4) consumer protection. This text focuses on consumer protection as the regulatory objective. Specifically, as will be discussed in more detail in Part II, this text focuses on the centralization of consumer protection as the mission of one federal agency rather than multiple agencies. Consider the following explanation concerning the challenges of different regulatory approaches:

> While the regulations imposed for systemic and prudential reasons may be similar (e.g. the establishment of capital requirements), they do not need to be (nor should they be) conducted by the same agency. The focus should be on the objectives of regulation. The danger is that, if a single regulatory agency conducts both systemic and prudential regulation, it might converge on the same requirements for different institutions, although the objectives might require different approaches.[21]

REGULATORY POWERS

What is meant by a regulator or "to regulate"? Regulatory power typically falls into three categories: (1) supervision, (2) rulemaking, and (3) enforcement. These powers will be discussed further in Part II. Rulemaking is the benchmark of regulatory power. Rulemaking requires establishing a set of permissible

---

[21] *See* GOODHART ET AL., *supra* note 12, at 6.

and prohibited behaviors. Further, agency rulemaking helps to clarify existing laws created by the legislature. Supervision may be described as the authority to monitor whether the established laws and rules are being adhered to. Supervision, in the context of financial services, typically amounts to examinations. An examination is conducted by a regulatory body, either remote or onsite, to gauge whether a financial institution is complying with established laws and rules. Enforcement is the authority to implement repercussions from violations of the rules. There can frequently be challenges inherent in the spread of supervision, rulemaking, and enforcement powers across different "regulating" bodies. The CFPB, discussed more in Part II, is notable because the CFPB's authority extends to all three regulatory powers for some institution types.

RESTRICTION v. DISCLOSURE

Finally, regulatory options may be furthered divided into two camps: (1) consumer protection through restrictions and (2) consumer protection through disclosure.[22] Prior to the 1960s and 1970s, consumer protection was achieved through restrictions. A restriction either prohibits the financial service provider from engaging in certain acts or affirmatively requires a financial service provider to engage in certain acts. Through restrictions, a consumer was directly protected. Government, at a state or federal level, determined that X was or was not a good practice in its effects to consumers and thus prohibited the practice or required the practice. A usury cap is an example of a restrictive consumer protection. The restrictive regulations seek to ensure "fair" business practices.

As consumer financial services expanded in availability and type, there was a push toward consumer access and choice. The result of having choices means that consumers must now choose among the choices. Because the state is not, effectively, making this decision for the consumer, there may inherently be more risk involved for the consumer as the consumer likely has access to less information than the government.[23]

How might consumers be able to make informed decisions?

1G

---

[22] RYAN ET AL., *supra* note 2, at 489.

[23] *See* John Y. Campbell, Howell E. Jackson, Brigitte C. Madrian, and Peter Tufano, *Consumer Financial Protection*, 25 J. ECON. PERSP. 91, 93 (2011) ("More generally, making sensible decisions about financial products often requires considerable information on terms and conditions, not just prices. [. . .] But in many cases, consumers cannot efficiently generate information on their own [. . .] Often the financial provider will be the most efficient supplier of information, which creates additional rationale for mandates that firms produce and disseminate certain types of information."); Campbell et al. 25 J. OF ECON. PERSP. 91, 95 (2011) ("Even if consumers cannot maximize their own welfare, regulators may not necessarily do better. But in certain cases, outcomes may be improved by regulations on market conduct that reflect the presumed judgment of what most consumers would want, were they fully informed and well advised.").

In the last fifty years, a shift occurred from restrictions to disclosure. With the demand of more choices, the means by which consumers could make "good" decisions was through receiving information—disclosure. The shift in the type of regulation could also be described as a shift toward deregulation. Disclosure laws typically have three important prongs: (1) **timing**, (2) **content**, and (3) **form**.

Through disclosure, rather than being restricted by government, financial institutions had the flexibility to innovate, to offer varying products and services, and to meet consumer demand. Consumers, in turn, had a variety of products, services, and institutions to choose from and could make decisions about what products, services, and institutions to choose. However, this decision-making assumption of risk[24] is legitimized only with the accompanying notion that the consumer is able to make informed decisions. Both restrictive regulations as well as disclosure regulations will be discussed throughout this text.

 1H   **Which regulatory method may yield greater consumer protection?**

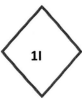 **1I**   **Which regulatory method may yield greater access to financial services and products?**

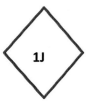 **1J**   **Do the social welfare costs of access to financial services and products outweigh the risks of the potential for poor decision-making?[25]**

Is all decision-making created equal?

In the article *Consumer Financial Protection*, the authors write that:

> Some consumers may lack the cognitive capacity to optimize their financial situation even if presented with all the information that in principle is required to do so.

---

[24] *See* RYAN ET AL., *supra* note 2, at 490.

[25] *See id.* at 496 ("Researchers have begun to explore the financial capability of consumers and their ability and preparedness to make household financial decisions. These studies illustrate the point that most consumers are ill equipped to make financial decisions that would keep their balance sheets healthy—whether that means having enough money in the bank to handle an emergency (or to expand wealth), or keeping their risk exposure low (by, for example, keeping their debt loads down).") ("[A]s Americans have been given more options and have been asked to make their own financial decisions, they remain ill equipped to make choices that foster household financial health or contribute to the development of a healthier national economy.").

Such biases and cognitive limitations may be particularly important in the financial context because learning from experience in major financial decisions is difficult. Many financial decisions like choosing a mortgage or investing in a retirement account are undertaken only infrequently. Moreover, the outcomes of these decisions are delayed, perhaps for decades, and are subject to large random shocks [. . .] Social taboos on discussing personal finances further reduce the effectiveness of social learning.[26]

In addition, if consumer financial behavior differs across different consumer groups, should there be a "one-size fits all" approach to consumer financial services regulation?[27]

There are at least three challenges to consumer protection through disclosure. First, this method of consumer protection requires that the information must actually be disclosed to the consumer. What constitutes disclosure can vary widely as there are a number of means to disclose the same information. Second, this method of consumer protection presupposes that the consumer can imbibe and understand the information disclosed. This lack of understanding, particularly if utilizing a "one-size fits all" approach to regulation, may result in disclosures that are not meaningful. In other words, the disclosures are so confusing that any benefit gained by having access to the information is negated.[28] There are perhaps different methods of increasing understanding, including ensuring that the information is disclosed uniformly across financial institutions using standard terms. Finally, if the goal is to protect the consumer and/or reduce risk, consumer protection through disclosure assumes that the consumer will make the logical choice. However, this is not always the case. Authors use the example of the "present-biased preferences"[29] of smoking and failing to save for retirement. In other words, cigarette companies disclose to individuals that smoking may have health risks. Individuals also have been informed that saving for retirement is a necessity. However, when given the choice to smoke (with disclosure of negative consequences of smoking) or not to smoke, and when given the choice to save for retirement or not to save for retirement (with the knowledge of the negative consequences of not saving for retirement), some individuals may still choose to smoke and to not save for retirement.[30]

Is it appropriate for the state or federal government to intervene in decision-making that may prove harmful? Alternatively, what level of importance do you attribute to freedom of choice? Can you think of any negative impacts to the whole that result from exercising individual choices in financial services? Rather than restricting individual freedoms, in financial services or otherwise, and rather than permitting individual choice to impose negative impacts on the whole, a policy compromise may be appropriate:

---

[26] Campbell et al. 25 J. OF ECON. PERSP. 91, 92 (2011).

[27] *See* Stephen Lumpkin, *Consumer Protection and Financial Innovation: A Few Basic Propositions*, 2010 OECD J.: FIN. MARKET TRENDS 117, 123 ("[C]onsumer financial behaviour can be distinguished across such demographic characteristics as age and gender, and also income levels, while culture and related social factors are also relevant in some contexts.").

[28] *See id.* at 124 (stating "excessive and overly complex disclosures tend to exacerbate matters.").

[29] Lane, *supra* note 5 ("[D]ecisions are affected by emotions and psychological experiences, by rules of thumb and accepted norms. For example, consumers can exhibit present-biased behaviour, which leads them to over-value payoffs today relative to payoffs in the future.").

[30] *See* Campbell et al., *supra* note 26, at 93.

Possible policy responses to such preferences are to constrain the present self from taking actions that would be too detrimental to the future self, for example, by limiting early access to retirement savings or taxing the sale of cigarettes.[31]

In other words, in some instances policy makers permit individual choice while creating incentives or disincentives for less "desirable" behaviors that could impact the financial system as a whole or consumers as a collective group. This may be described as "the role of the state versus the role of markets in achieving desirable outcomes."[32] Ultimately, it is difficult to determine when adequate consumer protection has been achieved as the goals are dynamic. However, disclosure consumer protection attempts to resolve the issue of access to information while consumer protection through restriction attempts to resolve the issue of access to financial markets. Consider which method of regulation may be advantageous for "sophisticated" consumers. Consider which method of regulation may be more advantageous for consumers who have various limitations, including lacking the ability to understand complex financial information, lacking access to markets, or lacking economic resources.[33]

Now that there exists an understanding of the historical context of financial services regulation, types of financial institutions, types of financial services, and types of regulatory policies or methods, the 5Ws of consumer financial services regulation may be discerned.

For the purposes of this text, the 5Ws are as follows:

- **(1)** **Who** is regulated?
- **(2)** **Who** is protected?
- **(3)** **What** is the protection? What is the appropriate law or regulation?
- **(4)** **When** is the protection applicable? (Under what circumstances does the protection apply?
- **(5)** **Why** does the protection exist? Would applying the law or rule make sense in context?

At the outset, at a basic level, it can be discerned that financial institutions are the: **WHO IS REGULATED?** However, we know that "financial institution" may be a defined term and defining financial institution may be challenging. In addition, as this text will reference, the scope of **Who** is regulated under any specific law could be broader, for example a "person," or narrower, for example a "creditor." Should entities that are providing services, that could be described as financial in nature, be required to comply with consumer financial protection laws? Who is regulated with respect to each consumer financial service law or regulation is explored later in the text.

It can be discerned that consumers are the: **WHO IS PROTECTED?** However, as will be discovered throughout the text, not all consumers are created equal. Therefore, lines must be drawn, and decisions made concerning whether some groups should receive more or less protection. For example, some consumers may be deemed "sophisticated." Alternatively, it is not uncommon for additional consumer

---

[31] Campbell et al., *supra* note 26, at 93.
[32] Lumpkin, *supra* note 27, at 118.
[33] *See id.* at 126-127.

protections to be built into laws for certain consumer groups, including students, the elderly, individuals for whom English is a second language, and servicemen.[34] Does greater protection and determinations of "suitability" reduce access? Consider:

> Access refers to a situation in which affordable, mainstream financial products are available to all segments of the population across the range of income levels and demographic characteristics. Suitability addresses the appropriateness of the products for particular consumer groups. That is, what products may safely be sold to retail financial consumers? By whom? Who decides? And whose fault is it if something goes wrong?[35]

We will later learn more about the specific laws and regulations that consider consumer financial services protection, namely the: **WHAT IS THE PROTECTION?**

Through reviewing the laws and rules in depth, we will discover under what circumstances the protections apply, the **WHEN IS THE PROTECTION APPLICABLE?**

Why is the determination of the five Ws essential to an understanding of consumer financial services regulation? Understanding these 5Ws will assist in problem-solving and aid in understanding consumer financial services protections.

---

[34] *See* 12 U.S.C. § 5493(e) (Fastcase 2018). The Consumer Financial Protection Bureau was required by statute to establish the Office of Service Member affairs which was to "be responsible for developing and implementing initiatives for service members and their families." For additional protections for service men, *see* The Servicemembers Civil Relief Act. The Consumer Financial Protection Bureau was required by statute to establish the Office of Financial Protection for Older Americans to protect seniors aged 62 years or more. *See* 12 U.S.C. § 5493(g) (Fastcase 2018).

[35] Lumpkin, *supra* note 27, at 118.

II. CONSUMER FINANCIAL PROTECTION BUREAU

In 2010, the Dodd-Frank Wall Street Reform and Consumer Protection Act was signed into law by President Barack Obama, following the 2008 financial crisis. No House Republicans initially voted for the law, and only four Senate Republicans initially voted for the law.[36] Of the four U.S. Republican Senators who voted for the law, one, Senator Scott Brown, was from the same state as the law's House sponsor Representative-D Barney Frank—Massachusetts.[37] Yale Law School Professor Roberta Romano notes that the passage of the Dodd-Frank Act differs from other reactive legislation because the law did not receive overwhelming support across the aisle; in other words, the law did not receive support from both Republicans and Democrats.[38]

The Dodd-Frank Wall Street Reform and Consumer Protection Act established the Consumer Financial Protection Bureau and the Consumer Financial Protection Bureau's powers.[39] Prior to the creation of the Consumer Financial Protection Bureau, federal consumer financial services regulatory oversight functions were held across a multitude of different **prudential**[40] regulators and agencies, including the Federal Reserve Bank Board of Governors, the Federal Deposit Insurance Corporation, the Federal Trade Commission; the National Credit Union Administration; the Office of the Comptroller of the Currency; the Office of Thrift Supervision; and the Department of Housing and Urban Development. These regulators/agencies are known as "legacy" regulators. Consumer financial protection functions/powers, including rule-making, supervision, and enforcement were transferred from legacy regulators to the CFPB pursuant to 12 U.S.C. § 5581. Adam Levitin, Professor of Law at Georgetown University Law Center, summarizes the "Problems with the Regulatory Architecture" pre-CFPB, namely:

(1) consumer protection was an "orphan" mission that had no regulatory "home" in any single agency;

(2) consumer protection was often subordinated to regulatory concerns about bank profitability;

---

[36] *See* GOVTRACK, https://www.govtrack.us/congress/votes/111-2009/h968 (last visited Dec. 8, 2018).

[37] *See id.*

[38] *See* Romano, *supra* note 4, at 12.

[39] *See generally* 12 U.S.C. § 5491 (Fastcase 2018) *et seq.*

[40] Prudential regulators are the federal banking agencies for insured depositories and the National Credit Union Administration for insured credit unions. *See* 12 U.S.C. § 5481(24). Prudential regulators include the Office of the Comptroller of the Currency for national banks, the Federal Deposit Insurance Corporation for state-chartered, insured banks who are not members of the Federal Reserve, and the Board of Governors of the Federal Reserve System for state-chartered member banks and bank holding companies. *See* 12 U.S. C. § 1813(q); *see also* 12 U.S. C. § 5301(10).

(3) there was a lack of regulatory expertise in consumer financial issues; and

(4) the diffusion of regulatory responsibility created regulatory arbitrage[41] opportunities that fueled a race to the bottom.[42]

One of the purposes of the CFPB is to ensure that consumer financial services laws are enforced consistently across different institution types.[43] In addition, a goal in the creation of the Consumer Financial Protection Bureau was to take the powers spread over various regulators and house these regulatory powers within one agency. Consider whether this goal resolves consumer protection issues or is helpful toward meeting challenges caused by the financial crisis, which will be discussed in more detail in Part IX. For example, Professor Romano refers to this transfer of powers from one agency to another as a "reshuffling of bureaucratic boxes."[44]

The CFPB is an independent government agency within the Federal Reserve.[45] The CFPB has its own Director.[46] **How is the Director of the Consumer Financial Protection Bureau determined?** The Director of the Consumer Financial Protection Bureau is appointed by the President of the United States with the advice and consent of the United States Senate.[47] The Director serves for a term of five years and may be removed for cause by the President of the United States.[48] Because the Director serves for a period of five years, the Director may be serving under a President that did not appoint the Director.

2A — **What impact, if any, may the term-length have on the Director's ability to function in the role? What impact, if any, may the President's ability to terminate the Director for cause have on the Director's ability to function in the role?**

This potentially, challenging dynamic was palatable with CFPB Director Richard Cordray. Richard Cordray was confirmed by the Senate on July 16, 2013 as the CFPB Director. This appointment occurred during the presidency of Barak Obama. Thereafter, Donald Trump was elected President in 2016. According to reports, Donald "Trump ha[d] on at least two occasions griped about Cordray in private and wondered what to do about his tenure [. . .] Under the agency's current structure, Trump could only fire Cordray for cause."[49] In November 2017, Richard Cordray announced that he would step down as CFPB Director.[50] That same month, Mick Mulvaney was appointed by Donald Trump as the interim

---

[41] Regulatory arbitrage will be discussed in more detail in Part IX.

[42] Levitin, *supra* note 6, at 329.

[43] *See* 12 U.S.C. § 5511(b)(4) (Fastcase 2018); 12 U.S. C. § 5495 (Fastcase2018).

[44] *See* Romano, *supra* note 4, at 27.

[45] *See* 12 U.S.C. § 5492(c)(2) (Fastcase 2018).

[46] *See* 12 U.S.C. § 5491(b)(1) (Fastcase 2018).

[47] *See* 12 U.S.C. § 5491(b)(2).

[48] *See* 12 U.S.C. § 5491(c)(1).

[49] *See* Renae Merle, *Richard Cordray is Stepping Down as Head of Consumer Financial Protection Bureau*, WASH. POST., Nov. 15, 2017, https://www.washingtonpost.com/news/business/wp/2017/11/15/richard-cordray-is-stepping-down-as-head-of-consumer-financial-protection-bureau/?noredirect=on&utm_term=.0fe48c7ec73e.

[50] *See id.*

CFPB Director pursuant to the Federal Vacancies Reform Act of 1998.[51] This change in CFPB director and shift in political party control was significant.[52] Since Mulvaney's appointment as Acting Director, Mulvaney "froze[] all new investigations"[53]and attempted to reduce the CFPB's power through limiting its funding.[54] Each political party may be in favor of different courses of action concerning the powers of the CFPB, depending upon which political party is "in power."[55]

2B **How was Acting Director Mick Mulvaney appointed by Donald Trump as the interim CFPB director without approval of the Senate?**

For an in-depth discussion of this issue, read *English v. Trump*, 279 F.Supp.3d 307 (D. D.C., 2018). On December 6, 2018, the U.S. Senate confirmed Kathleen Kraninger, nominated by President Donald Trump, to become the Director of the Consumer Financial Protection Bureau.

The primary objective of the Consumer Financial Protection Bureau is federal consumer protection with respect to consumer financial services and products. Specifically, the Consumer Financial Protection Bureau regulates the "offering and provision of consumer financial products or services under the Federal consumer financial laws.[56]

---

[51] *See* Alan S. Kaplinsky, *How Long Can Mick Mulvaney Serve as CFPB Acting Director*, BALLARD SPAHR LLP CONSUMER FIN. MONITOR BLOG (Feb. 27, 2018), https://www.consumerfinancemonitor.com/2018/02/27/how-long-can-mick-mulvaney-serve-as-cfpb-acting-director/.

[52] *See* Gregory Korte, *What Does Mulvaney's Appointment Mean for the Future of CFPB?*, USA TODAY, Nov. 28, 2017, https://www.usatoday.com/story/news/politics/2017/11/28/what-does-mulvaneys-appointment-mean-future-cfpb/901067001/.

[53] Glenn Thrush, *Mulvaney, Watchdog Bureau's Leader, Advises Bankers on Ways to Curtail Agency*, N.Y. TIMES, Apr. 24, 2018, https://www.nytimes.com/2018/04/24/us/mulvaney-consumer-financial-protection-bureau.html.

[54] *See* Stacy Cowley, *Consumer Bureau's Chief Gives Big Raises, Even as He Criticizes Spending*, N.Y. TIMES, Apr. 5, 2018), https://www.nytimes.com/2018/04/05/business/cfpb-mick-mulvaney-pay-raises.html; *see also* Stacy Cowley, *Consumer Watchdog's Latest Budget Request: $0*, N.Y. TIMES, Jan. 18, 2018, https://www.nytimes.com/2018/01/18/business/cfpb-mick-mulvaney.html?module=inline.

[55] *See* Alan Rappeport, *Mick Mulvaney, Consumer Bureau's Chief, Urges Congress to Cripple Agency*, N.Y. TIMES, Apr. 2, 2018, https://www.nytimes.com/2018/04/02/us/politics/cfpb-mick-mulvaney.html ("Last month, Representative Jeb Hensarling of Texas, the Republican chairman of the House Financial Services Committee and a longtime proponent for curbing the agency's power, said he was willing to get behind a financial regulation bill that left the consumer bureau untouched. The reason: He supports Mr. Mulvaney. 'Right now, I'm very happy,' he said of the bureau's direction under Mr. Mulvaney. 'May he rule forever.' "); *see also* Todd J. Zywicki, *The Consumer Financial Protection Bureau: Savior or Menace?* 81 GEO. WASH. L. REV. 856, 895 (2013) (stating "support for single-director design has often had an ideological motivation as well. As was the case the case with CFPB, advocacy groups with liberal policy orientations advocated a single-director design, under the impression that the Bureau's director would enact a liberal-friendly agenda.").

[56] 12 U.S.C. § 5491(a).

Considering that the Consumer Financial Protection Bureau protects consumers, how does the law, 12 U.S.C § 5481(4), define a consumer? A <u>consumer</u> is an individual or an agent, trustee, or representative acting on behalf of an individual.[57]

Considering that the Consumer Financial Protection Bureau regulates the provision of consumer financial products or services, how does the law, 12 U.S.C. § 5481(5), define a consumer financial product or service? A consumer financial service or product is any financial product or service that is provided for use by consumers primarily for personal, family, or household purposes.[58] A "financial product or service" is also defined in the law.[59] Recall the discussion in Part IB. Re-review the definition of "financial product or service" in 12 U.S.C. 5481(15).

The Consumer Financial Protection Bureau is funded by the Federal Reserve System.[60] Specifically, the CFPB Director requests from the Federal Reserve the "amount necessary to carry out the authorities of the Bureau."[61] The amount requested cannot exceed a specified percentage of the Federal Reserve System's operating expenses.[62]

The CFPB is not funded by and does not rely upon funding from Congress.[63] However, the Director is required to provide financial operating plans and forecasts to the Office of Management and Budget, and the CFPB is subject to annual audit by the Comptroller General with access by the Government Accountability Office.[64] The CFPB funding received from the Federal Reserve System may be used to carry out the CFPB functions.[65] In addition, a separate fund, the "Civil Penalty Fund," is also held by the Federal Reserve and is composed of civil penalties that the CFPB collects pursuant to its enforcement powers.[66] These funds may be used to pay victims of consumer financial services violations, for consumer education, and/or for financial literacy programs.[67]

2C   **How does the source of funding for the CFPB impact the CFPB's ability to function, if at all?**

Since Mick Mulvaney's appointment as Acting Director in November 2017, measures have been undertaken to reduce the power of the CFPB. Specifically, Mick Mulvaney requested $0 from the

---

[57] *See* 12 U.S.C. § 5481(4) (Fastcase 2018).
[58] *See* 12 U.S.C. § 5481(5).
[59] *See* 12 U.S.C. § 5481(15).
[60] *See* 12 U.S.C. § 5497(a) (Fastcase 2018)
[61] 12 U.S.C. § 5497(a)(1).
[62] *See* 12 U.S.C. § 5497(a)(2).
[63] *See id.*
[64] *See* 12 U.S.C. § 5497(a)(4)-(5); *see also* 12 U.S.C. § 5496a(b) (Fastcase 2018).
[65] *See* 12 U.S.C. § 5497(c).
[66] *See* 12 U.S.C. § 5497(d)(1).
[67] *See* 12 U.S.C. § 5497(d)(2).

Federal Reserve as the CFPB's budget, purportedly for the purpose of reducing the CFPB's power.[68] Recall that the CFPB Director is not removable at will by the President. Specifically, the CFPB Director is removable for cause, namely, inefficiency, neglect of duty, or malfeasance.[69]

2D   **Did Director Mulvaney neglect his duties by not requesting funding for the CFPB?**

The Consumer Financial Protection Bureau has varying degrees of authority in exercising its regulatory powers with respect to very large depository institutions, nondepository institutions, and other depository institutions (those with less than ten billion dollars in assets). In addition to these specified powers over depositories and nondepositories, which will be discussed in more detail in Parts IIA, IIB, and IIC, the Consumer Financial Protection Bureau may exercise regulatory authority over **larger participants** and **covered persons**.

How does 12 U.S.C. § 5481(6) define a covered person? A covered person is any person that engages in offering or providing a consumer financial product or service as well as an affiliate of such person if the affiliate acts as a service provider.[70]

The CFPB has at least three notable regulatory powers: (1) rulemaking, (2) supervision, and (3) enforcement. One of the CFPB's tasks includes the establishment and management of the Consumer Complaint Database.[71] The CFPB Consumer Complaint Database is public. The CFPB notes on its website that "all complaint data we publish is freely available for anyone to use, analyze, and build on."[72] In other words, individual consumers may visit the CFPB Consumer Complaint Database to read complaints posted by other consumers and to retrieve information about consumer financial services providers. Prior to the CFPB, no centralized consumer complaint database existed. As of December 2, 2018, the CFPB Consumer Complaint Database housed more than 1,170,000 consumer complaints.[73] By statute, the CFPB is required to share consumer complaint information with prudential regulators, the Federal Trade Commission, other Federal agencies, and state agencies, and these groups must share information with the CFPB.[74] In addition, the CFPB must coordinate with federal agencies and state

---

[68] *See* Stacy Cowley, *Consumer Bureau's Chief Gives Big Raises, Even as He Criticizes Spending*, N.Y. TIMES, Apr. 5, 2018), https://www.nytimes.com/2018/04/05/business/cfpb-mick-mulvaney-pay-raises.html; *see also* Stacy Cowley, *Consumer Watchdog's Latest Budget Request: $0*, N.Y. TIMES, Jan. 18, 2018, https://www.nytimes.com/2018/01/18/business/cfpb-mick-mulvaney.html?module=inline.

[69] *See* 12 U.S.C. § 5491(c)(3).

[70] *See* 12 U.S.C. § 5481(6).

[71] *See* 12 U.S.C. § 5493(b)(3); 12 U.S.C. § 5511 (c)(2).

[72] CONSUMER FIN. PROTECTION BUREAU, https://www.consumerfinance.gov/data-research/consumer-complaints/ (last visited Dec. 2, 2018).

[73] *See* CONSUMER FIN. PROTECTION BUREAU CONSUMER COMPLAINT DATABASE, https://www.consumerfinance.gov/data-research/consumer-complaints/search/?from=0&searchField=all&searchText=&size=25&sort=created_date_desc (last visited Dec. 2, 2018).

[74] *See* 12 U.S.C. § 5493(b)(3).

regulators "to promote consistent regulatory treatment" of consumer financial services.[75] Consumers must receive timely responses to complaints.[76] Finally, the CFPB is charged with ensuring that "markets for consumer financial products and services operate transparently and efficiently to facilitate access and innovation."[77] This mandate for transparency may support the purpose of the Consumer Complaint Database. However, this function may decrease under the guidance of the CFPB's Director, who likely sets the tone for the CFPB's focus consistent with its mandated objectives. Mick Mulvaney "announced a series of moves intended to reduce the [B]ureau's power [. . .] Such moves include cutting public access to the [B]ureau's database of consumer complaints, which the agency had used to help guide its investigations. 'I don't see anything in here that says I have to run a Yelp for financial services sponsored by the federal government,' [Mulvaney] said."[78]

2E

Would shifting the Consumer Complaint Database from public to nonpublic impact consumer protection? Why or Why Not?

The CFPB states that:

> Since we started accepting complaints in July 2011, we've helped consumers connect with financial companies to understand issues with their mortgages, fix errors on their credit reports, stop harassment from debt collectors, and get direct responses about problems with their credit cards, checking and savings accounts, student loans, and more. We analyze the data to identify trends and problems in the marketplace to help us do a better job supervising companies, enforcing federal consumer financial laws and writing rules and regulations. We publish reports on complaints and share information with state and federal agencies.[79]

---

[75] *See* 12 U.S.C. § 5511(b)(4); 12 U.S.C. § 5495.
[76] *See* 12 U.S.C. § 5534(a) (Fastcase 2018).
[77] 12 U.S.C. § 5511(b)(5).
[78] *See* Thrush, *supra* note 53.
[79] *See* CONSUMER FIN. PROTECTION BUREAU, https://www.consumerfinance.gov/data-research/consumer-complaints/ (last visited Dec. 2, 2018).

A. RULEMAKING

The CFPB's rulemaking power is one of its most controversial powers as rulemaking may fall into three categories. First, **express rulemaking** may involve creating an established, written rule for those who are subject to the rule to review and adhere to. Alternatively, some argue that establishing rules is too restrictive and does not allow for a quickly innovating market. Therefore, some are proponents of **incentive creation.** Finally, the CFPB has been criticized by financial industry participants for **"rulemaking by enforcement."**[80] In other words, rather than establishing new, express rules, the CFPB has been criticized for creating rules through its enforcement power.

Express rulemaking can present challenges. Establishing a specific, rigid rule allows for different institutions to manipulate express language, interpreting the express rule to their advantage, and/or seeking alternatives to compliance by highlighting what language is not in the rule. In other words, creating a rule may more easily allow for the proliferation of loopholes. Loopholes, in contrast to the "safe harbors" to be discussed in this text, are not expressed in the rule, and may result in unintentional opportunities to avoid compliance. Safe harbors, on the other hand, are typically express, intended exemptions provided for in the law or rule.

Correcting a loophole and drafting express rules may require a lot of time and resources.[81] For example, express rulemaking by the CFPB is subject to a public comment period.[82] In addition, express rulemaking requires consideration of certain factors specified by law.[83] In the time during which a regulator may be working to revise a rule to rid the rule of discovered loopholes, consumers may suffer. On the other hand, establishing an express rule in advance allows financial institutions to know what to expect. Theoretically, there is an objective, unambiguous delineation between what is permissible and what is not permissible, and results are predictable. In practice, however, there is always room for ambiguity. The comment period required for express rulemaking can also create challenges. In other words, as Yale Law School Professor Roberta Romano describes, "lobbying has been deliberately built into the

---

[80] Rulemaking by enforcement has also been described as "rulemaking by subterfuge." Romano, *supra* note 4, at 34.

[81] *See* Exec. Order No. 13771, 82 FR 9339 (Jan. 30, 2017), *available at* https://www.whitehouse.gov/presidential-actions/presidential-executive-order-reducing-regulation-controlling-regulatory-costs/ (stating "it is the policy of the executive branch to be prudent and financially responsible [. . .] Toward that end, it is important that for every one new regulation issued, at least two prior regulations be identified for elimination [. . .] [T]he heads of all agencies are directed that the total incremental cost of all new regulations, including repealed regulations [. . .] shall be no greater than zero [. . .]"); *see also* Romano, *supra* note 4, at 2 (stating that "rulemaking has also moved at a glacial pace due to intensive lobbying by affected parties who, given the stakes in the legislative delegation to agencies of the task of reconfiguring financial markets and institutions, have understandably sought to shape regulatory outcomes to their advantage.").

[82] *See* 12 U.S.C. § 5512 (d)(3) (Fastcase 2018).

[83] The CFPB must consider, when prescribing a rule: "the potential benefits and costs to consumers and covered persons, including the potential reduction of access by consumers to consumer financial products or services resulting from such rule; [. . .] the impact of proposed rules on covered persons, [. . .] and the impact on consumers in rural areas." 12 U.S.C. § 5512(b)(2)(a).

rulemaking process, and serves a critical function related to information and accountability, [. . .] Namely the notice and comment rulemaking procedure [. . .] intentionally encourages such a dialogue: agencies are expected to be responsive to issues raised by interested parties in rulemaking deliberations and informed by their input [. . .]."[84]

Incentive creation, on the other hand, may not necessarily produce predictable results. For example, consider the example in Part I about taxing the purchase of cigarettes.[85] Rather than restricting the behavior of smokers and banning cigarettes, disincentives, including increasing the costs of smoking, were imposed. Through creating incentives or disincentives, rather than an express rule, regulators may be able to steer financial institutions to desired behaviors. However, unlike with an express rule, the financial institution may have the choice of whether to succumb to the incentives or disincentives after considering the financial institutions' own unique circumstances.

Rulemaking by enforcement allows for regulatory flexibility. Rulemaking by enforcement allows the CFPB to adapt to dynamic innovation and new financial services, products, and providers. The administrative costs of creating a new rule to address a loophole is diminished. Instead, by rulemaking by enforcement, the CFPB can address emerging rule interpretation issues ad hoc. However, one of the primary challenges to this "rulemaking by enforcement" is that such ad hoc rulemaking is not predictable to financial industry participants. If the financial industry participant must rely on rulemaking by enforcement for direction, this may prove challenging; the institution may not be able to weigh risks adequately if it is not put on notice that certain behavior would be interpreted as law violations until *after* the violation is being enforced. The "notice" is, in fact, the enforcement action. As a result, many industry participants consider this "rulemaking" unfair.[86] Specifically, a frequent argument is that rulemaking by enforcement rather than by express rulemaking does not allow for due process.[87] In other words, the regulated entity does not have sufficient notice of what is prohibited.[88] CFPB Director Mick Mulvaney "advised that regulation by enforcement is dead, and that he does not care much for regulation by guidance either. He noted to the [Mortgage Bankers Association] members that they have a right to know what the law is."[89]

2F — Does rulemaking by enforcement negate due process? Why or why not?

---

[84] *See* Romano, *supra* note 4, at 16.

[85] Campbell et al., *supra* note 26, at 93.

[86] Note, however, that the Supreme Court has stated that "the choice made between proceeding by general rule or by individual, ad hoc litigation is one that lies primarily in the informed discretion of the administrative agency." *N.L.R.B. v. Bell Aerospace Co. Div. of Textron, Inc.*, 416 U.S. 267, 293 (1974) (quoting *SEC v. Chenery Corp.*, 332 U.S. 194, 203 (1947)).

[87] *See Consumer Fin. Prot. Bureau v. Think Fin., LLC*, No. CV-17-127-GF-BMM, *7-8 (D. Mont. Aug. 3, 2018).

[88] *See id.*

[89] *See* Richard J. Andreano, Jr., *Regulation by Enforcement is Dead*, BALLARD SPAHR CONSUMER FIN. MONITOR BLOG (Oct. 15, 2018), https://www.consumerfinancemonitor.com/2018/10/15/regulation-by-enforcement-is-dead/.

This text will primarily consider the CFPB's express rulemaking powers.

The Consumer Financial Protection Bureau ("CFPB") has rule-making authority.[90] Specifically, the CFPB has **<u>exclusive</u>** rule-making authority for federal consumer financial services laws.[91] This rulemaking authority includes writing rules, issuing orders, and issuing guidance.[92] The CFPB's express rulemaking is subject to public comment.[93] The CFPB receives deference in interpretation of laws and rules over which it has rulemaking authority.[94]

---

[90] *See* 12 U.S.C. § 5492 (a)(10); *see also* 12 U.S.C. § 5511 (c)(5); *see also* 12 U.S.C. § 5512.
[91] *See* 12 U.S.C. § 5512(b)(4)(A).
[92] *See* 12 U.S.C. § 5512(b)(1).
[93] *See* 12 U.S.C. § 5512 (d)(3).
[94] *See* 12 U.S.C. § 5512 (b)(4)(B).

B. SUPERVISION

Supervision means conducting examinations to (1) assess an institution's compliance with federal consumer financial services laws, (2) obtain information about the financial institution's activities and procedures, and (3) assess risks to consumers and to markets for consumer financial products and services.[95]

Examinations are typically periodic examinations or risk-based examinations. Periodic examinations are conducted by the regulator and occur at set intervals, usually determined by statute or rule. A risk-based examination is an examination that is initiated because the regulator has determined that the entity poses some risk. The risk and determination of the risk frequently varies by regulator. For example, some regulators may determine that businesses with large activity volume or market share pose significant risk. Other regulators may determine, based on consumer complaints, information provided by the entity's other regulators, or other confidential information received, that the entity poses a risk. Other regulators may determine that entities or institutions without other supervision pose significant risk. Finally, other regulators may focus on examining new licensees, institutions with new products or services, institutions that have not yet been examined, and/or institutions that may be under consent agreement or had negative findings in the institution's most recent examination.

Recall from the previous discussion of depository vs. nondepository institutions that nonbank/nondepository financial institutions did not have federal supervision of compliance with consumer financial protection laws prior to the creation of the Consumer Financial Protection Bureau. The Consumer Financial Protection Bureau has supervision authority regarding federal consumer financial services laws.[96] The CFPB has *exclusive* supervisory authority over nondepository institutions.[97] For the purposes of the CFPB's supervisory authority, the CFPB has *exclusive* authority over the nondepository institutions described in 12 U.S.C. § 5514, including mortgage companies, **larger participants**, private education loan companies, payday loan companies, and other **covered persons** who pose risks to consumers.[98] The CFPB's oversight concerning "larger participants" of a market extends to certain (1) **consumer reporting** companies, (2) **debt collectors**, (3) **student loan servicers**, (4) international money transfer companies, and (5) automobile financers.[99] Debt collection will be discussed more in Part V, and consumer reporting will be discussed more in Part VIII.

The CFPB has *exclusive* supervisory authority over depository institutions with assets in excess of ten billion dollars.[100] In 2012, this amounted to the CFPB having supervisory authority over less than one

---

[95] *See* 12 U.S.C. § 5514(b)(1) (Fastcase 2018).

[96] *See* 12 U.S.C. § 5511 (c)(4).

[97] *See* 12 U.S.C. § 5514(d).

[98] *See* 12 U.S.C. § 5514(a)(1); 12 U.S.C. §5514(d).

[99] *See* 12 C.F.R. § 1090.104 (Fastcase 2018); 12 C.F.R. §1090.105 (Fastcase 2018); 12 C.F.R. § 1090.106 (Fastcase 2018); 12 C.F.R. § 1090.107 (Fastcase 2018); 12 C.F.R. § 1090.108 (Fastcase 2018).

[100] *See* 12 U.S.C. § 5515(b) (Fastcase 2018).

percent of depository institutions.[101] The CFPB conducts examinations on a periodic basis for such institutions.[102]

The CFPB has **limited** supervisory authority over depository institutions with assets of ten billion dollars or less.[103] For example, the CFPB may participate in an examination performed by such an institution's prudential regulator.[104] Ultimately, the prudential regulator retains exclusive supervisory authority over consumer financial services with respect to depository institutions with assets of ten billion dollars or less.[105] In addition, the CFPB must coordinate with federal agencies and state regulators "to promote consistent regulatory treatment" of consumer financial services[106] and to reduce "regulatory burden."[107] Ultimately, the CFPB has access to examination reports of other prudential regulators and federal agencies supervising covered persons, and the prudential regulators, state agencies, and federal agencies have access to the CFPB's examination reports.[108]

Finally, the CFPB's supervisory authority does not extend to accountants and tax preparers, real estate brokerage activities, the practice of law; persons regulated by state insurance regulators; employee benefit and other compensation plans; persons regulated by state securities regulators; persons regulated by the Commodities Futures Trading Commission; and others.[109]

---

[101] *See* Levitin, *supra* note 6, at 357.

[102] *See* 12 U.S.C. § 5515(b)(1).

[103] *See* 12 U.S.C. § 5516(c)(1) (Fastcase 2018).

[104] *See id.*

[105] *See* 12 U.S.C. § 5581(c) (Fastcase 2018).

[106] 12 U.S.C. § 5495; *see* 12 U.S.C. § 5511(b)(4); 12 U.S.C. § 5515(e)(1)-(2).

[107] 12 U.S.C. § 5514(b)(3).

[108] *See* 12 U.S.C. § 5512(c)(6)(B)-(C).

[109] *See* 12 U.S.C. §5517 (Fastcase 2018).

C. ENFORCEMENT

REGULATORY CONSEQUENCES

Recall the discussion in Part IA: Types of Financial Institutions, about the different types of financial institutions. Additionally, recall the discussion in Part ID: Regulatory Policy, about the different methods of regulation, including regulating by financial institution type. One of the purposes of the CFPB is to ensure that consumer financial services laws are enforced consistently across different institution types.[110] The CFPB has *exclusive* authority to enforce federal consumer financial services laws against nondepository institutions.[111] The CFPB has *primary* authority to enforce federal consumer financial services laws against insured depository institutions with assets in excess of ten billion dollars.[112] Other federal agencies authorized to enforce federal consumer financial services laws have *backup* authority.[113] However, the CFPB has *limited* authority to enforce federal consumer financial services laws against insured depository institutions with assets totaling ten billion dollars or less while the institution's prudential regulator has exclusive authority.[114]

The CFPB's enforcement powers include initiating a civil action against the person, imposing civil penalties, or seeking legal or equitable relief.[115] Review 12 U.S.C. § 5565 for relief that is available for violation of rule or law enforced by the CFPB. Relief by the CFPB can include:

> (A) rescission or reformation of contracts;
> (B) refund of moneys or return of real property;
> (C) restitution;
> (D) disgorgement or compensation for unjust enrichment;
> (E) payment of damages or other monetary relief;
> (F) public notification regarding the violation, including the costs of notification;
> (G) limits on the activities or functions of the person; and
> (H) civil money penalties.[116]

Civil penalties may not be imposed without due process: notice and a hearing for the person accused of the violation.[117] In addition, the CFPB may "commence, defend, or intervene in an action" for violation of a consumer law.[118] Finally, the CFPB has investigative and administrative

---

[110] *See* 12 U.S.C. § 5511(b)(4); 12 U.S.C. § 5495.
[111] *See* 12 U.S.C. § 5514(c)(1).
[112] *See* 12 U.S.C. § 5515(c)(1).
[113] *See* 12 U.S.C. § 5515(c)(3); *see* 12 U.S.C.§ 5581(c)(2)(A).
[114] *See* 12 U.S.C. § 5516(d)(1); *see* 12 U.S.C. § 5581(c)(2)(B).
[115] *See* 12 U.S.C. § 5564(a) (Fastcase 2018).
[116] 12 U.S.C. § 5565(a)(2) (Fastcase 2018).
[117] *See* 12 U.S.C. § 5565(c)(5).
[118] *See* 12 U.S.C. § 5564(g)(2)(B).

discovery powers,[119] including through subpoenas and civil investigative demands,[120] and the power to conduct hearings and adjudication proceedings.[121]

While the CFPB's length of existence is short, the Bureau's use of its enforcement powers was initially swift and perceptible.[122] More recently, however, the exercise of enforcement authority has been quelled. Since Mick Mulvaney's appointment as Acting Director, Mulvaney "froze[] all new investigations."[123]

Does the CFPB have authority to close a bank for failure to meet capital requirements?

No. The CFPB's enforcement authority only extends to enforcing federal consumer financial services laws against insured depository institutions. The prudential regulator still maintains authority over the safety and soundness of the bank.

More information regarding the CFPB's enforcement power may be found in 12 U.S.C. § 5561 *et seq.*

If the CFPB has limited oversight, including enforcement of consumer financial service laws and supervision of entities with assets of ten billion dollars or less, who ensures that such entities are compliant with consumer financial protection laws and rules? Recall from Part IB that the Federal Reserve Bank has oversight over state-chartered member banks, and the Federal Deposit Insurance Corporation has oversight over state-chartered banks that are not members of the Federal Reserve System. These state-chartered banks may also be regulated by their individual state banking regulator. A general rule of thumb is that the banks that have assets of ten billion dollars or less are state-chartered, community banks. As a result, depository institutions with assets of ten billion dollars or less still have consumer protection regulatory oversight by the institutions' prudential regulator, usually either the Federal Deposit Insurance Corporation or the Federal Reserve Bank. However, even nationally-chartered banks may have assets that amount to ten billion or less. These banks will, of course, remain under the oversight of the Office of the Comptroller of the Currency.

Notable consumer protection laws and rules will be discussed *infra* in Parts III-VIII. Many of these laws and rules were created prior to the creation of the Consumer Financial Protection Bureau. Therefore, consider, as you learn more about these laws and rules, whether the creation of the CFPB and its objectives serve a tangible goal in context. Yale Law School Professor Roberta Romano argues:

> As often occurs with "off-the-rack" legislative responses to financial crises, Dodd-Frank's

---

[119] *See generally* 12 U.S.C. § 5562 (Fastcase 2018).
[120] *See* 12 U.S.C. § 5562(b), (c).
[121] *See generally* 12 U.S.C. § 5563 (Fastcase 2018).
[122] *See* Merle, *supra* note 49 (" 'In its short years as the nation's top consumer cop, all under Director Cordray, the young Bureau has returned $12 billion dollars to over 29 million consumer victims of financial schemes by wrongdoers ranging from Wall Street banks, mortgage companies and for-profit schools to debt collectors, credit bureaus and payday lenders,' said Ed Mierzwinski, director of the consumer program at U.S. Public Interest Research Group.").
[123] *See* Thrush, *supra* note 53.

administrative reorganization mismatches problem and solution because the U.S. regulatory architecture, and in particular, absence of a designated consumer-product regulator, did not contribute to the financial crisis. [. . .] Given the simultaneous regulatory failures and crises in nations with disparate financial products, markets and regulatory structures, it is improbable that any bureaucratic reorganization would address the causes of the recent financial crisis, let alone prevent a future one.[124]

ADDITIONAL CONSEQUENCES

Thus far, regulatory enforcement has been discussed with respect to the CFPB and regulatory and/or legal consequences. Many regulatory agencies may revoke or suspend licenses or charters and/or otherwise restrict the activities of the financial institution after failing to comply with requirements. Even if a financial services provider can escape regulatory consequences, in the form of actions or other enforcement powers imposed by the regulators, the financial institution may, nevertheless suffer other consequences stemming from alleged or confirmed law violations, including financial consequences. In addition to the financial consequences that the CFPB may impose, individual consumers may initiate actions against financial institutions under certain laws, discussed *infra*. In addition to penalties, fines, restitution, legal fees, and law suits, companies may suffer other financial consequences. For example, financial consequences can include a reduction in share price, a reduction in potential future earnings, and a loss of investor confidence. Note that correcting errors can be more expensive than proactive compliance. In other words, an "expanding business spends much more money on an unforeseen problem than it does on one for which it has prepared."[125]

The realities of business decision-making can often result in additional consequences. In addition to regulatory and financial consequences, institutions may also be impacted by reputational consequences. In 2016, Wells Fargo was fined $100 million by the CFPB for opening unauthorized consumer bank accounts.[126] Specifically, the CFPB alleged that:

> Spurred by sales targets and compensation incentives, [Wells Fargo] employees boosted sales figures by covertly opening accounts and funding them by transferring funds from consumers' authorized accounts without their knowledge or consent, often racking up fees or other charges [to the consumers].[127]

As a result of creating the fake accounts and charging erroneous fees to meet sales goals and employee incentives, Wells Fargo was in violation of consumer financial protection laws enforced by the CFPB.

---

[124] Romano, *supra* note 4, at 28.
[125] *See* Lawrence Uebel, *Why Startups Should Leverage Compliance*, TECHCRUNCH, https://techcrunch.com/2015/09/01/why-startups-should-leverage-compliance/, (last visited Dec. 13, 2018).
[126] *See* Press Release, Consumer Fin. Prot. Bureau, Consumer Fin. Prot. Bureau Fines Wells Fargo $100 Million for Widespread Illegal Practice of Secretly Opening Unauthorized Accounts, (Sept. 8, 2016), https://www.consumerfinance.gov/about-us/newsroom/consumer-financial-protection-bureau-fines-wells-fargo-100-million-widespread-illegal-practice-secretly-opening-unauthorized-accounts/.
[127] *Id.*

Knowledge of the fine and corresponding consent order between the CFPB and Wells Fargo is public and is accessible via the CFPB's website.[128] Public knowledge that a company is engaging in illegal activities can have negative reputational consequences for a company. Reputational consequences can include damage to the entity's brand, negative social media discussion or negative press, loss of customer trust, and decreased employee morale. In the 2016 American Banker article *How Wells Fargo Mishandled a Reputational Crisis*, author Kate Berry describes, that Wells Fargo "failed to hold senior leadership accountable," had a "late and halfhearted" apology, "missed opportunities to fix the problem," and sent mixed messaging.[129] Specifically, Wells Fargo terminated lower level employees but permitted a top executive to retire "with a reported $125 million pay package," apologized before the Senate Banking Committee and in newspapers but not directly to impacted customers, and failed to acknowledge wrong-doing and the contributing factors of company culture early on.[130] Finally, Wells Fargo apologized but also attempted to diminish the severity of its violations by retaining incentive pay and noting that the employees committing the violations represented a miniscule percent of Wells Fargo employees.[131]

In addition to the reputational backlash Wells Fargo experienced from consumers, the institution also had to contend with the damage done by its competitors in responding to the news. Specifically, community banks used the scandal as an opportunity to pounce on Wells Fargo's missteps by highlighting the questionable business practices.[132] These community banks may be described as "stakeholders." In other words, these banks are interested in the outcome of the alleged Wells Fargo compliance violations because of the negative or positive benefits that will accrue to them.

Wells Fargo's activities "undermined customer trust" and revealed "underlying systemic problems."[133] Negative reputational fallout can be very challenging for an institution like Wells Fargo that "grew into one of the largest financial institutions in the world by building a good reputation over a long period of time."[134] In other words, the reputational consequence of a public regulatory action could be more damaging to a company than a financial consequence, such as the cost to defend a private right of action and/or payment of a fine. In addition, reputational consequences may also spur additional financial consequences. For example, Wells Fargo stock dropped nine percent in the days after the

---

[128] *See id.*
[129] Kate Berry, *How Wells Fargo Mishandled a Reputational Crisis, American Banker,* AM. BANKER, Sept. 22, 2016, https://www.americanbanker.com/news/how-wells-fargo-mishandled-a-reputational-crisis.
[130] *See id.*
[131] *See id.*
[132] *See* Emily Glazer, *Next Test for Wells Fargo: Its Reputation*, WALL S. J., Sept. 9, 2016, https://www.wsj.com/articles/next-test-for-wells-fargo-its-reputation-1473462195.
[133] *See* Ben DiPietro, *Crisis of the Week: Fake Accounts Scandal Rocks Wells Fargo*, WALL S. J., Sept. 19, 2016, https://blogs.wsj.com/riskandcompliance/2016/09/19/crisis-of-the-week-fake-accounts-scandal-rocks-wells-fargo/.
[134] *See id.*

news of its violations.[135] Note that the low-level employees involved that represented a small percent of Wells employees amounted to over 5,000 employees. **Is it possible to have 5,000 "bad apple"[136] employees engaged in wrong-doing without the direction or consent of management or company culture influences? Why or Why not?**

In addition to competitors, consumers, and the CFPB/regulators, employees are also stakeholders in the Wells Fargo fake account scandal. Terminated employees may come forward and remaining employees may feel confused about future directives.[137]

Consider whether the potential for reputational risk serves to deter behavior/compliance violations.

Consider whether civil penalties are sufficient to deter behavior/compliance violations.

2G

Finally, in addition to competitors, consumers, regulators, and employees, investors, creditors, and partners may also be stakeholders. **Should regulators consider the impact to the company's investors when imposing fines that may prove detrimental, or should the CFPB only be concerned with resolving harm to consumers?**

Figure 2C

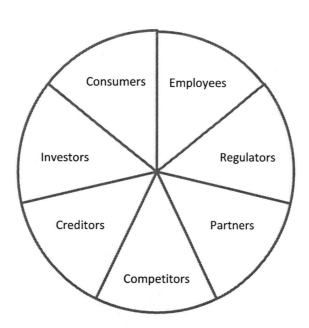

---

[135] *See* Jena McGregor, *Wells Fargo's Terrible, Horrible, No-Good, Very Bad Week* WASH. POST (Sept. 16, 2016), https://www.washingtonpost.com/news/on-leadership/wp/2016/09/16/wells-fargos-terrible-horrible-no-good-very-bad-week/?utm_term=.879d80638409.

[136] *See id* (" 'There are not 5000 bad apples,' said Maurice Schweitzer, a professor at the University of Pennsylvania's Wharton School who studies ethical decision-making.' ").

[137] *See id.*

 **What are the owners' and investors' interests?**

 **What are the interests of partners or suppliers that provide a service to the financial institution?**

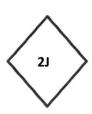 **What are the interests of the institutions' creditors?**

III. TRUTH-IN-LENDING ACT

A. LAWS AND RULES

The CFPB's powers are enumerated in the Dodd-Frank Wall Street Reform and Consumer Protection Act. The CFPB is charged with ensuring that consumers receive timely and understandable disclosures.[138] The 1968 Truth in Lending Act ("TILA") was transferred to the CFPB for regulatory oversight.[139] Specifically, the Truth in Lending Act provisions are located within 15 U.S.C. Chapter 41: Consumer Credit Protection.[140] TILA provisions are found within Subchapter I: Consumer Credit Cost Disclosure.[141] TILA is part of the Consumer Credit Protection Act of 1968.[142] The purpose of Truth in Lending is to "promote the informed use of consumer credit by requiring disclosures about its terms and cost."[143]

The informed use of credit and disclosure of costs appears noble and straightforward rather than a debatable topic. Why might a financial institution challenge the informed use of credit and disclosure costs? As is the case in most competitive markets, a financial institution contending for customers/consumers may wish to support those initiatives that will give that financial institution a competitive advantage. It is not surprising that the financial institution may be more likely to present information in a way that is advantageous to the financial institution and that leads to the consumer choosing the institution's product or service. [144] The article *A Brief Postwar History of U.S. Consumer Finance*, describes the historical context for TILA:

> We observe this close interconnection between regulation and competition in consumer credit markets. From the 1940s until the late 1960s, commercial banks fought fiercely to block laws that would force them to disclose their actual lending rates as annualized percentages. While consumer finance companies were bound by strict truth-in-lending laws, banks could use creative pricing, including discounting and add-on insurance, to advertise loans at 6 percent that had effective annual rates ranging from 20 percent to 25 percent.

---

[138] *See* 12 U.S.C. § 5511 (b)(1).

[139] *See* 12 U.S.C. § 5581(b).

[140] *See* 15 U.S.C. § 1601 (Fastcase 2018) *et seq.*

[141] *See id.*

[142] See id.

[143] 12 C.F.R. § 1026.1(b) (Fastcase 2018); *see* 15 U.S.C. § 1601(a) (stating that "The Congress finds that economic stabilization would be enhanced and the competition among the various financial institutions and other firms engaged in the extension of consumer credit would be strengthened by the informed use of credit. The informed use of credit results from an awareness of the cost thereof by consumers. It is the purpose of this subchapter to assure a meaningful disclosure of credit terms so that the consumer will be able to compare more readily the various credit terms available to him and avoid the uninformed use of credit[. . .].").

[144] *See* Lane, *supra* note 5 ("[F]raming matters – put simply, firms can present the same information in different ways and this can lead to different choices by consumers.").

With the passage of the 1968 Truth in Lending Act (TILA), banks were required to report the cost of their loans in a standardized fashion.[145]

The Consumer Financial Protection Bureau is tasked with regulatory oversight related to Regulation Z. Regulation Z, 12 C.F.R. Part 1026 *et seq.*, implements the Federal Truth in Lending Act, 12 U.S.C. § 1601 *et seq.* Regulation Z applies under the following circumstances: (1) **credit** is offered or extended to **consumers**, (2) the offering or extension of credit is done regularly, (3) the credit is subject to a finance charge or is payable by a written agreement in more than four installments; and (4) the credit is primarily for personal, family or household purposes.[146] In other words, Regulation Z applies to credit transactions to consumers. How is **credit** defined by Regulation Z? **Credit** is "the right to defer payment of debt or to incur debt and defer its payment."[147] Who is a **consumer** for Regulation Z purposes? A **consumer** is a "natural person to whom consumer credit is offered or extended."[148] A consumer credit transaction is credit extended to a natural person primarily for personal, family or household purposes.[149] **What transactions are exempt from compliance with Regulation Z?** Credit transactions primarily for business, commercial, or agricultural purposes are not generally subject to TILA.[150]

Regulation Z applies to both **open-end** and **closed-end** credit. How is **open-end credit** defined? **Open-end credit** is credit where repeated transactions are contemplated, the creditor assesses a finance charge on the outstanding unpaid balance, and additional credit up to a specified limit is made available so long as the outstanding balance is not in default.[151] **How is closed-end credit defined?** **Closed-end** credit is consumer credit "other than open-end credit" under Regulation Z.[152] Return to Part IC, Types of Financial Services.

3A   **How is closed-end credit different from open-end credit?**

This text focuses on closed-end credit. The Truth in Lending Act requires that a creditor disclose material information. How does the creditor know what disclosures are material to the transaction?[153] How is **creditor** defined? A creditor is a person who regularly extends consumer credit payable in more than

---

[145] RYAN ET AL., *supra* note 2, at 479.
[146] *See* 12 C.F.R. § 1026.1(c)(1).
[147] 12 C.F.R. § 1026.2(a)(14).
[148] 12 C.F.R. § 1026.2(a)(11).
[149] *See* 15 U.S.C. § 1602(i).
[150] *See* 15 U.S.C. § 1603(1) (Fastcase 2018).
[151] *See* 12 C.F.R. § 1026.2((a)20).
[152] *See* 12 C.F.R. § 1026.2(a)(10).
[153] 15 U.S.C. § 1602(v) defines "material disclosures" as the disclosure of the "annual percentage rate, the method of determining the finance charge and the balance upon which a finance charge will be imposed, the amount of the finance charge, the amount to be financed, the total of payments, the number and amount of payments, the due dates or periods of payments scheduled to repay the indebtedness [. . .]."

four installments or who assesses or may assess a finance charge and is the person to whom the consumer debt is initially payable.[154]

CONTENT

Read 15 U.S.C. § 1638 "Transactions Other Than Under an Open End Credit Plan" and 12 C.F.R. § 1026.18 "Content of Disclosures." **What must be included in the closed-end credit disclosures?** Generally speaking, the creditor must disclose its identity, the amount financed, the finance charge, the annual percentage rate; payment schedule; and total of payments, among other required disclosures mandated by 12 C.F.R. § 1026.18. In addition, for the amount financed disclosure, the creditor must provide to the consumer a statement that the consumer may request, in writing, a written itemization of the amount financed.[155] Read 12 C.F.R. § 1026.4 "Finance Charge." How does the regulation define **finance charge**? Regulation Z provides examples of finance charges[156] as well as lists charges that are excluded from inclusion in the finance charge.[157] The finance charge is the "cost of consumer credit as a dollar amount. It includes any charge payable directly or indirectly by the consumer and imposed directly or indirectly by the creditor as an incident to or a condition of the extension of credit. It does not include any charge of a type payable in a comparable cash transaction."[158]

FORM

How must information be disclosed? What is the form of the required disclosures? Generally speaking, "the disclosures shall be grouped together, shall be segregated from everything else, and shall not contain any information not directly related to the disclosures."[159] In addition, the disclosures must be disclosed "clearly and conspicuously," and the annual percentage rate and finance charge must be disclosed more conspicuously than other terms.[160] The disclosures must be in writing, in a form the consumer may keep, including in electronic form, and the itemization of the amount financed must be separate from other disclosures.[161] Finally, the right to the itemization of the amount financed must be presented via a "yes" and "no" space to be initialed by the consumer indicating the consumer's wishes.[162]

3B Why do you think the disclosures cannot contain any information not directly related? Why do you think the disclosures are required to be clear and conspicuous?

---

[154] *See* 15 U.S.C. §1602(g).
[155] *See* 15 U.S.C. § 1638(a)(2)(B) (Fastcase 2018).
[156] *See* 12 C.F.R. § 1026.4(b) (Fastcase 2018).
[157] *See* 12 C.F.R. § 1026.4(c).
[158] 12 C.F.R. § 1026.4(a).
[159] 12 C.F.R. § 1026.17(a)(1) (Fastcase 2018).
[160] 15 U.S.C. § 1632(a) (Fastcase 2018); *see* 12 C.F.R. § 1026.17(a)(1)-(2).
[161] *See* 12 C.F.R. § 1026.17(a)(1).
[162] *See* 15 U.S.C. § 1638(a)(2)(B).

Recall the discussion in Part I concerning methods of regulatory disclosure. Rather than restricting the financial products and services available to consumers, TILA requires that financial institutions/creditors subject to the law, disclose certain required information, as discussed above. **Does regulatory disclosure work as a successful method of consumer protection?**[163] Consider whether a "dizzying amount of information" may aid the consumer in decision-making.[164]

TIMING

When must the disclosures be provided to the consumer? The disclosures are required to be made prior to consummation of the transaction.[165] How is **consummation** defined? Consummation is "the time that a consumer becomes contractually obligated on a credit transaction."[166] Consummation is governed by state contract law.

Review Figure 1C.

To what part of the loan transaction process does the Truth in Lending Act and implementing regulations apply? Truth in Lending disclosures apply to the origination stage of the loan transaction process.

---

[163] Consider the statement that "most Americans fail to understand basic financial concepts, including how to calculate simple interest, how to account for inflation, and how to understand loan and mortgage terms." RYAN ET AL., *supra* note 2, at 496. If most Americans fail to understand information disclosed to them, is the disclosure useful in protecting the consumer and/or from reducing the consumer's risks?

[164] Campbell et al., *supra* note 26, at 91.

[165] *See* 12 C.F.R. § 1026.17(b).

[166] 12 C.F.R. § 1026.2(a)(13).

B. ENFORCEMENT

The Truth in Lending Act provides for civil liability for certain violations and additionally provides safe harbors for creditors.[167] Specifically, 15 U.S.C. §1640 provides for actual damages and statutory damages.[168] The consumer's ability to recover is limited to twice the creditor's finance charges, which amount is capped at a specified range dependent upon the type of credit extended.[169] As a result of the availability of statutory damages, a plaintiff may recover in a civil action based on a technical violation of TILA and without suffering any actual damages. The statute of limitations for a TILA violation is within one year of the violation.[170] Creditors may correct errors made within 60 days of discovering the error,[171] are not liable for unintentional violations,[172] and are not liable if the creditor's actions or lack thereof were a result of a good faith attempt to comply with a CFPB rule or regulation.[173] Assignees can also be held liable to consumers for violation of the Truth in Lending Act, if the violation is "apparent on the face of the disclosure statement."[174] A violation is apparent if, for example, the disclosure was incomplete or inaccurate on the face of the disclosure statement or the disclosure does not use the terms required by TILA.[175]

A consumer may rescind a consumer credit transaction **secured by the consumer's principal dwelling** within three business days following consummation, following delivery of the rescission notice, or following delivery of the required material TILA disclosures, whichever date is later.[176] How is **security interest** defined? A security interest is "an interest in property that secures performance of a consumer credit obligation and that is recognized by State or Federal law."[177] Upon notice and filing of rescission, the consumer is no longer obligated for any finance charge or other charges, the security interest is void, and the creditor must return any down payment, property, or earnest money.[178] In addition, the creditor is to be returned to the creditor's position prior to the credit transaction, namely, the consumer must return loan proceeds. An action for rescission must be brought within three years of the date of consummation.[179] Although included within TILA, the right of rescission is not necessarily tied to a TILA violation. Rather, the consumer can rescind the transaction within the three business days for a closed-end credit transaction without a TILA violation.[180] Creditors must provide borrowers with the Notice of Right to Rescind. The notice should disclose:

---

[167] *See generally* 15 U.S.C. § 1640 (Fastcase 2018).
[168] *See* 15 U.S.C. § 1640 (a)(1)-(2)(A)(i).
[169] *See* 15 U.S.C. § 1640(a)(2).
[170] *See* 15 U.S.C. § 1640(e).
[171] *See* 15 U.S.C. § 1640(b).
[172] *See* 15 U.S.C. § 1640(c).
[173] *See* 15 U.S.C. § 1640(f).
[174] *See* 15 U.S.C. § 1641(a) (Fastcase 2018).
[175] *See id.*
[176] *See* 15 U.S.C. § 1635(a) (Fastcase 2018).
[177] 12 C.F.R. § 1026.2(a)(25).
[178] *See* 15 U.S.C. § 1635(b).
[179] *See* U.S.C. § 1635(f).
[180] 15 U.S.C. § 1635(a).

(i) The retention or acquisition of a security interest in the consumer's principal dwelling.

(ii) The consumer's right to rescind the transaction.

(iii) How to exercise the right to rescind, with a form for that purpose, designating the address of the creditor's place of business.

(iv) The effects of rescission.

(v) The date the rescission period expires.[181]

If the creditor fails to provide the material disclosures or fails to provide the Notice of Right to Rescind, or if the material disclosures provided are not accurate, the consumer's right to rescind expires three years after consummation.[182]

Review Part IIC regarding the CFPB's enforcement authority. The CFPB has administrative enforcement authority over violations of the Truth in Lending Act.[183] Recall of course that this means that the CFPB has exclusive authority to enforce TILA against nondepository institutions.[184] The CFPB has primary authority to enforce TILA against insured depository institutions with assets in excess of ten billion dollars.[185] Other federal agencies namely, prudential and other regulators, have backup authority to enforce TILA against insured depository institutions with assets in excess of ten billion dollars and others.[186] In addition, the CFPB may use its enforcement powers, including initiating a civil action, imposing civil penalties, seeking legal or equitable relief,[187] or utilizing its investigative, subpoena, or hearing powers to enforce TILA.[188] The CFPB receives deference in interpretation of laws and rules over which it has rulemaking authority, including Regulation Z and the Truth in Lending Act.[189]

The U.S. Code provides for criminal liability for a willful and knowing violation of the Truth in Lending Act.[190] Penalties include a fine of up to $5,000 or imprisonment of one year or less, or both.[191]

The Consumer Financial Protection Bureau provides a safe harbor for use of model forms issued with rules.[192]

---

[181] *See* 12 C.F.R. § 1026.23(b) (Fastcase 2018).
[182] *See* 12 C.F.R. § 1026.23(a)(3).
[183] *See* 15 U.S.C. § 1607(a)(6) (Fastcase 2018).
[184] *See* 12 U.S.C. § 5514(c)(1).
[185] *See* 12 U.S.C. § 5515 (c)(1).
[186] *See* 12 U.S.C. § 5515 (c)(3); *see* 12 U.S.C.§ 5581(c)(2)(A).
[187] *See* 12 U.S.C. § 5564(a).
[188] *See generally* 12 U.S.C. § 5562; *see* 12 U.S.C. § 5562(b),(c). *See generally* 12 U.S.C. § 5563.
[189] *See* 15 U.S.C. § 1604(h) (Fastcase 2018).
[190] *See* 15 U.S.C. § 1611(3) (Fastcase 2018).
[191] *See id.*
[192] *See* 12 U.S.C. § 5532(d) (Fastcase 2018).

C. INTERPRETATION

Consider whether the Truth in Lending Act utilizes a restriction consumer protection method or a disclosure consumer protection method. Does TILA resolve the issue of access to information to create a "fair" playing field or does TILA resolve the issue of access to financial markets by encouraging financial inclusion? Consider the following cases interpreting provisions of TILA and/or Regulation Z. How do the courts rely on the definitions? What role does state law play in certain interpretations? Who is regulated? Who is protected? Are the protections the courts afford through their interpretations/decisions consistent with the purposes of TILA? Are TILA and Regulation Z construed in favor of the consumer?

Read *Jackson v. Grant*,[193] a 1989 case from the Ninth Circuit Court of Appeals, which considers the rescission right of consumers, consummation, and the timing of disclosures required by TILA.

---

[193] *See Jackson v. Grant*, 890 F.2d 118 (9th Cir. 1989).

JACKSON V. GRANT

CANBY, Circuit Judge:

Edna Jackson appeals the district court's judgment denying her rescission under the Federal Truth in Lending Act, ("TILA"), 15 U.S.C. Sec. 1601 *et seq.* Jackson seeks to rescind a loan transaction entered into with Union Home Loans ("Union"), a real estate loan broker. She contends that notice of her right to cancel the loan was not properly given and that other payment terms were insufficiently disclosed on the TILA Disclosure Statement. Reviewing the denial of rescission *de novo, Semar v. Platte Valley Fed. Sav. & Loan Ass'n*, 791 F.2d 699, 703 (9th Cir.1986), we reverse the judgment of the district court.

BACKGROUND

In June of 1982, Union instituted foreclosure proceedings on a $26,000 loan made to Jackson in 1981. The loan was secured by a deed of trust recorded against Jackson's residence in Richmond, California. A trustee's sale was scheduled for February 9, 1983. In January of 1983, Jackson and Union discussed takeout financing to avoid the pending foreclosure. Union loan officer, Dennis Moore, ordered an appraisal of Jackson's property and foreclosure was postponed.

On February 18, 1983, Jackson received, read and executed the following documents: (1) TILA Disclosure Statement; (2) Mortgage Loan Disclosure Statement; (3) Summary and Acknowledgment of the Terms of the Loan Transaction (hereinafter "Summary of Loan Terms"); (4) Deed of Trust; (5) Promissory Note; (6) Notice of Right to Cancel.

The TILA Disclosure Statement listed the annual percentage rate, the finance charge, the amount financed, the total payments, and the payment schedule for the loan. The Mortgage Loan Disclosure Statement and the Statement of Loan Terms informed Jackson that Union will not be the lender, that the lender is presently not known and that Jackson was not guaranteed a loan. The name of the lender was left blank on the Promissory Note and Deed of Trust. The Notice of Right to Cancel specified March 1, 1983 as the last date for cancellation.

Unable to find another lender, on April 28, 1983, Union sent a letter to Jackson advising her that the "loan will be made with funds owned or controlled by Union Home Loans." The terms of the loan were set out in the note and deed of trust executed, and the Disclosure Statement presented, on February 18, 1983, except that Jackson was required to pay an additional $700.00 and to delete credit life insurance from the loan. Jackson agreed to these changes and the loan closed on April 29, 1983.

On February 7, 1986, Jackson notified Syd and Belle G. Grant, assignees of the loan made by Union, of her election to cancel the loan transaction pursuant to the TILA. She filed a complaint seeking rescission on February 10, 1986. First, Jackson argued that the loan transaction was not "consummated" until April of 1983 and that she therefore did not receive proper notice of her right to cancel the transaction within three business days following consummation. Second, Jackson contended that the payment schedule for the loan as set forth in the TILA Disclosure Statement is insufficient. The district court made no findings with regard to the first contention but after a bench trial apparently stated on the record that the loan transaction had been consummated in February and therefore the Notice of Right to Cancel was properly given. In its order of November 26, 1986, denying the parties' cross-motions for summary judgment prior to trial, the district court held that the failure of the TILA Disclosure Statement to specify the exact payment due dates was not a material nondisclosure.

DISCUSSION

The TILA was enacted by Congress to "avoid the uninformed use of credit." *Mourning v. Family Publications Serv. Inc.*, 411 U.S. 356, 377, 93 S.Ct. 1652 1664, 36 L.Ed.2d 318 (1973) (quoting 15 U.S.C. Sec. 1601). In order to effectuate this purpose, the TILA has been liberally construed in this circuit. *Eby v. Reb Realty, Inc.*, 495 F.2d 646, 650 (9th Cir.1974). Even technical or minor violations of the TILA impose liability on the creditor. *Semar v. Platte Valley Fed. Sav. & Loan Ass'n*, 791 F.2d 699, 704 (9th Cir.1986). "'To insure that the consumer is protected ... [the TILA and accompanying regulations must] be absolutely complied with and strictly enforced.'" *Id.* (quoting *Mars v. Spartanburg Chrysler Plymouth, Inc.*, 713 F.2d 65, 67 (4th Cir.1983)).

Section 125(a) of the TILA, 15 U.S.C. Sec. 1635(a), provides that in credit transactions in which a security interest in a consumer's residence is retained:

> the [consumer] shall have the right to rescind the transaction until midnight of the third business day following the consummation of the transaction or the delivery of the information and rescission forms required under this section together with a statement containing the material disclosures required under this subchapter, whichever is later.

This right of rescission is further explained in Section 226.23(a)(3) of Regulation Z[194] of the Federal Reserve Board:

> The consumer may exercise the right to rescind until midnight of the third business day following consummation, delivery of the notice [of the right to rescind], or delivery of all material disclosures, whichever occurs last. If the required notice or material disclosures are not delivered, the right to rescind shall expire 3 years after consummation.

12 C.F.R. Sec. 226.23(a)(3).[195] Notice of the right to rescind must specify the date the rescission period expires. 12 C.F.R. Sec. 226.23(b)(5).[196] Jackson argues that because the loan transaction was not consummated until late April, the rescission period expired three business days *after* that date. Accordingly, the Notice of the Right to Cancel delivered to Jackson in February listed an incorrect expiration date of March 1, prior to the actual consummation of her loan. Therefore, the "required notice" was never delivered and the right to rescind the transaction extended until three years after the April consummation date.

---

[194] 12 C.F.R. § 1026.23(a)(3).
[195] *Id.*
[196] 12 C.F.R. § 1026.23(b)(5).

Jackson's argument has merit. Under Regulation Z, consummation "means the time that a consumer becomes contractually obligated on a credit transaction." 12 C.F.R. Sec. 226.2(a)(13).[197] When a consumer "becomes contractually obligated" is, in turn, determined by looking to state law:

> State law governs. When a contractual obligation on the consumer's part is created is a matter to be determined under applicable law; Regulation Z does not make this determination. A contractual commitment agreement, for example, that under applicable law binds the consumer to the credit terms would be consummation. Consummation, however, does not occur merely because the consumer has made some financial investment in the transaction ... unless, of course, applicable law holds otherwise.

Cal. Civ. Code §1550 sets forth the required elements of a contract under California law. They include:

> 1. Parties capable of contracting;
>
> 2. Their consent;
>
> 3. A lawful object; and,
>
> 4. A sufficient cause or consideration.

If an essential element of the contract is reserved for the future agreement of both parties, there is generally no legal obligation created until such an agreement is entered into. *Transamerica Equip. Leasing Corp. v. Union Bank*, 426 F.2d 273, 274 (9th Cir.1970); *Ablett v. Clauson*, 43 Cal.2d 280, 272 P.2d 753, 756 (1954); 1 Witkin SUMMARY OF CALIFORNIA LAW, Contracts Secs. 142, 156 (9th ed. 1987). It is essential not only that the parties to the contract exist, but that it is possible to identify them. Cal. Civ. Code 1558. *See San Francisco Hotel Co. v. Baior*, 189 Cal.App.2d 206, 11 Cal.Rptr. 32, 36 (1961) (names of seller and buyer are essential factors in considering whether contract is sufficiently certain to be specifically enforced); *Cisco v. Van Lew*, 60 Cal.App.2d 575, 141 P.2d 433, 437 (1943) (contract for sale of land must identify the parties to the transaction); *Losson v. Blodgett*, 1 Cal.App.2d 13, 36 P.2d 147, 149 (1934) (valid real property lease must contain names of parties).

In the present case, on February 18, 1983, Jackson executed a series of documents which designated herself as the borrower and Union as the "broker" or "arranger of credit." Several documents, including the Mortgage Loan Disclosure Statement and the Statement of Loan Terms, explicitly state that Union is not the lender and that Jackson was not guaranteed a loan by signing the loan documents. The Deed of Trust and the Promissory Note signed by Jackson leave the name of the beneficiary/lender blank, although Jackson granted Union the authority to fill in those blanks when a lender was arranged. While it is not necessary to decide what, if any, binding agreement was created by and between Jackson and Union on February 18, one conclusion is inescapable. No one, including Union, had agreed to extend

---

[197] 12 C.F.R. § 1026.23(a)(13).

credit to Jackson as of that date and no loan transaction was "consummated." The lender is unidentifiable and therefore no valid loan contract existed.

At most, the February 18 documents constituted an offer by Jackson to accept a loan under the terms specified. That offer was not "accepted" until Union agreed to fund Jackson's loan itself. *See* Cal.Civ.Code § 1586 ("[a] proposal may be revoked at any time before its acceptance is communicated by the proposer, but not afterwards"). Because no contract existed, Jackson was not "contractually obligated" within the meaning of 12 C.F.R. Sec. 226.2(a)(13).[198]

Murphy v. Empire of America, FSA, 746 F.2d 931 (2d Cir.1984), relied on by Union, is not controlling and can be distinguished from the instant case. In *Murphy*, the Second Circuit rejected an argument that "consummation" for TILA purposes does not occur until the closing of a loan transaction; it held that "[u]nder New York law the consumer's acceptance of a lender's commitment offer constitutes a binding contract." *Id.* at 934. "The transaction is consummated when the lender and borrower sign a contract obligating them, respectively, to lend and to borrow the funds." *Id.* Here, however, Union did not sign a commitment letter or any other contract obligating Union to lend funds in February. The identity of the lender remained unresolved, and any loan contract therefore unconsummated, until late April. *See also Baxter v. Sparks Oldsmobile, Inc.*, 579 F.2d 863, 864 (4th Cir.1978) (TILA does not apply when no binding contract consummated by parties; condition precedent necessary to consummate the extension of credit was "approval of an appropriate financier"). *Cf. Waters v. Weyerhaeuser Mortgage Co.*, 582 F.2d 503, 506 (9th Cir.1978) (consummation occurs at closing when no commitment letter sent and borrower had not accepted an offer to create a binding contract prior to closing).

Because the loan transaction was not consummated until late April and Jackson received no notice of her TILA cancellation right and the expiration date at that time, Jackson's right to rescind extended three years and her request for rescission several months before her balloon payment was due was timely. We reach this conclusion without great enthusiasm, for Jackson received many of the benefits of the agreement she is now rescinding. Nevertheless, Congress did not intend for TILA to apply only to sympathetic consumers; Congress designed the law to apply to all consumers, who are inherently at a disadvantage in loan and credit transactions.

Semar v. Platte Valley Fed. Sav. & Loan Ass'n, 791 F.2d 699, 705 (9th Cir.1986).

Our conclusion makes it unnecessary to address whether there was insufficient disclosure of the repayment terms. This case is remanded to the district court for proceedings not inconsistent with this opinion.

REVERSED AND REMANDED.

TROTT, Circuit Judge, dissenting:

---

[198] *Id.*

I respectfully dissent. I agree with Judge Conti and Judge Schnacke that consummation of Edna Jackson's loan occurred on February 18, 1983. As I see it, Union Home Loans and Jackson were parties to a binding contract as of that date, and the source of the funds was irrelevant. Union was obligated to come up with the money, and it did. Accordingly, the right to rescind extended only until March 1, 1983.

Under the circumstances her attempt to cancel the transaction almost three years later on February 7, 1986 was almost three years too late.

Today, the Grants learn a painful lesson. They learn that a law designed by Congress to shield the unwary consumer can also be a sword with which a wily borrower can sever financial responsibilities, leaving a trusting lender holding an empty bag. If the majority is correct that Jackson's arguments have technical merit—and I agree that the majority has made a strong case for its analysis—this result lends new meaning to the phrase "biting the hand that feeds you." I do share one sentiment with the majority: their lack of enthusiasm for this result.

What fails to come through in the majority's opinion is that Jackson was rescued from a trustees' sale by Dennis Moore who went out of his way to save Jackson's home. This is his business, so he gets no medals for his behavior, but neither he nor his assignees deserved what they got in return. Three years later, after enjoying the benefit of Mr. Moore's helping hand, Edna Jackson ducked out on her financial obligations on the eve of the required final payment of $38,570. The Grants now also know what a loophole is. It is possible for people to live up to moral obligations even if the cold letter of the law provides an easy out, but this case does not provide a display of that virtue. I am reminded of the observation of H.L. Mencken who said, "Injustice is relatively easy to bear; what stings is Justice." Mencken, H.L., *Prejudices*: Third Series (1922). If this is what Congress intended when it set out to protect the unwary from "... home improvement racketeers who trick homeowners, particularly the poor ...," I would be quite surprised. I fear instead that what we have before us is an example of a well-intentioned law being used for questionable purposes.

****

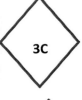

Review Figure 1C: What part of the loan transaction does Union represent? What part of the loan transaction do the Grants represent?

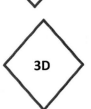

If Jackson did not rescind the loan, does she have a cause of action against the Grant's for Union's insufficient disclosure of payment terms? Why or Why Not?

3E   Is the dissent's comparison of a "wily borrower"[199] vs. an "unwary consumer"[200] consistent with the purposes of the Truth in Lending Act? Is a "wily borrower" entitled to accurate and complete disclosures? Why or why not?

3F   Is the dissent's characterization of Edna Jackson as a "wily borrower" who "ducked out on her financial obligations"[201] fair?

3G   What is the timeline for the loan at issue in *Jackson v. Grant*?

3H   At the time of the disclosure, the lender was not known. Is this significant? Why or Why not? Refer back to Part I. What is a loan broker? Who was the creditor in the February 1983 disclosure? Is the identity of the creditor significant? Why or Why Not?

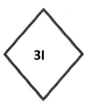

3I   Why does the case state that the right of rescission is further explained in Regulation Z of the *Federal Reserve Board?*

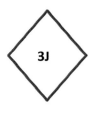

3J   12 C.F.R. § 1026.17(c) states, "if a disclosure becomes inaccurate because of an event that occurs after the creditor delivers the required disclosures, the inaccuracy is not a violation of this part, although new disclosures may be required." 12 C.F R § 1026.17(f) states that "if disclosures required by this subpart are given before the date of consummation of a transaction and a subsequent event makes them inaccurate, the creditor shall disclose before consummation [. . .] (1) Any changed term unless the term was based on an estimate in accordance with § 1026.17(c)(2) and was labeled an estimate; (2) All changed terms, if the annual percentage rate at the time of consummation varies from the annual percentage rate disclosed earlier by more than 1/8 of 1 percentage point in a regular transaction, or more than ¼ of 1 percentage point in an irregular transaction, as defined in § 1026.22(a)." **Could these**

---

[199] *See Jackson v. Grant*, 890 F.2d 118, 122 (9th Cir. 1989) (Trott, S., dissenting).
[200] *See id.*
[201] *See id.*

provisions of Regulation Z be useful to the court's interpretations in *Jackson v. Grant*? Why or Why Not?

3K

In footnote 2 to the case, omitted here, the court states that "Jackson also argues that even if the loan was 'consummated' in February, the March 1st rescission date was incorrect because the loan was not made on February 23, three business days before March 1. Because of our decision that the loan was consummated in April, we do not reach this issue."[202] **How would you decide this issue based on an interpretation of the regulation and its purposes?** Take a look at Figure 3C, a 1983 calendar, below. If the loan was consummated and Jackson signed the disclosure on February 18, 1983, **what date would be the last date for Jackson to rescind the loan under the regulation?**

Figure 3C

February 1983						
Sun	Mon	Tues	Wed	Thur	Fri	Sat
		1	2	3	4	5
6	7	8	9	10	11	12
13	14	15	16	17	18	19
20	21	22	23	24	25	26
27	28					
March 1983						
		1	2	3	4	5

3L

In footnote 5 to the case, omitted here, the court states that "the regulations define 'credit' as 'the right to defer payment of debt or to incur debt and defer its payment.' 12 C.F.R. Sec. 226.2(a)(14)."[203] **Did Jackson receive 'credit' from Union, as that term is defined by the regulation, in February 1983? Did Jackson receive 'credit' from Union, as that term is defined by the regulation, in April 1983?**

---

[202] *See id.* at 119 n.2.
[203] *See id.* at 121 n.5.

3M

In footnote 7 to the case, omitted here, the court states that "some courts have found that a consumer's right of action attaches under the TILA despite the failure to consummate a mutually binding contract. *See, e.g., Bryson v. Bank of New York*, 584 F.Supp. 1306, 1317 (S.D.N.Y.1984) (TILA attaches when consumer committed 'without regard for the degree of commitment of the lender"); *Madewell v. Marietta Dodge, Inc.*, 506 F.Supp. 286 (N.D.Ga.1980) (consumers obligated under Georgia law); *Copley v. Rona Enterprises, Inc.*, 423 F.Supp. 979, 982-83 (S.D.Ohio 1976). These decisions may be consistent with 12 C.F.R. Sec. 226.2(a)(13)[204] which defines consummation as the point at which "a consumer becomes contractually obligated.' However, they do not alter our reasoning in this case; namely, that Jackson was not contractually obligated in February because, under California law, no contract existed at all binding Jackson to Union or any other lender."[205] **Can a consumer's right of action attach when only the consumer is contractually obligated? In other words, can the consumer rescind the contract if only the consumer is obligated under the contract? Why or why not?**

3N

The dissent refers to a loophole.[206] **Is this characterization accurate? Can the CFPB exercise express rulemaking powers to correct such a "loophole?"**

Read the next case, *Egana v. Blair's Bail Bonds Inc.*,[207] a 2018 Eastern District of Louisiana case, in which the court considers a motion to dismiss with respect to the applicability of TILA and the definition of **creditor**.

---

[204] 12 C.F.R. § 1026.23(a)(13).
[205] *See Jackson*, 890 F.2d at 122 n.7.
[206] *See id.* at 122 (Trott, S., dissenting).
[207] *Egana v. Blair's Bail Bonds Inc.*, No. 17-5899 Section H, 2018 (E.D. La. June 1, 2018).

JANE TRICHE MILAZZO, District Judge.

Before the Court are a Motion to Dismiss filed by Bankers Insurance Company, Inc., Bankers Surety Services, Inc., and Bankers Underwriters, Inc. (the "Bankers Defendants"); a Motion to Dismiss filed by Blair's Bail Bonds, Inc. and New Orleans Bail Bonds, LLC (the "Blair's Defendants"); and a Motion to Dismiss filed by A2i LLC, Alternative to Incarceration NOLA, Inc., and Alternative to Incarceration, Inc. (the "A2i Defendants"). For the following reasons, the Motions are GRANTED IN PART.

In June 2016, Plaintiffs, Ronald Egana, his close friend Tiffany Brown, and his mother Samantha Egana, signed a contract and payment agreement with the Blair's Defendants in order to secure bail for Mr. Egana. The agreement provided that the Blair's Defendants would post bail in exchange for a $3,275.00 premium to be loaned to Plaintiffs and paid back in installments. Plaintiffs were also required to consent to having their payments applied to the preexisting balance that Mr. Egana owed to Defendants, which amounted to about $3,800.00. The Bankers Defendants acted as surety on the bonding agreement.

As a condition of the loan, Defendants required Mr. Egana to wear an ankle monitor, and he was charged a fee of $10 per day by the A2i Defendants in connection with the use of the ankle monitor. Although Plaintiffs allege that they were initially told that the ankle monitor would be removed after they paid $3,000.00, they were later told that the insurance company, the Bankers Defendants, had "changed its mind" and would require that Mr. Egana wear the ankle monitor longer.

. . .

Plaintiffs contend that the bonding agreement violated state and federal law by failing to disclose key terms of the loan and charging above the limit allowed by state law on bail bond premiums. Plaintiffs bring claims for violations of the Truth in Lending Act ("TILA") . . .The Blair's Defendants have moved for dismissal of Plaintiffs' . . . TILA claims against them. The Bankers Defendants and A2i Defendants separately move for dismissal of all claims against them.

. . .

TILA Claims

Plaintiffs bring claims under the Truth in Lending Act against the Blair's Defendants and the Bankers Defendants. These Defendants move for dismissal of Plaintiffs' TILA claims under several theories [. . .] they argue that TILA does not apply to the transaction at issue here. Finally, the Bankers Defendants argue that they are not a "creditor" under the terms of TILA.

. . .

Applicability of TILA

Defendants next argue that Plaintiffs cannot succeed on their TILA claims because they have not plead sufficient facts to establish that Defendants extended credit as required under the Act. TILA applies to each individual or business that offers or extends credit when four conditions are met: "(i) The credit is offered or extended to consumers; (ii) The offering or extension of credit is done regularly; (iii) The credit is subject to a finance charge or is payable by a written agreement in more than four installments; and (iv) The credit is primarily for personal, family, or household purposes." "A person regularly extends consumer credit only if it extended credit . . . more than 25 times . . . in the preceding calendar year." Defendants first argue that they are not subject to the provisions of TILA because they are not "in the business of extending credit." Defendants cite to two cases to support this proposition. In the first, *In re Gibbs*, the court noted, in *dicta*, that the Defendant was not in the business of extending credit and that the transaction at issue bore "no resemblance [to] transactions truth-in-lending laws were intended to cover." It based its decision, however, on the fact that the transaction was not subject to any finance charge. It held that the alleged finance charge was actually a late fee pursuant to a lease provision. The second case, *Bonfiglio v. Nugent*, held only that TILA does not apply to debts owed pursuant to a court order because such is not the extension of consumer credit. The Court does not find, as Defendants suggest, that these cases stand for the proposition that TILA does not apply to situations where a company is not involved in a lending-type business. Rather, these cases are simply situations in which a transaction did not satisfy the four conditions required for TILA to apply.

Next, Defendants argue that Plaintiffs cannot succeed on the TILA claims against them because the extension of credit was not subject to a finance charge. Plaintiffs argue that the ankle monitoring fees, other unexplained fees, and the bundling of outstanding balances constitute financing charges. Plaintiffs allege that they would not have been allowed to enter into the bail payment arrangement without these charges, and they are therefore charges incident to the extension of credit. TILA defines a "finance charge" as "the sum of all charges, payable directly or indirectly by the person to whom the credit is extended, and imposed directly or indirectly by the creditor as an incident to the extension of credit. The finance charge does not include charges of a type payable in a comparable cash transaction." Without considering whether the ankle monitoring fees or bundling of Mr. Egana's prior balances constitutes finance charges, this Court finds that Plaintiffs have alleged facts sufficient to establish that the credit transaction may have been subject to a finance charge. Plaintiffs' Complaint alleges that as part of the bail bond transaction they were charged an additional $130.00 for which no explanation was given. Viewing the Complaint in the light most favorable to Plaintiffs, this Court finds that such a charge could constitute a finance charge under TILA. Accordingly, this argument for dismissal of Plaintiffs' TILA claims fails.

Finally, the Bankers Defendants argue that they cannot be liable under TILA because they are not "creditors" as defined in the act. TILA defines a "creditor" as: [A] person who both (1) regularly extends, whether in connection with loans, sales of property or services, or otherwise, consumer credit which is payable by agreement in more than four installments or for which the payment of a finance charge is or may be required, and (2) is the person to whom the debt arising from the consumer credit transaction is initially payable on the face of the evidence of indebtedness or, if there is no such evidence of indebtedness, by agreement. The Bankers Defendants argue that the face of the bail bond agreement, attached to the Complaint, in no way indicates that the amounts are payable to them. Rather, the form merely states "Blair's Bail Bonds, LLC" at the top. Plaintiffs argue that this document does not represent the entirety of the agreement between the parties, and that regardless, it does not indicate to whom payments are due. Plaintiffs argue that the Blair's Defendants acted as an agent for the Bankers Defendants and that it is plausible that the Bankers Defendants also agreed to extend credit for the premium through their agent.

Even accepting Plaintiffs' arguments as true, however, their TILA claim against the Bankers Defendants cannot prevail. There are no facts in Plaintiffs' Complaint that would support an inference that the installment payments on the bail bond premium were initially payable to the Bankers Defendants. Even if the Bankers Defendants also extended credit and those amounts were ultimately owed to Bankers, the Complaint expressly alleges that the Blair's Defendants initially collect the payments. Accordingly, the Bankers Defendants cannot be said to be creditors under the terms of TILA. Plaintiffs' TILA claim against the Bankers Defendants is dismissed.

****

3O

The court does not decide whether the various fees amount to a finance charge. **Could the ankle monitoring fees constitute a finance charge? Why or Why Not? Could the "unexplained charge of $130.00"[208] constitute a finance charge? Why or Why Not? What additional information do you need, if any, to decide? If you represented the defendants, what type of fee would you advise would not constitute a finance charge regarding the $130.00? Could a TILA violation still be pursued if the $130 fee was, in fact, "unexplained"?[209] Why or Why Not? What additional information do you need, if any, to decide**?

3P

Is there a plausible argument that amounts owed in this case are not subject to TILA because, even if the amounts owed were credit, the credit is not primarily for personal, family, or household purposes? Why or why not?

3Q

How does the argument that the Defendants do not extend credit differ from the argument that Defendants are not creditors?

---

[208] *Egana v. Blair's Bail Bonds Inc.*, No. 17-5899 Section H, 2018, at *16 (E.D. LA. June 1, 2018).
[209] *Id.*

 **3R**   Would the defendants in *Egana* have a competitive advantage by not disclosing material terms subject to TILA?

 **3S**   If a consumer lender, bank, or other traditional financial institution loaned the plaintiffs the funds for bail, would the case be decided differently? Should the case be decided differently? Why or why not? What additional information do you need, if any, to decide?

 **3T**   Review 15 U.S.C. § 1640(c). Can the Defendants avoid TILA liability by demonstrating that the compliance failure was unintentional? Why or Why not? What additional information do you need, if any, to decide?

 **3U**   Would the CFPB have authority to enforce the proposed TILA violation with respect to the Defendants in this case? Why or Why not? What additional information do you need, if any, to decide?

Read the next case, *Lea v. Buy Direct, L.L.C.,*[210] a 2014 Fifth Circuit Court of Appeals case that considers whether a contract existed for TILA consummation purposes.

---

[210] 755 F.3d 250 (5th Cir., 2014).

LESLIE H. SOUTHWICK, Circuit Judge:

Angela Lea and Darrel Lea brought this action seeking statutory damages under the Truth in Lending Act. They claim that Buy Direct, L.L.C., doing business as Direct Buy of Houston North, failed to provide the dates that payments would be due on an installment contract for membership in Direct Buy's wholesale membership club. The district court granted summary judgment to Direct Buy. We REVERSE and REMAND for entry of judgment in favor of the Leas.

FACTUAL AND PROCEDURAL BACKGROUND

On May 16, 2012, Angela and Darrel Lea attended an "Open House" event at the Direct Buy Houston North location. Direct Buy is a wholesale membership club which offers members the opportunity to purchase home furnishings and electronics at wholesale prices through Direct Buy's vendor network. At the event, the Leas decided that they wished to join the Direct Buy membership club, at a cost of $3,995 for a three-year membership. Unable to make a required 10% down payment that day, the Leas agreed to pay $100 on May 16, and then $295 on June 5. The parties executed a Membership Agreement and a Retail Installment Contract, both post-dated June 5, 2012. On the form, the blanks for the "day of each month" the installment payments would be due and the "beginning" date of the Leas' payments were left blank, to be determined based upon the date the down payment was fully paid. The Leas and Direct Buy also executed a Payment Agreement, authorizing Direct Buy to charge the Leas' credit card for the $295 on June 5. At the Leas' request, this date was moved to June 8.

On June 8, Direct Buy attempted to charge the Leas' credit card for the $295, but the charge was declined. Pursuant to a provision in the Payment Agreement, on June 9, Direct Buy successfully charged the Leas' credit card for $100, leaving $195 of the down payment yet unpaid. On June 13, Direct Buy attempted to charge the Leas' card for the remaining $195, but the charge was declined. Finally, on June 21, Direct Buy successfully but erroneously charged the Leas' credit card for $295. Within the next 40 minutes, Direct Buy correctly refunded $100 to the Leas' credit card but then incorrectly refunded another $100. This meant that the Leas still had not paid the full $395 for the down payment. Also on June 21, the Leas attempted to cancel their Direct Buy membership in a telephone call to Direct Buy. On July 12, the Leas filed a chargeback request with their bank for the return of the $295 successfully charged to their credit card, citing the attempted cancellation from the June 21 telephone call. Direct Buy responded to the chargeback request from the Leas' bank with the Payment Agreement authorizing the charges and the Membership Agreement and Retail Installment Contract. Though the Leas' bank resolved the matter in Direct Buy's favor, Direct Buy canceled the Leas' membership on August 8 in accordance with the Leas' request. On October 29, the Leas sued in the United States District Court for the Southern District of Texas. On November 30, after the Leas filed a complaint with the Office of the Texas Attorney General, Direct Buy issued a check for $295 to the Leas, fully refunding all payments on their membership.

The Leas' suit alleged one cause of action: that Direct Buy had violated the Truth in Lending Act ("TILA") and its implementing regulations by failing to include the starting date and subsequent monthly payment due dates. *See* 15 U.S.C. § 1638(a)(6); 12 C.F.R. § 1026.18(g). Direct Buy moved to dismiss under Federal Rule of Civil Procedure 12(b)(6), which the district court later converted to a motion for summary judgment. The district court concluded that the contract was never "consummated" because the down payment was a condition precedent to the extension of credit, and the Leas never fully made their down payment. Thus, the district court concluded TILA did not apply and granted summary judgment in favor of Direct Buy. The Leas appeal.

DISCUSSION

"We review a grant of summary judgment *de novo*, applying the same legal standards as do the district courts." *Vuncannon v. United States*, 711 F.3d 536, 538 (5th Cir.2013). Summary judgment is proper when viewing the evidence in the light most favorable to the non-movant, "there is no genuine dispute as to any material fact and the movant is entitled to judgment as a matter of law." Fed.R.Civ.P. 56(a).

Under TILA, "a creditor ... shall disclose to the person who is obligated on a ... consumer credit transaction the information required under this subchapter." 15 U.S.C. § 1631(a). For a "consumer credit transaction other than an open end credit plan, the creditor shall disclose ... [t]he number, amount, and due dates or period of payments scheduled to repay the total of payments." 15 U.S.C. § 1638(a)(6). Successful plaintiffs may recover statutory damages against violators of TILA. 15 U.S.C. § 1640(a)(2)(A). The disclosures required by TILA must be made "before consummation of the transaction." 12 C.F.R. § 226.17(b). "Consummation means the time that a consumer becomes contractually obligated on a credit transaction." 12 C.F.R. 226.2(a)(13); *see also Davis v. Werne*, 673 F.2d 866, 869 (5th Cir.1982).

Here, the Leas agreed on May 16, 2012, to make a down payment in two separate credit card charges, one that day and a second on June 5. They also signed a Membership Agreement and Retail Installment Contract post-dated June 5. We first determine whether an agreement for the extension of credit was "consummated" on May 16 when the Leas signed the Membership Agreement, Payment Agreement, and paid the first $100 of their down payment. The district court analyzed the down payment as a condition precedent to the extension of credit. That is, Direct Buy was not obligated to extend the agreed-upon credit to the Leas until they made the down payment. Concluding that the Leas never fully paid the down payment, the district court reasoned that the condition precedent of the down payment was not met and the contract was never consummated. We disagree.

Precedent on consummation of credit transactions for TILA is sparse. Nonetheless, we find *Davis* instructive. In *Davis*, a seller of storm doors and window guards entered into an installment sales contract with a consumer, with the consumer to pay for those fixtures over a 48–month period. *Davis*, 673 F.2d at 868. When the seller-creditor was unable to assign the credit agreement, the agreement was rescinded and the parties arranged financing through another lender. *Id.* The district court there had concluded that because the parties mutually rescinded the contract later, it must not have been consummated for TILA purposes. *Id.* We rejected this conclusion, holding that "post-consummation abandonment of a financing agreement generally will have no effect upon a creditor's TILA liability." *Id.*

at 870. This is because TILA "is a disclosure law" designed to protect consumers and does not implicate "the duty of subsequent performance" on the relevant contract or contracts. *Id.*

We conclude that even though the Leas canceled their Direct Buy membership and sought to rescind the contract for credit before they completed the down payment, the contract was consummated for the purposes of TILA. The agreement was consummated when the Leas signed the Membership Agreement, Retail Installment Contract, and Payment Agreement and paid the first $100 of their down payment. That is when their obligations became fixed even though their performance was far from complete. It is important that those obligations included the need to comply with terms for the extension of credit. "Consummation does not occur when the consumer becomes contractually committed to a *sale* transaction, unless the consumer also becomes legally obligated to accept a particular *credit* arrangement."

. . . .

In sum, a credit transaction occurred on May 16 when the Leas paid $100, agreed to pay the remaining $295, and signed the Membership Agreement and Retail Installment Contract. To comply with its TILA duties, Direct Buy at that time was required to disclose a payment schedule, specifically, "[t]he number, amount, and due dates or period of payments scheduled to repay the total of payments." 15 U.S.C. § 1638(a)(6); *see also* 12 C.F.R. § 1026.18(g). The contracts did not show the day of the month that payments were due or the beginning date of the installment payments. They were intentionally left blank by Direct Buy, to be completed upon the receipt of the Leas' full down payment on an uncertain date. Neither the Membership Agreement nor Retail Installment Contract contained any language showing when the installment payments were to commence or at what interval they would be due. *See* 15 U.S.C. § 1638(a)(6); 12 C.F.R. § 1026.18(g). TILA is a private attorneys general statute enacted to "penalize noncomplying creditors and deter future violations." *Davis*, 673 F.2d at 869. Plaintiffs recover "even if they have not sustained any actual damages, or even if the creditors are guilty of only minute deviations from the requirements of TILA." *Id.*

Here, Direct Buy's failure to include the starting date and interval, or, alternatively, the day of each month the Leas' installment payments would be due, is a technical violation. Direct Buy's decision to leave the contract blanks unfilled was, at least in part, an accommodation to the Leas. A sister circuit suggested "it is not necessary or appropriate to hold creditors absolutely liable for every non-compliance and to disregard completely the factual situation out of which the claim has arisen." *Streit v. Fireside Chrysler–Plymouth, Inc.*, 697 F.2d 193, 196 (7th Cir.1983). "We believe that Congress would not have intended to impose liability on a creditor for a technical violation where [the transaction disintegrated] because of the consumer's complete failure to fulfill his obligations." *Id.* We acknowledge the equities but conclude that the statutory language is unqualified: a consumer is entitled to TILA disclosures prior to consummating a transaction. We find no basis in the statute to vary the application of TILA's requirements due to equitable considerations. Though we may see no harm here and find acquiescence by the consumer for whose protection the TILA requirement exists, we are compelled to apply TILA as written. When the parties entered into this agreement on May 16, the Leas became contractually obligated to make the down payment and installment payments. Accordingly, they were entitled to and did not receive all required disclosures under TILA.

Perhaps our reversal falls into the category of letting no good deed go unpunished. Another perspective, though, is that TILA provides an unvarying set of rules that protect consumers who might otherwise voluntarily waive what they should not. We do not perceive any harm here, but harm is not a prerequisite for relief. *See Davis*, 673 F.2d at 869.

Direct Buy failed to make the required disclosures to the Leas, who therefore are entitled to damages. 15 U.S.C. § 1640(a)(2)(A). As Direct Buy is a "creditor who fail[ed] to comply with" the disclosure requirements of TILA, it shall be liable as described in that statute, despite that the Leas suffered no injury due to Direct Buy's failure to provide the required disclosures. 15 U.S.C. § 1640(a); (a)(2)(A)(i); *see Davis*, 673 F.2d at 869. On remand, the district court shall determine the amount of damages, costs, and attorney's fees in accordance with the statute and enter judgment against Direct Buy for that amount. REVERSED and REMANDED.

****

In *Jackson v. Grant*, the court directly considers California law regarding the consummation of the credit transaction.[211] In *Lea v. Buy Direct*, the court considers other cases interpreting consummation as well as general principals of contract law, including conditions precedent and subsequent performance, etc. **Does the analysis differ in *Lea*[212]? Why or Why Not?**

Are the Leas the type of "wily borrowers" the dissent referenced in *Jackson v. Grant*?[213]

Would the CFPB have authority to enforce the proposed TILA violation with respect to the Defendants in this case? Why or Why not?

Read the next case, *Jager v. Bos. Rd. Auto Mall, Inc.*[214] This case considers the content [what must be disclosed to consumers] as well as the form of disclosures required by TILA.

---

[211] *See Jackson*, 890 F.2d at 120.
[212] 755 F.3d 250 (5th Cir., 2014).
[213] *See Jackson*, 890 F.2d at 122 (Trott, S., dissenting).
[214] *Jager v. Bos. Rd. Auto Mall, Inc.*, No. 14 Civ. 614, 2015 (S.D.N.Y. Jan. 15, 2015).

OPINION & ORDER

Plaintiff Peter Jager sued defendant Boston Road Auto Mall, Inc. ("BRAM") for violation of the Truth in Lending Act ("TILA"), 15 U.S.C. § 1601 *et seq.*, [. . .]

Jager moves for summary judgment in his favor on the TILA claim. BRAM moves for summary judgment dismissing the TILA [. . .] [claim].

FACTS

According to Jager's uncontradicted statement of facts, BRAM sells used cars and arranges financing for those sales. On November 21, 2013, Jager purchased a 2007 Chrysler Pacifica from BRAM. The purchase was financed by BRAM, and the only disclosure of the financing terms was a single-page summary ("pricing recap").

Sales Price:	$9,300
8.8750% Sales Tax:	825.38
Government Fees:	400.00
Tracking Device:	495.00
Dealer Fee:	395.00
Service Charge:	495.00
Total:	$11,910.38

Down Payment:	$2,500.00
Pick-Up Note:	$350.00
Amount Financed:	$9,060.38
Financing at 20.00% APR:	$3,530.36
Balance Due:	$12,590.74

Pick-Up Note Payment of $350.00 due on 12/21/13.

83 payments of $150.00 each

Payable Semi-Monthly beginning 11/30/13

Plus one final payment of $140.74

Final payment will be due on 5/15/17

. . . .

Truth in Lending Act

Jager seeks summary judgment in his favor on the TILA claim and an award of statutory damages. BRAM acknowledges that the transaction is a closed end consumer credit transaction and that it is a creditor subject to the TILA disclosure requirements of 15 U.S.C. § 1638(a). Accordingly, Jager must show that BRAM violated one of the TILA disclosure requirements that gives rise to statutory damages.

"It is the purpose of [the Truth in Lending Act] to assure a meaningful disclosure of credit terms so that the consumer will be able to compare more readily the various credit terms available to him and avoid the uninformed use of credit . . . ." 15 U.S.C. § 1601(a). " TILA endeavors to enable consumers to evaluate credit offers separately from the purchase of merchandise, and thereby to create an active market providing more efficient credit prices." *Poulin v. Balise Auto Sales, Inc.*, 647 F.3d 36, 39 (2d Cir.

2011) (quoting *Cornist v. B.J.T. Auto Sales, Inc.*, 272 F.3d 322, 326 (6th Cir. 2001)). "The Act is remedial in nature, designed to remedy what Congressional hearings revealed to be unscrupulous and predatory creditor practices throughout the nation. Since the statute is remedial in nature, its terms must be construed in liberal fashion if the underlying Congressional purpose is to be effectuated," *N.C. Freed Co. v. Bd. Of Governors of Fed. Reserve Sys.*, 473 F.2d 1210, 1214 (2d Cir. 1973); *see also Grant v. Imperial Motors*, 539 F.2d 506, 510 (5th Cir. 1976) ("[O]nce the court finds a violation, no matter how technical, it has no discretion with respect to the imposition of liability.").

TILA Liability

Jager argues that BRAM violated TILA by failing to comply with certain requirements of 15 U.S.C. § 1638(a): For each consumer credit transaction other than under an open end credit plan, the creditor shall disclose each of the following items, to the extent applicable: . . . . (3) The "finance charge," not itemized, using that term. . . . . (5) The sum of the amount financed and the finance charge, which shall be termed the "total of payments." . . . . (7) In a sale of property or services in which the seller is the creditor required to disclose pursuant to section 1631(b) of this title, the "total sale price," using that term, which shall be the total of the cash price of the property or services, additional charges, and the finance charge. (8) Descriptive explanations of the terms "amount financed," "finance charge," "annual percentage rate," "total of payments," and "total sale price" as specified by the [Consumer Financial Protection] Bureau.

Jager also contends that BRAM violated TILA by not complying with the requirement that "[t]he terms 'annual percentage rate' and 'finance charge' shall be disclosed more conspicuously than other terms." 15 U.S.C. § 1632(a).

Here, the pricing recap, which is the only financing disclosure, never uses the required terms "total of payments" or "total sale price." Rather the pricing recap uses the term "TOTAL" for the cash price of the car before the calculation of an additional $3,530.36 finance charge. The sum of the amount financed and the finance charge, which should be the "total of payments," is termed the "Balance Due." That does not comply with § 1638(a)(5). The "total of the cash price of the property or services, additional charges, and the finance charge," which is the "total sale price" defined in the statute (and which can be computed as $15,440.74), is not disclosed in the pricing recap anywhere. That does not comply with § 1638(a)(7).

The pricing recap also does not comply with TILA because it does not disclose the finance charge "using that term," as required by § 1638(a)(3), and the annual percentage rate and finance charge are not disclosed more conspicuously than other terms, as required by § 1632(a). Instead, those terms are combined on one line as "Financing at 20.00% APR: 3,530.36." By combining those terms, the pricing recap discloses them less conspicuously than other terms, each of which appear on their own line. Finally, § 1638(a)(8) requires that certain terms be accompanied by descriptive explanations specified by the Consumer Financial Protection Bureau. The terms and explanations are:

➢ amount financed: "the amount of credit provided to you or on your behalf" (12 C.F.R. § 1026.18(b))

> finance charge: "the dollar amount the credit will cost you" (*id.* Subsec. (d))

> annual percentage rate: "the cost of your credit as a yearly rate" (*id.* Subsec. (c))

> total of payments: "the amount you will have paid when you have made all scheduled payments" (*id.* Subsec. (h))

> total sale price: "the total price of your purchase on credit, including your downpayment of $___" (*id.* Subsec. (j)).

The pricing recap does not comply with those requirements: it includes no descriptive explanation for any of those terms.

TILA Damages

Jager seeks only statutory damages. TILA § 1640(a) provides that any creditor who fails to comply with any requirement imposed under this part . . . with respect to any person is liable to such person in an amount equal to the sum of-- . . . (2)(A)(i) in the case of an individual action twice the amount of any finance charge in connection with the transaction . . . . However not all, but only certain, TILA violations give rise to statutory damages. For those disclosures required by Section 1638(a) (as in this cases) statutory damages are only given for violations of paragraphs (2) ("insofar as it requires a disclosure of the 'amount financed'"), (3)-(6), and (9). 15 U.S.C. § 1640(a). Of BRAM's violations of § 1638(a),3 the provisions concerning the definition of the finance charge and the total of payments, § 1638(a)(3), (5), give rise to statutory damages. Those violations may be formal in nature, but they go to a core purpose of TILA. By mandating the use of standard terms, TILA enables the consumer "to compare more readily the various credit terms available to him." 15 U.S.C. § 1601(a). When a creditor uses non-standard terms, it frustrates the consumer's ability to compare different offers of credit.

On the basis of the undisputed facts, BRAM violated TILA by not correctly complying with the requirement of defining the finance charge and total of payments. Accordingly, Jager is granted summary judgment on the TILA claim, and because those violations give rise to statutory damages, he is awarded statutory damages.

The amount of statutory damages depends on the type of transaction. For an individual action concerning a closed end consumer credit transaction not secured by real property, statutory damages are "twice the amount of any finance charge in connection with the transaction." 15 U.S.C. § 1640(a)(2)(A)(i). However, statutory damages for such transactions are capped at $2,000. S*ee Koons Buick Pontiac GMC, Inc. v. Nigh*, 543 U.S. 50, 62-63, 125 S. Ct. 460, 468-69 (2004).

Here, the finance charge, as listed in the pricing recap, is $3,530.36. Twice that is $7,060.72, so Jager is awarded the maximum statutory damages of $2,000.

****

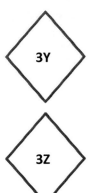

3Y   **Why does TILA require standard, defined terms?**

3Z   **Is the Plaintiff's claim a timing, form, and/or content TILA challenge?**

Consider the next case, *Yazzie v. Gurley Motor Co.*, No. CIV 14-555 JAP/SCY 2016 (D. N.M. Mar. 8, 2016)[215] where the District of New Mexico considers liability for content violations [what must be disclosed to consumers] as well as the form of disclosures required by TILA.

---

[215] *Yazzie v. Gurley Motor Co.*, No. CIV 14-555 JAP/SCY 2016 (D. N.M. Mar. 8, 2016).

YAZZIE V. GURLEY MOTOR CO.

MEMORANDUM OPINION AND ORDER

On January 6, 2016, Plaintiffs Eugene Yazzie and Phyllis Yazzie, class representatives, moved for summary judgment. Plaintiffs argue that the facts are undisputed and that they and similarly situated class members are entitled to judgment as a matter of law on the issue of liability and the proper formulae for calculating damages. Defendants Gurley Motor Co. (Gurley Motor) and Red Rock Investment Co. (Red Rock) oppose the motion. As described below, the Court will grant in part and deny in part Plaintiffs' motion.

Background

The following facts are undisputed. Defendant Gurley Motor is a licensed motor vehicle dealer located in Gallup, New Mexico that offers in-house financing to its customers. On or before June 16, 2013, Gurley Motor "developed a program of deferring a portion of the down payment which customers agreed to pay." Customers who participated in this program signed a standardized Motor Vehicle Installment Loan Contract and Security Agreement (Loan Contract) agreeing to repay the deferred down payment in addition to the regular loan payments. "Since at least June 16, 2013, in every car sale in which Gurley [Motor] agreed to accept a Deferred Down Payment from a customer, Gurley [Motor] disclosed the Deferred Down Payment as part of the Payment Schedule in the [Loan Contract], but failed to include the down payment in the Total of Payments." Plaintiffs maintain that this practice violated the mandatory disclosure provisions of the Truth in Lending Act of 1968 (TILA), 15 U.S.C. § 1601, *et seq.*

Defendant Red Rock acts as Gurley Motor's in-house financing company, with Gurley Motor assigning Loan Contracts to Red Rock. From June 16, 2013 to the present, Gurley Motor regularly assigned Loan Contracts to Red Rock, including every Loan Contract involving a deferred down payment. Some of the borrowers, like Plaintiffs, defaulted on their payments and Red Rock repossessed their vehicles.

. . . .

TILA Class Claims

"Congress enacted TILA in 1968 'to assure a meaningful disclosure of credit terms so that the consumer will be able to compare more readily the various credit terms available to him and avoid the uninformed use of credit.'" *Sanders v. Mt. Am. Fed. Credit Union*, 689 F.3d 1138 (10th Cir. 2012) (quoting 15 U.S.C. § 1601(a)). Relevant to this lawsuit, under TILA, in all closed consumer credit transactions, creditors must clearly and conspicuously disclose, among other things, (1) "the sum of the amount financed and the finance charge, which shall be termed the 'total of payments'" and (2) "the number, amount, and due dates or period of payments scheduled to repay the total of payments." 15 U.S.C. §§ 1632(a), 1638(a)(5-6). Disclosures of the "total of payments" and "schedule of payments" must be "in accordance with regulations of the Bureau." 15 U.S.C. § 1632(a).

Gurley Motor's TILA Liability

To prevail on their TILA class claims against Gurley Motor, Plaintiffs must show that (1) Gurley Motor is a creditor within the meaning of the statute, (2) the Loan Contracts qualify as consumer credit transactions, and (3) the Loan Contracts do not include the required TILA disclosures. *See* 15 U.S.C. § 1602, 1638. Defendants do not deny that Gurley Motor is a creditor or that the Loan Contracts constitute closed consumer credit transactions governed by 15 U.S.C. § 1638. Consequently, the only issue before the Court is whether Gurley Motor contravened § 1638(a)(5) of TILA (as Plaintiffs maintain) when it decided to omit deferred down payments from the total of payments disclosure on its standardized Loan Contract form.

It is clear from the statute and the briefing that the answer to this question is "yes." TILA directs creditors to provide consumers with (1) a list of scheduled payments and (2) a separate disclosure of the "total of payments," which is "the sum of the amount financed and the finance charge." 15 U.S.C. § 1638(a)(5). In other words, within the loan documents, creditors must list the required payments along with their sum – the "total of payments." *See* 15 U.S.C. § 1638(a)(6) (describing the schedule of payments as a list of the individual payments needed "to repay the total of payments"). The mandatory regulations make these requirements quite clear: "the creditor shall disclose" the payment schedule and "[t]he total of payments, using that term, and a descriptive explanation such as 'the amount you will have paid when you have made all scheduled payments.'" 12 C.F.R. § 1026.18(h). The official comments to this regulation even address how to handle deferred down payments: The total of payments is the sum of the payments disclosed under [the payment schedule]. For example, if the creditor disclosed a deferred portion of the downpayment as part of the payment schedule, that payment must be reflected in the total disclosed under this paragraph. Official Staff Interpretations of Regulation Z, 12 C.F.R. Part 226, Supplement I § 226.18.3 It is undisputed that Gurley Motor failed to comply with these directives. Gurley Motor listed deferred down payments as scheduled payments without including these amounts in the total of payments, with the result that the loan appeared cheaper than it really was.

Despite these facts, Defendants argue that they should not be held liable for Gurley Motor's inaccurate disclosure of the total of payments because Gurley Motor was attempting to help customers by offering interest-free deferred down payments and its failure to abide by TILA was inconsequential and harmless. To the extent Defendants are arguing that the Court can excuse Gurley Motor's TILA violation on the basis that Gurley Motor had good intentions and did not cause any harm to its customers, they have not cited to any case law to support such a result. Moreover, these requests are contrary to the statute's purpose as well as its language. Congress passed TILA to promote the use of standardized credit terms that consumers can more easily compare and understand. *Rosenfield v. HSBC Bank, USA*, 681 F.3d 1172, 1179-1180 (10th Cir. 2012). In accordance with this remedial purpose, TILA allows a plaintiff to recover statutory damages in the absence of actual harm. 15 U.S.C. § 1640. Additionally, while it contains a safe harbor provision for bona fide errors, *id.*, this provision is limited and Defendants' have not invoked its protections.

The thrust of Defendants' argument is that the Court should refrain from imposing liability on Defendants because the TILA violation at issue – failing to properly calculate the total of payments, separate from the schedule of payments – is trivial or as Defendants put it "hyper-technical." Defendants appear to be advocating for the position that partial compliance with TILA is sufficient as long as a court finds that any violations are undamaging or trifling. But even the cases cited by Defendants fall short of advancing such a lenient rule. For example, in *Smith v. Chapman*, 614 F.2d 968 (5th Cir. 1980), the Fifth Circuit explained that "the applicable standard is strict compliance with the technical requirements of [TILA]." *Id.* at 971. While it opined that this did not "necessarily mean punctilious compliance if, with minor deviations from the language described in the Act, there is still a substantial, clear disclosure of the fact or information demanded by the applicable statute or regulation," the Fifth Circuit stressed that creditors are required to make disclosures "in the proper technical form and in the proper locations" as mandated by TILA and its accompanying regulations. *Id.* at 971-972. In other words, disclosure need not be perfect, but they must include all of the information required under the statute and regulations, even if a creditor feels this information is unimportant. *See Ford Motor Credit Co. v. Milhollin*, 444 U.S. 555, 567-568 (1980) (warning that courts ought to refrain from "interstitial lawmaking" and treat "administrative rulemaking and interpretation under TILA as authoritative"); *Santos-Rodriguez v. Doral Mortg. Corp.*, 485 F.3d 12, 16 (1st Cir. 2007) (TILA requires "clear and conspicuous" notice, not perfect notice).

Gurley Motor's disclosure practices are actionable under these standards. The failure to include the deferred down payment in the total of payments was not a minor imperfection in the wording of the required disclosures. It was a purposeful, if unwitting, decision to understate a clearly required piece of information – the total sum of the payments the debtor would have to make. Defendants attempt to obfuscate this fact by focusing on the schedule of payments requirement and pointing out that the deferred down payments were identified on the Loan Contract, so consumers could properly calculate the amount owed. The problem with this argument is that Congress made a policy judgment that creditors should tell consumers both the number and amount of payments (the payment schedule) and the total amount that has to be paid, so that borrowers (1) know when payments are due and (2) have no confusion about the total cost of the loan, which is listed conspicuously for them. By understating the total of payments, Gurley Motor violated the second requirement. The Court will enter summary judgment on liability in favor of Plaintiffs and the TILA class members against Defendant Gurley Motor.

Red Rock's TILA Liability

Under TILA, an assignee of a deficient consumer loan contract bears the same liability as the creditor for any TILA violations that are "apparent on the face of the disclosure statement." 15 U.S.C. § 1641(a). TILA specifies that this includes all invalid disclosures (1) "which can be determined to be incomplete or inaccurate from the face of the disclosure statement or other documents assigned, or (2) . . . which does not use the terms required to be used by [TILA]." *Id.* Plaintiffs argues that Red Rock, the assignee of the class members' Loan Contracts, is liable for Gurley Motor's disclosure violations under this standard. Defendants take the position that Plaintiffs are not entitled to summary judgment on this issue because Gurley Motor's TILA violations "are by no means apparent to a reasonable person, particularly taken in the context of the relative lack of sophistication of [Red Rock,] [an] eight employee, family-owned, small town business."

Defendants' statement of the law belies its own argument. According to Defendants, "in considering a claim of assignee liability, the relevant inquiry is whether a reasonable person can spot any violations on the face of the disclosure statement or other assigned documents." In other words, the standard is objective. Here, the TILA violations – routinely uncalculating the total of payments – are discernible from the face of the Loan Contracts. Contrary to Defendants' assertions, it does not require a high degree of sophistication to read TILA, conclude that a loan contract must disclose the sum of the schedule of payments – the total of payments – and check loan contracts to ensure that this was done. Even if Red Rock somehow misconstrued TILA's mandate, ignorance of the law is not a defense. *See United States v. Reed*, 114 F.3d 1053, 1057 (10th Cir. 1997) ("an 'ignorance of the law' defense [is] a defense which is easily rejected"); *Gilbert v. Storage Tech. Corp.*, No. 95-1060, 1996 U.S. App. LEXIS 26656, at *13 (10th Cir. Oct. 11, 1996) (ignorance of the law is not a defense to unmet ADA and ADEA obligations). Because Red Rock could have discovered the TILA violation by reviewing the four corners of the Loan Contracts, without any additional investigation into Gurley Motor's lending practices, Red Rock is liable for Gurley Motor's TILA violation. The Court will enter summary judgment on the issue of TILA liability in favor of Plaintiffs and the TILA class against Defendant Red Rock.

. . .

****

3AA Review Figure 1C. What part of the loan transaction does Gurley Motors represent? What part of the loan transaction does Red Rock represent?

3BB Can the consumer rescind the loan contracts? Why or Why Not? What additional information do you need to know to decide?

3CC Is Plaintiff's claim a timing, content, and/or form TILA challenge?

Return to Figure 2C. The *Yazzie* Defendants argued that they were intending to be helpful to the consumer by deferring a portion of the car down payment.[216] **What stakeholders may be interested in how a deferred portion of the car down payment must be disclosed?**

---

[216] *See Yazzie*, No. CIV 14-555 JAP/SCY 2016 at *6.

Consider the following consumer complaint narrative, filed in the CFPB Consumer Complaint Database on April 4, 2018. Certain information concerning the complaint is redacted.

Consumer complaint narrative:[217]

> *Received an offer in the mail to obtain a personal loan from Prosper.com. I went online and filled out the required paperwork as to income verification etc. A couple of days later I received a truth in lending offer stating my loan had been approved at 9.57 %. Within a couple of days my money was in my personal account. This is where the deceit comes in. When I inquired from both Prosper.com and XXXX XXXX in Utah what the amortization schedule was it was like light in the eyes of a deer along the highway. No one wanted nor did they respond to my request. I have yet to receive a detailed break-down of interest vs principal for payments over the life of the loan. I assume that they intend to collect all of the interest payments up front??? Under TILA I should have gotten a much more detailed document prior to the execution of the loan and transfer of capital. Under TILA the Right of Recission must be done within 3 days but what are you walking away from … … ..?? There isn't any terms agreed to in writing. If you are a crook then its well thought out. If you are honest you may very well be getting scammed. I have also contacted XXXX XXXX as that is the financial source for Prosper.com.*

3DD The company responded timely, and the complaint was "closed with explanation" from the company. The company elected not to permit a response viewable to the public. **Does this consumer complaint amount to a TILA violation? Why or Why Not? What additional information would you need to decide?**

3EE **May the consumer rescind the personal loan obtained, as the consumer references in the complaint? Why or Why Not?**

---

[217] CONSUMER FIN. PROT. BUREAU ONLINE CONSUMER COMPLAINT DATABASE, https://www.consumerfinance.gov/data-research/consumer-complaints/search/detail/2867889, last visited Dec. 2, 2018.

3FF   **Is the clogging of courts with "technical" TILA violations consistent with the purpose of consumer financial services protection?** Consider that, due to litigation and an attempt to comply, disclosure forms have become increasingly complicated, and TILA and Regulation B have been revised more than fifty times collectively.[218]

3GG

Recall the discussion in Part ID concerning the 5Ws.

(1) **Who** is regulated under the Truth in Lending Act and its implementing regulations? **Who** is required to provide the mandated disclosures? **Who** is exempt from compliance with TILA?

(2) **Who** is protected under the Truth in Lending Act and its implementing regulations? **Who** must receive the mandated disclosures? **Who** is not protected under the Truth in Lending Act and its implementing regulations?

(3) **What** is the protection? What is the appropriate law or regulation?

(4) **When** is the protection applicable? (Under what circumstances does the protection apply?)

(5) **Why** does the protection exist? Would applying the law or rule make sense in context?

---

[218] Todd J. Zywicki, *The Consumer Financial Protection Bureau: Savior or Menace?* 81 Geo. Wash. L. Rev. 856, 904-05 (2013).

IV. EQUAL CREDIT OPPORTUNITY ACT

A. LAWS AND RULES

During the first half of the twentieth century the, now commonplace, use of credit reports was limited and unrecognizable from what we now recognize as a credit report today.[219] In extending credit, creditors needed some method by which to gauge an individual's credit-worthiness.[220] Equipped with data about borrowers, creditors could make informed decisions about whether to extend credit.[221] However, the determination of data to collect and how the information would be applied was ripe with subjectivity that created opportunities for discrimination.[222] There was a push toward laws and rules to encourage "fair lending." Fair lending is defined as "fair, equitable, and nondiscriminatory access to credit for consumers."[223]

The Equal Credit Opportunity Act of 1974 (hereinafter "ECOA") was passed post-Civil Rights Movement to combat challenges disadvantaged, creditworthy groups were facing in credit transactions. The Equal Credit Opportunity Act provisions are located within 15 U.S.C. Chapter 41: Consumer Credit Protection.[224]   Specifically, ECOA provisions are found within Subchapter IV: Equal Credit Opportunity.[225] ECOA is part of the Consumer Credit Protection Act of 1968.[226]

Regulation B is the corresponding regulation to the Equal Credit Opportunity Act. The CFPB is tasked with rulemaking/revising Regulation B.[227] Prior to the creation of the CFPB, the Federal Reserve Board was tasked with Regulation B rulemaking.[228] Supervision, i.e. oversight regarding compliance, with ECOA

---

[219] Consumer report is defined by the Fair Credit Reporting Act as "any written, oral, or other communication of any information by a consumer reporting agency bearing on a consumer's credit worthiness, credit standing, credit capacity, character, general reputation, personal characteristics, or mode of living which is used or expected to be used or collected in whole or in part for the purpose of serving as a factor in establishing the consumer's eligibility for" (1) credit or insurance to be used primarily for personal, family, or household purposes, (2) employment purposes; or (3) any other authorized purpose. *See* 15 U.S.C. § 1681a(d) (Fastcase 2018).

[220] *See* 15 U.S.C. § 1681(a)(3) (Fastcase 2018) ("Consumer reporting agencies have assumed a vital role in assembling and evaluating consumer credit and other information on consumers."); *see also* 15 U.S.C. § 1681g(f)(2) (Fastcase 2018) (defining credit score as "a numerical value or a categorization derived from a statistical tool or modeling system used by a person who makes or arranges a loan to predict the likelihood of certain credit behaviors, including default [. . .].").

[221] *See* 15 U.S.C. § 1681(a)(2) ("An elaborate mechanism has been developed for investigating and evaluating credit worthiness, credit standing, credit capacity, character, and general reputation of consumers.").

[222] *See* Dubravka Ritter, *Do We Still Need the Equal Credit Opportunity Act?*, FED. RESERVE BANK OF PHILA. PAYMENT CARDS CTR (Sept. 2012), at 1.

[223] 12 U.S.C. § 5481(13).

[224] *See* 15 U.S.C. § 1691 *et seq.* (Fastcase 2018).

[225] *See* 15 U.S.C. § 1691 *et seq.*

[226] *See* 15 U.S.C. § 1601 *et seq.*

[227] *See* 12 U.S.C. § 5492 (a)(10) (2018); *see* 12 U.S.C. § 5511 (c)(5); *see* 12 U.S.C. § 5512(b)(4)(A).

[228] *See* Ritter, *supra* note 222, at 12.

and Regulation B, is divided. Recall from Part IIB that the CFPB has exclusive supervisory authority over nondepository institutions and depository institutions with assets in excess of ten billion dollars. The CFPB has limited supervisory authority over depository institutions with assets of ten billion dollars or less.

Read 15 U.S.C. §1691 *et seq.* The Equal Credit Opportunity Act of 1974, 15 U.S.C. §1691 *et seq.* and its implementing regulation, Regulation B, 12 C.F.R. Part 1002 *et seq.*, have two important functions for the purposes of this text. The Equal Credit Opportunity Act is intended to "promote the availability of credit to all creditworthy applicants"[229] and to "notify applicants of action taken on their applications."[230] First, ECOA **prohibits discrimination** by **creditors** against **applicants** in **credit transactions**.[231] Creditors shall not discourage, on **prohibited bases**, applicants from making or pursuing an application.[232] How is **creditor** defined? A **creditor** is "any person who regularly extends, renews, or continues credit; any person who regularly arranges for the extension, renewal, or continuation of credit; or any assignee of an original creditor who participates in the decision to extend, renew, or continue credit."[233] Regulation B provides further guidance concerning creditors and defines a creditor as a person who regularly participates in a credit decision, including setting the terms of the credit, referring applicants or prospective applicants to creditors, or selecting or offering to select creditors to whom requests for credit may be made.[234] Further, creditor includes assignees and transferees.[235]

The laws and rules are limited in scope. First, the laws and rules are limited to discrimination under prohibited bases.[236] These bases include race, color, religion; national origin; sex or marital status; and/or age.[237] Second, the discrimination must involve (1) a creditor, (2) an applicant, and (3) a credit transaction. Not all instances of unequal treatment qualify as discrimination pursuant to the Equal Credit Opportunity Act.[238] How does Regulation B define to **discriminate against an applicant**? To **discriminate against an applicant** "means to treat the applicant less favorably than other applicants."[239] Finally, one of the bases upon which a creditor is prohibited from discriminating is with respect to marital status. How does Regulation B define **marital status**? Marital status is "the state of being unmarried, married, or separated, as defined by applicable state law. The term 'unmarried' includes persons who are single, divorced, or widowed."[240]

---

[229] 12 C.F.R. § 1002.1(b) (Fastcase 2018).
[230] *Id.*
[231] *See* 15 U.S.C. § 1691(a) (Fastcase 2018); 12 C.F.R. § 1002.4(a) (Fastcase 2018).
[232] *See* 12 C.F.R. § 1002.4(b).
[233] 15 U.S.C. § 1691a(e) (Fastcase 2018).
[234] *See* 12 C.F.R. § 1002.2(l) (Fastcase 2018).
[235] *See id.*
[236] *See* 15 U.S.C. § 1691(a)(1).
[237] *See* 15 U.S.C. § 1691(a)(1); *see* 12 C.F.R. § 1002.2(z).
[238] *See* 15 U.S.C. § 1691(b), (c).
[239] 12 C.F.R. § 1002.2(n).
[240] 12 C.F.R. § 1002.2(u).

Creditor has been defined *supra*. How is **applicant** defined? An **applicant** is "any person who applies to a creditor directly for an extension, renewal, or continuation of credit [. . .]."[241] Implementing Regulation B provides additional guidance, namely that an applicant is "any person who requests or who has received an extension of credit from a creditor, and includes any person who is or may be contractually liable regarding an extension of credit.[242] How is **credit transaction** defined? Review 12 C.F.R. § 1002.2(m), defining **credit transaction**. A credit transaction involves the advertising/prospective applicant stage, taking applications and information requested, the evaluation of the application, the extension of credit, and servicing/collection/default of the credit extension.

Consider Figure 4A below:

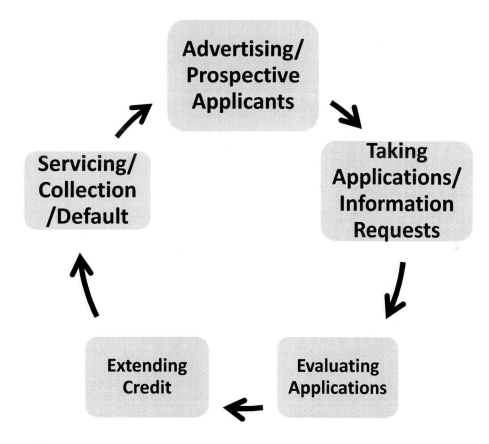

Figure 4A

Prohibited ECOA discrimination applies to all the stages of the loan transaction in Figure 4A. There are limitations to information that the creditor can advertise,[243] information that the creditor can request in taking an application,[244] information that the creditor may consider when evaluating a credit application,[245] and limitations to information that the creditor may use to make the credit decision.[246]

---

[241] 15 U.S.C. § 1691a(b).

[242] 12 C.F.R. § 1002.2(e).

[243] *See* 12 C.F.R. § 1002.4(b).

[244] 12 C.F.R. § 1002.5(b)-(d) (Fastcase 2018).

[245] 12 C.F.R. § 1002.6(a)-(b) (Fastcase 2018).

Review 12 C.F.R. § 1002.4(b), 12 C.F.R. § 1002.5, 12 C.F.R. § 1002.6, and 12 C.F.R. § 1002.7. **What limitations are placed on creditors to reduce/eliminate discrimination under a prohibited bases in credit transactions?**

Once a credit decision has been made, ECOA requires additional disclosures, in specified circumstances, intended to reduce discrimination. Specifically, the second important purpose of ECOA is to notify applicants of actions taken on applications, including **adverse actions**.[247] ECOA requires that **creditors** notify **applicants** of action on an **application** within thirty days of receiving a **complete** application.[248] Recall in the discussion above how applicant and creditor are defined by the Equal Credit Opportunity Act and Regulation B. How does Regulation B define **application**? An application is an "oral or written request for an extension of credit that is made in accordance with procedures used by a creditor for the type of credit requested."[249] How does Regulation B define a **complete application**? A completed application is an application where the "creditor has received all the information that the creditor regularly obtains and considers in evaluating applications for the amount and type of credit."[250] How does the Equal Credit Opportunity Act define **person**?

TIMING

What are the timing requirements for the adverse action notice required by the Equal Credit Opportunity Act?

Review Figure 1C.

To what part of the loan transaction process does the Equal Credit Opportunity Act and implementing regulations apply?

Creditors must notify applicants of action taken within thirty days after taking **adverse action** on an incomplete application.[251] If the creditor takes an adverse action against the application, the applicant is entitled to a statement of reasons for the adverse action.[252] An "adverse action" includes "a denial or revocation of credit, a change in the terms of an existing credit arrangement, and the refusal to grant credit in substantially the amount or on substantially the terms requested."[253] How does Regulation B define an **adverse action**?[254] Note that, under Regulation B, an adverse action notice is not required in instances where the creditor provides a counter-offer, and the counter-offer is accepted by the

---

[246] 12 C.F.R. § 1002.7(a), (d) (Fastcase 2018).

[247] 12 C.F.R. § 1002.1(b).

[248] *See* 15 U.S.C. § 1691(d)(1).

[249] 12 C.F.R. § 1002.2(f).

[250] 12 C.F.R. § 1002.2(f).

[251] *See* 12 C.F.R. § 1002.9(a) (Fastcase 2018).

[252] *See* 15 U.S.C. § 1691(d)(2).

[253] 15 U.S.C. § 1691(d)(6).

[254] *See* 12 C.F.R. § 1002.2(c).

applicant.[255] An example of a counteroffer by a creditor is when the creditor offers to extend credit on different terms or in a different amount than requested.[256]

Note that the ECOA requirement that creditors notify applicants of action on an application within thirty days of receiving a complete application,[257] is applicable regardless of whether the complete application decision is an approval, a counteroffer, or an adverse action.[258] In all cases, the creditor must notify the applicant of a decision on the completed application.[259] Read 12 C.F.R. § 1002.4(d)(1). Read 12 C.F.R. § 1002.9(b).

CONTENT

Read 12 C.F.R. § 1002.9(a)(2). **What are the content requirements for the adverse action notifications under ECOA?** The notice must identify the action taken, contain either a statement of reasons for the adverse action or a disclosure that the applicant is entitled to a statement of specific reasons, the name and address of the creditor, and the name and address of the federal agency that has oversight over the creditor.[260] If the creditor opts to notify the applicant of the applicant's right to a statement of specific reason, this notification must also detail the "identity of the person or office" where the statement of reasons may be obtained and that the applicant may obtain the statement of specific reasons within thirty days of requesting the statement from creditors.[261] Further, the applicant's request for the statement of reasons must be submitted within sixty days after receiving the adverse action notice, and the statement of the right to a list of specific reasons must also disclose this sixty-day deadline.[262] Finally, the adverse action notice must include the "ECOA notice" for which the regulation provides additional guidance.[263] **How do the content requirements under ECOA differ from the content requirements under the Truth in Lending Act discussed in Part IIIA?**

FORM

What are the requirements for the form of the adverse action notice required by the Equal Credit Opportunity Act? The creditor must provide the disclosures in writing or in electronic form, and the disclosures must be provided in a clear and conspicuous manner.[264] Regulation B further emphasizes that the statement of reasons must be specific.[265] Further, Regulation B additionally requires that the

---

[255] *See* 12 C.F.R. § 1002.2(c)(1).
[256] *See id.*
[257] *See* 15 U.S.C. § 1691(d)(1).
[258] *See* 12 C.F.R. § 1002.9(a)(1)(i).
[259] *See id.*
[260] *See* 12 C.F.R. § 1002.9(a)(2); *see* 15 U.S.C. § 1691(d)(2).
[261] *See* 15 U.S.C. §1691(d)(2(B); *see* 12 C.F.R. § 1002.9(a)(2)(ii).
[262] *See* 15 U.S.C. § 1691(d)(2)(B); *see* 12 C.F.R. § 1002.9(a)(2)(ii).
[263] 12 C.F.R. § 1002.9(a)(2)(ii).
[264] *See* 12 C.F.R. § 1002.4(d).
[265] *See* 12 C.F.R. § 1002.9(b)(2).

creditor "indicate the principal reason(s) for the adverse action."[266] Finally, Regulation B gives an example of language that is sufficient to serve as the ECOA notice part of the adverse action notice:

> *The Federal Equal Credit Opportunity Act prohibits creditors from discriminating against credit applicants on the basis of race, color, religion, national origin, sex, marital status, age (provided the applicant has the capacity to enter into a binding contract); because all or part of the applicant's income derives from any public assistance program; or because the applicant has in good faith exercised any right under the Consumer Credit Protection Act. The Federal agency that administers compliance with this law concerning this creditor is [name and address as specified by the appropriate agency or agencies listed in appendix A of this part].[267]*

How do the form of disclosures requirements under the Equal Credit Opportunity Act differ from the form of disclosure requirements under the Truth in Lending Act, discussed in Part IIIA?[268]

Read 12 C.F.R. § 1002.6. **What does ECOA state regarding age, income, immigration status, and marital status?** Does 12 C.F.R. § 1002.6 weaken or strengthen consumer protections?

Consider the following excerpt regarding access to credit as a consumer right:

> [T]he civil rights and women's movements in the late 1960s and 1970s [] portrayed consumer credit as a basic right that should be provided as broadly as possible. These social movements organized around credit began as a response to the urban riots that spread across the country between 1965 and 1969. Research into the sources of black urban violence led policymakers to conclude that the urban poor should be given greater economic access. In part, that meant access to credit. That conclusion reflected the findings of David Caplovitz, whose book *The Poor Pay More* documented the exploitative lending conditions faced by the urban poor, and of the government-appointed Kerner Commission, which concluded that urban blacks could be deradicalized if they were given greater access to credit at a fair price.[269]

How do you think these attitudes of the 1960s and 1970s impacted the prohibition against discrimination in credit transactions? Are there other groups that are denied access to equal credit opportunities that are not included in ECOA's definition of prohibited basis? Are these groups radical?

In addition to race and color, attitudes toward applicants' sex and/or marital status impaired access to credit:

> [T]he National Organization for Women (NOW) mobilized to promote credit access for[…] middle-class white women. Their grievances were broad ranging. Women who married had their credit information merged into their husbands' files, and credit cards

---

[266] *See* 12 C.F.R. § 1002.9(b)(2).

[267] 12 C.F.R. § 1002.9(b)(1).

[268] 12 C.F.R. §1002.4(d)(1); 12 C.F.R. §1026.17(a).

[269] RYAN ET AL., *supra* note 2, at 483.

were issued in their husbands' names. Mortgage lenders frequently discounted, or even ignored, a wife's income, in the belief that she would lose her salary once she had children. Many mortgage lenders would recognize women's salaries only if their doctor issued "baby letters," certifying that they were infertile or using birth control. Marriage was not the only source of discrimination. Young unmarried women were disproportionately denied educational loans because they were thought to be less serious students. Women who divorced or were widowed commonly found themselves without credit at the moment when they needed it the most.[270]

Does ECOA's federal prohibition against discrimination on the basis of sex and marital status in credit transactions sufficiently resolve the challenges faced by women in access to credit?

Consider the following example of the impact of discrimination in credit transactions:

To illustrate the effect of seemingly minor disparities in the APR on the lifetime cost of a loan, consider a hypothetical mortgage loan in the United States. Based on census data, the average home price in the U.S. stood at $272,900 in 2010. Assuming a 20 percent down payment (a conservative assumption) and a 5.5 percent interest rate (the average in 2010), the total amount paid by the borrower over a 30-year period would be $446, 255. Increasing the rate the 5.61 [. . .] percent would increase the total amount paid by nearly $5,000. . . This represents approximately $15 per month in additional interest charges on a $1,240 payment, which is roughly equivalent to a downgrade in FICO score of about 10 to 20 points at the time of application, which in this example is attributable solely to racial heritage.

Some fair lending investigations reveal differences in APRs paid by minority borrowers relative to similarly situated white borrowers that are substantially larger than the disparity identified in the Courchane (2007) study. Such disparities may represent an incremental cost that, for many families, would require either a reduction in other consumption, less saving for education or retirement, or perhaps increases in hours worked. Of course, this redistribution would occur only among minority applicants who are granted a loan; additional cost or other harm may be incurred among minority applicants who are either unable to obtain loans or who are discouraged from applying.[271]

---

[270] RYAN ET AL., *supra* note 2, at 484.
[271] Ritter, *supra* note 222, at 28.

B. ENFORCEMENT

The CFPB is tasked with enforcement of ECOA and Regulation B.[272] However, recall from Part IIC the division of financial services consumer protection laws enforcement. As a reminder, the CFPB has exclusive authority to enforce federal consumer financial services laws against nondepository institutions, primary authority to enforce federal consumer financial services laws against insured depository institutions with assets in excess of ten billion dollars, and limited authority to enforce federal consumer financial services laws against insured depository institutions with assets totaling ten billion dollars or less. As a reminder, the CFPB's enforcement powers include but are not limited to initiating a civil action against the violating institution, imposing civil penalties, or seeking legal or equitable relief.[273] Civil money penalties imposed by the CFPB may range from up to $5000 per day to up to $1,000,000 per day for a knowing violation.[274]

Prior to the creation of the CFPB, the creditor's regulator was tasked with ECOA enforcement. Now, both the CFPB and the prudential regulator have ECOA enforcement power. In 2017, the CFPB brought one enforcement action for ECOA violations.[275] Further, the CFPB refers "matters with ECOA violations to the [Department of Justice] when it has reason to believe that a creditor has engaged in a pattern or practice of lending discrimination."[276] The CFPB receives deference in interpretation of the Equal Credit Opportunity Act.[277]

Enforcement of ECOA typically included prohibition of either direct discrimination as well as effective discrimination, consistent with other federal laws prohibiting discrimination.[278] Direct discrimination may be characterized as "disparate treatment" while effective discrimination may be characterized as "disparate impact." Disparate treatment is "when a creditor treats an applicant differently based on a prohibited basis" while disparate impact is "when a creditor employs facially neutral policies or practices that have an adverse effect or impact on a member of a protected class unless it meets a legitimate business need that cannot be reasonably achieved by means that are less disparate in their impact."[279] Disparate treatment discrimination does not have to be intentional.[280] In the initial time following the creation of the CFPB, the CFPB indicated a commitment to enforcing prohibitions falling under both

---

[272] *See* 12 U.S.C. § 5493(c).

[273] *See* 12 U.S.C. § 5564(a).

[274] *See* 12 U.S.C. § 5565(c)(2).

[275] *See* CONSUMER FIN. PROT. BUREAU FAIR LENDING REP. (Dec. 2018), at 9, https://s3.amazonaws.com/files.consumerfinance.gov/f/documents/bcfp_fair-lending_report_12-2018.pdf.

[276] *See id.* at 20.

[277] *See* 15 U.S.C. § 1691b(g) (Fastcase 2018).

[278] *See* Ritter, *supra* note 222, at 1.

[279] CFPB CONSUMER L. & R., ECOA (Oct. 2015), at 1, https://s3.amazonaws.com/files.consumerfinance.gov/f/documents/201510_cfpb_ecoa-narrative-and-procedures.pdf.

[280] *See CFPB ECOA Baseline Review Examination Procedures,* CONSUMER FIN. PROT. BUREAU, at 2, https://s3.amazonaws.com/files.consumerfinance.gov/f/documents/102013_cfpb_equal_credit_opportunity_act_ecoa_baseline.pdf.

"tests" for discriminatory treatment.[281] Further, at least with respect to the evaluation of applications, Regulation B states that "Congress intended an 'effects test' concept . . . to be applicable to a creditor's determination."[282] In other words, a disparate impact test is intended for credit evaluation under the regulation. Recently, it has been argued that, due to a shift in CFPB directive, the CFPB may enforce credit discrimination in a more limited way: by potentially moving away from disparate impact cases.[283] BNA explains that, "the disparate impact theory states that lending practices can be discriminatory even if there was no intent by the lender to engage in racial discrimination if they are found to have a disparate impact on communities of color or other minorities."[284] In addition, disparate impact may be defined as "policies or practices that are applied consistently across groups of borrowers and yet have a disproportionately adverse impact on members of protected classes."[285] Steering the focus away from disparate impact ECOA violations to intentional discrimination violations can result in fewer determinations of ECOA violations and fewer enforcement actions.[286] Proponents of reduced use of disparate impact tests in potential ECOA violations note that a creditor is required to show that the practice, intended to determine creditworthiness but that also correlates to negative impact to protected groups, is justified by business necessity and "defend against a claim that an alternative practice would achieve the same business goal but with a lesser degree of disparate impact."[287]

The Equal Credit Opportunity Act allows for private rights of action for violations[288] but does not permit liability in instances where the creditor's actions or lack thereof were a result of a good faith attempt to comply with a CFPB rule or regulation.[289] Actual and punitive damages are permissible under ECOA[290] with a statute of limitations of within five years after the date of the occurrence of the violation.[291] Punitive damages are limited to $10,000 for individual actions.[292] Equitable and declaratory relief are also available to credit applicants.[293] A failure to comply with 12 C.F.R. § 1002.9, Notifications, is not a violation if the failure to comply resulted from an inadvertent error.[294]

Recall the discussion of TILA's civil liability regulatory reach in Part III. **Why do you think that TILA's statute of limitations is shorter than the ECOA statute of limitations for civil liability?**

---

[281] *See generally* Consumer Fin. Prot. Bureau, CFPB Bulletin 2012-04 Fair Lending (Apr. 18, 2012), *available at* https://files.consumerfinance.gov/f/201404_cfpb_bulletin_lending_discrimination.pdf.

[282] 12 C.F.R. § 1002.6(a).

[283] *See* Evan Weinberger, *CFPB to Review Use of Disparate Impact in Fair Lending Cases*, The Bureau of National Affairs, Inc. BNA (May 21, 2018); Consumer Fin. Prot. Bureau, *supra* note 281.

[284] Weinberger, *supra* note 283.

[285] *See* Ritter, *supra* note 222, at 11.

[286] *See* Weinberger, *supra* note 283.

[287] Ritter, *supra* note 222, at 37.

[288] *See* 15 U.S.C. § 1691e(a)-(c) (Fastcase 2018); 12 C.F.R. § 1002.16 (Fastcase 2018).

[289] *See* 15 U.S.C. § 1691e(e).

[290] *See* 15 U.S.C. § 1691e(a)-(b); 12 C.F.R. § 1002.16(b).

[291] *See* 12 C.F.R. § 1002.16(b)(2); 15 U.S.C. § 1691e(f).

[292] *See* 12 C.F.R. § 1002.16(b); 15 U.S.C. § 1691e(b).

[293] *See* 15 U.S.C. § 1691e(c); 12 C.F.R. § 1002.16(b).

[294] *See* 12 C.F.R. § 1002.16(c).

Why do you think that the safe harbor for inadvertent errors for notification requirements does not extend to ECOA violations based on discrimination?

C. INTERPRETATION

ECOA attempts to reduce discriminatory treatment of applicants seeking an extension of credit. Consider whether the Equal Credit Opportunity Act utilizes a restriction consumer protection method or a disclosure consumer protection method. Does ECOA resolve the issue of access to information to create a "fair" playing field or does ECOA resolve the issue of access to financial markets by encouraging financial inclusion? Consider the following cases interpreting provisions of ECOA/Regulation B. How do the courts rely on the definitions? Who is regulated? Who is protected? Are the protections the courts afford through their interpretations/decisions consistent with the purposes of ECOA?

Consider the next case, *Roberts v. Walmart Stores, Inc.*, 736 F.Supp. 1527 (E.D. Mo., 1990),[295] in which the court considers what constitutes **credit** for ECOA purposes.

---

[295] *Roberts v. Walmart Stores, Inc.*, 736 F.Supp. 1527 (E.D. Mo., 1990).

MEMORANDUM

LIMBAUGH, District Judge.

Plaintiffs are black citizens of the United States. Defendant is a retail department store. On December 5, 1989 plaintiffs were customers at a store operated by defendant in St. Charles, Missouri. During this visit plaintiffs purchased several items and presented defendant with a check in payment for the merchandise. Defendant recorded the race of plaintiffs on the check. Plaintiffs, upon becoming aware that their race was being recorded on the check, returned the merchandise and retrieved the check. Plaintiffs then filed a two-count amended complaint against defendant alleging that defendant's practice of recording the race of black citizens who pay for merchandise by check violates the Thirteenth Amendment, 42 U.S.C. § 1981, 42 U.S.C. § 1982, and 15 U.S.C. § 1691 *et seq.*

. . .

15 U.S.C. § 1691

The Equal Credit Opportunity Act, 15 U.S.C. § 1691(a)(1) provides, in part: It shall be unlawful for any creditor to discriminate against any applicant, with respect to any aspect of a credit transaction— (1) on the basis of race....

Defendant asserts that plaintiffs failed to plead a violation of the Equal Credit Opportunity Act because defendant's acceptance of a check is not an extension of credit pursuant to 15 U.S.C. § 1691a(d), which states: The term "credit" means the right granted by a creditor to a debtor to defer payment of debt or to incur debts and defer its payments or to purchase property or services and defer payments therefor.

Plaintiffs assert in their complaint that defendant's accepting payment by check constitutes credit because "the exchange of goods and merchandise for a check issued by a customer creates a valid debit or obligation on the part of the purchaser and defers payment until such time as the check is presented for payment to the debtor's bank and thereafter paid."

The Court concludes that the transaction between plaintiffs and defendant fails to meet the definition of "credit" in 15 U.S.C. § 1691a(d). Since plaintiffs' check was negotiable upon execution, defendant did not grant plaintiffs any right to purchase merchandise and defer payment for it. Although a delay in payment of the check may be necessary due to technology which does not currently allow for the immediate processing of a check, defendant maintained the right to present the check to the drawee immediately for payment.

In *Bailey v. Jewel Companies, Inc.*, No. 79 C 2400 (N.D.Ill.1979), the Court held that plaintiff failed to state a cause of action under 15 U.S.C. § 1691 because he was denied, on racial grounds, identical check cashing privileges at all defendant's retail stores. Plaintiff argued that defendant's check cashing service was an extension of credit within the purview of the Equal Credit Opportunity Act because defendant is deprived of the funds during the period it has accepted the check but has not yet received payment from the bank. Defendant, however, argued that its check cashing service was an exchange of cash or goods for a negotiable instrument, and the required element of deferred payment was not present. The Court stated: The Federal Reserve Board has stated that a bank is not extending credit when it permits a customer to overdraw its checking account without a pre-arranged right to impose a finance charge. If a bank, which is in the ordinary business of extending credit, is not extending credit by cashing a check when there is insufficient funds in the drawer's account to cover the check, it is difficult to see how defendant, which is not in the business of money lending, can be said to be extending credit by cashing a customer's check.

Plaintiffs cite *Sterling Brewers, Inc. v. Kile Williamson*, 269 S.W.2d 249 (Ky.App. 1954) as authority for their proposition that payment for merchandise by check constitutes an extension of credit by the seller. The facts of *Sterling Brewers, Inc.* are easily distinguishable from those in the instant matter. The purchaser in *Sterling Brewers, Inc.* paid for a shipment of alcohol with five post-dated checks payable one month apart. Two of the checks were returned after payment was stopped. In the instant matter plaintiffs paid for the merchandise with a check which was a negotiable instrument at the time of execution. Moreover, the *Sterling Brewers, Inc.* court held that the payment by check was not an extension of credit! The court stated: "The checks accepted by the seller were not an extension of credit for the sale of beer, but rather were an effort to collect a debt which had been created by the purchaser's breach of his contract to pay `cash on arrival.'"

There is no authority for plaintiffs' argument that payment by check, absent an agreement by the seller to hold the check for a period of time before presentment to the drawee, constitutes an extension of credit rather than a cash transaction. Therefore, the Court dismisses plaintiffs' claims under 15 U.S.C. § 1691.

****

4A   **Is the plaintiff's check in *Roberts* similar to an extension of credit or similar to cash in a different form? Is the retailer-Defendant risking nonpayment when the retailer-Defendant accepts cash? Is the retailer-Defendant risking nonpayment when the retailer-Defendant accepts a check? Why or Why Not?**

4B   The court notes in *Roberts*, that "a bank is not extending credit when it permits a customer to overdraw its checking account without a pre-arranged right to impose a finance charge."[296] Further, the court notes that "absent an agreement by the seller to hold the check for a period of time before presentment to the drawee,"[297] a check is not an extension of credit. **If plaintiffs were required to pay a fee for paying by check would this fee allow a check to constitute <u>credit</u> for ECOA purposes? Does the fee have to be applied only if the bank account amount funds prove insufficient to cover the check amount, similar to an overdraft fee applicable only in the case of an overdraft? Would it matter if such a charge was applied only to black patrons paying for goods by check?**

Consider the next case, *Laramore v. Ritchie Realty Management Co.*, 397 F.3d 544 (7th Cir., 2005),[298] in which the court considers what constitutes <u>**credit**</u> for ECOA purposes.

---

[296] *Id.* at 1530.
[297] *Id.* at 1530.
[298] *Laramore v. Ritchie Realty Management Co.*, 397 F.3d 544 (7th Cir., 2005).

LARAMORE V. RITCHIE REALTY MANAGEMENT CO.

MANION, Circuit Judge.

Brenda Laramore sued Ritchie Realty Management Company ("Ritchie") claiming that Ritchie violated the Equal Credit Opportunity Act, 15 U.S.C. § 1691 (the "ECOA") when it informed her that she could not apply to rent an apartment it managed because she received public assistance. The district court dismissed Laramore's complaint on the ground that the rental of residential property is not a credit transaction covered by the ECOA. We affirm.

Laramore receives federal assistance pursuant to Section Eight of the United States Housing Act, 42 U.S.C. § 1437f. "Section [Eight] is a federal program designed to assist the elderly, low income, and disabled pay rent for privately owned housing." *Allen v. Muriello*, 217 F.3d 517, 518 (7th Cir.2000). The assistance generally comes in the form of a voucher (often called a "Section 8 Voucher") that the recipient can use to pay a portion of their rent.

In October 2002, Laramore began a search for a new apartment for herself and her four children. She found a prospective apartment in Chicago via a search on the Internet. On October 21, 2002, after viewing the apartment, Laramore telephoned Ritchie, the company responsible for managing the apartment, to request an application for a lease. The woman who took the call initially told Laramore that the apartment was available to rent. After Laramore informed her that she intended to use a Section 8 Voucher to pay a portion of the rent, however, the woman told Laramore that the apartment was not available to persons using Section 8 Vouchers.

On February 21, 2003, Laramore filed suit in the United States District Court for the Northern District of Illinois (Eastern Division). In her suit, Laramore claimed that Ritchie and others not party to this appeal (the apartment's owners) violated the ECOA by denying her a rental application because she receives public assistance. Ritchie moved to dismiss the complaint pursuant to Fed.R.Civ.P. 12(b)(6) on the ground that a rental application is not a credit transaction under the ECOA. The district court agreed with Ritchie and dismissed the suit. This appeal followed.

We review de novo the dismissal of a complaint pursuant to Rule 12(b)(6). *Cole v. U.S. Capital*, 389 F.3d 719, 729 n. 10 (7th Cir.2004). "If the statute under which the plaintiff sued provides no relief in the circumstances alleged, the district court's decision was appropriate." *Pawlowski v. N.E. Ill. Reg'l Commuter R.R. Corp.*, 186 F.3d 997, 1000 (7th Cir.1999).

The ECOA makes it "unlawful for any creditor to discriminate against any applicant, with respect to any aspect of a credit transaction because all or part of the applicant's income derives from any public assistance program." 15 U.S.C. § 1691(a)(2). The ECOA is Title VII of the Consumer Credit Protection Act, 15 U.S.C. §§ 1601-1693r (the "CCPA").

A "creditor" is defined for the purposes of the ECOA as "any person who regularly extends, renews, or continues credit." 15 U.S.C. § 1691a(e). "Credit" is, in turn, defined by the ECOA as "the right granted by a creditor to a debtor to defer payment of debt or to incur debts and defer its payment or to purchase property or services and defer payment therefor." 15 U.S.C. § 1691a(d).

The question in this case, therefore, is whether Ritchie was acting as a creditor when it denied Laramore an application to rent the apartment she was interested in because the apartment was not available to persons receiving Section 8 Vouchers. As can be seen above, whether Ritchie was acting as a creditor is determined by whether Ritchie regularly extends credit. Put more clearly, Ritchie is a creditor if a residential lease amounts to the right of a lessee to defer payment of a debt for the purchase of property or services already purchased.

The district court found that a residential lease was not an extension of credit because a lease is not a deferred payment of a debt, "but prepaid advancement[] of a debt for contemporaneous use." *Laramore v. Ritchie Realty Mgmt. Co.*, No. 03 C 1333, 2003 WL 22227148, at *1 (N.D.Ill. Sept.25, 2003). The district court also noted that the Federal Reserve Board (the "Board") has stated that the ECOA should not be construed to cover lease transactions.

Laramore argues that a residential lease is an extension of credit. Laramore argues, in effect, that a residential lease is an agreement for occupancy for a term (typically a year) and that the agreement creates a debt as of the time of the agreement and that the lessee pays off the debt over the period of the term. In other words, when the lessor and the lessee sign a lease, the transaction is complete — the lessee has the right to use the premises for the duration of the term of the agreement and the lessee is paying off the amount owed for the entire term on a month-by-month basis. Another way of looking at it is that a tenant's monthly payments are not for the month's occupation of the apartment when the rent is paid (i.e., November's rent) but instead, simply 1/12th of the year's rent.

Courts that have considered whether leases are credit transactions are split. In *Brothers v. First Leasing*, 724 F.2d 789 (9th Cir.1984), the Ninth Circuit held the ECOA applies to consumer leases. The court concluded that applying the ECOA to consumer leases "is essential to the accomplishment of the [CCPA's] anti-discriminatory goals." *Id.* at 794. The court did note that it was "unclear" that the ECOA, when first enacted, applied to consumer leases. *Id.* at 793. The court concluded, however, that amendments to the Truth in Lending Act, 15 U.S.C. §§ 1601-1666j ("TILA"), another title of the CCPA, extending TILA's disclosure requirements to consumer leases suggested that the same should be done to the ECOA.

The Northern District of Illinois, in an unpublished decision, held that the ECOA applied to a lease transaction involving a mobile home. *Ferguson v. Park City Mobile Homes*, No. 89 C 1909, 1989 WL 111916, at *3 (N.D.Ill. Sept.18, 1989). The court, however, provided little analysis to support its decision. It did note that it did not follow the Ninth Circuit's analysis in *Brothers*, but concluded that "the language of the ECOA is certainly broad enough to cover the lease of a mobile home lot." *Id.* at *3. The court's decision also appears to have been motivated, at least in part, by the poor performance by counsel opposed to applying the ECOA. *Id.* ("[The defendant] has cited no case authority whatever in bringing its motion to dismiss, and its argument is almost wholly conclusory with no analysis of the interplay between the statutory provisions.").

The Western District of Washington, relying on *Brothers*, has held that the ECOA applies to cellular phone service agreements. *Williams v. AT & T Wireless Servs., Inc.*, 5 F.Supp.2d 1142, 1146-47 (W.D.Wash.1998). The court held that the application for a cell phone service agreement involved an application for credit. *Id.* The court determined that the agreement at issue gave the customer the right to use AT & T's phone services and pay for those services later. *Id.*

Other cases have held that leases are not subject to the ECOA. In *Liberty Leasing v. Machamer*, 6 F.Supp.2d 714 (S.D.Ohio 1998), the district court held that an equipment lease involving monthly payments was not a credit transaction because the lease involved a contemporaneous exchange of consideration — the lessee made monthly payments that allowed the lessee to continue to exercise its rights under the lease. *Id.* at 717. The Northern District of Illinois reached a similar conclusion in *Head v. North Pier Apt. Tower*, No. 02 C 5879, 2003 WL 22127885, at *3 (N.D.Ill. Sept.12, 2003). We find these cases persuasive.

We hold that a typical residential lease does not involve a credit transaction. The typical residential lease involves a contemporaneous exchange of consideration — the tenant pays rent to the landlord on the first of each month for the right to continue to occupy the premises for the coming month. A tenant's responsibility to pay the total amount of rent due does not arise at the moment the lease is signed; instead a tenant has the responsibility to pay rent over roughly equal periods of the term of the lease. The rent paid each period is credited towards occupancy of the property for that period (i.e., rent paid November 1 is credited towards the right of a tenant to occupy the premises in November). As such, there is no deferral of a debt, the requirement for a transaction to be a credit transaction under the Act.

We also find persuasive, at least insofar as residential leases are concerned, the conclusion of the Board that leases are not covered by the ECOA. Congress has delegated to the Board the authority to proscribe regulations concerning the Act. 15 U.S.C. 1691b(a)(1). In response, the Board promulgated Regulation B (12 C.F.R. Part 202). In a Supplementary Information issued in November 1985, as part of a periodic review of Regulation B, the Board, responding to the Ninth Circuit's decision in *Brothers*, stated "that the Ninth Circuit interpreted the ECOA's definition of credit too broadly when it concluded in the *Brothers* case that the granting of a lease is an extension of credit." 50 Fed.Reg. 48,018, 48,020.3 The Board then concluded that "Congress did not intend the ECOA, which on its face applies only to credit transactions, to cover lease transactions unless the transaction results in a 'credit sale' as defined in the Truth In Lending Act and Regulation Z." *Id.*

The ECOA prohibits discrimination against those who receive public assistance when they enter into a credit transaction. Because, however, a residential lease is not a credit transaction as that term is defined in the ECOA, Ritchie's refusal to provide Laramore with a rental application was not subject to the Act. The district court's decision to dismiss Laramore's complaint was appropriate and, therefore, that decision is

AFFIRMED.

****

Many leases require a one-year commitment rather than a month-to-month living arrangement. If a consumer "breaks a lease," in many instances, the consumer may be responsible to the lessor for payment of remaining months due on the lease, even if the consumer does not continue to live at the premises. **Is this lessee responsibility for payment of the remaining months more consistent with an extension of credit or with the lessee paying "rent to the landlord on the first of each month for the right to continue to occupy the premises for the coming month"?[299]**

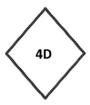

In footnote 3, omitted, the court states:

The parties spend a considerable amount of space in their briefs debating the significance of [the Federal Reserve Board] Supplementary Information. Laramore argues that the Supplementary Information is entitled to no deference while Ritchie argues that the Supplementary Information is entitled to significant deference or, at the very least, it is persuasive guidance in construing the ECOA. We need not resolve this dispute, however. We are convinced that the ECOA by its terms, and without need to resort to administrative interpretations of the Act, does not cover residential leases. The Supplementary Information is, however, at the least, persuasive.[300]

Why does the court consider interpretation from the *Federal Reserve Board*?

If residential leases constituted credit, was Laramore denied credit? Why or Why Not? Is the denial of an extension of credit the only relevant part of the credit transaction for ECOA purposes?

Consider the next case, *Rosa v. Park West Bank & Trust*, 214 F.3d 213 (1st Cir., 2000),[301] in which the court considers what constitutes sex discrimination for ECOA purposes.

---

[299] *Laramore*, 397 F.3d at 547.
[300] *Id.* at 548 n.3.
[301] *Rosa v. Park West Bank & Trust*, 214 F.3d 213 (1st Cir., 2000).

ROSA V. PARK WEST BANK & TRUST

Lynch, Circuit Judge.

Lucas Rosa sued the Park West Bank & Trust Co. under the Equal Credit Opportunity Act (ECOA), 15 U.S.C. §§§§ 1691-1691f, and various state laws. He alleged that the Bank refused to provide him with a loan application because he did not come dressed in masculine attire and that the Bank's refusal amounted to sex discrimination under the Act. The district court granted the Bank's motion to dismiss the ECOA claim, Fed. R. Civ. P. 12(b)(6); concurrently, the court dismissed Rosa's pendent state law claims for lack of subject matter jurisdiction. Rosa appeals and, given the standards for dismissing a case under Rule 12(b)(6), we reverse.

According to the complaint, which we take to be true for the purpose of this appeal, *see Duckworth v. Pratt & Whitney, Inc.*, 152 F.3d 1, 3 (1st Cir. 1998), on July 21, 1998, Rosa came to the Bank to apply for a loan. A biological male, he was dressed in traditionally feminine attire. He requested a loan application from Norma Brunelle, a bank employee. Brunelle asked Rosa for identification. Rosa produced three forms of photo identification: (1) a Massachusetts Department of Public Welfare Card; (2) a Massachusetts Identification Card; and (3) a Money Stop Check Cashing ID Card. Brunelle looked at the identification cards and told Rosa that she would not provide him with a loan application until he "went home and changed." She said that he had to be dressed like one of the identification cards in which he appeared in more traditionally male attire before she would provide him with a loan application and process his loan request.

Rosa sued the Bank for violations of the ECOA and various Massachusetts antidiscrimination statutes. Rosa charged that "[b]y requiring [him] to conform to sex stereotypes before proceeding with the credit transaction, [the Bank] unlawfully discriminated against [him] with respect to an aspect of a credit transaction on the basis of sex." He claims to have suffered emotional distress, including anxiety, depression, humiliation, and extreme embarrassment. Rosa seeks damages, attorney's fees, and injunctive relief.

Without filing an answer to the complaint, the Bank moved to dismiss pursuant to Federal Rule of Civil Procedure 12(b)(6). The district court granted the Bank's motion. The court stated:

> [T]he issue in this case is not [Rosa's] sex, but rather how he chose to dress when applying for a loan. Because the Act does not prohibit discrimination based on the manner in which someone dresses, Park West's requirement that Rosa change his clothes does not give rise to claims of illegal discrimination. Further, even if Park West's statement or action were based upon Rosa's sexual orientation or perceived sexual orientation, the Act does not prohibit such discrimination.

Price Waterhouse v. Hopkins, 490 U.S. 228 (1988), which Rosa relied on, was not to the contrary, according to the district court, because that case "neither holds, nor even suggests, that discrimination based merely on a person's attire is impermissible."

On appeal, Rosa says that the district court "fundamentally misconceived the law as applicable to the Plaintiff's claim by concluding that there may be no relationship, as a matter of law, between telling a bank customer what to wear and sex discrimination." Rosa also says that the district court misapplied Rule 12(b)(6) when it, allegedly, resolved factual questions.

The Bank says that Rosa loses for two reasons. First, citing cases pertaining to gays and transsexuals, it says that the ECOA does not apply to crossdressers. Second, the Bank says that its employee genuinely could not identify Rosa, which is why she asked him to go home and change.

We review a motion to dismiss *de novo*. *See Duckworth*, 152 F.3d at 3. In interpreting the ECOA, this court looks to Title VII case law, that is, to federal employment discrimination law. *See Mercado-Garcia v. Ponce Fed. Bank*, 979 F.2d 890, 893 (1st Cir. 1992) (applying the Title VII burden-shifting regime to ECOA); *see also, e.g., Lewis v. ACB Bus. Servs. Inc.*, 135 F.3d 389, 406 (6th Cir. 1998) (same). *But see Latimore v. Citibank Fed. Sav. Bank*, 151 F.3d 712, 713-15 (7th Cir. 1998) (rejecting the Title VII burden-shifting model for ECOA). The Bank itself refers us to Title VII case law to interpret the ECOA.

The ECOA prohibits discrimination, "with respect to any aspect of a credit transaction[,] on the basis of race, color, religion, national origin, sex or marital status, or age." 15 U.S.C. §§ 1691(a). Thus to prevail, the alleged discrimination against Rosa must have been "on the basis of . . . sex." *See Oncale v. Sundowner Offshore Servs., Inc.*, 523 U.S. 75, 78 (1998). The ECOA's sex discrimination prohibition "protects men as well as women." *Id.*

While the district court was correct in saying that the prohibited bases of discrimination under the ECOA do not include style of dress or sexual orientation, that is not the discrimination alleged. It is alleged that the Bank's actions were taken, in whole or in part, "on the basis of . . . [the appellant's] sex." The Bank, by seeking dismissal under Rule 12(b)(6), subjected itself to rigorous standards. We may affirm dismissal "only if it is clear that no relief could be granted under any set of facts that could be proved consistent with the allegations." *Hishon v. King & Spalding*, 467 U.S. 69, 73 (1984); *see also Correa-Martinez v. Arrillaga-Belendez*, 903 F.2d 49, 52 (1st Cir. 1990). Whatever facts emerge, and they may turn out to have nothing to do with sex-based discrimination, we cannot say at this point that the plaintiff has no viable theory of sex discrimination consistent with the facts alleged.

The evidence is not yet developed, and thus it is not yet clear why Brunelle told Rosa to go home and change. It may be that this case involves an instance of disparate treatment based on sex in the denial of credit. *See International Bhd. Of Teamsters v. United States*, 431 U.S. 324, 335 n.15 (1977) ("'Disparate treatment' . . . is the most easily understood type of discrimination. The employer simply treats some people less favorably than others because of their . . . sex."); *Gerdom v. Continental Airlines, Inc.*, 692 F.2d 602, 610 (9th Cir. 1982) (*en banc*), *cert. denied*, 460 U.S. 1074 (1983) (invalidating airline's policy of weight limitations for female "flight hostesses" but not for similarly situated male "directors of passenger services" as impermissible disparate treatment); *Carroll v. Talman Fed. Sav. & Loan Assoc.*,

604 F.2d 1028, 1033 (7th Cir. 1979), *cert. denied*, 445 U.S. 929 (1980) (invalidating policy that female employees wear uniforms but that similarly situated male employees need wear only business dress as impermissible disparate treatment); *Allen v. Lovejoy*, 553 F.2d 522, 524 (6th Cir. 1977) (invalidating rule requiring abandonment upon marriage of surname that was applied to women, but not to men). It is reasonable to infer that Brunelle told Rosa to go home and change because she thought that Rosa's attire did not accord with his male gender: in other words, that Rosa did not receive the loan application because he was a man, whereas a similarly situated woman would have received the loan application. That is, the Bank may treat, for credit purposes, a woman who dresses like a man differently than a man who dresses like a woman. If so, the Bank concedes, Rosa may have a claim. Indeed, under Price Waterhouse, "stereotyped remarks [including statements about dressing more 'femininely'] can certainly be evidence that gender played a part." *Price Waterhouse*, 490 U.S. at 251. It is also reasonable to infer, though, that Brunelle refused to give Rosa the loan application because she thought he was gay, confusing sexual orientation with cross-dressing. If so, Rosa concedes, our precedents dictate that he would have no recourse under the federal Act. *See Higgins v. New Balance Athletic Shoe, Inc.*, 194 F.3d 252, 259 (1st Cir. 1999). It is reasonable to infer, as well, that Brunelle simply could not ascertain whether the person shown in the identification card photographs was the same person that appeared before her that day. If this were the case, Rosa again would be out of luck. It is reasonable to infer, finally, that Brunelle may have had mixed motives, some of which fall into the prohibited category.

It is too early to say what the facts will show; it is apparent, however, that, under some set of facts within the bounds of the allegations and non-conclusory facts in the complaint, Rosa may be able to prove a claim under the ECOA. *See Conley v. Gibson*, 355 U.S. 41, 47-48 (1957) (stating that the notice pleading permitted by the federal rules requires only "'a short and plain statement of the claim' that will give the defendant fair notice of what the plaintiff's claim is and the grounds upon which it rests"); *Langadinos v. American Airlines, Inc.*, 199 F.3d 68, 72-73 (1st Cir. 2000); Fed. R. Civ. P. 8(a).   We reverse and remand for further proceedings in accordance with this opinion.

****

4F

Review Figure 4A. To what stage of the loan transaction does *Rosa* apply?

Would the CFPB have authority to enforce the proposed ECOA violation with respect to the Defendants in this case? Why or Why not?

4G

Recall that Regulation B defines "marital status," a prohibited basis for credit discrimination, as "the state of being unmarried, married, or separated, **as defined by applicable state law.**"[302] (emphasis added). **How might ECOA marital status discrimination prohibitions be impacted, if at all, by varying state definitions of marriage? Compare and contrast the reliance on state**

---

[302] 12 C.F.R. § 1002.2(u).

law definitions for "the state of being married" under ECOA with the reliance on the individual state definition of "contractually obligated" when determining consummation under TILA. Note that the CFPB, via Memorandum from former Director Richard Cordray in 2014 to CFPB Staff, has stated that, "the Bureau will regard a person who is married under the laws of any jurisdiction to be married nationwide for the purposes of the federal statutes and regulations under the Bureau's jurisdiction regardless of the person's place of residency."[303] In addition, Director Cordray stated that the "Bureau will use and interpret the terms 'spouse,' 'marriage,' 'married,' 'husband,' 'wife,' and any other similar terms related to family or marital status in statutes, regulations, and policies administered, enforced, or interpreted by the Bureau to include same-sex marriages and married same-sex spouses."[304] **Does the Memorandum to Bureau Staff constitute rulemaking? Why or Why Not? Does the Memorandum to Bureau Staff resolve any challenge in state definitions of marriage and protections against discrimination in credit transactions pursuant to ECOA? Why or Why Not?**

In footnote 3 in the Memorandum to Bureau Staff, it is stated:

> Regulation B defines "marital status" as "the state of being unmarried, married, or separated, as defined by applicable state law" and states that "unmarried includes persons who are single, divorced, or widowed" but does not state that those examples are exhaustive. 12 C.F.R. § 1002.2(u). While referring to "applicable state law," this definition does not specify which state's law is applicable. Consistent with the Bureau's policy, a person has the marital status of "married" by virtue of being in a marriage under the laws of any jurisdiction while a person has the marital status of "unmarried" by virtue of being in a domestic partnership, civil union, or other relationship not denominated as a marriage by a state.

> The text of Regulation B and the Regulation B commentary also use the words "married," "marriage," and "spouse" throughout. 12 C.F.R. pt. 1002. This guidance does not, however, address how consumers should respond to credit application inquiries into marital status. Nor does it address which state's law is applicable to determining whether the signature of a spouse is necessary to make community property available to satisfy the debt in the event of default.[305]

In 2016, the Consumer Financial Protection Bureau issued a response to the Services & Advocacy for GLBT Elders ("SAGE") concerning the "application of the Equal Credit Opportunity Act to Credit Discrimination on the Bases of Gender Identity and Sexual Orientation."[306] In that response letter, the

---

[303] *See* Memorandum on Ensuring Equal Treatment for Same-Sex Married Couples from the Consumer Fin. Prot Bureau 1 (June 25, 2014).
[304] *See id.* at 2.
[305] *See id.* at 2, n.3.
[306] *See generally* Consumer Fin. Prot. Bureau letter from Director Richard Cordray to Services & Advocacy for GLBT Elders ("SAGE") (Aug. 30, 2016), available at https://www.cfpbmonitor.com/wp-content/uploads/sites/5/2016/09/SAGE-Letter.pdf.

CFPB references *Rosa*, cases related to gender identity, and "legal doctrine that is pertinent to sexual orientation discrimination."[307] The CFPB concludes that:

> The current state of the law supports arguments that the prohibition of sex discrimination in ECOA and Regulation B affords broad protections against credit discrimination on the bases of gender identity and sexual orientation, including but not limited to discrimination based on actual or perceived nonconformity with sex-based or gender-based stereotypes as well as discrimination based on one's associations.[308]

The CFPB states:

> We would be interested to know about any situations in which creditors treat applicants less favorably because of gender identity or sexual orientation. For example, we would be interested in knowing if any creditors require married same-sex couples who apply for credit to provide different documentation of their marriage than married opposite-sex couples. We likewise would be interested in knowing if any creditors impose obstacles on transgender applicants who may submit applications designating their sex consistent with their gender identity.[309]

4H

Does this letter from Director Richard Cordray to SAGE, confirming gender identity and sexual orientation discrimination as constituting sex discrimination under ECOA, amount to "rulemaking"? Why or Why Not?

Return to Figure 2C. **Was the bank employee's requests aligned with the interests of Park West Bank & Trust at the time she requested that Rosa change clothes? Are the interests of the bank employee aligned with the interests of Park West Bank & Trust concerning the outcome of the case? What are the consequences to the employee as a result of a law violation? What are the consequences to the bank as a result of a law violation?**

Read the next case, *O'Dowd v. South Cent. Bell,* 729 F.2d 347 (5th Cir., 1984).[310]

---

[307] *See id.* at 4.

[308] *See id.* at 7.

[309] *See id.*

[310] *O'Dowd v. South Cent. Bell,* 729 F.2d 347 (5th Cir., 1984).

O'DOWD V. SOUTH CENT. BELL

TATE, Circuit Judge:

The plaintiffs, Rose Marie O'Dowd and George O'Dowd ("the O'Dowds"), brought suit under the Equal Credit Opportunity Act ("the Act"), 15 U.S.C. Sec. 1691 *et seq.* (1976), against the defendant South Central Bell Telephone Company ("South Central") to recover damages resulting from alleged violations of the Act. The district court dismissed by summary judgment the O'Dowds' claim upon finding, inter alia, (1) that the O'Dowds, a white couple, had no cause of action under the Act because they did not fall into a legally-recognized minority protected by the Act, and (2) that, if entitled to notice of "adverse action" under the Act, the statement of the reasons therefor supplied by South Central was adequate to satisfy the statutory requirement. We affirm, agreeing with the district court as to the latter holding, and finding that, under the undisputed showing, no discrimination affecting the Act's protected classifications was implicated, whether or not a non-minority applicant has a cause of action under the Act.

Facts

George O'Dowd, a well-respected white lawyer, and his wife had enjoyed residential telephone service supplied by South Central over twenty years previously. At the time this service was installed, no deposit was required by South Central. Through carelessness, O'Dowd was tardy in payment of his monthly telephone bill four times during the year preceding September 1980. The precipitating fact of this litigation arises out of South Central's notice to O'Dowd in September 1980 that, "due to [his] past payment record," a $100 deposit would be required and the telephone service disconnected if the deposit was not received in forty-five days. O'Dowd protested the demand, and South Central disconnected the service, whereupon he paid the deposit under protest and secured re-installation of his residential telephone service. (The deposit was subsequently refunded to him, with interest.)   The O'Dowds subsequently filed this action for damages, alleging two causes of action:

The first cause of action was based upon a violation of the Act "in denying credit on the bases of race, sex, creed, and/or other invalid or discriminatory basis," 15 U.S.C. Sec. 1691(a)(1), arising out of South Central's treatment of customer-applicants in the allegedly predominately black population of their "366" area exchange;

The second cause of action was based upon an additional violation by South Central of the Act's requirement that "[e]ach applicant [for credit] against whom adverse action is taken shall be entitled to a statement of reasons for such action from the creditor." 15 U.S.C. Sec. 1691(d)(2) (1976).

The Discrimination Claim under Section 1691(a)(1)

The O'Dowds do not claim that they themselves were discriminated against on the grounds of "race, color, religion, national origin, sex or marital status, or age," 15 U.S.C. Sec. 1691(a)(1), but rather that they were damaged as a result of South Central's discriminatory policies against customer-applicants in the "366" exchange (which the O'Dowds, a white couple, allege to have a large number of black and elderly customer-applicants). This cause of action would depend, for its predicate, upon a showing that South Central did not enforce a similar deposit-requirement, when presented with tardiness in payment, with regard to other exchange areas that were predominately white or predominately inhabited by younger persons.

We need not face the issue posed by the O'Dowds, however--that, contrary to the district court holding, not only members of Act-protected classifications, but also other applicants for credit damaged as a result of discrimination against the protected classifications, have a cause of action under the Act--because here, under the undisputed showing, South Central's request for a deposit was made pursuant to a standard policy applicable to all exchange areas serviced by it, and that, moreover, the exchange "366" area reflected a racially and sexually diverse "microcosm" reflecting South Central's entire customer population.

The district court granted South Central summary judgment on this claim. Initially, the party seeking summary judgment must demonstrate the absence of a genuine issue of material fact and the appropriateness of judgment as a matter of law. *Adickes v. S.H. Kress and Company*, 398 U.S. 144, 157, 90 S.Ct. 1598 1608, 26 L.Ed.2d 142 (1970). South Central presented various showings demonstrating that the basis for the deposit request to the O'Dowds was a pattern of lateness in payments (four times) during the previous twelve months. Presented by South Central for consideration on the motion for summary judgment were, inter alia, the affidavit of Beryle S. Ramsey, a supervisor handling accounts in the "366" telephone exchange area, and the deposition of Shari Hinojosa, the service representative who handled the request from the O'Dowds of the deposit. These factual submissions were sufficient to demonstrate, unless controverted, that South Central's deposit request was based upon a non-discriminatory motive, i.e., the O'Dowds' tardiness in payment of the telephone bill, and in accordance with a non-discriminatory general practice of requiring deposits in such instances.

Fed.R.Civ.P. 56(e) provides that, once motion for summary judgment is supported by affidavits and other evidence, "an adverse party may not rest on the mere allegations or denials of his pleading, but his response, by affidavits or as otherwise provided by this rule, must set forth specific facts showing that there is a genuine issue for trial." Fed.R.Civ.P. 56(e).

The O'Dowds' allegation that the deposit request was made on the basis of impermissible discrimination is refuted by the undisputed factual showing. The O'Dowds assert that South Central discriminates against "366" area applicants because the racial composition and age of the area's population indicate that residents in the area are a bad credit risk. When pressed for the factual basis of the allegation, however, O'Dowd was unable to identify his source. Further, O'Dowd admitted to having missed due dates in paying his telephone bills, and he admitted having received from South Central at least three "late" notices.

In short, the O'Dowds failed to produce any "specific facts," Fed.R.Civ.P. 56(e), to show there was a genuine factual issue with regard to South Central's undisputed showing of legitimate non-discriminatory reasons for the action taken, and that would tend to substantiate the O'Dowds' claims regarding the demography of the "366" area or the disparate treatment by South Central of customer-applicants in the area. Accordingly, the grant of summary judgment in favor of South Central was correct. *McKenzie v. U.S. Home Corp.*, 704 F.2d 778, 779 (5th Cir.1983); *White v. United Parcel Service*, 692 F.2d 1, 3 (5th Cir.1982).

The Adequate-Explanation-Failure Cause of Action Under Section 1691(d)(3)

 The Act affords a cause of action for damages against any creditor "who fails to comply with any requirement" imposed by the Act. 15 U.S.C. Sec. 1691e (emphasis added). The plaintiffs allege that they are entitled to damages for South Central's failure to comply with the requirements of 15 U.S.C. Sec. 1691(d)(3).

For present purposes, without necessarily so deciding, we accept the O'Dowds' contentions

(a) that South Central's new requirement that the O'Dowds furnish a deposit for continued credit service, after twenty years of such service without deposit, was an "adverse action" within the statutory definition as "a change in the terms of an existing credit arrangement," 15 U.S.C. Sec. 1691(d)(6), which thus entitled them to a "statement of reasons" for such adverse action, Sec. 1691(d)(2), that would contain "the specific reasons for the adverse action taken," Sec. 1691(d)(3), and

(b) that Sec. 1691(d), which was added to the Act by a 1976 amendment, required a creditor to notify any "credit applicant" of an adverse action and of the "specific reasons" therefor, Sec. 1691(d)(2), (3)--not just those within the classifications of race, gender, etc. protected against credit discrimination by the Act. *See, e.g., Fischl v. General Motors Acceptance Corporation*, 708 F.2d 143 (5th Cir.1983) (apparently accepting, without discussion, this construction of the Act).

As previously noted, pursuant to a standard policy, South Central sent a notice of its adverse action (i.e., requiring a deposit for continuation of credit), explaining the reason as "due to your [O'Dowd's] past payment record." The O'Dowds claim that this notice did not meet the statutory requirement that the notice contain "the specific reasons for the adverse action taken." 15 U.S.C. Sec. 1691(d)(3).   Before summarizing the present facts with more specificity, in the light of which we hold that the adverse-action notice did meet the statutory requirement, it is appropriate that, first, we advert to the statutory purposes designed to be served by this notice requirement. As explained in the Senate Report accompanying the 1976 notice-provision, which originated in the Senate and was added to the Act by the 1976 amendment:

The requirement that creditors give reasons for adverse action is, in the Committee's view, a strong and necessary adjunct to the antidiscrimination purpose of the legislation, for only if creditors know they must explain their decisions will they effectively be discouraged from discriminatory practices. Yet this requirement fulfills a broader need: rejected credit applicants will now be able to learn where and how their credit status is deficient and this information should have a pervasive and valuable educational benefit. Instead of being told only that they do not meet a particular creditor's standards, consumers particularly should benefit from knowing, for example, that the reason for the denial is their short residence in the area, or their recent change of employment, or their already overextended financial situation. In those cases where the creditor may have acted on misinformation or inadequate information, the statement of reasons gives the applicant a chance to rectify the mistake. S.Rep. No. 589, 94th Cong., 2d Sess. 4 (1976), reprinted in 1976 U.S.Code Cong. & Admin.News 403, 406. The notice provision was thought to have a long-term "beneficial educational effect on the credit-consuming public and a beneficial competitive effect on the credit marketplace." *Id.* at 409 (S.Rep. at 7).

The Senate Report concluded that it was not intended that "statements of reasons be given in the form of long, detailed personal letters, and that "a short, check-list statement will be sufficient so long as it reasonably indicates the reasons for adverse action." *Id.* at 410 (S.Rep. at 8). The report included a sample check-list letter regarded as sufficient, indicating that the reasons would be sufficiently stated by such notations as "length of employment," "lack of credit references," "time in residence," "too many other credit obligations at this time," etc. *Id.* at 410-11 (S.Rep. at 9). Consonantly with the legislative intent, the administrative regulation promulgated as authorized by the Act provided that the "statement of reasons for adverse action shall be sufficient if it is specific and indicates the principal reason(s)" for the action; the regulation furnished a form check-list that, if properly completed, would satisfy the Act's requirements, which includes such short-form summaries as "[d]elinquent credit obligations," "[i]nsufficient credit file," "[l]ength of employment," etc., 12 C.F.R. Sec. 202.9(b)(2).

Reverting to the present facts, in a letter of September 30, 1980, O'Dowd was informed by South Central that a deposit of $100 was requested "due to your past payment record" and that, if the deposit was not received by October 22, 1980, O'Dowd's telephone would be disconnected. As previously described, this letter was triggered by computer printout because O'Dowd's current telephone bill was overdue (by a day or so) and because, three times during the preceding year (October 1979, November 1979, and December 1979) the bill had been similarly overdue, resulting in each instance in a past-due notice that unless the rather nominal amounts owed were paid within a week, telephone service would be interrupted. (In each instance, O'Dowd promptly paid the overdue amounts, without further incident.)

Under these circumstances, O'Dowd was clearly informed, in our opinion, of the "specific reasons for the adverse action taken," as required by 15 U.S.C. Sec. 1691(d)(3). Within the meaning of the applicable administrative regulation, it was "specific and indicate[d] the principal reason(s) for the adverse action," 12 C.F.R. Sec. 202.9(b)(2), and it met the statutory purpose of informing the creditee of "where and how [his] credit status is deficient," S.Rep. No. 589, supra, at 4, U.S.Code Cong. & Admin.News 1976, at 406.

The present situation is thus distinguishable from that in *Fischl v. General Motors Acceptance Corporation*, 708 F.2d 143 (5th Cir.1983). There, a young homeowner with (actually) an A-1 credit rating, was denied financing on a new-car purchase with the check-listed reason, "credit references are insufficient," and with a check-list indication that no outside sources of information had been used. Actually, however, a credit-bureau report had been consulted, on which there was a mistaken although non-derogatory indication as to one account, and on which the applicant's present employment at $4,000 per month was not shown. In holding the statement of reasons insufficient in that instance, we pointed out that the creditor's statement of reasons inaccurately implied "some qualitative deficiency in Fishl's credit status" and that it did not "signal the nature of that deficiency and, since the name and address of the credit bureau was not supplied, did not provide the [statute] mandated opportunity for the applicant to correct erroneous information." 708 F.2d at 147.

Here, unlike in Fischl, the reason was not "misleading or at best excessively vague," and the O'Dowds were not " 'left to speculate' " as to the reasons for the adverse action here given, which stated reasons were not "misleading" but instead did "coincide with those in fact relied upon" by the creditor. *Fischl, supra*, 708 F.2d at 148. The holding and rationale in *Fischl* are thus consistent with ours in the instant decision.

Accordingly, we AFFIRM the district court's judgment summarily dismissing the O'Dowds' claims against South Central.

****

Review Figure 4A. To what stage of the loan transaction does *O'Dowd* apply?

Is O'Dowd's claim based on a timing, content, or form challenge concerning the adverse action notice?

Could South Central's requirement of a deposit constitute a counter-offer? Why or Why Not? Would an adverse action notice be required for a counter-offer?

4L

As an initial matter, the O'Dowds "do not claim that they themselves were discriminated against."[311] **Would such a claim be plausible?** Recall the Regulation B definition, defining to **discriminate against an applicant** as to treat the applicant less favorably than other applicants.[312]

---

[311] See *id.* at 349.
[312] *See* 12 C.F.R. § 1002.2(n).

MARTINEZ V. FREEDOM MORTG. TEAM, INC.[313]

MEMORANDUM OPINION AND ORDER

MILTON I. SHADUR, Senior District Judge.

Freedom Mortgage Team, Inc. ("Freedom") and Encore Credit Corporation ("Encore") move jointly under Fed. R.Civ.P. ("Rule") 12(b)(6) to be dismissed from this action brought against them and Freedom employee Gram Funes ("Funes") by Arturo Martinez ("Martinez").

. . .

Martinez is a Spanish-speaking Chicagoan of Hispanic origin, while Freedom is a mortgage broker and Encore is a residential mortgage lender. Martinez' relationship with them began when his real estate agent referred him to Funes to seek financing to purchase a home. Martinez met with Funes at Freedom's offices and eventually applied for a loan with Encore through Funes.

. . .

Funes told Martinez he was qualified for the loan and explained that the monthly payment would be $2,400, inclusive of amounts for escrow deposit, and that the monthly payments would later decline.

Although Martinez' dealings with Funes were conducted exclusively in Spanish, at the closing Martinez signed the mortgage documents prepared solely in the English language, with no accompanying Spanish translation or explanation . Martinez' actual mortgage was an adjustable rate mortgage with an interest rate that can only increase (and never decrease) from the initial rate.

Yield Spread Premiums

Encore paid Freedom a $3,390 yield spread premium ("Premium") in conjunction with the mortgage transaction. When a borrower agrees to pay interest rates higher than their "par" rate (the minimum interest rate at which the lender would make the loan), the lender may pay a Premium to the broker. Calculation of the Premium amount is based on how much the interest rate is above the "par" figure (formulas for determining such rates are sent by lenders to brokers on a regular basis), and a higher interest rate results in the broker receiving a larger Premium.

. . .

Freedom and Encore assert that Martinez' claims of discrimination in violation of the [...] Equal Credit Opportunity Act ("Credit Opportunity Act," 15 U.S.C. § 1691) fail because denial of credit is a required component of a successful claim of discriminatory treatment [...]. Martinez has not asserted a denial of

---

[313] 527 F.Supp.2d 827 (N.D. Ill., 2007).

credit, complaining instead of burdens associated with his receiving credit. But that contention by Freedom and Encore is dead wrong, because [the statute] clearly do[es] not require a denial of credit.

. . .

Congress spoke even more clearly (if possible) in setting out the Credit Opportunity Act provision that a creditor may not "discriminate against any applicant, with respect to any aspect of a credit transaction—on the basis of race" (15 U.S.C. § 1691(a)(1)). If anything, "any aspect of a credit transaction" meshes even more plainly with a case involving the granting of credit than with one where credit was denied, even though most litigation under that section has arisen from the latter situation. Simply put, a race-based loan rejection is merely a sufficient (but not a necessary) form of discrimination under the statute (*see JAT, Inc. v. Nat'l City Bank of Midwest*, 460 F.Supp.2d 812, 820 (E.D.Mich.2006)).

Martinez' discrimination-based contention asserts that in conjunction with loans made to minority borrowers, Encore pays and Freedom accepts higher Premiums than in loans made to non-minority borrowers. Higher Premiums stem from higher interest rates for borrowers (relative to their actual risk). If higher Premiums are indeed paid on minority borrowers' loans then on comparable loans, to their non-minority counterparts, that correlates with those minority borrowers having received loans on less favorable terms than their counterparts.

To be sure, Premiums are not inherently discriminatory. Lenders such as Encore provide brokers such as Freedom with rate sheets indicating what percentage of the total loan amount the broker will receive for inducing a borrower to accept an interest rate over the "par" rate. Lenders of course want to extend credit at as high an interest rate as possible. Premiums create the incentive for brokers, in an effort to obtain the highest possible commission, to induce borrowers to agree to the highest possible interest rate.

Any lender will pay the same Premium to a broker regardless of whether the broker convinced a non-minority person or a member of a racial minority to accept an interest rate higher than that individual's "par" rate. But discrimination can creep into that otherwise permissible equation if the broker makes disproportionate attempts to pressure racial minorities into accepting interest rates above their "par" rates (or rates disproportionately higher than their "par" rates).

At the core of Martinez' Complaint is the assertion that when Freedom saw someone of Hispanic origin such as himself walk into its office to apply for a mortgage, Freedom pushed harder for that person to agree to a higher interest rate than it would have had that applicant been white. Martinez' claim that "[d]efendants, on average, subjected plaintiff and other minority borrowers to more frequent and/or larger Premiums due to their race" is framed awkwardly, but its intended meaning is clear. Borrowers are not "subjected to" Premiums—Premiums are paid by lenders to brokers. If a broker talks a borrower into accepting a higher interest rate when he or she is qualified for a lower rate, that borrower is then "subjected to" the higher rate by the lender. Semantics notwithstanding, allegations of such conduct by Freedom properly plead actionable racial discrimination under [ ] the . . .Credit Opportunity Act.

In paying a Premium, a lender compares race-neutral factors (the borrower's "par" rate versus the actual interest rate accepted) in determining whether and to what extent to pay a Premium to the broker. But Martinez further alleges that Encore (1) knew that offering Premiums was causing its brokers to act in a discriminatory manner and (2) targeted minorities for higher cost loans by purposefully utilizing brokers who served minority communities. [. . .] targeting racial minorities for higher cost loans sets out a discrimination-based theory of recovery under [...] the Credit Opportunity Act.

****

Return to Figure 1C. What part of the loan transaction does Encore represent? What part of the loan transaction does Freedom Mortgage represent?

Return to Figure 4A. What part of the credit transaction is Martinez claiming involved prohibited discrimination?

Would the CFPB have authority to enforce the proposed ECOA violation with respect to the Defendants in this case? Why or Why not? Consider the CFPB and Department of Justice's 2015 joint complaint, filed in the United States District Court for the Northern District of California, pursuant to 12 U.S.C. §5565(a)(1), against Provident Funding Associates, L.P for charging higher prices on mortgage loans to African-American and Hispanic borrowers.[314] Provident was ultimately required to pay nine million dollars to harmed borrowers for the alleged discriminatory practices.[315]

Do consumers impacted by discrimination have a disincentive to develop a positive credit history?[316] Why or Why Not?

---

[314] *See* Patrice Ficklin, *African-American and Hispanic Borrowers Harmed by Provident Will Receive $9 million in Compensation* CONSUMER FIN. PROTECTION BUREAU BLOG (Nov. 2, 2017), https://www.consumerfinance.gov/about-us/blog/african-american-and-hispanic-borrowers-harmed-provident-will-receive-9-million-compensation/.
[315] *See id.*
[316] *See* Hynes, *supra* note 20, at 31 (stating "discrimination may cause minorities to underinvest in human capital and the development of a credit history, in anticipation of being denied credit on the account of their race.").

Return to Figure 2C. **Who are the various stakeholders in *Martinez*[317]?**

Consider the following consumer complaint narrative, filed in the CFPB Consumer Complaint Database on August 3, 2018. Recall that the CFPB Consumer Complaint Database is open to the public to submit complaints and to review complaints submitted by other consumers. Note that the CFPB does not "verify all the facts alleged in the complaints, but [the CFPB] take[s] steps to confirm a commercial relationship between the consumer and the company."[318] Certain information concerning the complaint is redacted.

Consumer complaint narrative:[319]

> *Received solicitation from Prosper to lend money to me. When I called they informed me that no one could speak XXXX (my first language). They also said all documents were in English therefore they could not do business with me. My husband asked if he could talk on my behalf and they refused saying they could only talk to me in English. My Husband spoke to a manager named XXXX who gave us a ticket number of XXXX for your information and files on XX/XX/18 at aprox. XXXX XXXX EST. My husband is of the opinion that this amounts to de facto lending discrimination against XXXX. He urged me to complain to the CFPB. This company is in Arizona and apparently they can not find XXXX speaking people there (even though there are a multitude of XXXX living in that area) to work for them who can conduct business with XXXX. Perhaps they also discriminate in hiring practices too considering the high percentage of XXXX speaking people living in Arizona.*

4Q The company responded timely, and the complaint was "closed with explanation" from the company. The company elected not to permit a response viewable to the public. **Does this consumer complaint amount to an ECOA violation? Why or Why Not? What additional information would you need to decide?**

4R **What are the consumer's potential remedies, if any? What are the CFPB's powers to resolve such an issue, if any? Should such protections be left to individual states to handle rather**

---

[317] 527 F.Supp.2d 827 (N.D. Ill., 2007).

[318] *See* CONSUMER FIN. PROT. BUREAU, https://www.consumerfinance.gov/data-research/consumer-complaints/ (last visited on Dec. 2, 2018).

[319] CONSUMER FIN. PROT. BUREAU ONLINE CONSUMER COMPLAINT DATABASE, https://www.consumerfinance.gov/data-research/consumer-complaints/search/detail/2981319, (last visited Dec. 2, 2018).

than a federal bureau?[320] Note that the consumer in the complaint above indicated that the consumer was from Florida, while complaining of a company based in Arizona.[321] Note further that Regulation B[322] and Regulation Z,[323] among other federal regulations, permit required disclosures to be provided in a language other than English so long as the disclosures are also available in English. However, creditors are not required to provide the disclosures in a language other than English.

4S **Does this consumer have reduced access to financial services? Why or Why Not?**

4T **Is disclosure meaningful to the consumer if the disclosure is not in the consumer's primary language? Why or Why Not?**

4U **Should a creditor be mandated to take on the expense of additional employees to ensure nondiscriminatory access to information and to credit? Why or Why Not?**

4V Recall *Yazzie*.[324] In that case, the Defendants argued that they were intending to be helpful to the consumer by deferring a portion of the car down payment.[325] Note, however, that this intent could also have been beneficial to the Defendants in attracting more consumers. **If a financial services provider attempts to be helpful by offering translated disclosures to consumers, and the translation is discovered to be unintentionally erroneous, would this**

---

[320] Limited English Proficient "individuals tend to be concentrated in the states with the largest populations [. . .]. Overall, LEP residents in California, Texas, and New York account for nearly 50 percent of the total LEP population in the United States." *See* CONSUMER FIN. PROT. BUREAU, *Spotlight on Serving Limited English Proficient Consumers: Language Access in the Consumer Financial Marketplace* (Nov. 2017), at 10-11 https://s3.amazonaws.com/files.consumerfinance.gov/f/documents/cfpb_spotlight-serving-lep-consumers_112017.pdf.

[321] CONSUMER FIN. PROT. BUREAU ONLINE CONSUMER COMPLAINT DATABASE, https://www.consumerfinance.gov/data-research/consumer-complaints/search/detail/2981319, (last visited Dec. 2, 2018).

[322] *See* 12 C.F.R. § 1002.4(e).

[323] *See* 12 C.F.R. 1026.27 (Fastcase 2018).

[324] *See Yazzie v. Gurley Motor Co.*, No. CIV 14-555 JAP/SCY 2016 (D. N.M. Mar. 8, 2016).

[325] *See id.* at *6.

constitute discrimination i.e. that the consumer was treated less favorably than other applicants[326] who received accurate disclosures? Further, consider that an institution can translate for meaning, or an institution can translate word-for-word.[327] Which translation type, if utilized, would be more likely to comply with TILA? Which translation type, if utilized, would be more likely to avoid an ECOA violation? Finally, consider also that the Limited English Proficient "population overlaps significantly with the immigrant population in the United States."[328]

What incentive does a bank or other financial institution have to provide such translation service, if not required by law? Note that consumers who are Limited English Proficient are also often "unbanked" not only with respect to credit, but also with respect to other financial services, including bank accounts, for example.[329]

4W

The cases in this text have considered "technical" violations of the Truth in Lending Act. **Can there be technical compliance with the Truth in Lending Act? For example, reconsider the consumer complaint above as a completed credit transaction. May a lender who has provided the written disclosures required under the Truth in Lending Act be held liable for a disclosure violation if the consumer cannot read[330] English language disclosures?   Why or Why Not?** Consider instead whether a lender who has provided the written disclosures required under the Truth in Lending Act may be held liable for a disclosure violation if the consumer cannot read.[331] Consider instead whether a lender who has provided the written disclosures required under the Truth in Lending Act may be held liable for a disclosure violation if the consumer has "mental disabilities."[332] Finally, consider whether a lender who has provided the written disclosures required under the Truth in Lending Act may be held liable for a disclosure violation if the consumer did not understand the disclosures provided.[333]

---

[326] *See* 12 C.F.R. § 1002.2(n).

[327] *See* CONSUMER FIN. PROT. BUREAU, *supra* note 320, at 8.

[328] *See id.* at 11.

[329] *See id.* at 12-13.

[330] Note that "to communicate the intended meaning, successful translation and interpretation of financial terms requires language fluency, cultural competency, and financial expertise." *See id.* at 9. Does TILA permit oral disclosures? Would oral disclosures be more helpful to some consumers? Why or Why Not?

[331] *See e.g. Gray v. First Century Bank*, 547 F.Supp.2d 815, 823 (E.D. Tenn., 2008) (stating, "though technical compliance with Truth in Lending Act regulations may not be sufficient in cases involving claims of illiteracy, *USLIFE Credit Corp. v. FTC*, 599 F.2d 1387, 1390 (5th Cir.1979)").

[332] *See id.* at *822.*

[333] How is protection balanced with access to choice, so as not to cross the line into "paternalistic" or so-called "nanny" regulation? Consider the following description: "[R]egulatory elitists were especially vigilant in their efforts to protect groups that they saw as vulnerable: the poor, immigrants, and perhaps most of all women, whom paternalists viewed as especially needing protection because of their purportedly poor math skills. The deregulatory reforms that began in the 1970s, by contrast, were grounded on the dual premises of treating borrowers like adults (even the supposedly "math-impaired" females) and the demonstrated inability of

Consider the following consumer complaint narrative, filed in the CFPB Consumer Complaint Database on July 7, 2018. Certain information concerning the complaint is redacted.

Consumer complaint narrative:[334]

> *I was declined a loan after I already have a loan with them. When I called to discuss why I was declined and to understand how they arrived at the XXXX I was put on hold. Then I was told they arent allowed to transfer me to talk to someone who could explain how they arrived at my XXXX. I believe they may have made a mistake and wanted to ensure they are calculating correctly. I feel it is not fair under and maybe against Regulation B for not explaining and giving me the chance to ensure they have my specific debts and income correctly. I currently have a loan with them and feel they could at least walk me through and explain. At least show me it was fair treatment and not based on discrimination. Instead I was provided with vague answers making it seem like who knows what the decision was really based on.*

The company responded timely, and the complaint was "closed with explanation" from the company. The company elected not to permit a response viewable to the public. **Does this consumer complaint amount to an ECOA violation? Why or Why Not? What additional information would you need to decide?**

Consider the following consumer complaint narrative, filed in the CFPB Consumer Complaint Database on November 14, 2017. Certain information concerning the complaint is redacted.

---

governmental regulators to improve matters by substantive regulation of consumer credit markets. *See* Zywicki, *supra* note 218, at 868.

[334] CONSUMER FIN. PROT. BUREAU ONLINE CONSUMER COMPLAINT DATABASE, https://www.consumerfinance.gov/data-research/consumer-complaints/search/detail/2956884, last visited Dec. 2, 2018.

Consumer complaint narrative:[335]

> *Applied Online and was Pre-approved for a personal loan of XXXX and XXXX secured with a vehicle. Based on a monthly income from all sources of XXXX. After discussing offer over the phone and learning I worked at a XXXX bar they 'forgot ' to include my stock dividends and capital gains income. So I was only approved for XXXX unsecured loan based on XXXX monthly income.. After documenting assets and income with bank statements, brokerage statements, profit and loss statements for self-employment ... They decided I did not qualify for a XXXX loan with proof of XXXX figure monthly income and XXXX of stocks and liquid assets. I think this decision not to lend is not based on any logical evaluation of my ability to repay. But rather discrimination against me on the basis of my assumed XXXX orientation XXXX XXXX nightlife entertainer) or religion XXXX my LinkedIn mentions an XXXX student group I led in college.)*

4Y

The company responded timely, and the complaint was "closed with explanation" from the company. The company elected not to permit a response viewable to the public. **Does this consumer complaint amount to an ECOA violation? Why or Why Not? What additional information would you need to decide?**

[335] CONSUMER FIN. PROT. BUREAU ONLINE CONSUMER COMPLAINT DATABASE, https://www.consumerfinance.gov/data-research/consumer-complaints/search/detail/2729390, last visited Dec. 2, 2018.

Consider the following consumer complaint narrative, filed in the CFPB Consumer Complaint Database on April 30, 2018. Certain information concerning the complaint is redacted.

Consumer complaint narrative:[336]

> *I am very concerned about policies limiting financing to companies engaged in the gun industry! I believe this is a violation of anti-discrimination law. What happens when the banks decide that we should no longer purchase vehicles which use fossil fuels, that we should all drive solar/battery powered cars? What happens when prolife organizations are deemed unacceptable by lenders? What would happen when black businesses are deemed too risky? What right do lenders have to pick the policies that we are all forced to live by and suppress policies with which they disagree? This is a very dark and dangerous path for us to choose and I would suggest BOA and XXXX XXXX need to take a step back and reconsider their policies regarding the gun industry and if they will not they should certainly be held accountable for this dangerous behavior! To me this is very comparable to the baker providing services to gay individuals, to separate restrooms for white versus black individuals, and even to equal pay for women versus men. We all supposedly ascribe to the principal of equality and these new policies of BOA and XXXX certainly violate these principals.*

4Z

The company responded timely, and the complaint was "closed with explanation" from the company. The company elected not to permit a response viewable to the public. **Does this consumer complaint amount to an ECOA violation? Why or Why Not? What additional information would you need to decide?**

---

[336] CONSUMER FIN. PROT. BUREAU ONLINE CONSUMER COMPLAINT DATABASE, https://www.consumerfinance.gov/data-research/consumer-complaints/search/detail/2891507, last visited Dec. 2, 2018.

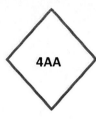

4AA

Note that one purpose of ECOA, as well as the use of consumer credit reports was to combat discrimination in subjective underwriting criteria. **If the underwriting criteria are well-defined rather than vague, can discrimination still occur?** Note that the CFPB considers, in its ECOA Examination Procedures Manual, whether the creditor allows exceptions to its underwriting policies.[337] **Could financial institutions permit a large number of exceptions, deviating from the defined underwriting criteria, for some consumers and not for others without violating ECOA? Why or Why Not? What additional information do you need to decide, if any?**

Many ECOA issues involve the beginning stages of a credit transaction. However, recall that ECOA also applies to the servicing stage of a credit transaction. Consider, for example, an entity's policies regarding which consumers the entity directs to "hardship" options, namely the ability to avoid foreclosure in the event of default.[338] An entity that offers hardship options to some consumers but not to others, on a prohibited basis, could be in violation of ECOA.

4BB

Recall the discussion in Part ID concerning the 5Ws.

Who is regulated under ECOA and its implementing regulations?

Who is protected under ECOA and its implementing regulations? Who is not protected under ECOA and its implementing regulations?

What is the protection? What is the appropriate law or regulation?

When is the protection applicable? (Under what circumstances does the protection apply?

Why does the protection exist? Would applying the law or rule make sense in context?

4CC

Consider whether ECOA utilizes a restriction consumer protection method or a disclosure consumer protection method. **Does ECOA resolve the issue of access to information to create a "fair" playing field or does ECOA resolve the issue of access to financial markets by encouraging financial inclusion?**

---

[337] *See* Consumer Fin. Prot. Bureau, *ECOA Examination Procedures Manual* (Oct. 2015), at 2, available at https://s3.amazonaws.com/files.consumerfinance.gov/f/documents/201510_cfpb_ecoa-narrative-and-procedures.pdf.

[338] *See* Consumer Fin. Prot. Bureau, *supra* note 280, at 22.

V. FAIR DEBT COLLECTION PRACTICES ACT

A. LAWS & RULES

The Fair Debt Collection Practices Act, 15 U.S.C. §1692 *et seq.*, was passed in 1977. The Fair Debt Collection Practices Act provisions are located within 15 U.S.C. Chapter 41: Consumer Credit Protection.[339] Specifically, FDCPA provisions are found within Subchapter V: Debt Collection Practices.[340] FDCPA is part of the Consumer Credit Protection Act of 1968.[341]

Debt collection is pervasive in American households.[342] Much of the debt is related to credit cards, student loans, and auto loans, rather than housing debt.[343] The Fair Debt Collection Practices Act serves three purposes. First, the Fair Debt Collection Practices Act serves to "eliminate abusive debt collection practices by debt collectors."[344] Second, the Fair Debt Collection Practices Act serves to "insure that debt collectors who refrain from using abusive debt collection practices are not competitively disadvantaged."[345] Do consumers benefit or suffer from increased competition? Creation of a fair market by reducing competitive advantages is a recurring theme in consumer protection regulation. If financial institutions' avoidance of certain laws is triggered by a need to remain competitive against other financial institutions, does establishing a balanced market help consumers? Finally, the Fair Debt Collection Practices Act ("FDCPA") serves to "promote consistent state action to protect consumers against debt collection abuses."[346]

"Creditor," "debt," and "debt collector" are defined terms under the FDCPA, and the definitions control the applicability of the statute.[347] A ***creditor*** is "any person who offers or extends credit creating a debt or to whom a debt is owed."[348] A creditor does not include a person "who receives an assignment or

---

[339] *See* 15 U.S.C. § 1692 *et seq.*

[340] *See* 15 U.S.C. § 1692 *et seq.*

[341] *See* 15 U.S.C. §1601 *et seq.*

[342] *See* CONSUMER FIN. PROT. BUREAU ANN. REP. Fair Debt Collection Practices Act, at 8, https://s3.amazonaws.com/files.consumerfinance.gov/f/documents/cfpb_fdcpa_annual-report-congress_03-2018.pdf ("Debt collection is a $10.9 billion dollar industry that employs nearly 120,000 people across approximately 8,000 collection agencies in the United States. The debt collection industry affects millions of Americans.").

[343] *See id.* at 11.

[344] 15 U.S.C. § 1692(e) (Fastcase 2018).

[345] *Id.*

[346] *Id.*

[347] *See* 15 U.S.C. § 1692a (Fastcase 2018).

[348] 15 U.S.C. § 1692a(4).

transfer of a debt in default solely for the purpose of facilitating collection of such debt for another."[349] Recall Part I.

A **_debt_** is "any obligation or alleged obligation of a consumer to pay money arising out of a transaction in which money, property, insurance or services which are the subject of the transaction are for primary personal, family, or household purposes, whether or not such obligation has been reduced to judgment."[350]

Debt collector means "any person who uses any instrumentality of interstate commerce or the mails in any business the principal purpose of which is the collection of any debts, or who regularly collects or attempts to collect, directly or indirectly, debts owed or due or asserted to be owed or due another."[351] Note that, although it is not expressly stated, the term debt collector does not include creditors. Therefore, creditors are not subject to FDCPA compliance. Recall the discussion in Part I concerning the options that a creditor may exercise after origination. To be a debt collector, the person must be collecting a debt owed _another_. By definition, a creditor, who has ownership of the debt/the right to enforce repayment on the debt cannot be a debt collector if the creditor is collecting on the debt. If the creditor is collecting on the debt, the debt is not owed or due another; the creditor would be collecting a debt owed or due itself. There are a few additional, important express exceptions to the term debt collector. Debt collector does not include a person collecting the debt of another person within the same corporate structure so long as the person collecting the debt (1) does not engage in debt collection as its principal business and (2) only collects debts for the person within the same corporate structure.[352] In addition, a debt collector does not include a person collecting a debt for another if the person collecting the debt originated the debt or if the debt was not in default at the time the person started collecting.[353] Review Figure 5A. Recall what type of entity is responsible for collecting debts of a creditor not in default when the entity starts collecting? A servicer is tasked with collecting debts owed another not in default. Return to Figure 2C. What type of stakeholder might a servicer be as to a lender?

Finally, there are limitations to the "exemption" for creditors. Creditors are not exempted from FDCPA compliance if the creditor uses a name other than the creditor's own name to collect the debt owed to the creditor.[354] **Why does FDCPA exempt creditors collecting their own debts? Why does the FDCPA not exempt creditors using names that indicate that a third person is collecting or attempting to collect such debts?** In some respects, FDCPA is intended to protect consumers against abuses by third-party debt collectors not so-called "first party debt collection" whereby the debt collector is the party to whom the debt is owed. Keep third party debt collection and first party debt collection in mind reading cases interpreting the FDCPA.

---

[349] _Id._
[350] 15 U.S.C. § 1692a(5).
[351] 15 U.S.C. § 1692a(6).
[352] _See_ 15 U.S.C. § 1692a(6)(B).
[353] _See_ 15 U.S.C. § 1692a(6)(F).
[354] _See id._

Consistent with other consumer protection statutes, the term consumer is defined under the FDCPA. **Consumer** is "any natural person obligated or allegedly obligated to pay any debt."[355] The FDCPA applies to consumer debts, for personal, family, or household purposes, only.

The FDCPA may be considered primarily in four consumer protections: (1) protection regarding communication, (2) protection from harassment or abuse, (3) protection from false or misleading representations, and (4) protection from unfair practices.[356] The FDCPA prohibits certain debt collection communications. Specifically, the FDCPA prohibits debt collectors from communicating with consumers at unusual times,[357] prohibits communicating with the consumer when the debt collector knows that the consumer is represented by an attorney with respect to the debt,[358] and prohibits communicating with consumers at the consumer's place of employment if the debt collector knows or has reason to know that the employer prohibits such communication.[359] Such communication with the consumer is prohibited unless the debt collector has the prior consent of the consumer or express permission of a court of competent jurisdiction.[360] Debt collectors are also prohibited from communicating with anyone other than the consumer, the consumer's attorney, a consumer reporting agency[361] as permissible, the creditor, the creditor's attorney, or the debt collector's attorney, without the consumer's prior consent or express permission from the court.[362] Finally, a debt collector is required to cease communicating with a consumer if the consumer notifies the debt collector in writing that the consumer refuses to pay the debt or that the consumer wishes the debt collector to cease further communication with the consumer.[363] There are a few limited exceptions to the communication cessation. "**Communication**" is a defined term under the FDCPA.[364] Communication is the "conveying of information regarding a debt directly or indirectly to any person through any medium."[365] Therefore, the prohibited debt collector communications, prohibited communications with third parties, and prohibited communication once communications must cease are communications regarding debts.[366] Finally, note that, with respect to communications, consumer is defined more broadly to include the spouse, parent (if the consumer is a minor), guardian, executor, or administrator.[367]

---

[355] 15 U.S.C. § 1692a(3).

[356] A large, and frequently challenging part of the FDCPA is debt validation under 15 U.S.C. § 1692g. While debt validation is an important consumer protection that is frequently utilized by consumers, particularly in the mortgage loan foreclosure context, this text will not discuss debt validation in detail.

[357] 15 U.S.C. § 1692c(a)(1) (Fastcase 2018).

[358] 15 U.S.C. § 1692c(a)(2).

[359] 15 U.S.C. § 1692c(a)(3).

[360] 15 U.S.C. § 1692c(a).

[361] Consumer reporting agencies will be discussed in detail in Part VIII.

[362] 15 U.S.C. § 1692c(b).

[363] 15 U.S.C. § 1692c(c).

[364] *See* 15 U.S.C. § 1692a(2).

[365] *Id.*

[366] *See id.*

[367] 15 U.S.C. § 1692c(d).

5A   **Does a voicemail message, where a "debt collector" does not actually speak to the consumer, constitute a communication?**

Recall the discussion in Part IV, ECOA, regarding the definition of marital status. Specifically, recall that the CFPB, via Memorandum from former Director Richard Cordray in 2014 to CFPB Staff, has stated that, "the Bureau will regard a person who is married under the laws of any jurisdiction to be married nationwide for the purposes of the federal statutes and regulations under the Bureau's jurisdiction regardless of the person's place of residency."[368] In addition, Director Cordray stated that the "Bureau will use and interpret the terms 'spouse,' 'marriage,' 'married,' 'husband,' 'wife,' and any other similar terms related to family or marital status in statutes, regulations, and policies administered, enforced, or interpreted by the Bureau to include same-sex marriages and married same-sex spouses."[369] Finally, the Memorandum to Bureau Staff notes, as referenced above, that the definition of consumer is broad and includes the consumer's spouse for the purposes of FDCPA communication protections/requirements under 15 U.S.C. §1692c.[370]

The FDCPA prohibits debt collectors from engaging in harassing, oppressive, and abusive behaviors, and the express language of the law controls what constitutes such prohibited behaviors sufficient to violate the law.[371] The use or threat of violence or other criminal means to harm the physical person, reputation, or property of any person is a violation.[372] The use of obscene or profane language or language the natural consequence of which is to abuse the hearer or reader is a violation.[373] Recall that "communication" is defined to include conveying information regarding a debt *through any medium*.[374] As a result, the profane or obscene language is prohibited in both oral and written communications regardless of whether the person is hearing or reading the communication.[375] The publication of a list of consumers who allegedly refuse to pay debts is a violation.[376] The advertisement for sale of any debt to coerce payment of the debt is a violation.[377] Causing a telephone to ring or engaging any person in telephone conversation repeatedly or continuously with intent to annoy, abuse, or harass any person at the called number is a violation.[378] Finally, calling without identifying the caller's identity is a violation.[379] Recall that one purpose of the Fair Debt Collection Practices Act is to "insure that debt

---

[368] Consumer Fin. Protection Bureau, *supra* note 303, at 1.

[369] *Id.* at 2.

[370] *See id.* at 2, n. 4.

[371] *See* 15 U.S.C. § 1692d (Fastcase 2018).

[372] 15 U.S.C. § 1692d(1).

[373] 15 U.S.C. § 1692d(2).

[374] 15 U.S.C. § 1692a(2).

[375] *See id.*; *see also* 15 U.S.C. § 1692d.

[376] 15 U.S.C. § 1692d(3).

[377] 15 U.S.C. § 1692d(4).

[378] 15 U.S.C. § 1692d(5).

[379] 15 U.S.C. § 1692d(6).

collectors who refrain from using abusive debt collection practices are not competitively disadvantaged."[380]

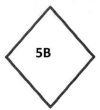

5B

If a debt collector employed harassing, oppressive, and abusive methods, how would these methods give such debt collectors a competitive advantage in collecting debts if the methods were not prohibited?

The FDCPA prohibits false, deceptive, or misleading representations or means in connection with debt collection, and the express language of the law controls what constitutes such prohibited behaviors sufficient to violate the law.[381] It is a violation of the FDCPA for a debt collector (1) to give the false representation or implication that the debt collector is vouched for, bonded by, or affiliated with the United States or any State, including the use of any badge, uniform, or facsimile thereof; (2) to give the false representation of the character, amount, or legal status of any debt or any services rendered or compensation which may be lawfully received by any debt collector for the collection of a debt; (3) to give the false representation or implication that any individual is an attorney or that any communication is from an attorney; (4) to give the representation or implication that nonpayment of any debt will result in the arrest or imprisonment of any person or the seizure, garnishment, attachment, or sale of any property or wages of any person unless such action is lawful and the debt collector or creditor intends to take such action; (5) to threaten to take any action that cannot legally be taken or that is not intended to be taken; (6) to give the false representation or implication that a sale, referral, or other transfer of any interest in a debt shall cause the consumer to lose any claim or defense to payment of the debt or become subject to any practice prohibited by the FDCPA; (7) to give the false representation or implication that the consumer committed any crime or other conduct in order to disgrace the consumer; (8) to communicate or threaten to communicate to any person credit information which is known or which should be known to be false, including the failure to communicate that a disputed debt is disputed; (9) to use or distribute any written communication which simulates or is falsely represented to be a document authorized, issued, or approved by any court, official, or agency of the United States or any State, or which creates a false impression as to its source, authorization, or approval; (10) to use a false representation or deceptive means to collect or attempt to collect any debt or to obtain information concerning a consumer; (11) to fail to disclose in the initial written communication with the consumer and, in addition, if the initial communication with the consumer is oral, in that initial oral communication, that the debt collector is attempting to collect a debt and that any information obtained will be used for that purpose, and the failure to disclose in subsequent communications that the communication is from a debt collector; (12) to use of any business, company, or organization name other than the true name of the debt collector's business, company, or organization; (13) to give the false representation or implication that documents are not legal process forms or do not require action by the consumer; and (14) to give the false representation or implication that a debt collector operates

---

[380] 15 U.S.C. § 1692(e) (Fastcase 2018).
[381] 15 U.S.C. § 1692e (Fastcase 2018).

or is employed by a consumer reporting agency, among others.[382] The FDCPA prohibits false, deceptive or misleading misrepresentations in the context of debt collection.[383] As referenced above, the FDCPA requires a debt collector to disclose, in the initial written communication with the consumer, and, in addition, if the initial communication with the consumer is oral, in that initial oral communication, that the debt collector is attempting to collect a debt and that any information obtained will be used for that purpose.[384] This disclosure is usually referred to as the "mini-Miranda."

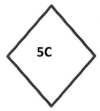

5C

Is the "mini-Miranda" a restrictive method of regulation or a disclosure method of regulation? Are the two types of regulatory methods mutually exclusive? Does the requirement to disclose that the person is a debt collector have specific form, timing, or content requirements?

The CFPB has not promulgated express rules for interpreting this FDCPA requirement, and there is no corresponding "model form." However, the requirement explicitly states timing requirements, namely "before the initial communication."[385] Further, the requirement explicitly states content requirements (what information must be disclosed to the consumer), namely that the person is a debt collector, the communication is an attempt to collect a debt, and any information obtained will be used for that purpose.[386]

Finally, FDCPA protects against unfair practices.[387] The law controls what practices amount to an FDCPA violation. Specifically, the FDCPA prohibits the following unfair debt collection practices:

> (1)The collection of any amount (including any interest, fee, charge, or expense incidental to the principal obligation) unless such amount is expressly authorized by the agreement creating the debt or permitted by law; (2) the acceptance by a debt collector from any person of a check or other payment instrument postdated by more than five days unless such person is notified in writing of the debt collector's intent to deposit such check or instrument not more than ten nor less than three business days prior to such deposit; (3) the solicitation by a debt collector of any postdated check or other postdated payment instrument for the purpose of threatening or instituting criminal prosecution; (4) depositing or threatening to deposit any postdated check or other postdated payment instrument prior to the date on such check or instrument; (5) causing charges to be made to any person for communications by concealment of the true purpose of the communication. Such charges include, but are not limited to, collect telephone calls and telegram fees; (6) communicating with a consumer regarding a debt by post card; and (7) using any language or symbol, other than the debt collector's

---

[382] 15 U.S.C. § 1692e.

[383] *See generally* 15 U.S.C. § 1692e.

[384] 15 U.S.C. § 1692e.

[385] 15 U.S.C. § 1692e.

[386] *See* 15 U.S.C. § 1692e.

[387] 15 U.S.C. § 1692f (Fastcase 2018).

address, on any envelope when communicating with a consumer by use of the mails or by telegram, among other prohibited practices.[388]

As a reminder, the FDCPA includes important exclusions, establishing who is not subject to the FDCPA. Specifically, the FDCPA excludes (1) persons collecting or attempting to collect debts that are owed to the person, (2) persons collecting debts that were not in default at the time obtained, (3) a person collecting a debt of another person to whom it is related by common ownership or control so long as the debt collection is only for the related entity.

Review Figure 1C.

To what part of the loan transaction process does the Fair Debt Collection Practices Act apply? The Fair Debt Collection Practices Act applies to the debt collection stage of the loan transaction process.

The CFPB has the authority to create implementing rules for the FDCPA.[389] Rules concerning FDCPA are found in 12 C.F.R. Part 1006 *et seq.* However, these rules, in Subpart A, currently govern a state's application for exemption from FDCPA provisions.[390] Subpart B is currently "reserved" but offers no further implementing guidance on FDCPA.[391]

---

[388] 15 U.S.C. § 1692f.
[389] *See* 15 U.S.C. § 1692l(d) (Fastcase 2018).
[390] *See* 12 C.F.R. § 1006 (Fastcase 2018).
[391] *See id.*

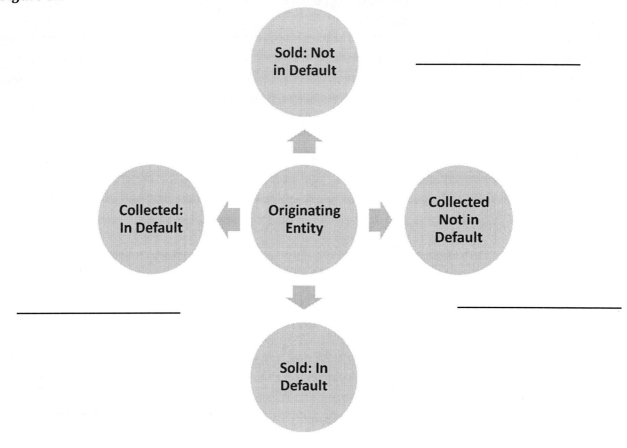

B. ENFORCEMENT

Recall that the CFPB has exclusive rulemaking, enforcement, and federal supervisory authority over nondepository institutions, including "larger participants."[392] The CFPB has oversight over larger participant debt collectors with annual receipts in excess of ten million dollars.[393] The Federal Trade Commission has authority to enforce compliance with the FDCPA, the FDIC has authority to enforce the FDCPA with respect to banks, the National Credit Union Administration has authority to enforce the FDCPA with respect to credit unions, and the CFPB has the authority to enforce the FDCPA with respect to anyone subject to the FDCPA.[394] In 2017, the CFPB issued a fine to a financial service provider that was accused of "illegal debt collection tactics, including making threats to contact servicemembers' commanding officers about debts."[395]

Violation of the FDCPA can also result in an individual action where actual or statutory damages of up to $1,000 may be awarded.[396] However, a debt collector is not liable in instances where the debt collector's actions or lack thereof were a result of a good faith attempt to comply with a CFPB advisory opinion.[397] Contrast this "good faith exemption" to the good faith exemption in TILA and ECOA. **What is different about the FDCPA "good faith exemption?"**

Obviously, ECOA and TILA exempt *creditors* while FDCPA exempts *debt collectors*. But more importantly, the FDCPA good faith exemption states that the debt collector will not be liable if the debtor is trying to comply with a CFPB *advisory opinion*. In contrast, the ECOA and TILA exemptions state that the creditor will not be liable if the creditor is trying to comply with a *rule or regulation*. Note that, in contrast to the existing rules for ECOA and TILA, the CFPB has not created express rules or regulations for debt collector compliance. Recall from Parts I and II that rulemaking authority includes prescribing rules, issuing orders, and issuing guidance.[398]

In addition, a debt collector is not liable for failure to comply with FDCPA if the debt collector can show that its violation was not intentional, considering procedures that the debt collector has in place to avoid such violations.[399] Notably, in an individual action for damages, FDCPA requires that a court

---

[392] *See* 12 U.S.C. § 5514.
[393] *See* 12 C.F.R. § 1090.105(b).
[394] 15 U.S.C. § 1692l.
[395] *See* Press Release, Consumer Fin. Protection Bureau, CFPB Issues $1.25 Million Fine to Servicemember Auto Lender for Violating Consent Order (Apr. 26, 2017), available at https://www.consumerfinance.gov/about-us/newsroom/cfpb-issues-125-million-fine-servicemember-auto-lender-violating-consent-order/.
[396] *See* 15 U.S.C. § 1692k (Fastcase 2018).
[397] *See* 15 U.S.C. § 1692k(e).
[398] *See* 12 U.S.C. § 5512(b)(1).
[399] *See* 15 U.S.C. § 1692k(c).

consider (1) the frequency and persistence of the debt collector's noncompliance, (2) the nature of the noncompliance, and (3) to what extent the noncompliance was intentional.[400]

5D   **Under what circumstances would noncompliance be intentional?**

The statute of limitations for a civil action is within one year from the date the violation occurs.[401] Consider that courts have held that any debt collector may be liable to any person, under the express language of the Fair Debt Collection Practices Act.[402] In other words, the potentially liability is not limited to causes of action by the consumer only.[403] In addition, courts have limited individual awards to $1,000 per case rather than $1,000 per violation or noncompliant instance, consistent with the language of 15 U.S.C. 1692k that damages are limited "in the case of **any action** by an individual" to no more than $1,000 (emphasis added).[404] In other words, any action has been interpreted to mean any legal proceeding and not to mean any action of the debt collector.[405]

5E   **Do you think this damages limitation reduces the likelihood of compliance?**

A debtor may decide that the potential liability of a violation is worth the risk in comparison to the ability to collect the debt through violative means to gain an advantage, especially when the likelihood of a lawsuit may be low. However, the FDCPA could still retain "deterrent value"[406] because the plaintiff can still recover actual damages.

---

[400] *See* 15 U.S.C. § 1692k(b)(1).

[401] *See* 15 U.S.C. § 1692k(d) (2018).

[402] *See Wright v. Finance Service of Norwalk, Inc.*, 22 F. 3d 647, 649-50 (6th Cir. 1994); *see also Whatley v. Universal Collection Bureau, etc.*, 525 F. Supp. 1204, 1205-06 (N.D.Ga 1981).

[403] *See Wright*, 22 F. 3d at 649-50; *see also Whatley*, 525 F. Supp. at 1205-1206.

[404] *See Wright*, 22 F. 3d at 650-51.

[405] *Id.*

[406] *See id.* at 651.

C. INTERPRETATION

The purpose of the FDCPA is to eliminate abusive debt collection practices by debt collectors. Consider whether the FDCPA utilizes a restriction consumer protection method or a disclosure consumer protection method. Does FDCPA resolve the issue of access to information to create a "fair" playing field or does FDCPA resolve the issue of access to financial markets by encouraging financial inclusion?

Consider the following cases interpreting provisions of the Fair Debt Collection Practices Act. How do the courts rely on the definitions? Who is regulated? Who is protected? Are the protections the courts afford through their interpretations/decisions consistent with the purposes of the Fair Debt Collection Practices Act?

MONTGOMERY V. HUNTINGTON BANK[407]

SILER, Circuit Judge.

Plaintiff Duane Montgomery, proceeding *pro se*, appeals the district court's judgment dismissing his claims against Huntington Bank and Silver Shadow Recovery, Inc. ("Silver Shadow"), filed under the Fair Debt Collection Practices Act (FDCPA), 15 U.S.C. § 1692 *et seq.* He argues that the district court erred in finding that he was not a party in interest with respect to all his claims, and that Huntington Bank and Silver Shadow (collectively, the "Defendants") were not "debt collectors," as that term is defined in the FDCPA. We AFFIRM.

BACKGROUND

In 1998, Montgomery's mother, Helen J. Smith, financed the purchase of a 1998 BMW by entering into a personal loan agreement with Huntington Bank. As collateral for the loan, Huntington Bank took a security interest in the car. As Montgomery has admitted in his complaint, the BMW in question was "owned by Helen Smith." Approximately one year later, Smith allegedly suffered an injury and was apparently unable to work. [. . .] Huntington Bank sought to take possession of the BMW. Thus, Huntington Bank retained Silver Shadow to repossess the vehicle pursuant to the terms of the loan agreement.

In 2000, while Montgomery was away from his home, two employees of Silver Shadow repossessed Smith's vehicle, which was parked in Montgomery's garage. Upon returning home, Montgomery discovered his mother's BMW was missing and immediately filed a police report with the West Bloomfield Township Police Department. The police report, which was attached to the complaint, stated that Montgomery had borrowed his mother's BMW in order to transport some personal items. The complaint averred that the vehicle removed from his home was in fact a "borrowed BMW."

. . .

He [] filed suit in federal court, claiming that Huntington Bank and Silver Shadow violated various provisions of the FDCPA. The Defendants moved to dismiss the complaint under Federal Rule of Civil Procedure 12(b)(1) for lack of subject matter jurisdiction, arguing that Montgomery was not a "consumer" within the meaning of the statute. Also, the Defendants moved to dismiss the complaint pursuant to Federal Rule of Civil Procedure 12(b)(6), arguing that neither Huntington Bank nor Silver Shadow met the statutory definition of a "debt collector" under the FDCPA. The district court granted the motions by dismissing the complaint as to each of the Defendants. In later ruling on Montgomery's motion for relief from judgment, the court determined that due to "Plaintiff's failure to make a claim upon which relief can be granted, to show that he is party in interest in this suit or that Defendants are

---

[407] 346 F.3d 693 (6th Cir., 2003).

`debt collectors' under the Consumer Credit Protection Act, the disposition of the case will not change in anyway [sic] upon rehearing or reconsideration."

STANDING

As an initial matter, both Huntington Bank and Silver Shadow contend that Montgomery lacks standing to pursue this litigation because he is not a "consumer" as defined by the FDCPA. As the Defendants see it, it was Smith, not Montgomery, who entered into the personal loan agreement with Huntington Bank for the purchase of the BMW, and, thus, it is Smith who is the real party in interest. Although the Defendants' assertion is correct for one of Montgomery's claims, the Defendants' standing analysis — more precisely its lack thereof — erroneously collapses the entire standing inquiry under the FDCPA into whether a particular plaintiff is a "consumer," completely ignoring that other sections of the FDCPA are either expressly available, or have been interpreted to be available, to "any person" aggrieved under the relevant statutory provision.

Montgomery brought suit under three separate provisions of the FDCPA: 15 U.S.C. §§ 1692c, 1692d and 1692e. Of these three sections, relief is limited to "consumers" only under § 1692c. As we have previously explained, "only a `consumer' has standing to sue for violations under 15 U.S.C. § 1692c." *Wright v. Fin. Serv. of Norwalk, Inc.*, 22 F.3d 647, 649 n. 1 (6th Cir.1994) (*en banc*). However, § 1692c "appears to be the most restrictive of the FDCPA's provisions. The other provisions are not limited to `consumers,' and thus are broader than § 1692c." *Id.*

By its express terms, § 1692d provides that "[a] debt collector may not engage in any conduct the natural consequence of which is to harass, oppress, or abuse any person in connection with the collection of a debt." We have interpreted this to mean that "any person who has been harmed by a proscribed debt collection practice under § 1692d ... [may] sue for damages under § 1692k(a)(2)(A)." *Wright*, 22 F.3d at 649 n. 1 (paraphrasing the court's holding in *Whatley v. Universal Collection Bureau, Inc.*, 525 F.Supp. 1204 (N.D.Ga.1981)). Likewise, § 1692e states that "[a] debt collector may not use any false, deceptive, or misleading representation or means in connection with the collection of any debt." 15 U.S.C. § 1692e. When read in conjunction with § 1692k(a),3 this means that "any aggrieved party may bring an action under § 1692e." *Wright*, 22 F.3d at 649-50. Accordingly, the Defendants are mistaken to suggest that Montgomery lacks standing to pursue his claims under §§ 1692d and 1692e. However, the Defendants are correct that he lacks standing under § 1692c, as he is not a consumer for purposes of the FDCPA.

Under the FDCPA, a "consumer" is defined as "any natural person obligated or allegedly obligated to pay any debt," 15 U.S.C. § 1692a(3), or "the consumer's spouse, parent (if the consumer is a minor), guardian, executor, or administrator." 15 U.S.C. § 1692c(d). *See also Wright*, 22 F.3d at 649 n. 1. In the instant case, Montgomery has admitted in his complaint that the personal loan agreement authorized Huntington Bank to "[t]ak[e] possession of the collateral (BMW) ... [held] in the name of Helen J. Smith" in the event of breach. His complaint further states that at the time of the repossession, the BMW was "owned by Helen Smith" and merely "borrowed" by him. Nowhere in his complaint does he allege that he is the legal guardian of his mother or that he is otherwise obligated or allegedly obligated to pay any debt in connection with the purchase of the BMW. Also, contrary to his suggestion, the mere fact that he possessed or borrowed his mother's car, and that the Defendants were aware of this possible arrangement and communicated this information to one another, does not show that he was responsible or allegedly responsible for paying any debt stemming from the purchase of the automobile. Accordingly, he fails to meet the statutory definition of "consumer," and, hence, lacks standing under § 1692c.

. . .

ANALYSIS

As a matter of law, liability under §§ 1692d and 1692e can only attach to those who meet the statutory definition of a "debt collector." The Defendants assert that they are not debt collectors within the meaning of the FDCPA. Thus, as a threshold matter, we must determine whether either of the Defendants falls within the FDCPA's definition of a "debt collector."

The FDCPA was enacted to "eliminate abusive debt collection practices by debt collectors, to insure that those debt collectors who refrain from using abusive debt collection practices are not competitively disadvantaged, and to promote consistent State action to protect consumers against debt collection abuses." 15 U.S.C. § 1692(e). The statute defines a "debt collector" as "any person who uses any instrumentality of interstate commerce or the mails in any business the principal purpose of which is the collection of any debts, or who regularly collects or attempts to collect, directly or indirectly, debts owed or due or asserted to be owed or due another." 15 U.S.C. § 1692a(6). Creditors who use names other than their own — such as a third-party name — to collect on their own debts also qualify as debt collectors under the Act. *See id.* Exempted from the definition of a debt collector, however, is any person collecting or attempting to collect any debt owed or due or asserted to be owed or due another to the extent such activity ... (ii) concerns a debt which was originated by such person ... [or] (iii) concerns a debt which was not in default at the time it was obtained by such person. 15 U.S.C. § 1692a(6)(F)(ii), (iii).

Finally, a "creditor" is "any person who offers or extends credit creating a debt or to whom a debt is owed...." 15 U.S.C. § 1692a(4). As the Fifth Circuit has concluded, "[t]he legislative history of section 1692a(6) indicates conclusively that a debt collector does not include the consumer's creditors...." *Perry v. Stewart Title Co.*, 756 F.2d 1197, 1208 (5th Cir.1985) (internal quotation marks and citation omitted); *see also Wadlington v. Credit Acceptance Corp.*, 76 F.3d 103, 106 (6th Cir.1996) (quoting *Perry* with approval for this proposition).

Based on the foregoing, it is clear that under the circumstances of this case, Huntington Bank is not a "debt collector" subject to liability under the FDCPA. First, Huntington Bank falls within the exemption contained in § 1692a(6)(F)(ii) because by retaining Silver Shadow to repossess the BMW that served as collateral for the car loan to Smith, it was collecting or attempting to collect on a debt that was owed, due, or asserted to be owed or due, and that originated with it. *See, e.g., Thomasson v. Bank One*, 137 F.Supp.2d 721, 724 (E.D.La.2001) (finding that "[i]n collecting on its own debts [through use of a third party or a subsidiary agent], [the] Bank... does not meet the criteria of a `debt collector' pursuant to [§

1692a(6)(F) of] the FDCPA"); *Zsamba v. Cmty. Bank*, 63 F.Supp.2d 1294, 1300 (D.Kan.1999) (finding that a creditor bank collecting on its own debt falls outside the purview of the FDCPA by virtue of § 1692a(6)(F)(ii)); *Vitale v. First Fidelity Leasing Group*, 35 F.Supp.2d 78, 81 (D.Conn.) (holding that "[a]lthough there are allegations to suggest that [the automobile leasing and financing company] was collecting a debt, the debt was one owed to it and thus its activities are not covered by the FDCPA"), aff'd, 166 F.3d 1202, 1998 WL 887171 (2d Cir.1998) (unpublished opinion). In other words, Huntington Bank was an actual, original, consumer creditor of Montgomery's mother collecting its account, and, as such, was exempted from the statutory definition of a "debt collector." To this, the federal courts are in agreement: A bank that is "a creditor is not a debt collector for the purposes of the FDCPA and creditors are not subject to the FDCPA when collecting their accounts." *Stafford v. Cross Country Bank*, 262 F.Supp.2d 776, 794 (W.D.Ky.2003) (citations omitted); *see, e.g., Russell v. Standard Fed. Bank*, 2000 WL 1923513, at *2 (E.D.Mich.2000); *James v. Ford Motor Credit Co.*, 842 F.Supp. 1202, 1206-07 (D.Minn.1994), aff'd, 47 F.3d 961 (8th Cir. 1995); *Meads v. Citicorp Credit Serv., Inc.*, 686 F.Supp. 330, 333 (S.D.Ga.1988).

Furthermore, Huntington Bank also does not qualify as a debt collector because it falls within the provision of § 1692a(6)(F)(iii), a "person collecting or attempting to collect any debt owed or due... to the extent such activity ... concerns a debt which was not in default at the time it was obtained by such person." Under Montgomery's version of the facts, at the time Huntington Bank extended a personal loan to Smith to purchase a car, and thus acquired a "debt," the personal loan was not "in default." In fact, the alleged default in this case did not occur until over a year after Smith entered into the loan agreement with Huntington Bank. Therefore, Huntington Bank is not a "debt collector" pursuant to § 1692a(6)(F)(iii). *See Wadlington*, 76 F.3d at 107 (finding that a corporation that obtained debts before they were in default did not fall within the definition of a debt collector). Accordingly, the district court was correct in dismissing the FDCPA claims against Huntington Bank.

As a repossession agency, Silver Shadow, likewise, does not fall within the definition of a "debt collector." Montgomery suggests that we give meaning to the term debt collector as it applies to Silver Shadow by looking at Michigan statutory law. State law, however, cannot be our reference point. Rather, to give proper meaning to a federal statute we must be guided by the plain meaning of the statute, canons of statutory construction, relevant legislative history, and other indicia that shed light on the statute's meaning, such as judicial precedent and administrative agency interpretations, which for purposes of the FDCPA, are interpretations given by the Federal Trade Commission ("FTC"). *See Jordan v. Kent Recovery Serv., Inc.*, 731 F.Supp. 652, 656 (D.Del. 1990). In *Jordan*, the court undertook a comprehensive analysis to determine whether those who enforce security interests, such as repossession agencies, fall outside the ambit of the FDCPA. It held that "an enforcer of a security interest, such as a repossession agency, falls outside the ambit of the FDCPA for all purposes, except for the purposes of § 1692f(6)." *Id.* at 659; *see also Seibel v. Society Lease, Inc.*, 969 F.Supp. 713, 716-17 (M.D.Fla. 1997) (concluding that except for purposes of § 1692f(6), a defendant in the business of repossessing vehicles does not fall within the FDCPA's definition of debt collector). We agree.

In *Jordan*, the court found that although Congress included within the definition of "debt collectors" those who enforce security interests, it limited this definition only to the provisions of § 1692f(6). As the court put it, "[s]uch a purposeful inclusion for one section of the FDCPA implies that the term `debt collector' does not include an enforcer of a security interest for any other section of the FDCPA." *Id.* at 657. The court further indicated that when § 1692f(6) is read in conjunction with its legislative history, the two provide "the key to understanding the reason Congress drew a distinction between a debt collector and an enforcer of a security interest." *Id.*

It went on to find that the FDCPA was enacted in order "to prevent the `suffering and anguish' which occur when a debt collector attempts to collect money which the debtor, through no fault of his own, does not have." *Id.* at 658 (citation omitted). In contrast, the court found that the evil sought to be prevented by proscribing the conduct of debt collectors, namely, "harassing attempts to collect money which the debtor does not have due to misfortune," is not implicated in the situation of a repossession agency that enforces a "present right" to a security interest because in the latter context, "an enforcer of a security interest with a 'present right' to a piece of secured property attempts to retrieve something which another person possesses but which the holder of the security interest still owns." *Id.* It noted that "[u]nlike the debtor who lacks the money sought, the possessor of secured property still has control of the property. Any failure to return the property to the rightful owner occurs not through misfortune but through a deliberate decision by the present possessor to avoid returning the property." *Id.* It was thus the court's view that "the legislative history confirms that Congress intended an enforcer of a security interest, such as a repossession agency, to fall outside the ambit of the FDCPA for all purposes except for the prohibitions described in § 1692f(6)." *Id.* In sum, we likewise conclude that except for purposes of § 1692f(6), an enforcer of a security interest, such as a repossession agency, does not meet the statutory definition of a debt collector under the FDCPA.

In the case at bar, Montgomery has not alleged any violation of § 1692f(6).8 Also, other than conclusorily stating that Silver Shadow is a "debt collector," he has not alleged that Silver Shadow is a business whose "principal purpose" is debt collection, or that it regularly collects or attempts to collect debts owed to another. His allegations reveal only that Silver Shadow was seeking recovery of the BMW that was posted as collateral for the personal loan given to Smith by Huntington Bank. In fact, Montgomery admits that Silver Shadow was simply acting as a repossession agency when it seized his mother's BMW. As such, Silver Shadow does not qualify as a debt collector under §§ 1692d and § 1692e, the only two claims remaining. Accordingly, the district court did not err in dismissing the complaint against Silver Shadow pursuant to Rule 12(b)(6) of the Federal Rules of Civil Procedure. AFFIRMED.

****

5F

Note the court's discussion of standing in the *Montgomery* case. **Are non-debtors permitted to initiate a civil action?**

5G   Would the CFPB have authority to enforce the proposed FDCPA violation with respect to the Defendants in this case? Why or Why not?

5H   Recall in Part I that there can oftentimes be additional consumer protections for the elderly. If Montgomery's mother was known to be elderly, would you be satisfied with the outcome of the case? Why or Why Not? If the Plaintiff's mother was determined to be both elderly and incapacitated would you be satisfied with the outcome of the case? Why or Why Not? Does it matter if the mother was incapacitated at the time of purchase? At the time of the default or repossession? Or at the time of the action? Why or Why Not?

Return to Figure 2C. **What is Silver Shadow Recovery's interest in the outcome of *Montgomery*[408]?**

---

[408] 346 F.3d 693 (6th Cir., 2003).

HORKEY V. J.V.D.B. & ASSOCIATES, INC.[409]

MANION, Circuit Judge.

Chris Romero, an employee of J.V.D.B. & Associates, Inc., a debt collection agency, attempted by telephone to collect a client's debt from Amanda Horkey while she was at work. Horkey asked him to give her a number she could call from her home. When he refused she hung up. Romero made a second call and left a profane message with Horkey's coworker. Horkey sued under the Fair Debt Collection Practices Act. J.V.D.B. appeals from the district court's entry of summary judgment in favor of Horkey, the denial of its motion for attorney's fees, and the awarding of statutory and compensatory damages in Horkey's favor. For the reasons set forth below, we affirm in all respects.

J.V.D.B. is a debt collection agency whose employee, identifying himself as Chris Romero, telephoned Amanda Horkey at her place of employment at least twice on January 9, 2001. In the first call, Romero demanded immediate payment of a debt of $817.00. Horkey told Romero that she could not talk to him at work and that she could call him back from her home and arrange a payment schedule. Romero, however, refused to end the conversation, so Horkey hung up on him. Shortly thereafter, Romero called back and spoke with Horkey's coworker, Jimmie Scholes. When Scholes told Romero that Horkey was away from the office and asked if Romero wished to leave a message, Romero told Scholes to "tell Amanda to quit being such a [expletive] bitch," and Romero then hung up the telephone. Scholes passed on the message to Horkey. Shortly after that, Horkey received a third telephone call, but the caller hung up when she answered.

Horkey brought suit under the Fair Debt Collection Practices Act (FDCPA), 15 U.S.C. § 1692 *et seq.* She alleged the following claims: (1) a violation of § 1692c(a)(3)'s prohibition on contacting the consumer at work in contravention of the employer's policy against such communication; (2) a violation of § 1692c(b)'s limits on contacting a third party about the consumer's debt; (3) a violation of § 1692d's prohibition of obscene or profane language . . . On January 4, 2002, the district court granted summary judgment in Horkey's favor on all claims except for her § 1692c(b) allegation. In later proceedings, the district court granted J.V.D.B.'s motion for summary judgment as to § 1692c(b) (third-party contact), but denied J.V.D.B.'s motion for attorney's fees pursuant to § 1692k(a)(3), which allows a defendant to recover sanctions for an action brought in bad faith and for the purpose of harassment. Ultimately, after a bench trial on the issue of damages, the district court awarded Horkey $1,000 in statutory and $350.00 in actual damages. J.V.D.B. appeals summary judgment as to Horkey's claims under § 1692c(a)(3) and § 1692d, the district court's denial of its motion for attorney's fees, and the district court's award of statutory and actual damages.

. . .

---

[409] 333 F.3d 769 (7th Cir., 2003).

The first issue on appeal is whether summary judgment in Horkey's favor was appropriate as to § 1692c(a)(3), which provides that

[w]ithout the prior consent of the consumer given directly to the debt collector or the express permission of a court of competent jurisdiction, a debt collector may not communicate with a consumer in connection with the collection of any debt ... at the consumer's place of employment if the debt collector knows or has reason to know that the consumer's employer prohibits the consumer from receiving such communication.

J.V.D.B. did not have Horkey's prior consent or a court's express permission to communicate with her at work, so the dispositive question is whether it knew or had reason to know that Horkey's employer prohibited such communication.

The only evidence to which Horkey points in support of the district court's conclusion, as a matter of law, that J.V.D.B. knew or should have known that her employer prohibited her from receiving calls from debt collectors is her statement to Romero that she could not talk to him at work and her request for a number she could call from her home. As Horkey paraphrased her protest in her affidavit, she "told Romero that [she] could not talk to him at work and asked him to give [her] his telephone number so that [she] could call him back from [her] home to set up a payment schedule." J.V.D.B. argues that this statement is susceptible to various interpretations and that Romero therefore was in no position to know that Horkey's employer prohibited her from receiving debt-related communication at work. The salient question is whether Horkey's statement was clear enough that, as a matter of law, J.V.D.B. knew or had reason to know that Horkey's employer prohibited her from receiving Romero's call at work.

We agree with the district court that it was. Horkey informed Romero that she could not discuss her debt while at work, and J.V.D.B. presents no evidence that Horkey's employer did allow her to take debt-related calls. Therefore we conclude that in this instance Romero had reason to know that Horkey's employer prohibited her from receiving communications related to debt collection while at work. *See United States v. Central Adjustment Bureau, Inc.*, 667 F.Supp. 370, 388 (N.D.Tex.1986), *aff'd* as modified, 823 F.2d 880 (5th Cir.1987) (holding that, after the consumer wrote the debt collector and "requested in writing that he not call her at work," further calls violated § 1692c(a)(3)).

It is true, as J.V.D.B. argues, that saying "I cannot talk with you at work" could conceivably be understood to mean something other than "my employer forbids me from talking with you at work." It could, for example, mean "I do not wish to talk with you at work" or "I am too busy to talk with you at work." But this observation does not create an issue of material fact because, as we observed in *Gammon v. GC Servs. Ltd. P'Ship*, 27 F.3d 1254 (7th Cir.1994), the FDCPA exists to protect the unsophisticated consumer. *Id.* at 1257. Unsophisticated consumers, whatever else may be said about them, cannot be expected to assert their § 1692c(a)(3) rights in legally precise phrases. It is therefore enough to put debt collectors on notice under § 1692c(a)(3) when a consumer states in plain English that she cannot speak to the debt collector at work. That is what Horkey did. Without evidence that J.V.D.B. knew, contrary to Horkey's assertion, that her employer did not prohibit her from taking debt-related calls at work, she is entitled to summary judgment on her § 1692c(a)(3) claim.

We now turn to Horkey's claim under § 1692d. Section 1692d provides that "a debt collector may not engage in any conduct the natural consequence of which is to harass, oppress, or abuse any person in connection with the collection of a debt." 15 U.S.C. § 1692d. Section 1692d(2), which is the specific subsection upon which the district court granted summary judgment, further provides that "[t]he use of obscene or profane language or language the natural consequence of which is to abuse the hearer or reader" is a violation of this section. *Id.* The uncontested evidence is that, within minutes after Horkey told Romero that she could not discuss the debt while at work, Romero called again and left a message with Horkey's coworker, Jimmie Scholes, asking Scholes to "tell Amanda to stop being such a [expletive] bitch." In an attempt to sidestep what would otherwise be a clear violation, J.V.D.B. asserts that Romero's message "was not spoken in connection with a debt collection nor was it meant to abuse the hearer or reader." Each half of this statement is preposterous.

To state the obvious, Romero's message was "in connection with the collection of a debt" because the undisputed evidence is that Romero called Horkey's workplace for only one reason: to collect a debt. In that context, when he told Horkey (via Scholes) to "stop being such a [expletive] bitch," Romero was not offering general advice about how Horkey could improve her disposition. He was telling her, crudely but specifically, to be more receptive to his entreaties regarding the debt. No other interpretation of the facts is reasonable and thus, as a matter of law, Romero's message to Horkey was "in connection with the collection of a debt."

J.V.D.B.'s assertion that Romero's message was not intended to abuse the hearer likewise fails. J.V.D.B. points to no evidence in the record regarding Romero's intent, which is just as well, because Romero's intent is irrelevant. What is determinative is whether "the natural consequence of" Romero's obscenity-laced message was to "abuse the hearer." 15 U.S.C. § 1692d(2). We need not examine the varying meanings of the words employed to determine that, in the context used, they were abusive as a matter of law. Unequivocally they were. We therefore affirm summary judgment as to Horkey's claim under § 1692d(2).1

. . .

For the reasons set forth above, we affirm in all respects.

****

Some courts have concluded that "the plain language of the FDCPA does not prohibit a debt collector from communicating with a consumer regarding future debts even if the debt collector receives a cease-and-desist letter from the consumer that can arguably be read as a request to cease communications regarding all currently existing as well as future debts."[410] Is this fair for the "unsophisticated consumer," in light of *Horkey*? In other words, should the unsophisticated consumer be required to specify in a cease and desist letter that the consumer does not want the debt collector to contact him or her with respect to all debts, *existing and future*? Could such a request be honored?

---

[410] *Udell v. Kansas Counselors, Inc.*, 313 F. Supp. 2d 1135, 1139 (D. Kansas 2004).

5I Would the CFPB have authority to enforce the proposed FDCPA violation with respect to the Defendants in *Horkey*? Why or Why not?

5J Does the court reach the correct conclusion concerning whether the communication to co-worker Scholes (a message that the co-worker then relayed to Horkey) was a communication for the purposes of 1692c(a)(3) and 1692d claims? Why or Why Not? How is communication defined? Does the communication to co-worker Scholes constitute a communication? Does the co-worker have standing? Why or Why Not?

In footnote 1, omitted, the court notes that:

> J.V.D.B. also points out that Romero "never spoke to" Horkey during his second call, apparently insinuating that there can be no liability under § 1692d(2) where the offending language is routed through an intermediary as opposed to being spoken directly to the consumer. Had the same message been left on Horkey's voicemail, a violation would be conclusive. This is worse because a third person received and relayed the statement. But because J.V.D.B. fails to develop this argument on appeal, the issue is waived. *Martin v. Shawano-Gresham Sch. Dist.*, 295 F.3d 701, 706 n. 4 (7th Cir.2002).[411]

Note that the district court did not grant summary judgment to Horkey on her §1692c(b) claim (third-party contact) and, in fact, granted the Defendant's motion for summary judgment as to the § 1692c(b) (third-party contact) claim. The Seventh Circuit Court of Appeals states in footnote 2, omitted, that:

> We need not address whether, as the district court reasoned, a violation of § 1692c(b) requires the debt collector to convey some information about the debt to a third party. At this point, it suffices to say that district courts are split on this question, and that we leave the matter for another day. Compare *Horkey v. J.V.D.B. ., Inc.*, 179 F.Supp.2d 861, 868 (N.D.Ill.2002) (holding that there can be no liability under § 1692c(b) where there is no discussion of the debt), with *West v. Nationwide Credit, Inc.*, 998 F.Supp. 642, 644-45 (W.D.N.C.1998) (reaching the opposite conclusion).[412]

5K Does liability under §1692c(b) require discussion of a debt? Why or Why Not?

---

[411] *Horkey*, 333 F.3d at 774.
[412] *Id.*

EDWARDS V. NIAGARA CREDIT SOLUTIONS, INC.[413]

CARNES, Circuit Judge:

In an oft-repeated statement from the Vietnam War, an unidentified American military officer reputedly said that "we had to destroy the village to save it." That oxymoronic explanation may be apocryphal, but the debt collection agency in this case offers up much the same logic to explain why it violated the Fair Debt Collection Practices Act: it was necessary to violate the Act in order to comply with the Act.

Brenda Edwards owed money to the Consumer Shopping Network. Her past due account was assigned to Niagara Credit Solutions, Inc. for collection. Niagara is a debt collection agency subject to the provisions of the Fair Debt Collection Practices Act, 15 U.S.C. §§ 1692-1692p, *et seq.* It attempts to collect debts by sending letters and making phone calls to debtors.

As part of its collection efforts, Niagara left over a dozen messages on Edwards' answering machine from July through October 2007. In September 2007, Niagara left a pre-recorded message on her machine stating: "This is an important message for Edwards Brenda. Please return this message at 1-800-381-0416, between the hours of 8 a.m. and 9 p.m. eastern standard time. It is important that you reach our office." The next month Niagara left another message on her answering machine: "This message is intended for Brenda Edwards. Please contact Jennifer [last name not clear] at 1-800-381-0416, my extension is 220. When returning my call have your file number available, it's 1250740."

At the time of those events Niagara had a well-defined policy about messages that it left on debtors' answering machines. That policy was to: leave a message asking the debtor to call back about an important matter; provide Niagara's phone number; supply the real first name of the person calling on behalf of Niagara; and give any reference number assigned to the account. Niagara purposefully left out of the messages any information disclosing that they were from Niagara Credit Solutions, Inc. or a debt collector or that the call had been made for the purpose of collecting a debt. The Fair Debt Collection Practices Act specifically requires that a debt collector disclose in all communications with a debtor that the message is from a debt collector. *See* 15 U.S.C. § 1692e(11). Niagara deliberately chose not to comply with that requirement because it feared that doing so would risk violating another provision of the Act, which generally forbids an agency from communicating about the debt with a third party. *See* 15 U.S.C. § 1692c(b). It was concerned that answering machine messages [584 F.3d 1352] might be played by or within the hearing of a family member or roommate, who would then know that a collection agency was calling the debtor.

In September 2007 Edwards filed a complaint against Niagara alleging that the messages it left on her answering machine violated § 1692e(11) of the Fair Debt Collection Practices Act, as well as § 1692d(6)

---

[413] 584 F.3d 1350 (11th Cir., 2009).

(requiring meaningful disclosure of the caller's identity). She sought an award of statutory damages, costs, and attorney's fees and moved for summary judgment. Niagara asserted a number of defenses, including the bona fide error defense contained in § 1692k(c). The district court granted summary judgment in favor of Edwards after concluding, among other things, that the messages Niagara left violated § 1692d(6) and § 1692e(11) and that the bona fide error defense did not apply. Niagara concedes at this stage that the messages it left violated § 1692e(11) and is only challenging the district court's conclusion that it is not protected by the bona fide error defense. The issue before us is whether a debt collector is entitled to the bona fide error defense when it intentionally violates one provision of the Act in order to avoid the risk of violating another provision.

The Fair Debt Collection Practices Act was enacted by Congress "to eliminate abusive debt collection practices by debt collectors" and "to protect consumers against debt collection abuses." 15 U.S.C. § 1692(e). Congress found abusive practices by debt collectors to be "serious and widespread." *Russell v. Equifax A.R.S.*, 74 F.3d 30, 33 (2d Cir.1996). The Act provides a civil cause of action against any debt collector who fails to comply with the requirements of the Act, including § 1692e(11). *See* 15 U.S.C. § 1692k(a). A debt collector can be held liable for an individual plaintiff's actual damages, statutory damages up to $1,000, costs, and reasonable attorney's fees. 15 U.S.C. § 1692k(a)(1)-(3).

The Act, however, provides debt collectors with an affirmative defense called the "bona fide error" defense, which insulates them from liability even when they have failed to comply with the Act's requirements. *Johnson v. Riddle*, 443 F.3d 723, 727 (10th Cir.2006). The defense is found in 15 U.S.C. § 1692k(c), which provides: A debt collector may not be held liable in any action brought under this subchapter if the debt collector shows by a preponderance of evidence that the violation was not intentional and resulted from a bona fide error notwithstanding the maintenance of procedures reasonably adapted to avoid any such error.

A debt collector asserting the bona fide error defense must show by a preponderance of the evidence that its violation of [584 F.3d 1353] the Act: (1) was not intentional; (2) was a bona fide error; and (3) occurred despite the maintenance of procedures reasonably adapted to avoid any such error. *Johnson*, 443 F.3d at 727-28. The failure to meet any one of those three requirements is fatal to the defense.

Niagara cannot make the first required showing. Section 1692e(11) requires a debt collector "to disclose in subsequent communications that the communication is from a debt collector." 15 U.S.C. § 1692e(11).3 By its own admission, Niagara deliberately decided not to disclose in the messages it left that the caller was a debt collector. Its failure to disclose was intentional.

Niagara has also failed to meet the second requirement of the bona fide error defense, which is that the violation actually be a "bona fide" error. Taking Niagara at its word, it was concerned that disclosing that the call was from a debt collector could result in a violation of 15 U.S.C. § 1692c(b), which prohibits a debt collector from communicating with third parties about the consumer's debt.4 Niagara feared that leaving a message on a debtor's machine stating that it was from a debt collector calling to collect a debt might be viewed as a violation of § 1692c(b) if the message were overheard by or played in the presence of someone other than the debtor, such as a family member or roommate. We do not need to decide whether that concern is well-grounded in the law. Even if there would be a violation of § 1692c(b) in those circumstances, involving fewer than all of the messages left on answering machines, Niagara's violation of § 1692e(11) with every message it left cannot be said to be a bona fide error.

As used in the Act "bona fide" means that the error resulting in a violation was "made in good faith; a genuine mistake, as opposed to a contrived mistake." *Kort v. Diversified Collection Servs., Inc.*, 394 F.3d 530, 538 (7th Cir. 2005); *see also* Black's Law Dictionary 186 (8th ed.2004) (defining "bona fide" as "1. Made in good faith; without fraud or deceit" and "2. Sincere; genuine"); *Garcia v. Vanguard Car Rental USA, Inc.*, 540 F.3d 1242, 1246 (11th Cir.2008) ("When statutory terms are undefined, we typically infer that Congress intended them to have their common and ordinary meaning, unless it is apparent from context that the disputed term is a term of art."). To be considered a bona fide error, the debt collector's mistake must be objectively reasonable. *Johnson*, 443 F.3d at 729 ("[I]n effect, [the bona fide] component serves to impose an objective standard of reasonableness upon the asserted unintentional violation." Just as it is not reasonable to destroy a village in order to save it, neither is it reasonable to violate an Act in order to comply with it. It was not reasonable for Niagara to violate § 1692e(11) of the Fair Debt Collection Practices Act with every message it left in order to avoid the possibility that some of those messages might lead to a violation of § 1692c(b).

Niagara complains that if it is not permitted to leave out of its answering machine messages the disclosure required by § 1692e(11), the result will be that it cannot leave any messages on answering machines. That assumes an answering machine message that includes the disclosure required by § 1692e(11), if heard by a third party, would violate § 1692c(b). We have not decided that issue, but even if Niagara's assumption is correct, the answer is that the Act does not guarantee a debt collector the right to leave answering machine messages.

Because Niagara has failed to meet either of the first two requirements of the bona fide error defense of § 1692k(c), we need not decide whether it also has failed to meet the third one, which requires the maintenance of procedures reasonably designed to avoid the violation of the Act. Although the district court's grant of summary judgment to Edwards was based on that ground, we can and do affirm on different grounds. *See Cuddeback v. Fla. Bd. of Educ.*, 381 F.3d 1230, 1235 (11th Cir.2004) ("This court may affirm [summary] judgment on any legal ground, regardless of the grounds ... relied upon by the district court."). AFFIRMED.

****

5L   **Would the CFPB have authority to enforce the proposed FDCPA violation with respect to the Defendants in this case? Why or Why not?**

BUCHANAN V. NORTHLAND GRP., INC.[414]

SUTTON, Circuit Judge.

Northland Group made a "settlement offer" to Esther Buchanan to resolve an unpaid debt without disclosing that the statute of limitations had run on the debt. Claiming that the letter falsely implied that Northland could enforce the debt in court, Buchanan filed a class action on behalf of herself and other similarly situated debtors under the Fair Debt Collection Practices Act. Northland filed a motion to dismiss under Rule 12(b)(6) of the Federal Rules of Civil Procedure, prompting this question: Could this offer plausibly mislead an unsophisticated consumer into thinking her lender could enforce the debt in court? Answer: Yes, at least at the pleading stage of the proceedings. We reverse the district court's contrary decision.

LVNV buys "uncollectable" debts at a discount—the older the debts, the greater the discount—and pays Northland Group to collect them. LVNV purchased a debt of Buchanan's and assigned it to Northland for collection. In late 2011, Northland sent Buchanan a letter attempting to collect part of the debt. Here is what the letter said: Your past due account balance: $4,768.43 Your settlement offer: $1,668.96 Dear Esther M Buchanan, LVNV Funding LLC, the current creditor of your account, has assigned the above referenced account to Northland Group, Inc. for collection. As of the date of this letter, you owe $4,768.43. Because of interest that may vary from day to day, the amount due on the day you pay may be greater. Hence, if you pay the amount shown above, an adjustment may be necessary after we receive your check, in which event we will inform you before depositing the check for collection. For further information, write the undersigned or call 866–699–2652 ext 3515. The current creditor is willing to reduce your balance by offering you a settlement. We are not obligated to renew this offer. Upon receipt and clearance of $1,668.96, your account will be satisfied and closed and a settlement letter will be issued. This offer does not affect your rights set forth below. LVNV Funding LLC has purchased the above referenced account from the above referenced Previous Creditor [National City Bank]. LVNV Funding LLC has placed your account with this agency for collection. Unless you notify this office within 30 days after receiving this notice that you dispute the validity of this debt or any portion thereof, this office will assume this debt is valid. If you notify this office in writing within 30 days after receiving this notice that you dispute the validity of this debt or any portion of it, this office will obtain verification of the debt or obtain a copy of a judgment and mail you a copy of such judgment or verification. If you request of this office in writing within 30 days after receiving this notice this office will provide you with the name and address of the original creditor if different from the current creditor. Sincerely, Northland Group, Inc. The "settlement offer" did not disclose two things. It did not say that the Michigan six-year statute of limitations had run on the debt, which would have provided a complete defense to any lawsuit to recover the money. *See* Mich. Comp. Laws § 600.5807(8). And it did not say that a partial

---

[414] 776 F.3d 393 (6th Cir., 2015).

payment on a time-barred debt—if, say, Buchanan had not accepted the offer but instead paid $500 to decrease her balance—restarts the statute-of-limitations clock under Michigan law. *See Yeiter v. Knights of St. Casimir Aid Soc'y*, 461 Mich. 493, 607 N.W.2d 68, 71 (2000). Such a settlement offer, to Buchanan's mind, falsely implied that Northland held a legally enforceable obligation. On her behalf and on behalf of similarly situated debtors, Buchanan sued Northland for violating the Fair Debt Collection Practices Act. *See* 15 U.S.C. §§ 1692 –1692p. Northland moved to dismiss the claim under Civil Rule 12(b)(6). In response, Buchanan claimed that the case implicated a question of fact—Was the letter misleading?— and required discovery, including with respect to the proposed testimony of Dr. Timothy E. Goldsmith, a professor of psychology who has studied consumers' attitudes toward time-barred debt and their understanding of communications like this one. *See* Timothy E. Goldsmith & Nathalie Martin, *Testing Materiality Under the Unfair Practices Acts: What Information Matters when Collecting Time–Barred Debts?*, 64 CONSUMER FIN. L.Q. REP. 372 (2010). The district court rejected Buchanan's discovery request and granted Northland's motion to dismiss, concluding that Northland's letter was not misleading as a matter of law. Buchanan appeals the dismissal of her lawsuit.

The Fair Debt Collection Practices Act bans all "false, deceptive, or misleading" debt-collection practices. 15 U.S.C. § 1692e. As the addition of the term "misleading" confirms, the statute outlaws more than just falsehoods. That is why "[t]ruth is not always a defense," *Grden v. Leikin Ingber & Winters PC*, 643 F.3d 169, 172 (6th Cir.2011), and that is why even a true statement may be banned for creating a misleading impression. In its illustrative (and non-exhaustive) list of violations, the statute prohibits a false representation of "the character, amount, or legal status of any debt." 15 U.S.C. § 1692e(2)(A). The Act protects "all consumers," the "shrewd" as well as the "gullible," *Fed. Home Loan Mortg. Corp. v. Lamar*, 503 F.3d 504, 509 (6th Cir.2007), from practices that would mislead the "reasonable unsophisticated consumer," one with some level of understanding and one willing to read the document with some care, *Wallace v. Wash. Mut. Bank, F.A.*, 683 F.3d 323, 327 (6th Cir.2012). Dunning letters that appear misleading only by way of "bizarre," "idiosyncratic," or "nonsensical" readings do not violate the Act. *Lamar*, 503 F.3d at 510, 514 (internal quotation marks omitted). In considering whether this letter creates a cognizable claim, we agree with two premises of Northland's argument (and the district court's holding). Under Michigan law, as under the law of most states, a debt remains a debt even after the statute of limitations has run on enforcing it in court. *See De Vries v. Alger*, 329 Mich. 68, 44 N.W.2d 872, 876 (1950) ; *see also, e.g., Ingram v. Earthman*, 993 S.W.2d 611, 634 n. 19 (Tenn.Ct.App.1998), abrogated on other grounds by *Fahrner v. SW Mfg., Inc.*, 48 S.W.3d 141 (Tenn.2001), as recognized by *Redwing v. Catholic Bishop for Diocese of Memphis*, 363 S.W.3d 436, 461 n. 25 (Tenn.2012). As a result, when the six-year limitations period ran on Buchanan's debt, that meant only that the creditor—LVNV today—could not enforce the debt in court without facing a complete legal defense to it. Legal defenses are not moral defenses, however. And a creditor remains free, in the absence of a bankruptcy order or something comparable preventing it from trying to collect the debt, to let the debtor know what the debt is and to ask her to pay it. There thus is nothing wrong with informing debtors that a debt remains unpaid or for that matter allowing them to satisfy the debt at a discount. For some individuals, such letters may offer a welcome solution to an outstanding debt. Nor does a "settlement offer" with respect to a time-barred debt by itself amount to a threat of litigation. Even an unsophisticated consumer could not reasonably draw such an inference, as the dissent and we both agree. *See Huertas v. Galaxy Asset*

Mgmt., 641 F.3d 28, 33 (3d Cir.2011) ; *Freyermuth v. Credit Bureau Servs., Inc.*, 248 F.3d 767, 771 (8th Cir.2001). If we grant these two premises of Northland's argument, doesn't its conclusion follow—that this lawsuit should be dismissed as a matter of law? We think not, for three reasons. First, whether a letter is misleading raises a question of fact. Generally speaking, "a jury should determine whether the letter is deceptive and misleading." *Kistner v. Law Offices of Michael P. Margelefsky, LLC*, 518 F.3d 433, 441 (6th Cir.2008) ; *see Grden*, 643 F.3d at 172 (same); *Hartman v. Great Seneca Fin. Corp.*, 569 F.3d 606, 613 (6th Cir.2009) (same). Courts do not lightly reject fact-based claims at the pleading stage. They may do so only after drawing all reasonable inferences from the allegations in the complaint in the plaintiff's favor and only after concluding that, even then, the complaint still fails to allege a plausible theory of relief. *See* Fed.R.Civ.P. 12(b)(6) ; *Ashcroft v. Iqbal*, 556 U.S. 662, 677–79, 129 S.Ct. 1937, 173 L.Ed.2d 868 (2009). That is not to say that all such claims will go to a jury merely because they implicate a question of fact. A claim may be implausible on its face because even an unsophisticated consumer would not be confused, making discovery pointless and jury resolution unnecessary. *See Evory v. RJM Acquisitions Funding L.L.C.*, 505 F.3d 769, 776–77 (7th Cir.2007). Or the claimant may not wish to seek discovery and may agree that a court should resolve the claim as a matter of law. *See Walker v. Nat'l Recovery, Inc.*, 200 F.3d 500, 503 (7th Cir.1999). Or the claim may warrant discovery but be appropriate for summary judgment after that. *Lamar*, 503 F.3d at 508 n. 2. Through it all, the hurdle to proceed from pleading to discovery remains a low one, requiring only that the plaintiff plead a plausible theory of relief. That reality favors Buchanan. Second, Buchanan submits that evidence supports her claim, and in this instance her theory is sufficiently plausible that she deserves an opportunity to show how. She has already identified an expert in the area, Dr. Timothy E. Goldsmith, a professor of psychology, who plans to testify about consumers' attitudes toward, and their understanding of, time-barred debt. This is not the time or the place to assess whether this evidence will be admissible, whether it will satisfy *Daubert* (if need be), and whether it will materially inform the inquiry. For now, it suffices to say that parties who wish to present evidence in support of their claim usually will be given an opportunity to do so, making summary judgment, not a motion to dismiss, the relevant time for ascertaining whether the claim should be resolved as a matter of law. The Goldsmith testimony is not the only relevant piece of evidence that could bear on this dispute. The relevant agencies charged with enforcing the Act are in the midst of studying this precise problem. *See* Br. for Federal Trade Commission and Consumer Financial Protection Bureau as Amici Curiae Supporting Appellant at 2–3. In November 2013, the Consumer Financial Protection Bureau asked for input on potential rulemaking regarding time-barred debt. Debt Collection (Regulation F), 78 Fed.Reg. 67,848, 67,875 –76 (advance notice of proposed rulemaking given Nov. 12, 2013). According to the CFPB, "[c]onsumers, in some circumstances, may infer from a collection attempt the mistaken impression that a debt is enforceable in court even in the absence of an express or implied threat of litigation." *Id.* at 67,875. The CFPB posed several questions for public comment directly relevant to this lawsuit, including these: What kinds of data exist with respect to consumers' beliefs about debt collection? Has there been any consumer testing? Do debtors receiving collection letters think they might get sued? Do they understand the consequences of partial payment? Should the agency require additional disclosures when a debt is time barred? If so, what information, and using what language? Are there studies of sample language? The answers to these questions bear on Buchanan's claims. Beyond collecting public comments, the CFPB plans to conduct its own "consumer testing and other research" on these questions. *Id.* at 67,875 –76. At this preliminary stage of the case, it seems fair to infer that, if the agency deems these same questions worthy of further study, Buchanan deserves a shot too. A contrary conclusion—that consumer confusion is not even plausible here—would amount to our own declaration that the CFPB's efforts on this score are a waste of time. We are not prepared to say that at this stage of the case. Nothing, it is true, compels us to defer to the agencies' view, whether now or after their further study. But their position remains "instructive." *Bridge v. Ocwen Fed. Bank, FSB*, 681 F.3d 355, 361 (6th Cir.2012). The FTC sometimes is "in a better position than are courts to determine when a practice is 'deceptive' within the meaning of the [Federal Trade Commission] Act," and thus its judgment deserves respect. *FTC v. Colgate–Palmolive Co.*, 380 U.S. 374, 385, 85 S.Ct. 1035, 13 L.Ed.2d 904 (1965). That is all the more true when it comes to factual plausibility in a setting that may turn as much on empirical data as on anything else. *See McMahon v. LVNV Funding, LLC*, 744 F.3d 1010, 1021 (7th Cir.2014). Third, Buchanan offers a plausible theory of consumer deception and confusion that "nudge[s] [her] claims across the line from conceivable to plausible." *Bell Atl. Corp. v. Twombly*, 550 U.S. 544, 570, 127 S.Ct. 1955, 167 L.Ed.2d 929 (2007). The question is whether Northland's letter could plausibly mislead a "reasonable unsophisticated consumer" into thinking her debt is enforceable in court. *See Wallace*, 683 F.3d at 327. One part of this inquiry is easy. When a dunning letter creates confusion about a creditor's right to sue, that is illegal. The Act singles out as unlawful the "false representation of ... the character, amount, or legal status of any debt." 15 U.S.C. § 1692e(2)(A). "Whether a debt is legally enforceable is a central fact about the character and legal status of that debt." *McMahon*, 744 F.3d at 1020. A misrepresentation about the limitations period amounts to a "straightforward" violation of § 1692e(2)(A). *Id.* The other part is more difficult. Was this letter misleading? One reason to say yes is that a "settlement offer" with respect to a time-barred debt may falsely imply that payment could be compelled through litigation. Formal and informal dictionaries alike contain a definition of "settle" that refers to concluding a lawsuit. On the formal side, one defines the verb as "to conclude (a lawsuit) by agreement between the parties usu[ally] out of court." Webster's Third New International Dictionary 2079 (2002). Another defines it as "[t]o decide (a case) by arrangement between the contesting parties." OED Online, Oxford University Press (September 2014), http://goo.gl/yd1KF6. A third defines "settlement" as "[t]he resolution of a lawsuit or dispute by settling." The American Heritage Dictionary of the English Language (5th ed.2014), *available at* http://goo.gl/dPSCMH. On the informal side, Wiktionary defines "settlement agreement" as "[a] contractual agreement between parties to actual or potential litigation by which each party agrees to a resolution of the underlying dispute." *See* http://goo.gl/00xE9s.AndDictionary.com defines "settle" as "to terminate (legal proceedings) by mutual consent of the parties." *See* http://goo.gl/vOmoty. Perhaps the best definition, one that accounts for the various ways an everyman individual might read the terms, appears oddly enough in Black's Law Dictionary. It acknowledges that the word is one of "equivocal meaning," "meaning different things in different connections, and the particular sense in which it is used may be explained by the context or surrounding circumstances." Black's Law Dictionary 1372 (6th ed.1990). All of these definitions make it plausible to allege that a "settlement offer" falsely implies that the underlying debt is enforceable in court. The other problem with the letter is that an unsophisticated debtor who cannot afford the settlement offer might nevertheless assume from the letter that some payment is better than no payment. Not true: Some payment is worse than no payment. The general rule in Michigan is that partial payment restarts the statute-of-limitations clock, giving the creditor a new opportunity to sue for the full debt. *See Yeiter*, 607 N.W.2d at 71. As a result, paying anything less than the settlement offer exposes a debtor to substantial new risk. This point is almost assuredly not within the ken of most people, whether sophisticated, whether reasonably unsophisticated, or whether unreasonably unsophisticated. It thus is not hard to imagine how attempts to collect time-barred debt might mislead consumers trying their best to repay. *See McMahon*, 744 F.3d at 1021. Without disclosure, a well-meaning debtor could inadvertently dig herself into an even deeper hole. *See* Debt Collection, 78 Fed.Reg. at 67,876 ("[C]onsumers may believe that when they make a partial payment on a time-barred debt they have only obligated themselves in the amount of the partial payment but in many circumstances that is not true."). Northland claims that this approach puts us at odds with two fellow circuits. No such conflict exists. In turning two claims under the Act aside, *Huertas* and *Freyermuth* held only that an attempt to collect a time-barred debt is not a thinly veiled threat to sue. *See Huertas*, 641 F.3d at 33 ; *Freyermuth*, 248 F.3d at 771. On that point we agree, as shown above. But neither case addressed the possibility that consumers might still be confused about the enforceability of a debt or the pitfalls of partial payment. And neither case, most pertinently, featured a letter offering a "settlement." To the contrary, the one circuit that has reached this issue, the Seventh Circuit, adopted an approach similar to ours. *See McMahon*, 744 F.3d at 1020–22. Northland further objects that our reasoning is inconsistent with this circuit's prior application of the "least sophisticated consumer" standard. But the cited cases (two-thirds of which are unpublished) do not support its argument. All three arose on summary judgment, not on a motion to dismiss, and all three rejected claims based on bizarre interpretations. *See Lamar*, 503 F.3d at 511; *Clark v. Main St. Acquisition Corp.*, 553 Fed.Appx. 510, 516 (6th Cir.2014); *Webb v. Asset Acceptance, LLC*, 486 Fed.Appx. 596, 597 (6th Cir.2012). There is nothing bizarre about our interpretation of Northland's letter. Northland and its amici add that this interpretation will require debt collectors to give legal advice to every debtor about the statute of limitations. But if a debt collector is unsure about the applicable statute of limitations, "it would be easy to include general language about that possibility," *McMahon*, 744 F.3d at 1022, correcting any possible misimpression by unsophisticated consumers without venturing into the realm of legal advice. Proving this is not a herculean task is one of Northland's new letters: "The law limits how long you can be sued on a debt. Because of the age of your debt, LVNV Funding LLC will not sue you for it, and LVNV Funding LLC will not report it to any credit reporting agency." For these reasons, we reverse and remand for further proceedings consistent with this opinion.

KETHLEDGE, Circuit Judge, dissenting. Some lawsuits make sense only to lawyers. Here, it is undisputed that Buchanan's debt remains entirely valid, notwithstanding that the debt is no longer enforceable in court. And it is likewise common ground in this appeal—since the majority agrees, Buchanan agrees (she has not challenged the district court's determination to the contrary) and even the amici agencies agree—that Northland would have been within its lawful rights to send her a letter that simply recited the amount of her long-unpaid debt and demanded payment in full. The ostensible basis for this lawsuit, rather, is that Northland offered Buchanan a discount—that it offered to accept about 35 cents on the dollar of what she owed, rather than demand payment in full. One might expect a conscientious debtor either to accept this offer or, at worst, to ignore it. But Buchanan chose to sue Northland for making it. Buchanan's claim, such as it is, is that in making this offer, Northland's use of a single word— "settlement"—was misleading as a matter of federal law. Specifically, in a letter to Buchanan, Northland stated that her creditor "is willing to reduce your balance by offering you a settlement [,]" and that, upon receipt of the discounted amount ($1,668, rather than $4,768), "your account will be satisfied and closed and a settlement letter will be issued." As a statement of Northland's willingness to accept a reduced amount in satisfaction of Buchanan's debt, that language is straightforward and direct. But her reading is more gossamer: Buchanan says that the word "settlement" is one frequently used in connection with lawsuits, which means that the word "settlement" intimates the prospect of legal action, which means that the settlement offer was actually an implied threat to sue, which would amount to a representation that the debt remained enforceable in court, which would be a "misleading representation" in violation of the Fair Debt Collection Practices Act. This reading of Northland's offer is implausible. The relevant perspective here is that of an unsophisticated debtor—an unsophisticated debtor, moreover, who by definition has received dunning letters for years without a lawsuit ever having been brought against her. In that context, the mere fact of another collection letter is itself no reason to think that a lawsuit might follow close behind. And the letter here says nothing about any lawsuit—which is good reason, so far the threat of a lawsuit is concerned, not to distinguish this letter from the legions of letters that surely preceded it. If anything, Northland's willingness to settle the debt at a discount should make the letter seem less threatening, not more. Buchanan's arguments to the contrary (or more precisely, the arguments of her counsel) reflect a different perspective. Not the perspective of the unsophisticated debtor, but rather our own perspective as lawyers and judges— whose work, by definition, is done through the vehicle of lawsuits. And from that lawsuit-saturated perspective, Buchanan suggests, we should conclude that, of the many different meanings of the word "settle"—many of which have nothing to do with lawsuits—the unsophisticated debtor would read Northland's offer to accept a 65% discount in "settlement" of her account as a threat to sue her instead. But we have no basis to read a single word—"settlement"—from a lawyerly perspective and the rest of Northland's letter from an unsophisticated one. To the contrary, we are bound to apply the unsophisticated-debtor standard all the way through. Buchanan also argues that Northland's use of the word "settlement" is misleading because "[a]n offer to settle implies a colorable obligation to pay." But Buchanan's premise is wrong—she does have a legal obligation to pay her debt, even though that obligation is no longer enforceable in court. *See De Vries v. Alger*, 329 Mich. 68, 44 N.W.2d 872, 876 (1950) ("The running of the statute of limitations does not cancel the debt, it merely prevents a creditor from enforcing his claim"). Indeed the validity of Buchanan's debt—she did, after all, receive goods or services that she did not pay for—is the reason why Northland undisputedly would have been within its rights simply to demand that she pay all the money she owes. There remains, as the majority points out, an equitable point—that if a debtor sends a creditor less than the settlement amount, then under Michigan law (and that of many states) the limitations period runs anew and the debt becomes enforceable again in court. Virtually no one, save the creditors themselves, would welcome that result. But Northland's letter nowhere invites that result; and if it arose, that result would be the fault of state substantive law, which we have no license to change. In any event, that case is not the case before us here. In this case, rather, Buchanan seeks up to $1,000 in statutory damages—for herself, and also for each member of a putative statewide class—for the trouble of reading a letter that offered her a discount on an entirely valid debt that for years she failed to pay. I would reject this claim as a matter of law, rather than continue to make a federal case out of it. I respectfully dissent.

****

5M   Do you agree or disagree with the dissent that the offer to Buchanan was inviting rather than threatening?

5N   Is Buchanan the type of consumer that FDCPA is intended to protect?

5O   Would debt collection regulations be helpful? Why or Why Not?

5P   Do you agree or disagree with the characterization of settlement as a lawsuit, as a construct of a legal mind rather than a plausible conclusion of an unsophisticated consumer?[415]

5Q   Could this action be brought against LVNV by the consumer? Why or Why Not? Could this action be brought against National City Bank by the consumer? Why or Why Not?

5R   Are companies that must advise that a debt is time-barred in certain circuits at a competitive disadvantage in collecting the debt than are other companies that do not have to advise consumers of this fact? Why or Why Not? Return to Figure 2C. Who are the stakeholders in the *Buchanan* case?[416]

---

[415] 776 F.3d at 401 (Kethledge, R. dissenting).
[416] 776 F.3d 393 (6th Cir., 2015).

FRANKLIN V. PARKING REVENUE RECOVERY SERVS., INC.[417]

Before Flaum, Ripple, and Sykes, Circuit Judges. Sykes, Circuit Judge.

Carmen Franklin and Jenifer Chism parked their cars in a Chicago-area lot owned by Metra, the public commuter railroad, and operated by CPS Chicago Parking, LLC. ("CPS"). The lot offers parking spaces to the public at the rate of $1.50 per day. CPS says the two failed to pay and sent them violation notices demanding payment of the $1.50 fee and a $45 nonpayment penalty. When they still did not pay, CPS referred the matter for collection to Parking Revenue Recovery Services, Inc. ("Parking Revenue"), which sent them collection letters for the $46.50 total due. Franklin and Chism responded with this class action against Parking Revenue alleging violations of the Fair Debt Collection Practices Act ("FDCPA"), 15 U.S.C. §§ 1692 *et seq.* The district court entered summary judgment for Parking Revenue, holding that the FDCPA does not apply because the unpaid parking obligations are not "debts" as that term is defined in § 1692a(5). We reverse. The obligations at issue here—unpaid parking fees and nonpayment penalties—are "debts" within the meaning of the FDCPA. That statutory term comprises obligations "arising out of" consumer "transactions." Parking in a lot that is open to all customers subject to stated charges is a "transaction." The obligation that arises from that transaction is a "debt," and an attempt to collect it must comply with the FDCPA.

In June 2012 Franklin and Chism parked their cars in a Chicago-area lot owned by Metra (the Commuter Rail Division of the Regional Transportation Authority) and operated by CPS, a wholly owned subsidiary of Central Parking System, Inc. CPS is a private company that contracts with Metra to manage parking lots adjacent to commuter rail stations throughout the Chicago area. Under its contract with Metra, CPS keeps a percentage of the gross revenues collected from the lots that it operates. The signage and the pay machine at the lot plainly state that it costs $1.50 for daily parking. And CPS tells us that the signage also states that a fee of up to $60 will be assessed to parkers who fail to pay. Franklin and Chism both insist that they paid the $1.50 upon parking, but CPS claims they parked without paying and now owe the $1.50 parking fee and a $45 nonpayment penalty. CPS referred the matter to Parking Revenue, which in turn sent the women collection letters. The letters noted that Franklin and Chism had previously received one or more parking-violation notices and demanded payment of "this debt" within 30 days or alternatively, notification in writing that they dispute the debt's validity. Franklin and Chism responded with this class action against Parking Revenue alleging that the collection letters violated the FDCPA in numerous ways. The suit alleges that parking in the lot was a "transaction"—Central Parking offers parking to all comers, which the plaintiffs accepted by parking in the lot—and the payment obligation therefore was a debt, the collection of which is governed by FDCPA. The district judge disagreed. He characterized the collection letters as attempts to collect fines imposed for violating the parking lot's rules. The judge said that the payment obligation was "materially indistinguishable from a

---

[417] 832 F.3d 741 (7th Cir., 2016).

ticket issued for failure to feed a parking meter." As such, it did not reflect a consensual transaction; Franklin and Chism essentially stole the parking spaces from CPS. On this reasoning, the judge concluded that the obligations were not debts within the meaning of the FDCPA and granted Parking Revenue's motion for summary judgment.

We review the court's order granting summary judgment de novo, evaluating the record in the light most favorable to Franklin and Chism and drawing all reasonable inferences from the evidence in their favor. *Townsend v. Cooper*, 759 F.3d 678, 685 (7th Cir. 2014). The FDCPA prohibits various "abusive debt collection practices," 15 U.S.C. § 1692(e), including the use of false or misleading representations, *id.* § 1692e, and other unfair practices, *id.* § 1692f, to collect any debt. Franklin and Chism contend that Parking Revenue's collection letters violate the FDCPA in several ways. Our present concern, however, is limited to the threshold question whether the FDCPA even applies. That question turns on whether the underlying payment obligations are debts within the meaning of § 1692a(5). If they are, then the FDCPA applies and summary judgment was improper. Section 1692a(5) defines a "debt" as "any obligation or alleged obligation of a consumer to pay money arising out of a transaction in which the money, property, insurance, or services which are the subject of the transaction are primarily for personal, family, or household purposes." Two parts of the definition need further explanation. First, although the statute does not define "transaction," we have held that the term is "a broad reference to many different types of business dealings between parties." *Bass v. Stolper, Koritzinsky, Brewster & Neider, S.C.*, 111 F.3d 1322, 1325 (7th Cir. 1997). Next, the "arising out of" language limits the FDCPA's reach to only those obligations that are created by the contracts the parties used to give legal force to their transaction. *Id.* at 1326. This means that, in general, efforts to collect on obligations that are created by other kinds of legal authorities, like tort law or traffic regulations, are not covered by the FDCPA. The parties rightly agree that if Franklin's and Chism's obligations arise out of contract law, they are debts covered by the FDCPA. And it's clear that contract law is the source of the obligations at issue here. Indeed, at oral argument Parking Revenue's attorney was unable to explain what source of law other than contract could have created the obligations that its letters attempted to collect. By parking in the lot, Franklin and Chism accepted CPS's offer to park at the stated cost. At that moment a contract was formed obligating them to pay the stated price or pay a higher price if they left the parking lot without paying. It matters not that Metra owns the lot, or that the contract between Metra and CPS sometimes refers to the $45 nonpayment charge as a "fine." The crucial question is the legal source of the obligation. Although Metra is a governmental agency, no municipal ordinance or regulation obligates park-and-dashers to pay the $45; that obligation comes from the contract that is formed when a customer parks in the lot. Metra owns these lots like any other parking-lot proprietor and contracts with CPS to operate them. That contract provides that any dispute between "patron[s]" (parkers) and "[o]perator" (CPS) shall be handled "as a matter of contract." So the district judge's analogy to fines assessed for nonpayment at municipal parking meters was inapt. These obligations have no source in municipal law.

The judge's analogy to theft was also inapt. The judge thought a car parker's failure to pay resembled the condition of the thief that we described in *Bass*. There we noted that the FDCPA doesn't cover a thief's obligation to pay for the goods he steals if his obligation is created by tort law (e.g., the tort of conversion), *see* RESTATEMENT (SECOND) OF TORTS § 222A (Am. Law Inst. 1965), rather than by contract law, *see Bass*, 111 F.3d at 1326. The obligations at issue here, however, are not premised on the tort of conversion; they are premised exclusively on the contract that was formed between Franklin and Chism on one side and CPS on the other. This distinction between contract and tort is the reason that the obligation incurred after paying with a bad check gives rise to a "debt" under the FDCPA while shoplifting does not. *See id.* at 1325. When the check is tendered for payment, a contract is formed. *See id.*

To conclude: The signs at the parking lot offered a parking spot to all comers for $1.50 per day and noted a penalty for failing to pay. Franklin and Chism each accepted this offer—and thus formed a contract—when they parked in the lot. Their obligation to pay the $46.50 is premised entirely on this contract. Parking Revenue was therefore attempting to collect debts, and its attempts are regulated by the FDCPA's protections. REVERSED.

****

Is CPS subject to the FDCPA? Why or Why Not?

The court notes that payment of the $45 late penalty is not required by municipal ordinance but rather via contract.[418] **If the late penalty was imposed as a result of municipal ordinance, how does this change the analysis? Would the analysis be based upon the entire amount owed or just the amount imposed via ordinance?**

Would the CFPB have authority to enforce the proposed FDCPA violation with respect to the Defendants in this case? Why or Why not?

Review 1692a prior to reading the next case.

---

[418] *See Franklin*, 832 F.3d at 744.

Justice GORSUCH delivered the opinion of the Court.

Disruptive dinnertime calls, downright deceit, and more besides drew Congress's eye to the debt collection industry. From that scrutiny emerged the Fair Debt Collection Practices Act, a statute that authorizes private lawsuits and weighty fines designed to deter wayward collection practices. So perhaps it comes as little surprise that we now face a question about who exactly qualifies as a "debt collector" subject to the Act's rigors. Everyone agrees that the term embraces the repo man—someone hired by a creditor to collect an outstanding debt. But what if you purchase a debt and then try to collect it for yourself—does that make you a "debt collector" too? That's the nub of the dispute now before us. The parties approach the question from common ground.

The complaint alleges that CitiFinancial Auto loaned money to petitioners seeking to buy cars; that petitioners defaulted on those loans; that respondent Santander then purchased the defaulted loans from CitiFinancial; and that Santander sought to collect in ways petitioners believe troublesome under the Act. The parties agree, too, that in deciding whether Santander's conduct falls within the Act's ambit we should look to statutory language defining the term "debt collector" to embrace anyone who "regularly collects or attempts to collect ... debts owed or due ... another." 15 U.S.C. § 1692a(6). Even when it comes to that question, the parties agree on at least part of an answer. Both sides accept that third party debt collection agents generally qualify as "debt collectors" under the relevant statutory language, while those who seek only to collect for themselves loans they originated generally do not. These results follow, the parties tell us, because debt collection agents seek to collect debts "owed ... another," while loan originators acting on their own account aim only to collect debts owed to themselves. All that remains in dispute is how to classify individuals and entities who regularly purchase debts originated by someone else and then seek to collect those debts for their own account. Does the Act treat the debt purchaser in that scenario more like the repo man or the loan originator?

For their part, the district court and Fourth Circuit sided with Santander. They held that the company didn't qualify as a debt collector because it didn't regularly seek to collect debts "owed ... another" but sought instead only to collect debts that it purchased and owned. At the same time, the Fourth Circuit acknowledged that some circuits faced with the same question have ruled otherwise—and it is to resolve this conflict that we took the case. Compare 817 F.3d 131, 133–134, 137–138 (2016) (case below); *Davidson v. Capital One Bank (USA), N.A.,* 797 F.3d 1309, 1315–1316 (C.A.11 2015), with *McKinney v. Cadleway Properties, Inc.,* 548 F.3d 496, 501 (C.A.7 2008) ; *FTC v. Check Investors, Inc.,* 502 F.3d 159, 173–174 (C.A.3 2007).

Before attending to that job, though, we pause to note two related questions we do not attempt to answer today. First, petitioners suggest that Santander can qualify as a debt collector not only because it regularly seeks to collect for its own account debts that it has purchased, but also because it regularly

---

[419] 137 S. Ct. 1718, 198 L. Ed. 2d 177 (2017).

acts as a third party collection agent for debts owed to others. Petitioners did not, however, raise the latter theory in their petition for certiorari and neither did we agree to review it. Second, the parties briefly allude to another statutory definition of the term "debt collector"—one that encompasses those engaged "in any business the principal purpose of which is the collection of any debts." § 1692a(6). But the parties haven't much litigated that alternative definition and in granting certiorari we didn't agree to address it either.

With these preliminaries by the board, we can turn to the much narrowed question properly before us. In doing so, we begin, as we must, with a careful examination of the statutory text. And there we find it hard to disagree with the Fourth Circuit's interpretive handiwork. After all, the Act defines debt collectors to include those who regularly seek to collect debts "owed ... another." And by its plain terms this language seems to focus our attention on third party collection agents working for a debt owner— not on a debt owner seeking to collect debts for itself. Neither does this language appear to suggest that we should care how a debt owner came to be a debt owner—whether the owner originated the debt or came by it only through a later purchase. All that matters is whether the target of the lawsuit regularly seeks to collect debts for its own account or does so for "another." And given that, it would seem a debt purchaser like Santander may indeed collect debts for its own account without triggering the statutory definition in dispute, just as the Fourth Circuit explained.

Petitioners reply that this seemingly straightforward reading overlooks an important question of tense. They observe that the word "owed" is the past participle of the verb "to owe." And this, they suggest, means the statute's definition of debt collector captures anyone who regularly seeks to collect debts previously "owed ... another." So it is that, on petitioners' account, the statute excludes from its compass loan originators (for they never seek to collect debts previously owed someone else) but embraces many debt purchasers like Santander (for in collecting purchased debts they necessarily seek to collect debts previously owed another). If Congress wanted to exempt all present debt owners from its debt collector definition, petitioners submit, it would have used the present participle "owing." That would have better sufficed to do the job—to make clear that you must collect debts currently "owing ... another" before implicating the Act. But this much doesn't follow even as a matter of good grammar, let alone ordinary meaning. Past participles like "owed" are routinely used as adjectives to describe the present state of a thing—so, for example, burnt toast is inedible, a fallen branch blocks the path, and (equally) a debt owed to a current owner may be collected by him or her. *See* P. Peters, THE CAMBRIDGE GUIDE TO ENGLISH USAGE 409 (2004) (explaining that the term "past participle" is a "misnomer[ ], since" it "can occur in what is technically a present ... tense"). Just imagine if you told a friend that you were seeking to "collect a debt owed to Steve." Doesn't it seem likely your friend would understand you as speaking about a debt currently owed to Steve, not a debt Steve used to own and that's now actually yours? In the end, even petitioners find themselves forced to admit that past participles can and regularly do work just this way, as adjectives to describe the present state of the nouns they modify. *See* Brief for Petitioners 28; *see also* B. Garner, MODERN ENGLISH USAGE 666 (4th ed. 2016) (while "owing ... is an old and established usage ... the more logical course is simply to write owed "). Widening our view to take in the statutory phrase in which the word "owed" appears—"owed or due ... another"—serves to underscore the point. Petitioners acknowledge that the word "due" describes a debt currently due at the time of collection and not a debt that was due only in some previous period. So to rule for them we would have to suppose Congress set two words cheek by jowl in the same phrase but meant them to speak to entirely different periods of time. All without leaving any clue. We would have to read the phrase not as referring to "debts that are owed or due another" but as describing "debts that were owed or are due another." And supposing such a surreptitious subphrasal shift in time seems to us a bit much. Neither are we alone in that assessment, for even petitioners acknowledge that theirs "may not be the most natural interpretation of the phrase standing in isolation." *Id.*, at 26–27. Given that, you might wonder whether extending our gaze from the narrow statutory provision at issue to take in the larger statutory landscape might offer petitioners a better perspective. But it does not.

Looking to other neighboring provisions in the Act, it quickly comes clear that Congress routinely used the word "owed" to refer to present (not past) debt relationships. For example, in one nearby subsection, Congress defined a creditor as someone "to whom a debt is owed." 15 U.S.C. § 1692a(4). In another subsection, too, Congress required a debt collector to identify "the creditor to whom the debt is owed." § 1692g(a)(2). Yet petitioners offer us no persuasive reason why the word "owed" should bear a different meaning here, in the subsection before us, or why we should abandon our usual presumption that "identical words used in different parts of the same statute" carry "the same meaning." *IBP, Inc. v. Alvarez*, 546 U.S. 21, 34, 126 S.Ct. 514, 163 L.Ed.2d 288 (2005). Still other contextual clues add to petitioners' problems. While they suggest that the statutory definition before us implicitly distinguishes between loan originators and debt purchasers, a pass through the statute shows that when Congress wished to distinguish between originators and purchasers it left little doubt in the matter. In the very definitional section where we now find ourselves working, Congress expressly differentiated between a person "who offers" credit (the originator) and a person "to whom a debt is owed" (the present debt owner). § 1692a(4). Elsewhere, Congress recognized the distinction between a debt "originated by" the collector and a debt "owed or due" another. § 1692a(6)(F)(ii). And elsewhere still, Congress drew a line between the "original" and "current" creditor. § 1692g(a)(5). Yet no similar distinction can be found in the language now before us.

To the contrary, the statutory text at issue speaks not at all about originators and current debt owners but only about whether the defendant seeks to collect on behalf of itself or "another." And, usually at least, when we're engaged in the business of interpreting statutes we presume differences in language like this convey differences in meaning. *See, e.g., Loughrin v. United States*, 573 U.S. ——, ——, 134 S.Ct. 2384 2391, 189 L.Ed.2d 411 (2014). Even what may be petitioners' best piece of contextual evidence ultimately proves unhelpful to their cause. Petitioners point out that the Act exempts from the definition of "debt collector" certain individuals who have "obtained" particular kinds of debt—for example, debts not yet in default or debts connected to secured commercial credit transactions. §§ 1692a(6)(F)(iii) and (F)(iv). And because these exemptions contemplate the possibility that someone might "obtain" a debt "owed or due ... another," petitioners submit, the word "owed" must refer only to a previous owner. *Ibid.* This conclusion, they say, necessarily follows because, once you have "obtained" a debt, that same debt just cannot be currently "owed or due" another. This last and quite essential premise of the argument, however, misses its mark.

As a matter of ordinary English, the word "obtained" can (and often does) refer to taking possession of a piece of property without also taking ownership—so, for example, you might obtain a rental car or a hotel room or an apartment. *See, e.g.,* 10 OXFORD ENGLISH DICTIONARY 669 (2d ed. 1989) (defining "obtain" to mean, among other things, "[t]o come into the possession or enjoyment of (something) by one's own effort or by request"); *Kirtsaeng v. John Wiley & Sons, Inc.,* 568 U.S. 519, 532–533, 133 S.Ct. 1351, 185 L.Ed.2d 392 (2013) (distinguishing between ownership and obtaining possession). And it's easy enough to see how you might also come to possess (obtain) a debt without taking ownership of it. You might, for example, take possession of a debt for servicing and collection even while the debt formally remains owed another. Or as a secured party you might take possession of a debt as collateral, again without taking full ownership of it. *See, e.g.,* U.C.C. § 9–207, 3 U.L.A. 197 (2010). So it simply isn't the case that the statute's exclusions imply that the phrase "owed ... another" must refer to debts previously owed to another. By this point petitioners find themselves in retreat. Unable to show that debt purchasers regularly collecting for their own account always qualify as debt collectors, they now suggest that purchasers sometimes qualify as debt collectors. On their view, debt purchasers surely qualify as collectors at least when they regularly purchase and seek to collect defaulted debts—just as Santander allegedly did here. In support of this narrower and more particular understanding of the Act, petitioners point again to the fact that the statute excludes from the definition of "debt collector" certain persons who obtain debts before default. 15 U.S.C. § 1692a(6)(F)(iii). This exclusion, petitioners now suggest, implies that the term "debt collector" must embrace those who regularly seek to collect debts obtained after default. Others aligned with petitioners also suggest that the Act treats everyone who attempts to collect a debt as either a "debt collector" or a "creditor," but not both. And because the statutory definition of the term "creditor" excludes those who seek to collect a debt obtained "in default," § 1692a(4), they contend it again follows as a matter of necessary inference that these persons must qualify as debt collectors. But these alternative lines of inferential argument bear their own problems. For while the statute surely excludes from the debt collector definition certain persons who acquire a debt before default, it doesn't necessarily follow that the definition must include anyone who regularly collects debts acquired after default. After all and again, under the definition at issue before us you have to attempt to collect debts owed another before you can ever qualify as a debt collector. And petitioners' argument simply does not fully confront this plain and implacable textual prerequisite. Likewise, even spotting (without granting) the premise that a person cannot be both a creditor and a debt collector with respect to a particular debt, we don't see why a defaulted debt purchaser like Santander couldn't qualify as a creditor. For while the creditor definition excludes persons who "receive an assignment or transfer of a debt in default," it does so only (and yet again) when the debt is assigned or transferred "solely for the purpose of facilitating collection of such debt for another." *Ibid.* (emphasis added). So a company collecting purchased defaulted debt for its own account—like Santander—would hardly seem to be barred from qualifying as a creditor under the statute's plain terms.

Faced with so many obstacles in the text and structure of the Act, petitioners ask us to move quickly on to policy. Indeed, from the beginning that is the field on which they seem most eager to pitch battle. Petitioners assert that Congress passed the Act in large measure to add new incentives for independent debt collectors to treat consumers well. In their view, Congress excluded loan originators from the Act's demands because it thought they already faced sufficient economic and legal incentives to good behavior. But, on petitioners' account, Congress never had the chance to consider what should be done about those in the business of purchasing defaulted debt. That's because, petitioners tell us, the "advent" of the market for defaulted debt represents " 'one of the most significant changes' " to the debt market generally since the Act's passage in 1977. Had Congress known this new industry would blossom, they say, it surely would have judged defaulted debt purchasers more like (and in need of the same special rules as) independent debt collectors. Indeed, petitioners contend that no other result would be consistent with the overarching congressional goal of deterring untoward debt collection practices. All this seems to us quite a lot of speculation. And while it is of course our job to apply faithfully the law Congress has written, it is never our job to rewrite a constitutionally valid statutory text under the banner of speculation about what Congress might have done had it faced a question that, on everyone's account, it never faced. *See Magwood v. Patterson*, 561 U.S. 320, 334, 130 S.Ct. 2788, 177 L.Ed.2d 592 (2010) ("We cannot replace the actual text with speculation as to Congress' intent"). Indeed, it is quite mistaken to assume, as petitioners would have us, that "whatever" might appear to "further[ ] the statute's primary objective must be the law." *Rodriguez v. United States*, 480 U.S. 522, 526, 107 S.Ct. 1391, 94 L.Ed.2d 533 (1987) (*per curiam*). Legislation is, after all, the art of compromise, the limitations expressed in statutory terms often the price of passage, and no statute yet known "pursues its [stated] purpose [ ] at all costs." *Id.*, at 525–526, 107 S.Ct. 1391. For these reasons and more besides we will not presume with petitioners that any result consistent with their account of the statute's overarching goal must be the law but will presume more modestly instead "that [the] legislature says ... what it means and means ... what it says." *Dodd v. United States*, 545 U.S. 353, 357, 125 S.Ct. 2478, 162 L.Ed.2d 343 (2005).

Even taken on its own terms, too, the speculation petitioners urge upon us is far from unassailable. After all, is it really impossible to imagine that reasonable legislators might contend both ways on the question whether defaulted debt purchasers should be treated more like loan originators than independent debt collection agencies? About whether other existing incentives (in the form of common law duties, other statutory and regulatory obligations, economic incentives, or otherwise) suffice to deter debt purchasers from engaging in certain undesirable collection activities? Couldn't a reasonable legislator endorsing the Act as written wonder whether a large financial institution like Santander is any more or less likely to engage in abusive conduct than another large financial institution like CitiFinancial Auto? Especially where (as here) the institution says that its primary business is loan origination and not the purchase of defaulted debt? We do not profess sure answers to any of these questions, but observe only that the parties and their amici manage to present many and colorable arguments both ways on them all, a fact that suggests to us for certain but one thing: that these are matters for Congress, not this Court, to resolve. In the end, reasonable people can disagree with how Congress balanced the various social costs and benefits in this area. We have no difficulty imagining, for example, a statute that applies the Act's demands to anyone collecting any debts, anyone collecting debts originated by another, or to some other class of persons still. Neither do we doubt that the evolution of the debt collection business might invite reasonable disagreements on whether Congress should reenter the field and alter the judgments it made in the past. After all, it's hardly unknown for new business models to emerge in response to regulation, and for regulation in turn to address new business models. Constant competition between constable and quarry, regulator and regulated, can come as no surprise in our changing world. But neither should the proper role of the judiciary in that process—to apply, not amend, the work of the People's representatives. The judgment of the Court of Appeals is Affirmed.

****

This case is the first opinion authored by Supreme Court Justice Neil Gorsuch. **How might this decision impact the ability of consumers to bring FDCPA actions if the scope of who qualifies as a "debt collector" is narrowed?** Prior to *Santander*, a so-called "debt buyer," was considered a debt collector and subject to FDCPA. In other words, an entity that did not originate the debt, was collecting for itself, but was collecting on a debt that was in default when the debt was acquired, was subject to FDCPA compliance. **Does Santander "step into the shoes" of CitiFinancial Auto? If debt buyers did not exist in 1977 and Congress did not contemplate the FDCPA applicability with respect to debt buyers, may the CFPB implement a regulation regarding debt collection?** Compare the Court's determination that an entity collecting for itself on a debt in default is not subject to FDCPA compliance with the court's reasoning in the next case.

The Supreme Court briefly references the alternative argument of whether Santander could qualify as a debt collector if Santander's principal purpose is the collection of debt.[420] A debt collector also includes "any person who uses any instrumentality of interstate commerce or the mails in any business the principal purpose of which is the collection of any debts."[421]

5V   **Would the CFPB have authority to enforce the proposed FDCPA violation with respect to the Defendants in this case, if the Defendants were deemed debt collectors? Why or Why not?**

5W   **Can the CFPB issue a rule, guidance or order revising the law to make clear that debt collectors include debt buyers collecting on debts in default?**

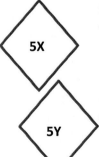

5X   **Has Santander discovered a loophole or is Santander merely invoking an exemption for creditors?**

5Y   **Review Figure 5A. What role does Santander play? What role does CitiFinancial Auto play?**

---

[420] *Henson*, 137 S. Ct. at 1721.
[421] 15 U.S. C. § 1692a(6).

MCKINNEY V. CADLEWAY PROPERTIES, INC.[422]

SYKES, Circuit Judge.

This case requires us to determine whether the defendant, Cadleway Properties, Inc., is a "debt collector" under the Fair Debt Collection Practices Act, 15 U.S.C. §§ 1692 et seq. ("FDCPA"). If it is, then the FDCPA applies [. . .]

Reverend Versia McKinney's Chicago home was damaged by a flood in 1996. To help with repair costs, she obtained a disaster assistance loan from the Small Business Administration ("SBA"). After McKinney ceased making payments in 2002, the SBA sold the debt to a third party, and Cadleway subsequently acquired it. In an attempt to collect on the debt, Cadleway sent McKinney a collection letter that included a notice of her right to dispute and obtain verification of the debt and of the original creditor as required by the FDCPA. McKinney responded with this lawsuit alleging the notice was confusing.

The district court entered summary judgment for McKinney, concluding that Cadleway is a debt collector and its collection letter was confusing to the unsophisticated consumer and therefore violated the FDCPA. We agree with the former conclusion but not the latter. The FDCPA covers debt collectors, not creditors, and these categories are "mutually exclusive." *Schlosser v. Fairbanks Capital Corp.*, 323 F.3d 534, 536 (7th Cir.2003); *see also* 15 U.S.C. § 1692a(4), (6) & (6)(F). The undisputed evidence here establishes that Cadleway is a debt collector, not a creditor.

. . .

Reverend Versia McKinney's Chicago home was damaged in 1996 when a sewer backed up into her basement due to flooding. Unable to afford the repairs, McKinney applied for and received a disaster loan for $5,200 from the [Small Business Administration]. The loan agreement authorized the SBA to demand immediate payment of the entire balance should McKinney fail to make a scheduled payment. Indeed, at some point after disbursement of the loan, McKinney was unable to keep up with the payments and ceased making them altogether, although the SBA never demanded that she pay the outstanding balance.

Instead, in 2002 the SBA sold McKinney's loan to Lehman Capital/Aurora Loan Servicing Inc., which eventually sold it to Cadleway. Cadleway's first contact with McKinney was in September 2004 when it issued a collection letter informing her that it had purchased the debt and that she should begin making payments to the new address provided.

. . .

---

[422] 548 F.3d 496 (7th Cir., 2008).

McKinney sent the letter to Michelle Weinberg, an attorney with the Legal Assistance Foundation of Metropolitan Chicago. Weinberg replied to Cadleway, asking it to "cease all further communications regarding this account" because Cadleway was not a licensed debt collector and McKinney "is simply unable to pay this debt." McKinney then filed this action in the district court under 15 U.S.C. § 1692k, which makes debt collectors who violate the FDCPA civilly liable for actual and statutory damages as well as attorney's fees and court costs. McKinney alleged that Cadleway's collection letter violated the FDCPA because an unsophisticated consumer would be confused about her right to dispute the debt and obtain verification of its validity. McKinney asked only for statutory damages and attorney's fees; she did not claim actual damages.

. . .

Cadleway's Status as a "Debt Collector"

The FDCPA applies only to "debt collectors" seeking satisfaction of "debts" from "consumers"; it does not apply to "creditors." *Schlosser*, 323 F.3d at 536. The Act defines "creditor" as follows: The term "creditor" means any person who offers or extends credit creating a debt or to whom a debt is owed, but such term does not include any person to the extent that he receives an assignment or transfer of a debt in default solely for the purpose of facilitating collection of such debt for another.

§ 1692a(4) (emphasis added). The Act defines "debt collector" as follows:

The term "debt collector" means any person who uses any instrumentality of interstate commerce or the mails in any business the principal purpose of which is the collection of any debts, or who regularly collects or attempts to collect, directly or indirectly, debts owed or due or asserted to be owed or due another.

§ 1692a(6) (emphasis added).

The statutory definition of "debt collector" thus has two subcategories. It includes any person who: (1) uses an instrumentality of interstate commerce or the mails in "any business the principal purpose of which is the collection of any debts"; or (2) "regularly collects or attempts to collect . . . debts owed or due or asserted to be owed or due another." This second subcategory of debt collectors refers back to a group specifically excluded from the Act's definition of creditors— those who receive "an assignment or transfer of a debt in default" for the purpose of "facilitating [the] collection of such debt for another."

The definition of debt collector also contains certain enumerated exclusions, one of which is relevant here:

The term [debt collector] does not include ...

(F) any person collecting or attempting to collect any debt owed or due or asserted to be owed or due another to the extent such activity ... (iii) concerns a debt which was not in default at the time it was obtained by such person ....

§ 1692a(6)(F)(iii)

We have held that "[f]or purposes of applying the Act to a particular debt, these two categories—debt collectors and creditors—are mutually exclusive." *Schlosser*, 323 F.3d at 536. We have also observed, however, that "for debts that do not originate with the one attempting collection, but are acquired from another, the collection activity related to that debt could logically fall into either category." *Id. Schlosser* noted that in such a case— one involving a debt originated by another and subsequently acquired by the entity attempting collection—"the Act uses the status of the debt at the time of the assignment" to distinguish between a debt collector and a creditor. *Id.*

The Act draws this distinction in a rather indirect way, however—by the exclusionary language, quoted above, in the statutory definitions of creditor and debt collector. That is, the definition of creditor excludes those who acquire and attempt to collect a "debt in default," § 1692a(4), while the definition of debt collector excludes those who acquire and attempt to collect "a debt which was not in default at the time it was obtained," § 1692a(6)(F). So one who acquires a "debt in default" is categorically not a creditor; one who acquires a "debt not in default" is categorically not a debt collector.

Thus, we held in *Schlosser* that the Act "treats assignees as debt collectors if the debt sought to be collected was in default when acquired by the assignee, and as creditors if it was not." 323 F.3d at 536; *see also Bailey v. Sec. Nat'l Servicing Corp.*, 154 F.3d 384, 387 (7th Cir.1998) ("The plain language of § 1692a(6)(F) tells us that an individual is not a `debt collector' subject to the Act if the debt he seeks to collect was not in default at the time he purchased (or otherwise obtained) it."). We explained that "[f]ocusing on the status of the obligation asserted by the assignee is reasonable in light of the conduct regulated by the statute," which generally covers debt collection, not debt servicing:

For those who acquire debts originated by others, the distinction drawn by the statute—whether the loan was in default at the time of the assignment— makes sense as an indication of whether the activity directed at the consumer will be servicing or collection. If the loan is current when it is acquired, the relationship between the assignee and the debtor is, for purposes of regulating communications and collection practices, effectively the same as that between the originator and the debtor. If the loan is in default, no ongoing relationship is likely and the only activity will be collection. *Schlosser*, 323 F.3d at 538. Accordingly, the purchaser of a debt in default is a debt collector for purposes of the FDCPA even though it owns the debt and is collecting for itself. *Id.* at 538-39; see also *FTC v. Check Investors, Inc.*, 502 F.3d 159, 171-74 (3d Cir.2007) (holding that an entity engaged in collection activity on a defaulted debt acquired from another is a "debt collector" under the FDCPA even though it "may actually be owed the debt").

Cadleway argues that the evidence on the cross-motions for summary judgment is insufficient to establish its status as a debt collector. We disagree. FDCPA does not define "default," but it is undisputed that McKinney's debt had been delinquent for at least two years when Cadleway purchased it, and we think this suffices to establish that it was a "debt in default" when it was acquired. Accordingly, under *Schlosser's* interpretation of the "mutually exclusive" statutory definitions of "creditor" and "debt collector," Cadleway is a debt collector.

Cadleway maintains there is insufficient evidence in the record to establish that the "principal purpose" of its business was the collection of debts or that it "regularly collects" debts owed to "another." § 1692a(6). As we have discussed, however, under *Schlosser*, an agency in the business of acquiring and collecting on defaulted debts originated by another is a debt collector under the FDCPA even though it actually may be collecting for itself. In its answers to McKinney's interrogatories, Cadleway admitted to issuing nearly 3,500 letters identical to the one it sent to McKinney during the year-and-a-half period surrounding the collection activity in this case. It is reasonable to infer that at least some—perhaps most—of this voluminous collection activity related to debts, like McKinney's, that were in default when acquired by Cadleway. There is no evidence in the record to support an inference more favorable to Cadleway. Cadleway's interrogatory answer is therefore sufficient to establish that it "regularly collects" defaulted debts. We agree with the district court that Cadleway is a debt collector under the FDCPA.

. . .

****

5Z   **Is McKinney's loan from the Small Business Administration a debt subject to FDCPA protections? Why or Why Not?**

5AA   **How did the Seventh Circuit Court of Appeals' interpretation of the FDCPA definitions differ from the Supreme Court's decision in *Santander*[423]?**

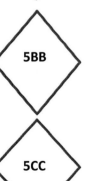

5BB   **Would the CFPB have authority to enforce the proposed FDCPA violation with respect to the Defendants in this case? Why or Why not?**

5CC   **Review Figure 5A. What role does Cadleway play? What role does the Small Business Administration play? What role does Aurora Loan Servicing play?**

Note that *McKinney*, a 2008 case,[424] occurred prior to the Supreme Court's 2017 clarifying decision in *Santander*.[425] Compare the next case, which also preceded *Santander*.

---

[423] 137 S. Ct. 1718, 198 L. Ed. 2d 177 (2017).
[424] 548 F.3d 496 (7th Cir., 2008).
[425] 137 S. Ct. 1718, 198 L. Ed. 2d 177 (2017).

F.T.C. V. CHECK INVESTORS, INC.[426]

McKEE, Circuit Judge.

Check Investors, Inc., Check Enforcement, Inc., Jaredco, Inc., Barry Sussman (hereinafter collectively "Check Investors") and Charles T. Hutchins appeal the district court's grant of injunctive relief and $10.2 million in fines in this action that the Federal Trade Commission initiated against them. The FTC claimed that their debt collection practices violated the Federal Trade Commission Act ("FTC Act"), 15 U.S.C. §§ 41 *et seq.*, and various provisions of the Fair Debt Collection Practices Act ("FDCPA"), 15 U.S.C. §§ 1692 *et seq.* For the reasons that follow, we will affirm.

Check Investors is in the business of purchasing large numbers of checks written on accounts with insufficient funds ("NSF checks"). The payors of those checks typically wrote them in connection with retail transactions and purchases. Check Investors purchased over 2.2 million NSF checks having an estimated face value of approximately $348 million. The checks were purchased from companies such as Telecheck, Inc., Certegy, Inc., and Cross Check, Inc. (collectively "Telecheck").

Telecheck is in the business of guaranteeing checks tendered to pay for consumer transactions. When checks are dishonored, Telecheck pays the merchant/payee the full face value of the check, thereby making the merchant whole. The merchant therefore has no need to attempt to collect the check from the payor/customer. In return for the payment, the merchant assigns all of its rights and benefits to Telecheck, and Telecheck then attempts to collect on the defaulted check to reimburse itself for its payment.

Telecheck first attempts to collect by making three electronic re-presentments of an NSF check to the financial institution the instrument was drawn on. If unsuccessful, Telecheck then sends the payor notices and attempts to contact him/her by telephone. This process may continue for approximately sixty to ninety days. If these efforts fail, Telecheck hires a debt collector, who makes further attempts to collect on the check from the payor. If the debt collector is not able to collect after six months to a year, Telecheck contracts with a second debt collector. Both the first and second debt collectors work on a contingency basis, and, if successful, will receive one-third of the payment received. If the second debt collector is also unsuccessful, Telecheck sells the rights it acquired from the original merchant to Check Investors, and Check Investors initiates additional collection efforts.

Initially, Check Investors collected NSF checks on behalf of large retail clients. However, by 2002 it was purchasing NSF checks from check guarantee companies such as Telecheck for pennies on the dollar and collecting on its own behalf as part of the process we have just described.   According to the Federal Trade Commission, Check Investors was the brainchild of Barry Sussman. After graduating from law

---

[426] 502 F.3d 159 (3rd Cir., 2007).

school (and after serving time in prison for attempting to collect debts by posing as an FBI agent), Sussman theorized that if a debt collection business collected only debts it actually owned based on purchasing NSF checks, it would not be subject to the FDCPA, and would therefore be free to use collection techniques prohibited by the FDCPA such as harassment and deception.

In collecting checks, Check Investors routinely added a fee of $125 or $130 to the face amount of each check; an amount that exceeded the legal limit for such fees under the laws of most states. Check Investors would then aggressively dun the defaulting payors without disclosing either the original face amount of the check, or that the amount it was demanding in "satisfaction" of the check included a fee that was higher than permitted under the laws of the applicable state.

Check Investors used both dunning letters and phone calls to collect debts. However, its primary modus operandi was to accuse consumers of being criminals or crooks, and threatening them with arrest and criminal or civil prosecution. The collectors it employed were provided with a script that directed them to begin calls by advising consumers that a "criminal complaint recommendation" was pending, and that the consumer would be arrested and prosecuted if he/she did not pay the amount demanded in full. Collectors were allowed to personalize the approach they used, but the approach always focused on threats of prosecution. By way of example, one of Check Investor's collectors left the following message on a consumer's answering machine:

This message is for the criminal check writer, Stephanie _____. If you think that you could rip these merchants off with your hot checks and hide behind your telephone, I guess you'll just have to explain to the judge why you stole from this merchant, from [name of merchant], with your fraudulent check. At this moment, we do not have any intentions of working this matter out with you voluntarily. You may need to turn yourself in to the local county sheriff's office.   Another consumer was told that if she did not pay, her children would "watch their mother being taken away in handcuffs," and they would "be bringing their mommy care packages in prison."

Check Investors also threatened consumers by sending a form collection letter that purported to be from defendant Hutchins, who is an attorney. The letter informed the recipient that Hutchins had been retained by a client who was considering taking criminal or civil action. Hutchins did not actually send the letters or sign them, he had no idea about the number of letters that were sent out purporting to be from him, and he made no inquiry about the status of any of the debts underlying the letters that were sent.

Check Investors' threats of prosecution were made without regard to the amount of the underlying obligation. Employees of Check Investors told one consumer who allegedly wrote an NSF check for $14.70 that she would be "sitting in jail" unless she immediately paid $144.70 (the amount of the original check plus Check Investors' additional fee of $130). Faced with the threat, the consumer paid the full amount demanded.

Check Investors' threats of prosecution were all false. It never notified law enforcement authorities, nor did it take any steps to initiate civil suit against any consumer. Indeed, perhaps because of the small face amount of many of the debts it was collecting, Hutchins conceded that it would have been a "ridiculous proposition" to file suit.

Check Investors' tactics apparently knew no limits. It routinely contacted family members of obligors. In one case, Check Investors' repeatedly called a 64-year old mother regarding her son's debt; fearing that her son would be arrested and carted off to jail, she paid the amount of the demand. Another technique that Check Investors employed can best be described as "saturation phoning." One consumer stated that Check Investors' collectors called him 17 times in 10 minutes. Collectors also used abusive language, referring to consumers as "deadbeats," "retards," "thieves," and "idiots." The tactics often yielded results. Between January 1, 2000, and January 6, 2003, Check Investor's collection efforts netted $10.2 million from more than 42,000 consumers.

DISTRICT COURT PROCEEDINGS

On May 12, 2003, the Federal Trade Commission filed a seven-count complaint in the United States District Court for the District of New Jersey against Check Investors and Hutchins alleging that they had violated Section 5(a) of the FTC Act, 15 U.S.C. § 45(a), and various provisions the FDCPA, in their attempts to collect from consumers who had written NSF checks. More specifically, the FTC alleged that Check Investors was a "debt collector," collecting "debts", within the meaning of the FDCPA. The complaint further alleged that, in the course of collecting debts, Check Investors had violated, inter alia, 15 U.S.C. § 1692d (by using abusive language, and calling consumers repeatedly); § 1692e (by falsely representing that communications came from an attorney, by falsely representing that the consumer would be arrested or imprisoned or had committed a crime, and by falsely threatening legal action); and § 1692f (by adding impermissible charges to the face amounts of the debts it was collecting). The complaint also alleged that many of the acts that violated the FDCPA also violated the FTC Act. The FTC sought to enjoin Check Investors' conduct and obtain restitution for injured consumers, including a refund of the money Check Investors had collected using these techniques.

The district court issued a temporary restraining order enjoining Check Investors from engaging in the conduct alleged in the FTC's complaint, and the court also froze most of Check Investors' assets. On August 14, 2003, the district court entered a preliminary injunction against Check Investors, which continued the injunctive provisions and the asset freeze of the TRO.

Both parties thereafter filed cross-motions for summary judgment. The district court granted the FTC's motion and denied Check Investors' motion. Check Investors did not dispute that it engaged in any of the conduct alleged in the FTC's complaint, and there was therefore no genuine issue of material fact about its collection tactics. Rather, Check Investors opposed the FTC's motion for summary judgment (and supported its own motion for summary judgment) by arguing that the FDCPA did not apply because it was collecting NSF checks that it had purchased outright from the original payees. According to Check Investors, it was therefore acting as a creditor collecting its own obligations rather than as debt collector collecting obligations owed to a third party.

Check Investors also argued that the payors on the NSF checks it had purchased had violated state laws pertaining to presenting "bad checks" and by committing fraud. Accordingly, in Check Investors view, the payors should be considered criminals or tortfeasors, not consumers, and they were therefore not entitled to the consumer protection of the FDCPA.

The district court rejected these arguments, in part because Check Investors presented no evidence to show that all the payors in question had the intent required for criminal or civil liability when they wrote the checks. The court also held that persons who write NSF checks are entitled to the FDCPA's protections in any event. The district court thus held that Check Investors was a "debt collector" collecting "debts" within the meaning of the FDCPA, and that it was therefore subject to the prohibitions that Act places on debt collectors' efforts to collect debts. Finally, the court held that Check Investors made material misrepresentations in the course of its collections, and that these misrepresentations also violated the FTC Act.

The district court permanently enjoined Check Investors from engaging in any debt collection activities or selling any of the debts that consumers purportedly owed to it. The court concluded that all defendants were jointly and severally liable to the FTC for restitution in the amount of $10,204,445.00. Thereafter, Hutchins and Check Investors appealed the court's ruling.

THE FAIR DEBT COLLECTION PRACTICES ACT

The FDCPA was enacted in 1977 as an amendment to the Consumer Credit Protection Act `to protect consumers from a host of unfair, harassing, and deceptive collection practices without imposing unnecessary restrictions on ethical debt collectors.'" *Staub v. Harris*, 626 F.2d 275, 276-77 (3d Cir.1980) (quoting Consumer Credit Protection Act, S.Rep. No. 95-382, at 1-2 (1977), reprinted in 1977 U.S.C.C.A.N. 1695, 1696). "The primary goal of the FDCPA is to protect consumers from abusive, deceptive, and unfair debt collection practices, including threats of violence, use of obscene language, certain contacts with acquaintances of the consumer, late night phone calls, and simulated legal process." *Bass v. Stolper, Koritzinsky, Brewster & Neider, S.C.*, 111 F.3d 1322, 1324 (7th Cir.1997). "A basic tenet of the Act is that all consumers, even those who have mismanaged their financial affairs resulting in default on their debt, deserve the right to be treated in a reasonable and civil manner." *Id*.

Although Check Investors uses broad strokes to paint all of the payors of its NSF checks as deadbeats, criminals and/or tortfeasors, Congress's findings in enacting the FDCPA are to the contrary. The relevant Senate report noted, *inter alia*, that [o]ne of the most frequent fallacies concerning debt collection legislation is the contention that the primary beneficiaries are "deadbeats." In fact, however, there is universal agreement among scholars, law enforcement officials, and even debt collectors that the number of persons who willfully refuse to pay debts is minuscule. S.Rep. No. 93-382, at 2 (1977), reprinted in 1977 U.S.C.C.A.N. at 1696. Rather, Congress recognized that "the vast majority of consumers who obtain credit fully intend to repay their debts. When default occurs, it is nearly always due to an unforeseen event such as unemployment, overextension, serious illness or marital difficulties or divorce." *Id*. Congress also recognized that "[a]busive debt collection practices contribute to the number of personal bankruptcies, to marital instability, to the loss of jobs, and to invasions of individual privacy." 15 U.S.C. § 1692a. Thus, Congress concluded that "[t]he issue is not one of uncollected debts, but rather whether or not consumers must lose their civil rights and be terrorized and abused by unethical debt collectors." H.R.Rep. No. 95-131, at 3 (1977).

"In the most general terms, the FDCPA prohibits a debt collector from using certain enumerated collection methods . . . to collect a `debt' from a consumer." *Bass*, 111 F.3d at 1324. The FDCPA prohibits debt collectors from, *inter alia*, engaging in any conduct "the natural consequence of which is to harass, oppress, or abuse any person," 15 U.S.C. § 1692d; from using "any false, deceptive, or misleading representations or means in connection with the collection of any debt," 15 U.S.C. § 1692e; or from using "unfair or unconscionable means to collect or attempt to collect any debt," 15 U.S.C. § 1692f.

Within each broad category of prohibited conduct, the FDCPA includes examples of specific practices that are prohibited. Those prohibited practices could have been modeled on the various tactics Check Investors employed to collect the NSF checks it purchased. For example, the prohibition on harassing, oppressive or abusive practices precludes a debt collector from using abusive language, 15 U.S.C. § 1692d(2), or from repeatedly calling a consumer, 15 U.S.C. § 1692d(3). The prohibition on false, deceptive or misleading representations precludes a debt collector from falsely representing that a dunning letter was sent by an attorney, 15 U.S.C. § 1692e(3), from falsely representing that nonpayment will result in arrest or imprisonment, 15 U.S.C. § 1692e(4), or that a consumer committed a crime, 15 U.S.C. § 1692e(7). The prohibition on unfair or unconscionable practices precludes a debt collector from adding any charge to the underlying debt unless that charge is authorized by law or the agreement creating the debt. 15 U.S.C. § 1692f(1).

The FDCPA allows consumers to sue an offending creditor for actual damages, attorney's fees and costs, as well as statutory damages up to $1,000. 15 U.S.C. § 1692k(a). The FDCPA also provides the FTC with enforcement authority. 15 U.S.C. § 1692l(a).

Are the NSF Checks "Debts" Under the FDCPA?

"A threshold requirement for application of the FDCPA is that the prohibited practices are used in an attempt to collect a `debt.'" *Zimmerman v. HBO Affiliate Group*, 834 F.2d 1163, 1167 (3d Cir.1987). Congress incorporated a broad definition of both "debt" and "debt collector" into the FDCPA in order to achieve its remedial purpose. 15 U.S.C. §§ 1692a(5), 1692a(6).

The FDCPA defines a "debt" as

any obligation or alleged obligation of a consumer to pay money arising out of a transaction in which the money, property, insurance, or services which are the subject to the transaction are primarily for personal, family, or household purposes, whether or not such obligation has been reduced to judgment. 15 U.S.C. § 1692a(5)

Appellants claim that the FDCPA does not apply to them because the NSF checks they purchased were not "debts" within the meaning of the FDCPA. They begin by noting that all 50 states criminalize the act of writing a check knowing that it will be dishonored; and that the law of many states creates a presumption of knowledge and/or willfulness when a check is written on insufficient funds and not paid within a certain period after it has been dishonored, or after the payor receives notice that it has been dishonored. Appellants also stress that since writing a fraudulent check gives rise to tort liability, and since they only attempted to collect NSF checks after a presumption of knowledge or willfulness arose under state law, their NSF checks were not "debts" within the meaning of the FDCPA because they did not arise out of a consumer "transaction." Rather, according to Appellants, their NSF checks arose out of criminal or tortious conduct.

Four Courts of Appeals have rejected this argument and held that payment with a NSF check creates a "debt" as defined in the FDCPA. *See Bass*, 111 F.3d at 1322; *Duffy v. Landberg*, 133 F.3d 1120 (8th Cir.1998); *Charles v. Lundgren & Assocs.*, 119 F.3d 739 (9th Cir.1997); *Snow v. Riddle*, 143 F.3d 1350 (10th Cir.1998).

The Court of Appeals for the Seventh Circuit was first to reject this argument in *Bass*, and its analysis has been followed by three other courts of appeals. In Bass, the court explained:

[T]he plain language of the Act defines "debt" quite broadly as "any obligation to pay arising out of a [consumer] transaction." In examining this definition, we first focus on the clear and absolute language in the phrase, "any obligation to pay." Such absolute language may not be alternatively read to reference only a limited set of obligations as appellants suggest. As long as the transaction creates an obligation to pay, a debt is created. We harbor no doubt that a check evidences the drawer's obligation to pay for the purchases made with the check, and should the check be dishonored, the payment obligation remains. 111 F.3d at 1325; *see also Duffy*, 133 F.3d at 1123 ("Since a check written by a consumer in a transaction for goods or services evidences the `drawer's obligation to pay' and this obligation remains even if the check is dishonored, abusive collection practices related to the dishonored check are prohibited by the FDCPA.") (quoting *Bass*, 111 F.3d at 1325).

Although we have not yet addressed this precise issue, we have held that a transaction's status as a "debt" under the FDCPA must be determined at the time that the obligation first arose. *See Pollice v. National Tax Funding*, L.P., 225 F.3d 379, 400 (3d Cir.2000). In *Pollice*, we held that water and sewer obligations constituted a "debt" based on their status when they first arose, and they remained a "debt" after assignment to a collection agency. Thus, our view of a "debt" under the FDCPA is consistent with the four courts of appeals that have held that an NSF check is a "debt."

Nonetheless, Check Investors and Hutchins attempt to circumvent the impact of our analysis in *Pollice* by relying on our earlier decision in *Zimmerman v. HBO Affiliate Group*, 834 F.2d 1163 (3d Cir. 1987). In *Zimmerman*, we held that the FDCPA did not apply to attempts by cable television companies to collect money from people who allegedly stole cable television signals by installing illegal antennas. *Id.* at 1167-69. Check Investors and Hutchins now argue that since the payors on its NSF checks were also subject to criminal or tort liability, Zimmerman compels the conclusion that the FDCPA does not apply to their collection efforts. We disagree.

In *Zimmerman*, we explained that the FDCPA was enacted to protect people who have "contracted for goods or services and [are] unable to pay for them," and that it was not intended to "protect against a perceived problem with the use of abusive practices in collecting tort settlements from alleged tortfeasors through threats of legal action." *Id.* at 1168. We also explained this in *Pollice*, 225 F.3d at 401 n. 24, by noting: "[c]learly, there was no `debt' in *Zimmerman* because the obligations arose out of a theft rather than a `transaction.'"

Check Investors and Hutchins argue that the payors on their NSF checks are similarly situated to the "consumers" who stole cable television signals in *Zimmerman*, and that, like those "consumers," the payors here are not entitled to the protection embodied in the FDCPA because they are criminals and tortfeasors rather than "consumers." They argue that, as in Zimmerman, no "debt" was created by executing the NSF checks here because there was no "transaction," as that term is commonly understood and as it is used in the FDCPA.

As the court explained in *Bass* when rejecting identical arguments there:

Appellants misstate the law when they categorize all dishonored checks as criminal and tortious. Both under the common law of fraud, a specific intent crime, and under most criminal statutes which specifically address dishonored checks, liability attaches only if the drawer either knew or intended that the check be dishonored at the time the check was drawn. A bank may refuse payment on a check for a variety of reasons lacking in the necessary fraudulent intent: administrative holds on the account of which the drawer is unaware, bank error, and the drawer's reliance on deposited checks that themselves are dishonored, to name a few. Even when the drawer is at fault for the dishonor, the requisite intent may be absent — for example, when the drawer makes a simple miscalculation or has a subsequent emergency need for funds.

We recognize that by the time a dishonored check has been turned over to a third party collector, the issuer has typically received notice of dishonor yet has still refused to pay. Nevertheless, an issuer whose intention not to pay the check arises only at some point after it is issued has still not, in most jurisdictions, committed a fraudulent or criminal act. The requisite knowledge or intent that the check be dishonored must arise at the time the check is written. We therefore must reject appellants' argument that all dishonored checks are fraudulent and thus not covered by the [FDCPA]. 111 F.3d at 1329 (emphasis in original) (footnote omitted).

Moreover, even if some of the payors of NSF checks had engaged in fraud at the time of the transaction, the court held in *Bass* that there is no "fraud exception" in the FDCPA. Given the explicit and unambiguous text of the FDCPA, we agree.

In *Bass*, a debt collector argued that the FDCPA should not apply to debts it was collecting because it was attempting to collect an NSF check that was presumed to be fraudulent under Wisconsin law. 111 F.3d at 1329. The court of appeals rejected that argument because the presumption that the check writer engaged in fraud was rebuttable under Wisconsin law, and because the debt collector had not made the showing required to establish fraudulent intent under state law. Id. In rejecting the defendants' argument, the court commented that, even if the requisite intent had been established, the court would be reluctant to "create a fraud exception where none exists in the [FDCPA's] text." *Id.* at 1329-30. The court explained:

A review of the legislative history reveals that Congress considered the entire field of defaulting debtors, stating its belief that most debtors fully intended to repay their debts. "Most" is not "all," however, yet Congress still chose not to exempt debt collectors from following the Act if they could prove that the consumer intended his check to be dishonored or accepted credit from a merchant intending default. No section of the Act requires an inquiry into worthiness of the debtor, or purports to protect only "deserving" debtors. To the contrary, Congress has clearly indicated its belief that no consumer deserves to be abused in the collection process. Moreover, we think that such a fraud exception would violate the spirit of the Act. The Act's singular focus is on curbing abusive and deceptive collection practices, not abusive and deceptive consumer payment practices. We are not unaware that in some cases . . . the absence of a fraud exception will allow consumers who intend to pass worthless checks to invoke the protections of the FDCPA. . . . Absent an explicit showing that Congress intended a fraud exception to the Act, the wrong occasioned by debtor fraud is more appropriately redressed under the statutory and common law remedies already in place, not by a judicially-created exception that selectively gives a green light to the very abuses proscribed by the Act. *Id.* at 1330.

The court thereafter amplified this discussion in *Keele v. Wexler*, 149 F.3d 589 (7th Cir.1998). There, the court explained:

We touched upon a similar request in *Bass* without formally deciding the issue, but did express at length "our discomfort with the proposition that the courts should create a fraud exception where none exists in the Act's text." Unfortunately for the [debt collector], this "discomfort" has not subsided since *Bass*, and it is time we put to rest any lingering doubts as to the nonexistence of a fraud exception to the FDCPA. *Id.* at 595 (citation omitted). The court's analysis continued:

[T]he FDCPA's legislative history reflects that Congress acknowledged there may be a "number of persons who willfully refuse to pay just debts," but apparently "believe[d] that the serious and widespread abuses" of debt collectors outweighed the necessity to carve out an exception for these so called "deadbeats." If the Act was designed to protect those who willfully refused to pay their debts, it makes little sense why consumers who write checks, knowing they will be dishonored, should not enjoy the same protections. *Id.* at 596 (citations omitted).

We agree that, given the legislative history of the FDCPA, its structure and text, we could not craft the kind of fraud exception that underlies the arguments of Check Investors without amending the statute.

The Payors of the NSF Checks are "Consumers" under the FDCPA.

As noted earlier, "[t]he FDCPA was enacted in 1997 as an amendment to the Consumer Credit Protection Act to protect consumers from a host of unfair, harassing, and deceptive collection practices without imposing unnecessary restrictions on ethical debt collectors." *Staub*, 626 F.2d at 276-77. Check Investors and Hutchins argue that the payors of the NSF checks are not "consumers" and therefore are not protected by the FDCPA. More specifically, they argue that

[a]n individual's conduct, when taken as a whole, determines whether he or she qualifies as a consumer for FDCPA purposes. An individual who issues a NSF check or a closed account check, in exchange for

money, goods, services or insurance, and who subsequently fails to make restitution within the criminal code statutory period established by the state legislature, is not a FDCPA consumer because the individual has not acted like a consumer.

However, the argument ignores that the FTC's cause of action is controlled by the FDCPA. That governing statute defines "consumer" as "any natural person obligated or allegedly obligated to pay any debt." 15 U.S.C. § 1692a(3). Even if we accept the claim that these payors are criminals and tortfeasors, those labels would advance neither our inquiry, nor Appellants' position, because "any" is all inclusive and does not exclude criminals or tortfeasors. Rather, it unambiguously includes them. As noted above in our discussion of the analysis in *Bass* and *Keele*, it is clear that Congress realized that some people who write "bad checks" do so knowingly and willfully and that their conduct is fraudulent. It is just as clear that Congress enacted a definition of "consumer" that did not exclude such persons from the protections they would otherwise be afforded under the FDCPA. Yet, Appellants' argument requires that we ignore the phrase: "any natural person," that Congress used to define "consumer."

Just as the obligations underlying the NSF checks are "debts" that the payor remains obligated to pay, *see Duffy*, 133 F.3d at 1123 ("[A] check written by a consumer in a transaction for goods or services evidences the "drawer's obligation to pay" and this obligation remains even if the check is dishonored. . . ."), the payors of those checks are "consumers" within the meaning of the FDCPA.

Appellants are "Debt Collectors" and not "Creditors" Under the FDCPA.

"The FDCPA's provisions generally apply only to debt collectors." *Pollice*, 225 F.3d at 403 "Creditors — as opposed to debt collectors — generally are not subject to the FDCPA." *Id.* A "debt collector" is broadly defined as one who attempts to collect debts "owed or due or asserted to be owed or due another," 15 U.S.C. § 1692a(6). A "creditor" is one who "offers or extends to offer credit creating a debt or to whom a debt is owed." 15 U.S.C. § 1692a(4).

The district court held that Check Investors and Hutchins are "debt collectors" as defined by the FDCPA because Check Investors obtained the "debts," i.e., the NSF checks, after they were in default. It relied on our decision in *Pollice v. National Tax Funding, L.P., supra*. There, National Tax Funding ("NTF") purchased homeowner's water and sewer obligations from a municipality and sought to collect on those obligations for its own benefit. We held that water and sewer obligations are "debts" within the meaning of the FDCPA. We also held that NTF was a "debt collector" and that the district court should not have dismissed FDCPA claims against it. We explained:

Courts have indicated that an assignee of an obligation is not a "debt collector" if the obligation is not in default at the time of assignment; conversely, an assignee may be deemed a "debt collector" if the obligation is already in default when it is assigned. . . . Here, there is no dispute that the various claims assigned to NTF were in default prior to their assignment to NTF. Further, there is no question that the "principal purpose" of NTF's business is the "collection of any debts," namely defaulted obligations which it purchases from municipalities. 225 F.3d at 403-404. This is equally true of Hutchins and Check Investors. Nevertheless, they contend that the district court's holding that they are "debt collectors" was error because they are actually "creditors" collecting debts actually owed to them, as opposed to "debt collectors" collecting obligations owed to someone else. The FDCPA defines "creditor" as

any person who offers or extends credit creating a debt or to whom a debt is owed, but such term does not include any person to the extent he receives an assignment or transfer of a debt in default solely for the purpose of facilitating collection of such debt for another.

15 U.S.C. § 1692a(4) (emphasis added). Appellants contend that because Check Investors bought the NSF checks from Telecheck, Check Investors is the actual owner of those checks and is therefore not collecting "debts of another," as a debt collector would. Rather, according to Appellants, Check Investors is actually the entity "to whom a debt is owed." They claim further that because Check Investors is owed the debt, it did not "receive[] an assignment or transfer" of the NSF checks "solely for the purpose of" collecting the debt for Telecheck. Thus, Appellants argue that Check Investors satisfies the statutory definition of a "creditor," and, therefore, they are not subject to the provisions of the FDCPA. Although the argument is rather clever, it is wrong. It would elevate form over substance and weave a technical loophole into the fabric of the FDCPA big enough to devour all of the protections Congress intended in enacting that legislation.

Admittedly, Check Investors appears at first blush to satisfy the statutory definition of a creditor. As the Court of Appeals for the Seventh Circuit noted in *Schlosser v. Fairbanks Capital Corp.*, 323 F.3d 534, 536 (7th Cir.2003), "for debts that do not originate with the one attempting collection, but are acquired from another, the collection activity related to that debt could logically fall into either category."

However, as to a specific debt, one cannot be both a "creditor" and a "debt collector," as defined in the FDCPA, because those terms are mutually exclusive. As the court explained in *Schlosser*, "[i]f the one who acquired the debt continues to service it, it is acting much like the original creditor that created the debt. On the other hand, if it simply acquires the debt for collection, it is acting more like a debt collector." *Id.* Thus, in determining if one is a "creditor" or a "debt collector," courts have focused on the status of the debt at the time it was acquired. 15 U.S.C. § 1692a controls that inquiry. That provision provides in relevant part:

(6) The term "debt collector" means any person who uses any instrumentality of interstate commerce or the mails in any business the principal purpose of which is the collection of any debts, or who regularly collects or attempts to collect, directly or indirectly, debts owed or due or asserted to be owed or due another. . . . The term does not include — (F) any person collecting or attempting to collect any debt owed or due or asserted to be owed or due another to the extent such activity . . . (iii) concerns a debt which was not in default at the time it was obtained by such person. . . . 15 U.S.C. § 1692a(6)(F)(iii). In *Pollice*, we relied on this provision of the FDCPA to hold that one attempting to collect a debt is a "debt collector" under the FDCPA if the debt in question was in default when acquired. Conversely, we concluded that § 1692a means that an entity is a creditor if the debt it is attempting to collect was not in default when it was acquired. 225 F.3d at 403-04. Other courts agree. *See Schlosser*, 323 F.3d at 536; *Bailey v. Security Nat'l Servicing Corp.*, 154 F.3d 384, 387 (7th Cir.1998); *Whitaker v. Ameritech Corp.*,

129 F.3d 952, 958 (7th Cir.1997); *Wadlington v. Credit Acceptance Corp.*, 76 F.3d 103, 106-07 (6th Cir.1996); *Perry v. Stewart Title Co.*, 756 F.2d 1197, 1208 (5th Cir.1985).

Admittedly, focusing on the status of the debt when it was acquired overlooks the fact that the person engaging in the collection activity may actually be owed the debt and is, therefore, at least nominally a creditor. Nevertheless, pursuant to § 1692a, Congress has unambiguously directed our focus to the time the debt was acquired in determining whether one is acting as a creditor or debt collector under the FDCPA. The legislative history explains the wisdom of that provision. The term "debt collector," subject to the exclusions discussed below, was intended to cover all third persons who regularly collect debts. "The primary persons intended to be covered are independent debt collectors." S.Rep. No. 95-382, at 2, 1997 U.S.C.C.A.N. at 1697. The Senate Committee explained that the FDCPA was limited to third-party collectors of past due debts because, unlike creditors, "who generally are restrained by the desire to protect their good will when collecting past due accounts," independent collectors are likely to have "no future contact with the consumer and often are unconcerned with the consumer's opinion of them." *Id.* at 1696.

Thus, as the court explained in Schlosser:

Focusing on the status of the obligation asserted by the assignee is reasonable in light of the conduct regulated by the statute. For those who acquire debts originated by others, the distinction drawn by the statute — whether the loan was in default at the time of the assignment — makes sense as an indication of whether the activity directed at the consumer will be servicing or collection. If the loan is current when it is acquired, the relationship between the assignee and the debtor is, for purposes of regulating communications and collections practices, effectively the same as that between originator and the debtor. If the loan is in default, no ongoing relationship is likely and the only activity will be collection. 323 F.3d at 538.

Here, Check Investors acquired the defaulted checks only for collection purposes. Indeed, it is in business to do just that: acquire seriously defaulted debt, the age of which allows Check Investors to acquire it for a few pennies on the dollar. The low cost of acquisition allows for substantial profit if the checks are subsequently collected. This is particularly true given the size of the "fees" that Check Investors adds on to each check.

The fact that the NSF checks were purchased and owned outright by Check Investors, rather than Check Investors merely receiving an assignment of the rights of the original payee is therefore irrelevant for purposes of determining whether Check Investors was acting as a debt collector or creditor. Check Investors clearly had no intention of servicing the debt. Check Investors and Hutchins do not dispute the FTC's claim that they employed harassing and abusive tactics to collect the debts they acquired and added "collection fees" that exceeded limitations imposed by state laws. No merchant worried about goodwill or the future of his/her business would have engaged in the kind of conduct that was the daily fare of the collectors at Check Investors. Neither Check Investors nor Hutchinson intended any future contact with the payees of the NSF checks they acquired, and their collection practices reflected as much. The collectors working there resorted to whatever harassment appeared likely to succeed; the only limit appears to have been a given tactic's likelihood of bearing fruit by yielding a profit. If the future of Appellants' business was in any way dependent upon their goodwill, they would not have dreamed of unleashing their collectors in this manner. Not only do we conclude that Appellants are "debt collectors" rather than "creditors," we believe that their course of conduct exemplifies why Congress enacted the FDCPA and the wisdom of doing so. It also shows why Congress has directed us to focus on whether a debt was in default when acquired to determine the status of "creditor" vs. "debt collector."

The Federal Trade Commission Act

As noted earlier, Hutchins and Check Investors do not dispute the FTC's claim that their collection practices constituted unfair and deceptive practices under the FTC Act. Instead, they argue that the payors of their NSF checks were not "consumers." "[T]he deceptive acts or practices forbidden by the [FTC Act] include those used in the collection of debts." *Trans World Accounts, Inc. v. FTC*, 594 F.2d 212, 214 (9th Cir.1979). Accordingly, [502 F.3d 175] we must also reject the argument that the payors of the NSF checks were not "consumers" under the FTC Act.

Nevertheless, Check Investors argues that

[t]his is not a case where consumers are being solicited to buy time-shares in non-existent condos or swamp land in Florida, and that the district court erred in determining that the Check Investors' practices were, in fact, deceptive as to a consumer.

Selling time shares for swamp land in Florida is but one kind of deceptive business practice. The collection techniques involved here are another. Moreover, Check Investors offered nothing in the district court to challenge the FTC's allegations that its collection practices included material misrepresentations in violation of the FTC Act. Accordingly, we will not consider that argument, raised for the first time on appeal, absent a compelling circumstance requiring us to consider it. *Srein v. Frankford Trust Co.*, 323 F.3d 214, 224 n. 8 (3d Cir.2003). Check Investors does not allege the existence of any compelling circumstance, and we can think of none. Thus, we will not consider its argument that the district court erred in finding that its practices were deceptive to a consumer.

For all of the above reasons, we will affirm the district court.

****

Compare *Check Investors*[427] to *Roberts v. Walmart Stores*[428]. In *Check Investors*, the Third Circuit determines that a check is a debt for the purposes of the FDCPA. However, in *Roberts v. Walmart Stores*, the court determines that the check is not an extension of credit for the purposes of an ECOA violation.

---

[427] 502 F.3d 159 (3rd Cir., 2007).
[428] *Roberts v. Walmart Stores, Inc.*, 736 F.Supp. 1527 (E.D. Mo., 1990).

While "debt collector" is defined in FDCPA, what activities constitute "debt collection" is not expressly defined by the law.

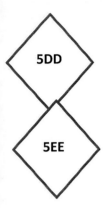

Are debts not in default subject to the FDCPA?

Review Figure 5A. What role does Telecheck play? What role does the merchant play? What role does the first debt collector play? What role does the second debt collector play? What role does Check Investors play?

Does the CFPB have the authority to write rules removing FDCPA protections for consumers who commit fraud? Why or Why Not?

Would the CFPB have authority to enforce the proposed FDCPA violation with respect to the Defendants in this case, if the Defendants were deemed debt collectors? Why or Why not?

As of December 2, 2018, the CFPB Consumer Complaint Database housed more than 1,170,000 consumer complaints.[429] Note that, as of December 2, 2018, 225,117 complaints were identified by the "Debt Collection" product/sub-product category.[430] "Cont'd attempts to collect debt not owed" represented 60,695 complaints as the complaint issue or sub-issue in the CFPB Consumer Complaint Database as of December 2, 2018. [431] "Improper contact or sharing of info" including talking to a third party about the consumer's debt, contacting the consumer after the consumer asked not to be contacted, contacting the employer after the consumer asked the debt collector not to contact the employer, and contacting the consumer instead of the consumer's attorney, accounted for 10,069 complaints as the complaint issue or sub-issue in the CFPB Consumer Complaint Database as of

---

[429] *See* CONSUMER FIN. PROT. BUREAU ONLINE CONSUMER COMPLAINT DATABASE, https://www.consumerfinance.gov/data-research/consumer-complaints/search/?from=0&searchField=all&searchText=&size=25&sort=created_date_desc, last visited Dec. 2, 2018.

[430] *See* CONSUMER FIN. PROT. BUREAU ONLINE CONSUMER COMPLAINT DATABASE, https://www.consumerfinance.gov/data-research/consumer-complaints/search/?from=0&searchField=all&searchText=&size=25&sort=created_date_desc, last visited Dec. 2, 2018.

[431] *See* CONSUMER FIN. PROT. BUREAU ONLINE CONSUMER COMPLAINT DATABASE, https://www.consumerfinance.gov/data-research/consumer-complaints/search/?from=0&searchField=all&searchText=&size=25&sort=created_date_desc, last visited Dec. 2, 2018.

December 2, 2018.[432] "Taking/Threatening an Illegal Action" including but not limited to threatening to sue on a too old debt and threatening the consumer with an arrest or jail time if the consumer did not pay the debt, amounted to 8,869 consumer complaints as the complaint issue or sub-issue in the CFPB Consumer Complaint Database as of December 2, 2018.[433] "False Statements or Representation," including but not limited to, impersonating an attorney, member of law enforcement or government official, indicating to the consumer that the consumer was committing a crime by not paying the debt, and attempting to collect the wrong amount represented 18,557 consumer complaints as the complaint issue or sub-issue in the CFPB Consumer Complaint Database as of December 2, 2018.[434] "Communication tactics," including but not limited to frequent or repeated calls, the use of obscene, profane, or abusive language, and calling outside of 8am-9pm amounted to 33,214 consumer complaints as the complaint issue or sub-issue in the CFPB Consumer Complaint Database as of December 2, 2018.[435]

Consider the following consumer complaint narrative, filed in the CFPB Consumer Complaint Database on June 12, 2018. Certain information concerning the complaint is redacted.

Consumer complaint narrative:[436]

---

[432] *See* CONSUMER FIN. PROT. BUREAU ONLINE CONSUMER COMPLAINT DATABASE, https://www.consumerfinance.gov/data-research/consumer-complaints/search/?from=0&searchField=all&searchText=&size=25&sort=created_date_desc, last visited Dec. 2, 2018.

[433] *See* CONSUMER FIN. PROT. BUREAU ONLINE CONSUMER COMPLAINT DATABASE, https://www.consumerfinance.gov/data-research/consumer-complaints/search/?from=0&searchField=all&searchText=&size=25&sort=created_date_desc, last visited Dec. 2, 2018.

[434] *See* CONSUMER FIN. PROT. BUREAU ONLINE CONSUMER COMPLAINT DATABASE, https://www.consumerfinance.gov/data-research/consumer-complaints/search/?from=0&searchField=all&searchText=&size=25&sort=created_date_desc, last visited Dec. 2, 2018.

[435] *See* CONSUMER FIN. PROT. BUREAU ONLINE CONSUMER COMPLAINT DATABASE, https://www.consumerfinance.gov/data-research/consumer-complaints/search/?from=0&searchField=all&searchText=&size=25&sort=created_date_desc, last visited Dec. 2, 2018.

[436] CONSUMER FIN. PROT. BUREAU ONLINE CONSUMER COMPLAINT DATABASE, https://www.consumerfinance.gov/data-research/consumer-complaints/search/detail/2933981, last visited Dec. 2, 2018.

> *XX/XX/XXXX @ XXXX XX/XX/XXXX @ XXXX XX/XX/XXXX @ XXXX XX/XX/XXXX @ XXXX XX/XX/XXXX @ XXXX Calling from : XXXX I've been receiving calls from this number since XX/XX/XXXX at what would be just about XXXX in the evening. It's unusual for someone to call my line after XXXX XXXX regular work day as I'm usually not available at this time. I actually have the publicly registered number (s) from this company saved on my phone and that is where I was expecting to be contacted from. I found it odd that a local number would call so many times without leaving a voicemail but ignored it nonetheless because no one who knows me calls without texting me first unless it's an emergency. Due to the amount of times this number appeared in my logs alone, I decided to call them back on the XX/XX/XXXX. When I dialed the number, it rang once, then bounced me to the queue for Simm Associates Incorporated and immediately puts me in line to speak to a live agent. My phone number works perfectly fine and I'm open to returning calls of those who leave voicemails, but these practices are done in a way that I believe is in violation of my rights as a consumer under the FDCPA [. . .] because not only is it deceptive, but because the company masking their number with a local line to establish contact with me in a way that misrepresents the nature of their calls [. . .]*

5HH

The company responded timely, and the complaint was "closed with explanation" from the company. The company elected not to permit a response viewable to the public. **Does this consumer complaint amount to an FDCPA violation? Why or Why Not? What additional information would you need to decide?**

5II

Would the CFPB have authority to enforce the proposed FDCPA violation with respect to the Defendants in this case, if the Defendants were deemed debt collectors? Why or Why not?

Consider the following consumer complaint narrative, filed in the CFPB Consumer Complaint Database on September 14, 2017. Certain information concerning the complaint is redacted.

Consumer complaint narrative:[437]

---

[437] CONSUMER FIN. PROT. BUREAU ONLINE CONSUMER COMPLAINT DATABASE, https://www.consumerfinance.gov/data-research/consumer-complaints/search/detail/2674454, last visited Dec. 2, 2018.

> *Credence Resource Management has been calling my cell phone for the last 2-3 months trying to collect {$180.00} for an old XXXX XXXX XXXX bill my wife did not pay. I tell them that they are calling the wrong number and give them my wife 's cell number. They continue to call me from an offshore call center speaking XXXX with an unusual accent. They only ask my relationships with the debtor, not my name, then give me her address and only ask if it is right. I say yes and then they continue to tell me who they are, what company they work for for, that it is an attempt to collect a debt and the phone call may be recorded. After about 15 calls I asked to speak to a supervisor. I notified him that my wife wanted to take care of the debt but was disputing the amount. The supervisor " checked " the amount and verbally confirmed it was the right balance. I informed the supervisor that I wished to dispute the balance and requested a breakdown or proof of the debt by mail. We never received the proof and now the phone calls are coming more often. I received yet another call just a few minutes ago. I let the gentleman on the other end know that he was violating FDCPA laws by giving me information about the debtor and her account. The gentleman who stated he was in XXXX was not aware of any laws transfered me to another supervisor. The supervisor said he was going to check the times I had been called. He came back on the line very apologetic and informed me that he would remove my number and that I would not receive any more calls from their company. I thanded him but asked him for his company 's information so I could file a complaint. The supervisor hesitated then hesitantly gave me the company name. I asked him for the company address. He said he was not authorized to give me anymore information. He then put me on hold then returned with a company e-mail to file my complaint. I informed him that I would be filing a complaint with the authorities. He said that it was not necessary and asked me not to file a complaint.*

5JJ The company responded timely, and the complaint was "closed with explanation" from the company. The company elected not to permit a response viewable to the public. **Does this consumer complaint amount to an FDCPA violation? Why or Why Not? What additional information would you need to decide?**

5KK The individual that submitted this complaint in the CFPB Consumer Complaint Database identified as a servicemember. **Should this individual be entitled to more consumer**

protection? Why or Why Not? Consider that "financial concerns can distract from military readiness for servicemembers being asked to serve our nation at home and abroad."[438]

Consider the following consumer complaint narrative, filed in the CFPB Consumer Complaint Database on June 12, 2018. Certain information concerning the complaint is redacted.

Consumer complaint narrative:[439]

XXXX of 2016 I started to receive letters telling me I'd face criminal prosecution if I didn't pay the debt in full. They followed that by calling me a piece of XXXX XXXX and you're all alike. Since then they have sent threatening letters to my place of resident insinuating I would face legal ramification if I did't pay {$2000.00} immediately to them even though the courts instructed me to pay the state of Pennsylvania. I recently had an influx in my bills and am giving them XXXX per month from XXXX more letter. I was trying to be polite to give them a heads up so I wouldn't have to receive anymore threatening letters from them. Every time I receive a letter its signed with another name but in the same handwriting. I receive XXXX Benefits so I am on a fixed income and don't have the money to pay in full. They don't seem to care and I believe their modo is " We Collect No Matter What ". Well after I just called to let them to let them know my bills went up so there forI would be making {$20.00} less a month on my payments. Prior to this they would call all night until I XXXX PM. I just want the letters to stop because in no way my judge said that payments will be to XXXX XXXX collection agency. I pay through the Pennsylvania EPay website instead because I simply won't pay this debt collector. I make the payments I can. I am trying to return the money I owe and looking for any kind of job now that I have a vehicle to use. I just want to be left alone by these people. they harass you at every turn, they use profain language, and scare tactics at all time. I thank you for your time looking into this I also have reciepts from all payments.

---

[438] *See* Chris Johnson, *Complaints Show Military Families and Nonmilitary Families Have Different Experiences in the Financial Marketplace* CONSUMER FIN. PROT. BUREAU BLOG (Oct. 31, 2017), https://www.consumerfinance.gov/about-us/blog/complaints-show-military-families-and-non-military-families-have-different-experiences-financial-marketplace/.

[439] CONSUMER FIN. PROT. BUREAU ONLINE CONSUMER COMPLAINT DATABASE, https://www.consumerfinance.gov/data-research/consumer-complaints/search/detail/3008227, last visited Dec. 2, 2018.

5LL

The company responded timely, and the complaint was "closed with explanation" from the company. The company elected not to permit a response viewable to the public. **Does this consumer complaint amount to an FDCPA violation? Why or Why Not? What additional information would you need to decide?**

5MM

Return to Figure 2C. **Are the stakeholder interests of Romero, the offending employee in** *Horkey* **aligned with the interests of the debt collection institution? Why or Why Not? Recall the discussion of Wells Fargo's response to the fake account scandal, namely the difference in its treatment of employees in comparison to top-level executives. Do you think the actions of employee Romero in** *Horkey* **are representative of corporate culture? Why or Why Not?**

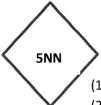

5NN

Recall the discussion in Part ID concerning the 5Ws.

(1) **Who** is regulated under the FDCPA? Who is exempt from compliance with the FDCPA
(2) **Who** is protected under the FDCPA?
(3) **What** is the protection? What is the appropriate law or regulation?
(4) **When** is the protection applicable? (Under what circumstances does the protection apply?
(5) **Why** does the protection exist? Would applying the law or rule make sense in context?

VI. UNFAIR, DECEPTIVE or ABUSIVE ACTS or PRACTICES

A. LAWS AND RULES

Thus far, in the review of the Truth in Lending Act, the Equal Credit Opportunity Act, and the Fair Debt Collection Practices Act, statutory provisions have been located within 15 U.S.C. Chapter 41: Consumer Credit Protection.[440] Specifically, TILA, ECOA, and FDCPA provisions are found within Subchapter I: Consumer Credit Cost Disclosure, Subchapter IV: Equal Credit Opportunity, and Subchapter V: Debt Collection Practices, respectively.[441] Collectively, these subchapters, among others, make up the Consumer Credit Protection Act of 1968.[442] The prohibition against unfair, deceptive or abusive acts or practices, however, is found within the Dodd-Frank Wall Street Reform and Consumer Protection Act.[443]

Prior to the creation of the CFPB, the Federal Trade Commission was responsible for rulemaking and guidance with respect to unfair and deceptive acts and practices. This rulemaking power, as it relates to consumer financial services and products, transferred to the CFPB.[444] Therefore, now the CFPB is charged with protecting consumers from unfair, deceptive and/or abusive acts and practices.[445] The CFPB may promulgate implementing regulations applicable to covered persons and service providers identifying or preventing unfair, deceptive, or abusive acts or practices in consumer financial services products. [446] Thus far, the CFPB has not used its authority to create implementing regulations.[447]

Unfair means that the "act or practice causes or is likely to cause substantial injury to consumers which is not reasonably avoidable by consumers, and such substantial injury is not outweighed by countervailing benefits to consumers or to competition."[448] The CFPB has indicated in its Supervision and Examination Manual that "injury" is typically monetary harm and that "an act or practice that

---

[440] *See* 15 U.S.C. §1601 *et seq.*; *see* 15 U.S.C. § 1691 *et seq.*; *see* 15 U.S.C. § 1692 *et seq.* (Fastcase 2018).

[441] *See* 15 U.S.C. §1601 *et seq.*; *see* 15 U.S.C. §1691 *et seq.*; *see* 15 U.S.C. §1692 *et seq.*

[442] *See generally* 15 U.S.C. §1601 *et seq.*

[443] *See* 12 U.S.C. §5531 (Fastcase 2018).

[444] 12 U.S.C. § 5581(5).

[445] *See* 12 U.S.C. § 5511(b)(2).

[446] *See* 12 U.S.C. § 5531(b).

[447] *See id.*

[448] *See* 12 U.S.C. § 5531(c).

causes a small amount of harm to a large number of people" can be "substantial."[449] Further, an act or practice is not reasonably avoidable if the consumer's decision-making is impeded or if an overwhelming majority of financial services providers engage in the same act or practice, impeding the consumer's ability to avoid the injury.[450]

Abusive means that the act or practice:

> (1) materially interferes with the ability of a consumer to understand a term or condition of a consumer financial product or service; or
> (2) takes unreasonable advantage of—
> (A) a lack of understanding on the part of the consumer of the material risks, costs, or conditions of the product or service;
> (B) the inability of the consumer to protect the interests of the consumer in selecting or using a consumer financial product or service; or
> (C) the reasonable reliance by the consumer on a covered person to act in the interests of the consumer.[451]

Abusive was added as a violation source through the Dodd-Frank Act.[452]

Deceptive is not defined in the Dodd-Frank Act. However, prior to the transfer of regulatory oversight to the CFPB, the Federal Trade Commission provided guidance concerning "deceptive" acts and practices. Therefore, the CFPB has inherited some historical context for what constitutes a deceptive act or practice. An act or practice is deceptive if:

> (1) There is a representation, omission, or practice that misleads or is likely to mislead.
> (2) The act or practice has been reasonably interpreted by the consumer.
> (3) The representation, omission, or practice is material.
> (4) No disclosure or qualifying statement is provided to the consumer to prevent the deception. [453]

The Federal Trade Commission has previously provided guidance on what is likely to mislead via the "four Ps" test, namely:

> Is the statement prominent enough for the consumer to notice?
> Is the information presented in an easy-to-understand format that does not contradict other information in the package and at a time when the consumer's attention is not distracted elsewhere?

---

[449] CONSUMER FIN. PROT. BUREAU, *UDAAP Supervision and Examination Manual* (Oct. 2012), at 2, available at https://s3.amazonaws.com/files.consumerfinance.gov/f/documents/102012_cfpb_unfair-deceptive-abusive-acts-practices-udaaps_procedures.pdf.
[450] *Id.*
[451] *See* 12 U.S.C. § 5531(d).
[452] *See id.*
[453] *See* CONSUMER FIN. PROT. BUREAU, *supra* note 449, at 5.

Is the <u>placement</u> of the information in a location where consumers can be expected to look or hear?

Finally, is the information in close <u>proximity</u> to the claim it qualifies?[454]

There have been no express implementing regulations issued by the CFPB regarding unfair, deceptive and abusive acts or practices. However, the CFPB has issued some unofficial guidance in the form of bulletins, commenced enforcement actions and/or filed complaints pursuant to its enforcement authority.[455] Recall the discussion in Part II regarding express rulemaking.

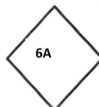

6A   **Does the CFPB's issuance of bulletins amount to express rulemaking?**

The CFPB includes the following disclaimer in a 2015 FDCPA bulletin:

> This compliance bulletin [. . .] is a non-binding general statement of policy articulating considerations relevant to the Bureau's exercise of its supervisory and enforcement authority. It is therefore exempt from notice and comment rulemaking requirements.[456]

The CFPB has indicated that it is "considering how rulemaking may be helpful to further clarify the meaning of "abusiveness."[457]

Recall that the FDCPA prohibits false, deceptive, or misleading representations or means in connection with debt collection.[458] Note that a violation of the FDCPA is also usually considered an unfair or deceptive act or practice in violation of UDAAP with regard to the Federal Trade Commission's enforcement authority.[459] In addition, in contrast to ECOA, TILA, and FDCPA, which are applicable to credit transactions, lending, and debt collection, respectively, UDAAP is not limited to a specific part of a consumer transaction nor to a specific consumer financial service. This is recognizable in at least three ways. First, the reading of the code section does not indicate a restriction to a particular product, transaction, or consumer financial service. Second, as noted above, the prohibition against unfair, deceptive or abusive acts or practices is located in the Dodd-Frank Wall Street Reform and Consumer

---

[454] CONSUMER FIN. PROT. BUREAU, *supra* note 449 at 5-6.

[455] *See* 12 U.S.C. § 5564(a).

[456] *See* CFPB Bulletin 2015-07, In-Person Collection of Consumer Debt, (Dec. 16, 2015), at 3, *available at* https://files.consumerfinance.gov/f/201512_cfpb_compliance-bulletin-in-person-collection-of-consumer-debt.pdf

[457] *See* Kelly Cochran, *Fall 2018 Rulemaking Agenda* CONSUMER FIN. PROT. BUREAU BLOG (Oct. 17, 2018), https://www.consumerfinance.gov/about-us/blog/fall-2018-rulemaking-agenda/.

[458] 15 U.S.C. § 1692e.

[459] 15 U.S.C. § 1692l(a).

Protection Act. This chapter title, alone, referencing "consumer protection" generally, contrasts with the chapter title of the Consumer *Credit* Protection Act of 1968 (emphasis added). Finally, interestingly, the Consumer Credit Protection Act of 1968, and therefore TILA, ECOA, and FDCPA are located in Title 15 of the United States Code, reserved for Commerce and Trade. In contrast, the Dodd-Frank Wall Street Reform and Consumer Protection Act, and consequently UDAAP authority, is located in Title 12, reserved for Banks and Banking.

B. ENFORCEMENT

The CFPB has authority to take action against covered persons for violation of 12 U.S.C. §5531.[460] No private right of action exists for consumers for federal UDAAP violation. However, many states have their own state UDAAP laws that include civil liability protections for individuals.

Why would an institution engage in unfair, deceptive, or abusive acts and practices with the threat of action by a federal bureau? Adam Levitin, Professor of Law at Georgetown University Law Center, explains that, prior to the CFPB, "unfair, deceptive, and abusive practices [could] be highly profitable, even accounting for regulatory and reputational risk. Indeed that is the very reason to engage in them."[461]

In 2017 the CFPB and New York Attorney General brought an action against RD Legal for deceptive practices.[462] The action included both federal and state violations. RD Legal was accused of deceiving 9/11 first responders and National Football League concussion victims who received settlement awards.[463] Specifically, RD Legal offered the consumers advances of the anticipated settlement awards before the consumers received the settlement awards to which they were entitled.[464] However, the terms of RD Legal's deal with consumers were elaborate, deceptive, and led to consumers' owing RD Legal almost twice the amount that was advanced, in some cases.[465]

---

[460] *See* 12 U.S.C. § 5531.

[461] *See* Levitin, *supra* note 6, at 331.

[462] *See* Press Release, Consumer Fin. Prot. Bureau, CFPB and New York Attorney General Sue RD Legal for Scamming 9/11 Heroes Out of Millions of Dollars in Compensation Funds, (Feb. 7, 2017), available at https://www.consumerfinance.gov/about-us/newsroom/cfpb-and-new-york-attorney-general-sue-rd-legal-scamming-911-heroes-out-millions-dollars-compensation-funds/.

[463] *See id.*

[464] *See id.*

[465] *See id.*

C. INTERPRETATION

Recall that the CFPB's enforcement powers include initiating a civil action against the person, imposing civil penalties, or seeking legal or equitable relief.[466] Consider whether UDAAP utilizes a restriction consumer protection method or a disclosure consumer protection method. Does UDAAP resolve the issue of access to information to create a "fair" playing field or does UDAAP resolve the issue of access to financial markets by encouraging financial inclusion? Because a private right of action is not available to individuals for federal UDAAP violations, the following cases include actions initiated by the CFPB.

Consider the following complaint filed by the Consumer Financial Protection Bureau against Mission Settlement Agency in 2013 in the Southern District of New York.

CONSUMER FIN. PROT. BUREAU V. MISSION SETTLEMENT AGENCY (COMPLAINT)

---

[466] *See* 12 U.S.C. § 5564(a)(2).

UNITED STATES DISTRICT COURT
SOUTHERN DISTRICT OF NEW YORK

--- x

CONSUMER FINANCIAL PROTECTION : BUREAU,

:

Plaintiff, :

: Case No. 1:13-cv-_____

v. :

: **COMPLAINT**

MISSION SETTLEMENT AGENCY, d/b/a :
MISSION ABSTRACT LLC, MICHAEL LEVITIS, :
in his individual and official capacity, LAW :
OFFICE OF MICHAEL LEVITIS, PREMIER :
CONSULTING GROUP LLC, LAW OFFICE OF :
MICHAEL LUPOLOVER, :

:

Defendants. :

--- x

The Consumer Financial Protection Bureau (the Bureau) alleges the following against

Mission Settlement Agency, d/b/a Mission Abstract LLC (Mission), the Law Office of Michael

Levitis, Premier Consulting Group LLC (Premier), and the Law Office of Michael Lupolover

(together, the Corporate Defendants); and against Michael Levitis:

INTRODUCTION

1.   The Bureau brings this action under sections 1031(a), 1036(a), 1054(a), and 1061 of the Consumer Financial Protection Act of 2010 (CFPA), 12 U.S.C. §§ 5531(a), 5536(a), 5564(a), 5581, and under the Telemarketing and Consumer Fraud and Abuse Prevention Act, 15 U.S.C. §§ 6102(c)(2), 6105(d), based on violations of the Telemarketing Sales Rule (TSR), 16 C.F.R. § 310 *et seq.*, in connection with the marketing and sale of debt-relief services and based on unfair and deceptive practices in violation of the CFPA, 12 U.S.C. §§ 5531, 5536.

JURISDICTION AND VENUE

2.   This Court has subject-matter jurisdiction over this action because it is brought under a federal consumer financial law, 12 U.S.C. § 5565(a)(1), presents a federal question, 28 U.S.C. § 1331, and is brought by an agency of the United States, 28 U.S.C. § 1345.

3.   Venue is proper in this district under 28 U.S.C. § 1391(b), (c), and 12 U.S.C. § 5564(f).

PARTIES

4.   The Bureau is an agency of the United States created by 12 U.S.C. § 5491(a). It has independent litigating authority, 12 U.S.C. § 5564(a), (b), including to enforce the TSR as it applies to persons covered by the CFPA, 15 U.S.C. §§ 6102(c)(2), 6105(d); 12 U.S.C. § 5531(a).

5.   Mission is a for-profit company that is located and does business in this district. Mission has used office space at 280 Madison Avenue, Suite 300, New York, NY 10017 and has offices at 2713 Coney Island Avenue, Brooklyn, NY 11235.

6.   The Law Office of Michael Levitis is a law firm located at 1729 E. 12th Street, Brooklyn, NY 11229. It does business in this district.

7.   Premier is a for-profit company with offices at 180 Sylvan Avenue, 2nd Floor,

Englewood Cliffs, NJ 07632 and 1130 Hooper Avenue, Toms River, NJ 08753. It does business in this district.

8.   The Law Office of Michael Lupolover is a law firm located at 180 Sylvan Avenue, 2nd Floor, Englewood Cliffs, NJ 07632. It does business in this district.

9.   Each Corporate Defendant engages in offering or providing a consumer financial product or service and is therefore a "covered person" under the CFPA. 12 U.S.C. § 5481(15)(A)(viii)(II), (6).

10.   Levitis is the principal of Mission and the Law Office of Michael Levitis, and is heavily involved in their day-to-day operations. He approved, ratified, endorsed, directed, controlled, managed, and otherwise materially participated in the conduct of their affairs. Levitis is a "related person" under the CFPA. 12 U.S.C. § 5481(25). Because of his status as a related person, Levitis is a "covered person" for purposes of the CFPA. *Id.* Levitis does business in this district.

SUMMARY OF COMPLAINT

11.   Since at least September 2010, Defendants have marketed and sold debt-relief services to consumers. Defendants attracted financially distressed consumers through phone calls, mailings, and other solicitations promising substantial reductions in outstanding debts owed to unsecured creditors. In the course of offering their services, Defendants unlawfully collected fees in advance of providing any debt-relief services.

12.   In addition, since at least July 2011, Mission and Levitis committed deceptive and unfair acts and practices causing substantial financial injury to consumers. Specifically, they misled consumers, impersonated a government agency, and gave false statements regarding fees for Mission's debt-relief service. Instead of being applied towards repayment of consumers'

195

debts, a large percentage of the amounts that consumers paid into Mission's debt-relief services program went to Mission, which provided scant meaningful assistance to resolve consumers' debts and often left consumers in worse financial positions than before they enrolled.

THE CORPORATE DEFENDANTS' BUSINESS PRACTICES

13.   The Corporate Defendants sold or offered to sell debt-relief services to consumers. In exchange for a fee, the Corporate Defendants promised to renegotiate, settle, reduce, or otherwise alter the terms of at least one debt between a consumer and one or more unsecured creditors or debt collectors in accordance with a settlement agreement or other contractual agreement executed by the consumer.

14.   The Corporate Defendants marketed their debt-relief services via the U.S. Mail, the Internet, and outbound or inbound telephone calls to or from consumers, including via at least more than one interstate telephone call.

15.   The Corporate Defendants requested or received enrollment fees, processing fees, debt-relief service fees, and other types of fees in advance of settling at least one of the consumer's debts.

16.   Each of the Corporate Defendants separately entered into a contract with a payment processor to receive services for the management, processing, and administration of payments. Under this contract, the payment processor managed the savings account (Dedicated Account) of each and every consumer who contracted for debt-relief services from each of the Corporate Defendants.

17.   When consumers signed up to receive debt-relief services through the Corporate Defendants' respective debt-relief programs, the Corporate Defendants directed consumers to sign up for the Dedicated Account with the payment processor. The Corporate Defendants also

instructed consumers to stop paying their creditors and instead to start making payments into the Dedicated Account managed by the payment processor.

18.   The Corporate Defendants represented to consumers that, if and when a consumer's Dedicated Account reached a sufficient balance, they would instruct the payment processor to transmit funds to a consumer's creditors to help satisfy the consumer's debts.

19.   At all times relevant to this Complaint, the Corporate Defendants required and relied on assistance from the payment processor to collect and disburse monies through the consumer's Dedicated Accounts.

20.   Consistent with the Corporate Defendants' direction, the payment processor: (i) withdrew funds from a consumer's bank account through ACH transfer and deposited them into the Dedicated Account, and (ii) transmitted funds from the Dedicated Account to itself and to the Corporate Defendants to cover processing and servicing fees, including the fee the Corporate Defendants charge to consumers for its debt-relief services. The transactions managed by the payment processor reflected that funds were routinely transferred out of a consumer's Dedicated Account to pay the Corporate Defendant's debt-relief fees before payments went to any creditors.

21.   With respect to Dedicated Accounts that were established on or after October 27, 2010, the effective date of the TSR's advance-fee ban, Mission and the Law Office of Michael Levitis collected fees from consumers in advance of settling the consumers' debts totaling approximately $1.1 million.

22.   With respect to Dedicated Accounts that were established on or after October 27, 2010, Premier collected fees from consumers in advance of settling the consumers' debts totaling approximately $187,830.

23.   With respect to Dedicated Accounts that were established on or after October 27, 2010, the Law Office of Michael Lupolover collected fees from consumers in advance of settling the consumers' debts totaling approximately $111,809.

ADDITIONAL DEBT-RELIEF ACTIVITES OF MISSION

24.   At Levitis's direction, Mission impersonated a government agency to induce a higher volume of sales calls from consumers who incorrectly believed that Mission offered a government program. Mission routinely disseminated a written solicitation to consumers in an envelope bearing an image of the Great Seal of the United States for what Mission called the "Office of Disbursement." Mission circulated this solicitation in order to cause consumers to believe Mission was affiliated with a government program and to enhance Mission's ability to attract financially distressed consumers to receive debt-relief services. Mission's debt-relief service was in fact not affiliated with the government.

25.   Mission also misled consumers about the timing of fees for debt-relief services. Mission falsely asserted in the written solicitation that there were no "Upfront Fees" when in fact Mission charged them. Mission, at Levitis's direction, did not inform consumers that Mission charges advance fees, and otherwise concealed and misrepresented the size of Mission's fees.

26.   Mission, at Levitis's direction, also committed unfair acts and practices causing consumers substantial injury. Despite promising consumers that it would settle their unsecured debts for typically 55% of consumers' total outstanding credit-card balances, Mission often: (i) concealed the fact that creditors will not be paid by the time that consumers expect, or might not be paid at all; (ii) charged exorbitant debt-relief services fees often without settling any debts; and (iii) left consumers in worse financial positions than before they enrolled in Mission's program.

27.   Specifically, many consumers enrolled in Mission's program received zero or scant benefit in the form of settled debts and suffered net losses of approximately $1,300 to $3,000 per person. Consumers often learned from creditors that Mission had never contacted them. Unaware that this would occur, consumers had stopped communicating with and paying their creditors based on Mission's representation that it would handle consumers' debts on their behalf and based on Mission's instruction to cease communicating with the creditors and to cease paying these creditors directly. Because Mission did not often make negotiated payments to creditors as it promised it would, many consumers suffered additional financial injury in the form of credit-card penalties, higher interest rates, and adverse effects on their credit. Many consumers faced lawsuits commenced by their creditors or had to file for bankruptcy.

28.   By virtue of Mission's own conduct, the substantial injury that Mission caused was not reasonably avoidable by consumers: Mission systematically erected barriers to prevent consumers from obtaining information regarding the disadvantages of its debt-relief program. Whether Mission was originating new consumer accounts or working to maintain existing consumer accounts, Mission communicated with consumers in a manner that prevented consumers from learning of the debt-relief program's risks, costs, and conditions – the disclosures of which would have permitted consumers to ascertain the likelihood of consumer injury. For example:

a. At Levitis's direction, Mission staff enrolled as many consumers as possible regardless of whether consumers understood Mission's fee structure or other attributes of its debt-relief program.

b. Levitis directed Mission's staff to conceal the debt-relief services fees when enrolling new customers. If a consumer made specific inquiries regarding fees, Levitis told staff to explain that the fee was embedded in the overall amount that consumers contributed on a monthly basis to their Dedicated Accounts so that Mission could obscure how much money accrued to pay off underlying debts versus went to Mission. If the consumer continued seeking more information, Levitis, at times, allowed the Mission employees to reveal the size of the fee (18%) but even then instructed them to withhold other information, including the timing of fees. Mission staff followed Levitis's instructions.

c. Mission employees avoided answering consumers' questions about termination policies or the consequences of ineffective debt negotiations. Mission staff, at Levitis's direction, used deliberate obfuscation – by providing nonresponsive or misleading answers – to confuse consumers about the program's risks and costs. At other times, Mission staff dodged consumers' questions by assuring consumers that answers would be provided by more knowledgeable Mission employees during a later meeting with the consumers – despite knowing that no such meeting would occur.

d. To retain the exorbitant fees paid into the program by consumers, Levitis instructed staff during periodic staff meetings not to issue refunds and to delay responding to consumers' refund requests until they ceased to be made.

e. Before obtaining the consumer's consent to pay for the program, Mission failed to disclose the time by which it would make a *bona fide* settlement offer to the consumer's creditors or debt collectors, or the amount that the consumer would have to accumulate in the Dedicated Account before Mission would initiate settlement attempts or make a *bona fide* settlement offer to the consumer's creditors.

29.   Mission's conduct as described above ensured that consumers could not avoid substantial injury. Mission prevented consumers from learning information that would lead consumers to decide to forgo participation in the program.

30.   Mission's conduct did not generate any meaningful countervailing benefit to consumers or to competition.

LEVITIS'S INVOLVEMENT IN MISSION'S DEBT-RELIEF ACTIVITIES

31.   Levitis managed Mission's day-to-day operations, including activities that form the basis for this Complaint. Levitis approved the use of marketing materials bearing counterfeit government seals, demanded regular reports on sales and consumer complaints, directed employees to provide misleading information to consumers, and determined the outcome of consumer complaints and refund requests. Accordingly, Levitis engaged in the sale of debt-relief services provided by Mission.

32.   Levitis also designed and implemented the business model through which Mission charged advance fees from consumers while often providing consumers little to no debt-relief services.

33.   Levitis also retained payment processors on Mission's behalf.

34.   Since Mission's inception, Levitis knew that Mission routinely charged fees before settling consumers' debts and that Mission engaged in unfair and deceptive acts and practices.

COUNT ONE (VIOLATIONS OF THE TSR'S ADVANCE-FEE BAN) ASSERTED AGAINST ALL DEFENDANTS

35.   The allegations in paragraphs 1 to 34 are incorporated here by reference.

36.   In the course of telemarketing debt-relief services, the Corporate Defendants requested or received fees from consumers for debt-relief services before renegotiating, settling, reducing, or otherwise altering the terms of at least one of the consumer's debts. The Corporate Defendants requested or received payment of these fees prior to consumers making at least one payment pursuant to any settlement agreement or other valid contractual agreement between consumers and their creditors.

37.   The Corporate Defendants' acts or practices from October 27, 2010 to present violate the TSR, 16 C.F.R. § 310.4(a)(5)(i), and are unlawful acts or practices in telemarketing. Because each Corporate Defendant is a "covered person," each Corporate Defendant's conduct in violation of the TSR is unlawful under sections 1031(a) and 1036(a)(1)(A) of the CFPA, 12 U.S.C. §§ 5531(a), 5536(a)(1)(A). 15 U.S.C. § 6102(c)(2).

38.   Levitis is a "related person" and a "covered person." 12 U.S.C. § 5481(25). He is liable for violating the TSR, 16 C.F.R. § 310.4(a)(5)(i), and sections 1031(a) and 1036(a)(1) of the CFPA, 12 U.S.C. §§ 5531(a), 5536(a)(1).

COUNT TWO (DECEPTIVE ACTS AND PRACTICES IN VIOLATION OF THE CFPA) ASSERTED AGAINST MISSION AND LEVITIS

39.   The allegations in paragraphs 1-34 are incorporated here by reference.

40.   In numerous instances, in the course of advertising, marketing, promoting, offering for sale, the sale, or the performance of debt-relief services, Mission and Levitis have represented, directly or indirectly, that: Mission's program was affiliated with the government and Mission did not charge advance fees for debt-relief services. Both of these representations

were material, false, and likely to mislead a reasonable consumer at the time they were made.

41. Therefore, the representations made by Mission and Levitis constitute deceptive acts and practices in violation of section 1036(a)(1)(B) of the CFPA, 12 U.S.C. § 5536(a)(1)(B).

42. Levitis is a "related person" and a "covered person." 12 U.S.C. § 5481(25). He is liable for the deceptive misrepresentations described above, in violation of sections 1031(a) and 1036(a)(1) of the CFPA, 12 U.S.C. §§ 5531(a), 5536(a)(1).

COUNT THREE (UNFAIR ACTS AND PRACTICES IN VIOLATION OF THE CFPA) ASSERTED AGAINST MISSION AND LEVITIS

43. The allegations in paragraphs 1-34 are incorporated here by reference.

44. Under the CFPA, an act or practice is unfair if it causes or is likely to cause consumers substantial injury which is not reasonably avoidable and if the substantial injury is not outweighed by countervailing benefits to consumers or to competition.

45. The acts and practices of Mission and Levitis – in particular the acts and practices set out in paragraphs 26 to 34 above – caused consumers substantial injury.

46. The substantial injury inflicted upon consumers was not reasonably avoidable.

47. The substantial injury inflicted on consumers was not outweighed by countervailing benefit to consumers or to competition.

48. Therefore, Mission engaged in unfair acts and practices in violation of sections 1036(a)(1)(B) and 1031(c)(1) of the CFPA. 12 U.S.C. §§ 5536(a)(1)(B) and 5531(c)(1).

49. Levitis is a "related person" and a "covered person." 12 U.S.C. § 5481(25). He is liable for the unfair acts and practices described above, in violation of sections 1031(a) and 1036(a)(1) of the CFPA, 12 U.S.C. §§ 5531(a), 5536(a)(1).

COUNT FOUR (DECEPTIVE ACTS AND PRACTICES IN VIOLATION OF THE TSR) ASSERTED AGAINST MISSION AND LEVITIS

50.   The allegations in paragraphs 1-34 are incorporated here by reference.

51.   It is a violation for a debt-relief service provider to fail to disclose before the consumer consents to pay, or to misrepresent in the sale of debt-relief services, the amount of money or percent of debt that the consumer must accumulate before the debt-relief service provider will initiate attempts to settle the debt or before it will make a *bona fide* settlement offer to them. 16 C.F.R. § 310.3(a)(1)(viii)(B), (2)(x). It is also a violation for a debt-relief service provider to fail to disclose before the consumer consents to pay the time by which it will make a *bona fide* settlement offer to the consumer's creditors or debt collectors. 16 C.F.R. § 310.3(a)(1)(viii)(A).

52.   From September 27, 2010 to present, Mission did not disclose either the amounts that must accumulate or the time by which Mission will make a *bona fide* settlement offer, in violation of the TSR.

53.   Because Mission is a "covered person," its conduct in violation of the TSR is unlawful under sections 1031(a) and 1036(a)(1)(A) of the CFPA, 12 U.S.C. §§ 5531(a), 5536(a)(1)(A). 15 U.S.C. § 6102(c)(2).

54.   Levitis is a "related person" and a "covered person." 12 U.S.C. § 5481(25). He is liable for violating sections 1031(a) and 1036(a)(1) of the CFPA, 12 U.S.C. §§ 5531(a), 5536(a)(1).

DEMAND FOR RELIEF

WHEREFORE, the Bureau requests that the Court:

a. permanently enjoin Defendants from committing future violations of the CFPA, 12 U.S.C. §§ 5531, 5536, and the TSR, 16 C.F.R. § 310 *et seq.*;

b. award restitution against Defendants in the amount of all unlawfully collected fees;

c. order disgorgement of ill-gotten profits against Defendants;

d. award civil money penalties against Defendants;

e. award attorneys' fees and costs against Defendants; and

f. award additional relief as the Court may determine to be just and proper.

Dated: May 7, 2013   Respectfully submitted,

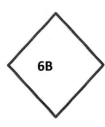 **In what ways does the CFPB have power to enforce UDAAP against Defendants as covered persons?**

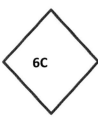 **What is the substantial injury to consumers in this case?**

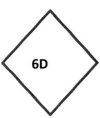 **May consumers bring an action under UDAAP against the Defendants in this case to recover their losses?**

MEMORANDUM OPINION

This case requires the Court to resolve several issues of statutory interpretation with respect to Title X of the Dodd-Frank Wall Street Reform and Consumer Protection Act as well as address whether the structure of the independent executive agency created by the Act, the Consumer Financial Protection Bureau, offends the Constitution. For the reasons that follow, the Court finds (1) the Bureau was within its statutory authority to bring an enforcement action without first engaging in rulemaking, (2) there are no constitutional defects with the structure of the Consumer Financial Protection Bureau, and (3) the Bureau's Complaint against Navient is adequately pleaded.

INTRODUCTION AND PROCEDURAL HISTORY

Plaintiff, the Consumer Financial Protection Bureau ("CFPB" or "Bureau"), filed a Complaint in the above captioned action on January 18, 2017. The eleven count Complaint alleges that Defendants, Navient Corporation, Navient Solutions, Inc., and Pioneer Credit Recovery, Inc., (collectively "Navient"), committed various violations of the Consumer Financial Protection Act ("CFP Act" or "Act"), 12 U.S.C. §§ 5531, 5536 (Counts I-VIII), the Fair Debt Collection Practices Act, 15 U.S.C. § 1692e (Counts IX-X), and Regulation V of the Fair Credit Reporting Act, 12 C.F.R. §1022.42 (Count XI). On March 24, 2017, Navient filed a Motion to Dismiss or, in the alternative, for a More Definite Statement. Specifically, Navient raised the following arguments: (1) Counts I-VIII should be dismissed because the Bureau lacks authority to bring suit under the CFP Act without first engaging in rulemaking to declare specific acts or practices unfair, deceptive, or abusive; (2) the entire Complaint should be dismissed because the structure of the CFPB is unconstitutional and therefore the Director of the Bureau was acting without authority when he authorized the present suit; (3) Counts I-IV and Counts VII-X fail to state a claim for which relief can be granted; and (4) Count VI is so vague that Navient is unable to respond to it by way of an answer. For the reasons that follow, the Court will deny Navient's Motion in its entirety.

FACTUAL ALLEGATIONS

Plaintiff's Complaint alleges the following facts which this Court accepts as true for the purposes of this Motion:

Navient Corporation is a company specializing in loan management, loan servicing, and asset recovery. In that role, Navient Corporation holds contracts with the U.S. Department of Education for the servicing of over six million federal student loans. In turn, Navient Solutions (formerly Sallie Mae) and Pioneer Credit Recovery are both wholly-owned subsidiaries of Navient Corporation. As relevant to this action,

---

[467] *Consumer Fin. Prot. Bureau v. Navient Corp.*, No. 3:17-CV-101, 2017 (M.D. Pa. Aug. 4, 2017).

Navient Solutions services federal and private student loans while Pioneer Credit Recovery performs debt collection activities on delinquent and defaulted student loans.

As a loan servicer, Navient Solutions is responsible for managing student loan borrowers' accounts, which includes activities such as processing monthly payments and communicating with borrowers about repayment of their loans. Navient Solutions has repeatedly encouraged those borrowers who are having trouble paying their monthly bill to contact Navient Solutions. For example, Navient Solutions' webpage contained the following statement: "If you're experiencing problems making your loans payments, please contact us. Our representatives can help you by identifying options and solutions, so you can make the right decision for your situation." The U.S. Department of Education's webpage has similarly encouraged financially troubled borrowers to contact their loan servicer for help.

Most federal loan borrowers experiencing financial difficulties have several options to address unaffordable monthly payments. One such option is forbearance. Although forbearance allows a borrower to stop making payments temporarily, interest continues to accrue and will eventually capitalize on the principal of the loan. Thus, a borrower who places his or her loan in forbearance for a long period of time is likely to see a significant increase in the total amount he or she must ultimately pay back and, upon resuming repayment, may be required to make a larger monthly payment than was required before entering forbearance. As a result, forbearance is not a good option for those experiencing long-term financial hardship.

Another option for borrowers with certain eligible federal loans is to enter into one of several different types of income-driven repayment plans that calculate a borrower's monthly payment based on his or her income and family size and result in an affordable monthly payment that can be as low as $0 per month. For some borrowers, income-driven repayment plans offer several secondary benefits as well, including (1) an interest subsidy where the government pays off the unpaid accruing interest, preventing it from being added to the principal, and (2) treating low payments as "qualifying payments" for certain programs that forgive the balance of the loan after a borrower makes a certain number of qualifying payments. Because of these benefits, income-driven repayment plans are usually the best option for those borrowers experiencing long-term financial hardship.

Nevertheless, entering a borrower into an income-driven repayment plan is more time-intensive and expensive for Navient Solutions then putting a borrower's loan into forbearance. While a Navient Solutions customer service representative can put a borrower's loan into forbearance quickly over the phone, generally without filling out any paperwork, entering a borrower into an income-driven repayment plan involves lengthy conversations about different plans, helping a borrower fill out the initial application, and possessing both the initial and annual renewal paperwork. Thus, Navient Solutions has had to increase its staff size—and overall operating costs—as the number of borrowers entering income-driven repayment plans has increased. Additionally, taking the time to enter a borrower into an income-driven repayment plan is less appealing to Navient Solutions' customer service representatives because they are compensated, in part, based on how short they can keep their average call. As a result, Navient Solutions, through its customer service representatives, routinely entered financially distressed borrowers into forbearance without adequately discussing—or sometimes discussing at all—the option of income-driven repayment plans. As a consequence of guiding borrowers—including those borrowers who had demonstrated long-term financial difficulties—into forbearance and even multiple consecutive forbearances, Navient Solutions routinely had more borrowers with loans in forbearance then in income-driven repayment plans. This has imposed significant monetary costs on those borrowers who qualified for an income-driven repayment plan but whose loans were placed in forbearance.

For those borrowers who did enroll in an income-driven repayment plan, Navient Solutions was obligated to send a written notice with the requirements for annual renewal of the plan. Unless a borrower properly recertified his or her income and family size once a year, the borrower would automatically be removed from the income-driven repayment plan. Even temporary removal from the plan would result in one or more of the following negative consequences for borrowers: (1) an immediate increase in his or her monthly payment; (2) the addition of any unpaid, accrued interest onto the principal; and (3) the loss of an interest subsidy.

From mid-2010 to March of 2015, for those borrowers who had consented to receiving electronic communication, Navient Solutions sent borrowers an email with the subject line of either "Your Sallie Mae Account Information" or "New Document Ready to View," when the borrower's annual renewal notice was available. Upon opening the email, a borrower would be instructed that "a new education loan document is available. Please log in to your account to view it." The email would also contain a hyperlink to Navient Solutions' website, where a borrower could log in to his or her account and view the renewal notice. Upon changing both the subject line and body of the email in March of 2015 to contain more descriptive information concerning which specific document was available, renewal rates for borrowers more than doubled.

For those borrowers who had not consented to receiving electronic communication, Navient Solutions would send the annual renewal notice through the mail. From January of 2010 until December of 2012, the mailed notice stated that the borrower's participation in an income-driven repayment plan would "expire in approximately 90 days" and that the "renewal process may take at least 30 days." It further told borrowers to fill out the renewal forms completely and that if a borrower "provid[ed] incorrect or incomplete information the [renewal] process will be delayed." The renewal notice, however, did not (1) provide any specific date for which a borrower's participation in an income-driven repayment plan would expire, (2) specify that submitting an incomplete or inaccurate renewal form may result in his or her removal, at least temporarily, from the plan, or (3) explain that certain irreversible consequences such as the capitalization of unpaid interest would occur if the plan expired, even temporarily.

Another one of Navient Solutions' responsibilities was the processing of student loan payments. This involved receiving a borrower's check and both allocating the payment between his or her multiple loans and applying the payment to each loan according to the terms of the promissory note. Many payments, however, were either misallocated or misapplied by Navient Solutions. These errors occurred for multiple reasons, including that Navient Solutions (1) did not disclose its payment allocation methodology, (2) failed to read borrowers' allocation and application instructions, and (3) failed to implement borrowers' instructions properly. Such processing errors resulted in a range of negative consequences for borrowers including the assessment of improper late fees and interest, the loss of certain benefits, and having inaccurate negative information about them shared with consumer reporting agencies.

If a borrower discovered such a processing error, he or she would need to contact Navient Solutions to correct it. Nevertheless, even after reporting an error, some borrowers experienced the same processing errors month after month. This occurred because an error reported only to the first level of Navient Solutions' customer service was not categorized or tagged in such a manner as to allow the company to identify the underlying issues causing the errors. As a result, Navient Solutions was generally unable to prevent the reoccurrence of errors that borrowers were experiencing month after month.

For those borrowers who failed to make payments on their student loans, after a certain number of missed payments, the loan would enter default status. Some student loans which entered default were referred to Pioneer Credit Recovery for collection. In addition to being referred to collection, there are at least two other negative consequences of a federal student loan entering default. First, multiple negative notations indicating the default are placed on the borrower's credit report. Second, the U.S. Department of Education begins assessing collection fees on the loan.

When certain federal student loans entered default, Pioneer could enroll borrowers into the federal loan rehabilitation program. The federal loan rehabilitation program helps borrowers get their loan out of default status and back into active repayment status. Additionally, completion of the program removes some, but not all, of the negative notations from a borrower's credit history and forgives any remaining unpaid collection fees. Nevertheless, in calls with borrowers, Pioneer collectors routinely overstated the benefits of the rehabilitation program by claiming that all negative information on a borrower's credit history would be removed and all collection fees would be forgiven.

. . .

Statutory Authority to Bring Suit before Rulemaking

Navient first argues that the CFPB lacks statutory authority to bring an enforcement action without first engaging in rulemaking to declare a specific act or practice unfair, deceptive, or abusive. This argument requires the Court to interpret provisions of Title X of the Dodd-Frank Wall Street Reform and Consumer Protection Act. "The first step in interpreting a statute is to determine 'whether the language at issue has a plain and unambiguous meaning with regard to the particular dispute in the case.'" *Marshak v. Treadwell*, 240 F.3d 184, 192 (3d Cir. 2001) (quoting *Robinson v. Shell Oil Co.*, 519 U.S. 337, 340, 117 S. Ct. 843, 136 L. Ed. 2d 808 (1997)). "The plainness or ambiguity of statutory language is determined by reference to the language itself, the specific context in which that language is used, and the broader context of the statute as a whole." *Robinson*, 519 U.S. at 341. "When the statutory language has a clear meaning, [a court] need not look further." *Valansi v. Ashcroft*, 278 F.3d 203, 209 (3d Cir. 2002).

Here, the statutory provision at issue provides, in relevant part,

(a) In general

The Bureau may take any action authorized under part E to prevent a covered person or service provider from committing or engaging in an unfair, deceptive, or abusive act or practice under Federal law in connection with any transaction with a consumer for a consumer financial product or service, or the offering of a consumer financial product or service.

(b) Rulemaking

The Bureau may prescribe rules applicable to a covered person or service provider identifying as unlawful unfair, deceptive, or abusive acts or practices in connection with any transaction with a consumer for a consumer financial product or service, or the offering of a consumer financial product or service. Rules under this section may include requirements for the purpose of preventing such acts or practices. 12 U.S.C. § 5531. Part E of the Act, titled "Enforcement Powers," provides, in part, that "[i]f any person violates a Federal consumer financial law, the Bureau may . . . commence a civil action against such person to impose a civil penalty or to seek all appropriate legal and equitable relief including a permanent or temporary injunction as permitted by law." 12 U.S.C. § 5564(a).

In addition to section 5531, section 5492 states that "[t]he Bureau is authorized to establish the general policies of the Bureau with respect to all executive and administrative functions, including . . . implementing the Federal consumer financial laws through rules, orders, guidance, interpretations, statements of policy, examinations, and enforcement actions." 12 U.S.C. § 5492(a)(10). Further, section 5512 provides that "[t]he Director may prescribe rules and issue orders and guidance, as may be necessary or appropriate to enable the Bureau to administer and carry out the purposes and objectives of the Federal consumer financial laws, and to prevent evasions thereof," and then delineates standards for rulemaking. 12 U.S.C. § 5512(b).

Navient's argument is in essence that the CFPB is authorized to "take any action authorized under part E"—which includes enforcement actions—only to prevent a regulated entity "from committing or engaging in an unfair, deceptive, or abusive act or practice under Federal law." 12 U.S.C. § 5531(a). According to Navient, the use of the term "under Federal law" looks to the following subsection on rulemaking which allows the CFPB to "identify[ ] as unlawful unfair, deceptive, or abusive acts or practices." Thus, Navient argues that until the CFPB uses its rulemaking authority to declare an act or practice unlawful, that act or practice is not unlawful under federal law, and therefore cannot serve as a basis for an enforcement action.

This argument fails in light of another section of the Act that plainly declares that "[i]t shall be unlawful for . . . any covered person or service provider . . . to engage in any unfair, deceptive, or abusive act or practice." 12 U.S.C. § 5536(a)(1)(B). Thus, there appears to be no reason why the CFPB cannot base an enforcement action on a violation of this provision of federal law. Indeed, reading sections 5531(a), 5536(a)(1)(B), and 5564(a) together, their plain language provides that the CFPB may, among other things, commence a civil action "to prevent a covered person or service provider from committing or engaging in an unfair, deceptive, or abusive act or practice under Federal law," 12 U.S.C. § 5531(a), and that one such violation of federal law occurs when a "covered person . . . engage[s] in any unfair, deceptive, or abusive act[s] or practice[s]," 12 U.S.C. § 5536(a)(1)(B).

At oral argument, Navient argued that subsections (c) and (d) of section 5531 support its position:

(c) Unfairness

(1) In general The Bureau shall have no authority under this section to declare an act or practice in connection with a transaction with a consumer for a consumer financial product or service, or the offering of a consumer financial product or service, to be unlawful on the grounds that such act or practice is unfair, unless the Bureau has a reasonable basis to conclude that— (A) the act or practice causes or is likely to cause substantial injury to consumers which is not reasonably avoidable by consumers; and (B) such substantial injury is not outweighed by countervailing benefits to consumers or to competition. . . .

(d) Abusive

The Bureau shall have no authority under this section to declare an act or practice abusive in connection with the provision of a consumer financial product or service, unless the act or practice— (1) materially interferes with the ability of a consumer to understand a term or condition of a consumer financial product or service; or (2) takes unreasonable advantage of— (A) a lack of understanding on the part of the consumer of the material risks, costs, or conditions of the product or service; (B) the inability of the consumer to protect the interests of the consumer in selecting or using a consumer financial product or service; or (C) the reasonable reliance by the consumer on a covered person to act in the interests of the consumer. 12 U.S.C. § 5531. Navient argues that these provisions—specifically, the use of the word "declare" in each subsection—constrain the CFPB's authority to engage in rulemaking. According to Navient, because "declare" refers to rulemaking, and not litigation, the only way the CFPB would be statutorily authorized to initiate litigation is in the circumstances where the Bureau first declares an act or practice unlawful through rulemaking. Otherwise, Navient contends, the CFPB could avoid these limitations by bringing a lawsuit and arguing that unfairness and abusiveness mean whatever the Bureau wanted it to mean without constraint from the Act.

Navient, however, has failed to explain—or cite to any authority which would explain—why "declare" must refer only to rulemaking and not litigation, and why it would be improper for the CFPB to declare something unlawful through litigation. *See generally FTC v. Wyndham Worldwide Corp.*, 799 F.3d 236 (3d Cir. 2015). The Court is not persuaded that the language of section 5531 should be read in the manner advocated by Navient. Subsections (c) and (d) of section 5531 fall within the section of the Act titled "Prohibiting unfair, deceptive, or abusive acts or practices." That section states that the Bureau may (a) "take any action authorized under part E to prevent a covered person or service provider from committing or engaging in an unfair, deceptive, or abusive act or practice under Federal law," and (b) "prescribe rules applicable to a covered person or service provider identifying as unlawful unfair, deceptive, or abusive acts or practices." 12 U.S.C. § 5531(a)-(b). The section then states the requirements that must be met before the Bureau can declare an act or practice unfair or abusive. 12

U.S.C. § 5531(c)-(d). There is no reason, therefore that subsections (c) and (d) should not constrain the CFPB equally in litigation and in rulemaking.

In the end, Navient is unable to point to any clear language in the statutory scheme that requires the CFPB to first engage in rulemaking before bringing an enforcement action for unfair, deceptive, or abusive acts or practices. The plain meaning of the statutory language provides that the CFPB has both the power to engage in rulemaking, 12 U.S.C. §§ 5512(b)(1), 5531(b), and litigation, 12 U.S.C §§ 5531(a), 5564(a), to address unfair, deceptive, or abusive acts or practices. The most harmonious construction of these provisions is that the CFPB may proceed either via rulemaking or an enforcement action. This interpretation is supported not only by the plain language of the provisions at issue, but finds support in other places as well.

First, all of the language regarding rulemaking is permissive. *See* 12 U.S.C. § 5531(b) ("The Bureau may prescribe rules . . . ."); 12 U.S.C. § 5512(b)(1) ("The Director may prescribe rules . . . ."). Nevertheless, the Act provides that the Bureau "shall regulate the offering and provision of consumer financial products or services under the Federal consumer financial laws." 12 U.S.C. § 5491(a); *see also* 12 U.S.C. § 5511(a) ("The Bureau shall seek to implement and, where applicable, enforce Federal consumer financial law consistently for the purpose of ensuring that all consumers have access to markets for consumer financial products and services and that markets for consumer financial products and services are fair, transparent, and competitive."). Thus, if rulemaking was a prerequisite for the Bureau to exercise any of its enforcement powers under Part E, it would make little sense for rulemaking to be designated permissive in the language of the statute itself.

Second, this interpretation is consonant with how courts have interpreted the older but analogous language found in the Federal Trade Commission Act ("FTC Act"). That scheme provides, in part, that the Federal Trade Commission ("FTC") shall have no authority under this section . . . to declare unlawful an act or practice on the grounds that such act or practice is unfair unless the act or practice causes or is likely to cause substantial injury to consumers which is not reasonably avoidable by consumers themselves and not outweighed by countervailing benefits to consumers or to competition. 15 U.S.C. § 45(n). This Court is unaware of any court that has held that the use of "declare" in section 45(n) requires the FTC to proceed via rulemaking before institution of an enforcement action. Instead, "Circuit Courts of Appeal have affirmed FTC unfairness actions in a variety of contexts without preexisting rules or regulations specifically addressing the conduct-at-issue." *FTC v. Wyndham Worldwide Corp.*, 10 F. Supp. 3d 602, 618 (D.N.J. 2014) aff'd, 799 F.3d 236 (3d Cir. 2015).

In sum, the Court finds that the plain language of the CFP Act does not impose a requirement on the Bureau to engage in rulemaking before bringing an enforcement action. Nonetheless, Navient contends that dismissal of Counts I-VIII are still warranted because the CFPB's failure to promulgate rules before filing the present action has left Navient without fair notice of what acts or practices the Bureau considered unfair, deceptive, or abusive. The Navient Defendants, however, do not contend that the CFP Act is unconstitutionally vague on its face. Instead, they are arguing that "[t]he CFPB's suit is an attempt to retroactively 'declare' new student loan servicing obligations."

Navient's argument misstates the nature of this lawsuit. The CFP Act makes it "unlawful for . . . any covered person or service provider . . . to engage in any unfair, deceptive, or abusive act or practice." 12 U.S.C. § 5536(a)(1)(B). The CFPB's lawsuit does not retroactively impose any requirements on Navient. Instead, it seeks to impose liability for Navient's alleged acts or practices that the CFPB believes violates section 5536(a)(1)(B) of the CFP Act. As discussed further below, this case involves "ordinary judicial interpretation of a civil statute." *Wyndham*, 799 F.3d at 253. As such, the relevant legal question is not whether Navient had fair notice of what acts or practices the CFPB has interpreted as unlawful under the Act, but only whether Navient had fair notice of what the Act requires.

This same argument, within the context of the FTC Act, arose in *FTC v. Wyndham Worldwide Corporation*, 799 F.3d 236 (3d Cir. 2015). In *Wyndham*, the FTC filed a lawsuit against Wyndham Worldwide Corporation alleging that the company's deficient cybersecurity, which had led to customer data being stolen, was an unfair practice in violation of the FTC Act. *Id.* at 240. Wyndham moved to dismiss, arguing that because there was no relevant FTC rule or adjudication on the matter, it lacked fair notice that its cybersecurity practices could violate the unfairness provision of the FTC Act. *Id.* On interlocutory appeal of the denial of Wyndham's motion, the Third Circuit held that if the federal courts are to decide whether Wyndham's conduct was unfair in the first instance under the statute without deferring to any FTC interpretation, then this case involves ordinary judicial interpretation of a civil statute . . . . The relevant question is not whether Wyndham had fair notice of the FTC's interpretation of the statute, but whether Wyndham had fair notice of what the statute itself requires. *Id.* at 253-54. With the issue properly framed, the Third Circuit found that "for civil statutes that regulate economic activities," such as the FTC Act, "a party lacks fair notice when the relevant standard is 'so vague as to be no rule or standard at all.'" *Id.* at 250, 255 (quoting CMR D.N. Corp. v. City of Phila., 703 F.3d 612, 631-32 (3d Cir. 2013)). Stated otherwise, "[f]air notice is satisfied . . . as long as the company can reasonably foresee that a court could construe its conduct as falling within the meaning of the statute." *Id.* at 256.

Therefore, in light of *Wyndham*, Navient's fair notice argument fails if it was reasonably foreseeable to Navient that a court could construe their alleged conduct as unfair, deceptive, or abusive under the CFP Act. Navient, however, has only advanced arguments as to why it did not have fair notice of the Bureau's interpretation of the CFP Act. But, as discussed above, the CFPB's interpretation of whether its allegations constitute unfair, deceptive, or abusive acts or practices is irrelevant to whether Navient had fair notice of the conduct the CFP Act itself proscribes. Stripped of these irrelevant arguments, Navient's position reduces to its assertion that it complied with the Higher Education Act, the Department of Education's regulations related to the Higher Education Act, and Navient's contracts with the Department of Education. Nevertheless, even assuming the truth of these assertions, complying with other statutory, regulatory, and contractual obligations does not relieve Navient of its obligation to refrain from committing acts that are unlawful under the CFP Act. Nor does it begin to explain why it was not reasonably foreseeable to Navient that a court could construe the acts or practices alleged in the Complaint as violations of the CFP Act. As Navient has put forth no specific argument as to how or why the standards found in the CFP Act are so vague as to be no standards at all when applied to the facts of this case, the Court need not address this argument further. *See Commonwealth of Pa. v. HHS*, 101 F.3d. 939, 945 (3d Cir. 1996) (noting that arguments that are not squarely argued are waived).

In sum, the Court finds no merit in Navient's assertion that the CFP Act requires the CFPB to engage in rulemaking before initiating an enforcement action, or that Navient lacked fair notice of what the CFP Act proscribes.

Constitutionality of the Agency's Structure

Next, Navient argues that the CFPB's structure improperly interferes with the President's powers under Article II of the Constitution because it combines the following three characteristics: (1) the agency is headed by a single director who wields executive power; (2) the director is only removable for cause; and (3) the agency is funded outside the normal budgetary process. At oral argument, counsel for Navient made clear that it is not any one of these attributes in isolation that renders the Bureau constitutionally problematic, but the combination of all three together. Thus, to fully understand Navient's arguments, it is important to first understand how the CFPB is structured.

The Consumer Financial Protection Bureau is an independent agency within the Federal Reserve System created by the Consumer Financial Protection Act of 2010, otherwise known as Title X of the Dodd-Frank Wall Street Reform and Consumer Protection Act. 12 U.S.C. § 5491(a); Pub. L. No. 111-203, § 1001, 124 Stat. 1376, 1955 (2010). The Bureau is headed by a single director, appointed by the President with the advice and consent of the Senate, who serves a fixed five year term. 12 U.S.C. § 5491(b)(1)-(2), (c)(1). "The President may remove the Director for inefficiency, neglect of duty, or malfeasance in office." 12 U.S.C. § 5491(c)(3). As for funding, the Director determines the amount of the Bureau's yearly operating expenses and that amount is transferred to the CFPB from the Federal Reserve System. 12 U.S.C. § 5497(a)(1). In a given fiscal year, however, the Bureau is prohibited from receiving more than twelve percent of the Federal Reserve System's operating expenses. 12 U.S.C. § 5497(a)(2)(A)(iii).

The CFP Act instructs that the Bureau "shall regulate the offering and provision of consumer financial products or services under the Federal consumer financial laws." 12 U.S.C. § 5491(a). To accomplish this directive, the Bureau can "prescribe rules and issue orders and guidance," 12 U.S.C. § 5512(b)(1), "engage in joint investigations and requests for information," 12 U.S.C. § 5562(a)(1), "conduct hearings and adjudication proceedings," 12 U.S.C. § 5563(a), "commence a civil action," 12 U.S.C. § 5564(a), and refer appropriate matters for criminal prosecution, 12 U.S.C. § 5566. Generally speaking, the CFPB may only exercise these authorities within the realm of federal consumer financial law, but the Act also provides more specific subject matter limitations on the Bureau's powers. 12 U.S.C. § 5517.

In both their brief and at oral argument, Navient argued that this structure brings the CFPB so far outside of the control of the President that it violates Article II of the Constitution. To address this argument, the Court begins by reviewing the underlying principles that will guide its analysis of the issue at hand.

Article II of the Constitution begins by proclaiming that "[t]he executive Power shall be vested in a President of the United States of America." U.S. CONST. art. II, § 1, cl. 1. It further instructs that the President "shall take Care that the Laws be faithfully executed." U.S. CONST. art. II, § 3. With respect to the appointment of officers, the Constitution provides that the President shall nominate, and by and with the Advice and Consent of the Senate, shall appoint Ambassadors, other public Ministers and Consuls, Judges of the supreme Court, and all other Officers of the United States, whose Appointments are not herein otherwise provided for, and which shall be established by Law: but the Congress may by Law vest the Appointment of such inferior Officers, as they think proper, in the President alone, in the Courts of Law, or in the Heads of Departments. U.S. CONST. art. II, § 2, cl. 2. Thus, under the Appointments Clause, officers are divided into two classes. *United States v. Germaine*, 99 U.S. 508, 509, 25 L. Ed. 482 (1878). "Principal officers are selected by the President with the advice and consent of the Senate. Inferior officers Congress may allow to be appointed by the President alone, by the heads of departments, or by the Judiciary." *Buckley v. Valeo*, 424 U.S. 1,132, 96 S. Ct. 612, 46 L. Ed. 2d 659 (1976).

Nevertheless, while the Constitution provides some detail concerning the appointment of officers, the document does not speak to the President's power to remove either principal or inferior officers. Accordingly, in 1926, the Supreme Court took up the question of what limits could properly be placed on the President's power to remove appointed officers within the executive branch. *Myers v. United States*, 272 U.S. 52, 47 S. Ct. 21, 71 L. Ed. 160 (1926). *Myers* involved a postmaster of the first class who was appointed by the President with the advice and consent of the Senate for a four year term. *Id.* at 106. The relevant statute provided that postmasters of the first class could only "be removed by the President by and with the advice and consent of the Senate." *Id.* at 107. Nevertheless, two and a half years into Myers's term, the President demanded his resignation. *Id.* at 106. When Myers refused, the President, through the Postmaster General, terminated him without Senate approval. *Id.* Myers then filed a lawsuit for back pay. *Id.* In a lengthy opinion authored by former President and then Chief Justice Taft, the Supreme Court, after a thorough review of the historical record, held that Congress could not "draw to itself, or to either branch of it, the power to remove or the right to participate in the exercise of that power." *Id.* at 161.

Nine years later, the Supreme Court addressed a slightly different question in *Humphrey's Executor v. United States*, 295 U.S. 602, 55 S. Ct. 869, 79 L. Ed. 1611 (1935). Humphrey was a principal officer appointed by President Hoover, with the advice and consent of the Senate, to serve a seven year term as a commissioner on the FTC. *Id.* at 618. Unlike *Myers*, the relevant statute in this case did not condition removal of the commissioner on Senate approval, but instead provided "that 'any commissioner may be removed by the President for inefficiency, neglect of duty, or malfeasance in office.'" *Id.* at 619 (quoting 15 U.S.C. § 41). Two years into Humphrey's term, President Roosevelt was elected and requested Humphrey's resignation so that the President could appoint someone of his own choosing. *Id.* at 618-19. After Humphrey refused to resign, the President terminated him. *Id.* at 619.

After first determining that the language of the statute restricted the President's power to remove commissioners at will, the Court turned to the question of whether such a restriction was an unconstitutional limit on the President's Article II powers. *Id.* at 621-26. On that point, the government argued that language in Myers supported an unfettered presidential power of removal, such that any limitation on the President's ability to terminate executive officers at will was unconstitutional. *Id.* at 626. The Court responded that the narrow point actually decided [in *Myers*] was only that the President had power to remove a postmaster of the first class, without the advice and consent of the Senate as required by act of Congress. In the course of the opinion of the court, expressions occur which tend to sustain the government's contention, but these are beyond the point involved and, therefore, do not come within the rule of *stare decisis*. In so far as they are out of harmony with the views here set forth, these expressions are disapproved. *Id.* The Court then went on to describe the FTC as "an administrative body created by Congress to carry into effect legislative policies embodied in the statute in accordance with the legislative standard therein prescribed, and to perform other specified duties as a legislative or as a judicial aid." *Id.* at 628. Therefore, according to the Court, the FTC could not "in any proper sense be characterized as an arm or an eye of the executive," but instead "acts in part quasi legislatively and in part quasi judicially."

Accordingly, the unanimous Court held that the "illimitable power of removal is not possessed by the President in respect of officers of the character of those just named." *Id.* at 629. Looking to future cases, the Court instructed that "[w]hether the power of the President to remove an officer shall prevail over the authority of Congress to condition the power by fixing a definite term and precluding a removal except for cause will depend upon the character of the office." *Id.* at 631.

The Court reaffirmed this principle in 1958 when it held that the President could not, without cause, remove a member of the War Claims Commission—a body set up to adjudicate certain classes of claims involving those who sustained an injury during World War II—because that agency was judicial in nature. *Wiener v. United States*, 357 U.S. 349, 355-56, 78 S. Ct. 1275, 2 L. Ed. 2d 1377 (1958). In response to "the claim that the President could remove a member of an adjudicatory body like the War Claims Commission merely because he wanted his own appointees on such a Commission," the Court "conclude[d] that no such power is given to the President directly by the Constitution, and none is impliedly conferred upon him by statute simply because Congress said nothing about it." *Id.* at 356.

Over thirty years later, in *Morrison v. Olson*, 487 U.S. 654, 108 S. Ct. 2597, 101 L. Ed. 2d 569 (1988), the Supreme Court addressed the question of whether Congress may place restrictions on the President's power to remove an inferior officer within the executive branch who performs core executive functions. Specifically, *Morrison* involved Title VI of the Ethics in Government Act, 28 U.S.C. §§ 591-599, which allowed a special court, upon request by the Attorney General, to appoint "an 'independent counsel' to investigate and, if appropriate, prosecute certain high-ranking Government officials for violations of federal criminal laws." *Id.* at 660-61. The Office of the Independent Counsel automatically terminated upon completion of his or her investigations or prosecutions, but otherwise the independent counsel could only be removed by the Attorney General and only for cause. *Id.* at 663-64. After one such independent counsel was appointed pursuant to the Ethics Act, she caused a grand jury to issue subpoenas to several government officials. *Id.* at 668. Those officials moved to quash the subpoenas on the basis that, among other reasons, the Ethics Act violated Article II and the principle of separation of powers. *Id.* at 668-69.

Responding to the argument that Myers was controlling because the independent counsel exercised core executive powers, the Court held that the determination of whether the Constitution allows Congress to impose a "good cause"-type restriction on the President's power to remove an official cannot be made to turn on whether or not that official is classified as "purely executive." The analysis contained in our removal cases is designed not to define rigid categories of those officials who may or may not be removed at will by the President, but to ensure that Congress does not interfere with the President's exercise of the "executive power" and his constitutionally appointed duty to "take care that the laws be faithfully executed" under Article II. . . . [T]he characterization of the agencies in *Humphrey's Executor* and *Wiener* as "quasi-legislative" or "quasi-judicial" in large part reflected our judgment that it was not essential to the President's proper execution of his Article II powers that these agencies be headed up by individuals who were removable at will. We do not mean to suggest that an analysis of the functions served by the officials at issue is irrelevant. But the real question is whether the removal restrictions are of such a nature that they impede the President's ability to perform his constitutional duty, and the functions of the officials in question must be analyzed in that light. *Id.* at 689-91 (footnotes omitted). The Court then analyzed whether the for cause removal provision inhibited the President's ability to perform his constitutional functions under Article II. *Id.* at 691. After determining that the independent counsel was "an inferior officer under the Appointments Clause, with limited jurisdiction and tenure and lacking policymaking or significant administrative authority," but one who "exercise[d] no small amount of discretion and judgment," the Court found that "the President's need to control the exercise of that discretion" was not "so central to the functioning of the Executive Branch as to require as a matter of constitutional law that the counsel be terminable at will by the President." *Id.* at 691-92. Further, with respect to the President's Article II powers, the Court also found that the removal provision did not impermissibly burden[ ] the President's power to control or supervise the independent counsel, as an executive official, in the execution of his or her duties under the Act. This is not a case in which the power to remove an executive official has been completely stripped from the President, thus providing no means for the President to ensure the "faithful execution" of the laws. Rather, because the independent counsel may be terminated for "good cause," the Executive, through the Attorney General, retains ample authority to assure that the counsel is competently performing his or her statutory responsibilities in a manner that comports with the provisions of the Act. . . . *Id.* at 692. Thus, the Court concluded that the for cause removal provision did not "sufficiently deprive[ ] the President of control over the independent counsel" so as "to interfere impermissibly with his constitutional obligation to ensure the faithful execution of the laws." *Id.* at 693.

Turning to the question of whether the Ethics Act violated the principle of separation of powers, the Court first observed that this was not a case in which there was any legislative or judicial usurpation of executive functions. *Id.* at 693-95. The Court then held that the Ethics Act did not "impermissibly undermine[ ] the powers of the Executive Branch, or disrupt[ ] the proper balance between the coordinate branches by preventing the Executive Branch from accomplishing its constitutionally assigned functions." *Id.* at 695. In coming to this conclusion, the Court found that the Act does give the Attorney General several means of supervising or controlling the prosecutorial powers that may be wielded by an independent counsel. Most importantly, the Attorney General retains the power to remove the counsel for "good cause," a power that we have already concluded provides the Executive with substantial ability to ensure that the laws are "faithfully executed" by an independent counsel. *Id.* at 696.

Most recently, in 2010, the Court in *Free Enterprise Fund v. Public Company Accounting Oversight Board*, 561 U.S. 477, 483-84, 130 S. Ct. 3138, 177 L. Ed. 2d 706 (2010), addressed the question of whether an inferior officer on the Public Company Accounting Oversight Board may be given for cause removal protection when the principal officers of the Securities and Exchange Commission who oversee the Board can themselves only be removed for cause. Finding such a structure unconstitutional, the Court distinguished prior decisions that had upheld for cause removal restrictions, reasoning that [t]he added layer of tenure protection makes a difference. Without a layer of insulation between the Commission and the Board, the Commission could remove a Board member at any time, and therefore would be fully responsible for what the Board does. The President could then hold the Commission to account for its supervision of the Board, to the same extent that he may hold the Commission to account for everything else it does. A second level of tenure protection changes the nature of the President's review. Now the Commission cannot remove a Board member at will. The President therefore cannot hold the Commission fully accountable for the Board's conduct, to the same extent that he may hold the Commission accountable for everything else that it does. *Id.* at 495-96. Thus, the Court concluded, "[b]y granting the Board executive power without the Executive's oversight, this Act subverts the President's ability to ensure that the laws are faithfully executed." *Id.* at 498.

With this line of cases to guide its analysis, the Court addresses whether the structure particular to the CFPB violates the Constitution. Even on this narrow point, however, the Court does not write on a blank slate. Four published cases have addressed this topic as of this writing.

The first two published opinions, *CFPB v. Morgan Drexen, Inc.*, 60 F. Supp. 3d 1082 (C.D. Cal. 2014), and *CFPB v. ITT Educational Services, Inc.*, 219 F. Supp. 3d 878 (S.D. Ind. 2015), found no constitutional deficiencies. Relying on *Humphrey's Executor* and *Morrison*, both district courts found the for cause removal provision did not impermissibly invade the President's Article II powers. *Morgan Drexen*, 60 F. Supp. 3d at 1087-89; *ITT Educ. Servs.*, 219 F. Supp. 3d at 893-94. Similarly, both courts also rejected the idea that there was any constitutional significance to the fact that (1) the CFPB is funded outside the normal appropriation process, and (2) the CFPB is run by a single director, as opposed to a multi-member board or commission. *Morgan Drexen*, 60 F. Supp. 3d at 1089, 1092; *ITT Educ. Servs.*, 219 F. Supp. 3d at 894-97. Finally, both courts also rejected the argument that the combination of the above characteristics in one agency rendered the CFPB unconstitutional. *Morgan Drexen*, 60 F. Supp. 3d at 1092; *ITT Educ. Servs.*, 219 F. Supp. 3d at 895.

The Court of Appeals for the District of Columbia was the next court to issue a published opinion on this topic. *See PHH Corp. v. CFPB*, 839 F.3d 1, (D.C. Cir. 2016), *reh'g en banc granted, order vacated*, (Feb. 16, 2017). In a lengthy and detailed opinion, the PHH court found it constitutionally untenable for the CFPB to be headed by a single director who could only be removed for cause. *Id.* at 8. The panel's majority summarized their rationale as follows: In order to preserve individual liberty and ensure accountability, Article II of the Constitution assigns the executive power to the President. The President operates with the assistance of subordinates, but the President acts as a critical check on those subordinates. That check provides accountability and protects against arbitrary decision-making by executive agencies, thereby helping to safeguard individual liberty. Article II has been interpreted by the Supreme Court to allow independent agencies in certain circumstances. Independent agencies lack the ordinary constitutional checks and balances that come from Presidential supervision and direction. But to ensure some check against arbitrary decision-making and to help preserve individual liberty, independent agencies have traditionally been structured as multi-member bodies where the commissioners or board members can check one another. The check from other commissioners or board members substitutes for the check by the President. As an independent agency with just a single Director, the CFPB represents a sharp break from historical practice, lacks the critical internal check on arbitrary decision-making, and poses a far greater threat to individual liberty than does a multi-member independent agency. *Id.* at 30-31. To remedy the constitutional deficiency, the court severed the for cause removal provision, making the Director removable at the will of the President. *Id.* at 39.

Subsequently, the Court of Appeals for the District of Columbia granted a rehearing en banc and the PHH opinion was vacated. *See PHH Corp. v. CFPB*, 2017 U.S. App. LEXIS 2733 (D.C. Cir. 2017). As of this writing, the en banc court has not issued an opinion.

The latest published opinion to address the constitutionality of the CFPB's structure is *CFPB v. Future Income Payments, LLC*, ___ F. Supp. 3d. ___, 2017 WL 2190069 (C.D. Cal. 2017). Applying *Humphrey's Executor* and *Morrison*, the Future Income court found that "the CFPB's structure is at least as constitutionally sound as the FTC" and that "there [was] no textual basis in the Constitution for concluding that independent agencies must be led by multimember commissions." *Id.* at *6. Addressing the PHH decision, the court observed that whether to structure an independent agency as a multimember or director-led body depends on the proper weighing of the advantages and drawbacks of each structure. But neither the text of the Constitution nor any Supreme Court precedent supports drawing a constitutional distinction between multimember and director-led independent agencies, so the question is properly reserved for the political branches and the democratic process. *Id.* at *9.

This Court comes to the same conclusion as that reached by our sister district courts, namely that *Humphrey's Executor* and *Morrison* compel the conclusion that the CFPB's structure does not violate the Constitution. As discussed above, Navient has argued that the combination of three characteristics of the Bureau's structure render it unconstitutional: (1) the agency is headed by a single director who wields executive power; (2) the director is only removable for cause; and (3) the agency is funded outside the normal budgetary process. Although it is not entirely clear whether Navient has argued that this structure violates Article II by impermissibly interfering with the President's duty to "take Care that the Laws be faithfully executed," or whether they have argued that it violates the principle of separation of powers by undermining the President's executive powers—*Morrison* clearly addressed these as two separate and distinct concerns—this Court is convinced that, under either analysis, the Bureau's structure is not constitutionally deficient.

With respect to whether CFPB's structure violates Article II, the Court first notes that the provision providing that the Director of the Bureau may only be removed for cause is nearly identical to the for cause removal provision found to be constitutionally permissible in Humphrey's Executor. Compare 12 U.S.C. § 5491(c)(3) ("The President may remove the Director for inefficiency, neglect of duty, or malfeasance in office") with 15 U.S.C. § 41 ("Any Commissioner may be removed by the President for inefficiency, neglect of duty, or malfeasance in office."). The similarities between *Humphrey's Executor* and this case do not end there. First, both the CFPB and the agency at issue in *Humphrey's Executor*, the FTC, are charged with similar tasks in comparable subject matter. In 1935, the FTC was tasked with "prevent[ing] persons, partnerships, or corporations . . . from using unfair methods of competition in commerce." Federal Trade Commission Act, Pub. L. No. 63-203, § 5, 38 Stat. 717, 719 (1914). The Bureau is similarly directed to "regulate the offering and provision of consumer financial products or services under the Federal consumer financial laws," 12 U.S.C. § 5491(a), and "prevent a covered person or service provider from committing or engaging in an unfair, deceptive, or abusive act or practice under Federal law in connection with" consumer financial products, 12 U.S.C. § 5531(a).

Second, "[t]he CFPB's authority closely parallels the FTC's powers considered in Humphrey's Executor." *Future Income Payments, LLC*, 2017 WL 2190069, at *6. Just as the CFPB does now, in 1935 the FTC had the power to conduct investigations, promulgate rules, conduct administrative adjudications, and issue cease-and-desist orders. Compare 12 U.S.C. §§ 5512(b), 5562-5563 with Federal Trade Commission Act, §§ 5-6, 9. Unlike the CFPB, however, in 1935 the FTC could not bring a civil action in a district court for monetary penalties. Nevertheless, the FTC could bring actions in court to enforce its orders and regulated entities were subject to fines for failing to comply with lawful requests of the Commission. Federal Trade Commission Act, §§ 5, 10. Further, in 1975, the FTC gained the explicit authority to "commence a civil action to recover a civil penalty in a district court of the United States." *See* Magnuson-Moss Warranty—Federal Trade Commission Improvement Act, Pub. L. No. 93-637, § 205(a), 88 Stat. 2183, 2200-01 (1975) (codified as amended at 15 U.S.C. § 45(m)(1)(A)). In the intervening forty years no court questioned the continued validity of the holding of *Humphrey's Executor* in light of the change.

In addition to *Humphrey's Executor*, the Supreme Court's decision in *Morrison* supports the conclusion that the removal provision here does not violate the Constitution. Even though *Morrison* involved an inferior officer "with limited jurisdiction and tenure and lacking policymaking or significant administrative authority," the Court made clear that a provision limiting removal "only for good cause, physical disability, mental incapacity, or any other condition that substantially impairs the performance of such independent counsel's duties" did not "impermissibly burden[ ] the President's power to control or supervise the independent counsel, as an executive official, in the execution of his or her duties under the Act." *Morrison*, 487 U.S. at 663, 691-92; *see also Bowsher v. Synar*, 478 U.S. 714, 729, 106 S. Ct. 3181, 92 L. Ed. 2d 583 (1986) ("The statute permits removal for 'inefficiency,' 'neglect of duty,' or 'malfeasance.' These terms are very broad and, as interpreted by Congress, could sustain removal of a Comptroller General for any number of actual or perceived transgressions of the legislative will."). There is no basis to characterize the CFP Act's removal provision as more burdensome.

Finally, the removal provision does not have any of the qualities that the Supreme Court found constitutionally troubling in *Free Enterprise Fund*. The Director of the CFPB is not insulated by a second layer of tenure and is removable directly by the President. As such, the President "may hold the [Director] to account for everything . . . [he or she] does." *Free Enter. Fund*, 561 U.S. at 495-96. Accordingly, in light of the above, *Humphrey's Executor* and *Morrison* are controlling with respect to the for cause removal provision. *See Future Income Payments, LLC*, 2017 WL 2190069, at *6, *Morgan Drexen*, 60 F. Supp. 3d at 1087-89; *ITT Educ. Servs.*, 219 F. Supp. 3d at 893-94.

Next, looking at the other two characteristics of the Bureau's structure that Navient identified—its funding and single director structure—neither is constitutionally concerning by itself. With respect to the fact that the CFPB is funded by a percentage of the Federal Reserve System's earnings, 12 U.S.C. § 5497(a), and not through the normal appropriations process, Navient argues that this makes the Director unaccountable to both Congress and the President. Congress, however, "may choose . . . to loosen its own reins on public expenditure . . . [and] decide not to finance a federal entity with appropriations." *Am. Fed'n of Gov't Emps., AFL-CIO, Local 1647 v. Fed. Labor Relations Auth.*, 388 F.3d 405, 409 (3d Cir. 2004). Moreover, although the CFPB is funded outside of the appropriations process, Congress has not relinquished all control over the agency's funding because it remains free to change how the Bureau is funded at any time. Navient's argument in this regard does not support its claim that the President's powers under Article II have been curtailed.

Nor does the Court see how the agency's funding significantly removes the CFPB from the control of the President. Navient argues that the President lacks control over the CFPB because the President cannot annually propose the level of funding the President believes the agency should receive and cannot veto a congressional budget that funds the CFPB. Although the President does propose a budget that includes levels of funding that he or she believes an agency should receive, it is Congress that actually sets the agency's level of funding in the appropriations bill. And although the President may veto an appropriations bill, the President lacks the power to veto a specific budget line such as an individual agency's funding. In order for the President to reject a specific agency's funding through the exercise of a veto, the President would have to veto the entire appropriations bill. U.S. CONST. art. I, § 7, cl. 2. Thus, while this presidential power serves as an important check on Congress's power, its application is too diluted at the agency level for this Court to find that removal of the CFPB from the appropriations process inhibits the President from executing his or her Article II powers.

More importantly, however, this argument ignores the fact that an independent agency with funding outside the normal appropriations process has existed for over one hundred years. *See* Federal Reserve Act, Pub. L. No. 63-43, § 10, 38 Stat. 251, 261 (1913) (codified as amended at 12 U.S.C. § 243). Moreover, the Federal Reserve Board of Governors' composition presents no anomaly. There are at least five other independent agencies that operate completely outside of the normal annual appropriations process. *See* 12 U.S.C. § 1811, *et seq.* (Federal Deposit Insurance Corporation);6 12 U.S.C. § 1755 (National Credit Union Administration); 12 U.S.C. § 4516 (Federal Housing Finance Agency); 12 U.S.C. § 2250 (Farm Credit Administration); 15 U.S.C. § 7219 (Public Company Accounting Oversight Board). None of these agencies' funding structures, however, have ever been held to violate Article II of the Constitution. Consequently, the Court cannot say that the CFPB's system of funding, by itself, violates the Constitution.

Nor can the Court say that a single director structure by itself violates the Constitution. Indeed, many executive agencies are headed by a single individual. In addition, at least three other independent agencies are headed by a single individual. *See* 5 U.S.C. § 1211 (Office of Special Counsel); 12 U.S.C. § 4512 (Federal Housing Finance Agency); 42 U.S.C. § 902 (Social Security Administration). Thus, the CFPB's single director structure, in and of itself, does not offend the Constitution.

At oral argument, counsel for Navient agreed that each of the structural aspects of the CFPB could be found in other agencies. Consequently, Navient does not argue that any of these attributes in isolation violates the Constitution. Instead, Navient argues that these three otherwise unoffending attributes, when combined together in a single agency, run afoul of Article II and bring this case outside of the holdings of *Humphrey's Executor* and *Morrison*. (*Id.* at 78-79, 81).

As outlined above, two of the core holdings in *Morrison* were that (1) the mere fact that an agency exercises executive functions does not necessarily mean it falls outside of the holding of Humphrey's Executor, and (2) a for cause removal provision is not a significant bar to the President's ability to supervise and control heads of independent agencies. *Morrison*, 487 U.S. at 688-91, 696. Navient has failed to put forth any persuasive arguments as to why the three characteristics Navient has identified combine to unconstitutionally prevent the President from ensuring that the Bureau is performing its functions under the CFP Act. Indeed, to the contrary, there is good reason to believe that these characteristics function to increase the President's ability to supervise the Bureau over other independent agencies.

As the CFPB argues in its brief, because the Bureau is headed by a single Director instead of a multi-member body, it is easier for the President to hold the director accountable for the actions of the agency. With a multi-member body, it is more difficult to assess or allocate responsibility among the members of the body for policy decisions or actions taken because decision making is made within the group and may be the product of compromise. In contrast, with a single director, it is very clear who made the decision. Further, it is a similarly difficult task to hold an individual commissioner or board member responsible for the acts or omissions of the agency. This is not the case with a single director whose responsibility for any agency action or omission is easily assessed.

Further, the President's appointment of a single director, as opposed to a member of a multi-member commission or board, has an immediate impact because the appointee, and the appointee alone, now heads the agency. In contrast, in the case of a multi-member agency, the establishment of majority control of the agency requires successive appointments by the President and, at least in some instances, will take more time. For example, because the President serves a four year term and the Director serves a five year term, eighty percent of presidential terms will enable the President to appoint a Director. In contrast, the FTC has five commissioners with staggered seven year terms. 15 U.S.C. § 41. Because of the manner in which the commissioners' terms are staggered, only four-sevenths, or approximately fifty-seven percent, of presidential terms will enable a president to appoint a controlling majority of three or more commissioners.

Navient, however, points to the *PHH* decision. As a reminder, the PHH panel held that the for cause removal provision in combination with the single director structure was unprecedented and unconstitutional. The panel's holding proceeded on the basis that, because independent agencies lack presidential supervision and direction, they are traditionally set up as multi-member bodies so that "[t]he check from other commissioners or board members substitutes for the check by the President." *PHH Corp.*, 839 F.3d at 30-31. No Supreme Court decision has adopted the principle that the

Constitution allows multi-member bodies whose members are removable only for cause because, in lieu of checks from the President, the members provide checks on each other.

To the extent that Navient also argues that CFPB's structure violates the principle of separation of powers, this argument fares no better. As laid out above, this is not a case, and Navient does not so argue, that either the legislative or judicial branch has usurped executive power. Nevertheless, legislation may still violate the principle of separation of powers if it "impermissibly undermines the powers of the Executive Branch, or disrupts the proper balance between the coordinate branches by preventing the Executive Branch from accomplishing its constitutionally assigned functions." *Morrison*, 487 U.S. at 695. Given this Court's above analysis and its conclusion that the CFPB's structure does not impede a president's ability to execute his or her Article II powers, the Court sees no reason to conclude differently here.

In sum, the Court finds that the CFPB's structure does not violate Article II or the principle of separation of powers in that it does not impede the President's ability to "take Care that the Laws be faithfully executed." Accordingly, the Court will deny Navient's Motion to Dismiss on these grounds.

In any event, were this Court, or any other, to find that the CFPB's structure violates Article II, Dodd-Franks has a severance clause that provides that "[i]f any provision of this Act . . . or the application of such provision . . . to any person or circumstance is held to be unconstitutional, the remainder of this Act . . . and the application of the provisions of such to any person or circumstance shall not be affected thereby." 12 U.S.C. § 5302. Accordingly, when the *PHH* court found the for cause provision violated the Constitution, the panel "remed[ied] the constitutional violation . . . by severing the for-cause removal provision from the statute" and making the Director of the CFPB removable by the President at will. *PHH Corp.*, 839 F.3d at 37-39.

If any of the provisions Navient has identified were to be held unconstitutional and are severed from the CFP Act, the question then presented is how would such a ruling affect the present lawsuit. At oral argument, Navient advocated for the position that, if the CFPB's structure is unconstitutional, then the Director is acting outside of Executive control and therefore the actions of the Director in bringing the current lawsuit are unauthorized and void. As a result, Navient argues that the present lawsuit should be dismissed if any provision is found unconstitutional. Conversely, the CFPB argued that if the for cause provision was severed, the President, if he did not approve of the current lawsuit, could simply instruct the Director to dismiss the action. If the present Director refused, the President could simply remove the Director and replace him with someone who would dismiss the lawsuit.

This Court views the latter position as the more prudent course of action for two reasons. First, and most importantly, it finds support in the case law. *See, e.g., Buckley*, 424 U.S. at 142 (according "de facto validity" to the past acts of the Federal Election Commission even though four members of the Commission were appointed in violation of the Appointments Clause); *John Doe Co. v. CFPB*, 849 F.3d 1129, 1133 (D.C. Cir. 2017) ("[T]he Supreme Court and this court have often accorded validity to past acts of unconstitutionally structured governmental agencies."). Second, it affords the President the

224

ability to make the determination as to whether or not he or she wishes for the Director to continue with the present litigation.

Accordingly, in the event that the Bureau's structure is found to be unconstitutional and the problematic provisions are severed from the CFP Act, the severance would not affect the CFPB's ability to maintain the present suit.

Count I

Turning to the individual claims against Navient, Count I of the CFPB's Complaint alleges that Navient violated the CFP Act's prohibition on abusive acts or practices. Specifically, the Complaint alleges that Navient's webpage stated that Navient would help borrowers find a repayment option appropriate for the individual borrower's situation but that Navient instead steered borrowers into forbearance without adequately advising them about other repayment options. Navient argues that Count I should be dismissed because they had no duty to provide individualized financial counseling to borrowers.

The CFP Act makes it "unlawful for . . . any covered person or service provider . . . to engage in any unfair, deceptive, or abusive act or practice." 12 U.S.C. § 5536(a)(1)(B). An act or practice is not abusive unless it meets certain statutory criteria. 12 U.S.C. § 5531(d). One way an act or practice can be abusive is if it "takes unreasonable advantage of . . . the reasonable reliance by the consumer on a covered person to act in the interests of the consumer." 12 U.S.C. § 5531(d)(2)(C).

Navient argues that Count I is deficient because it only alleges an omission on their part. The Complaint, Navient contends, does not allege that they made any false statements or misrepresentations, but only that Navient did not provide adequate financial counseling. Navient therefore argues that "[b]orrowers could not reasonably rely on Navient to counsel them into alternative payment plans unless Navient had an affirmative duty to provide such individualized financial counseling." The law, according to Navient, imposes no such duty because Navient is a loan servicer, not a fiduciary.

Navient's arguments cloud, rather than clarify, the issue. Navient's alleged practice is abusive under the CFP Act if Navient took unreasonable advantage of a borrower's reasonable reliance that Navient would act in the borrower's interest. The CFPB has alleged that Navient made various statements on their webpage that indicated that if a borrower in financial distress contacted them, Navient would give them enough information about different repayment options so the borrower could make an informed decision about which repayment plan was right for them. For example, the Complaint alleges that Navient's webpage contained the following statement: "If you're experiencing problems making your loans payments, please contact us. Our representatives can help you by identifying options and solutions, so you can make the right decision for your situation." The Complaint further alleges that, when borrowers called, Navient representatives did not give complete information on income-driven repayment plans and instead pushed borrowers into forbearance. Finally, the Complaint alleges that this was both detrimental to borrowers and beneficial to Navient. This is sufficient at the pleading stage to allege that Navient took unreasonable advantage of borrowers' reasonable reliance on Navient's statements that Navient would give them adequate information to properly choose a repayment plan.

Navient's focus on whether the law imposes an underlying duty is misplaced for two reasons. First, the statutory language does not state that a duty is an element of an abusive act or practice but instead states that a loan servicer cannot take unreasonable advantage of "the reasonable reliance by the consumer" that the loan servicer will "act in the interests of the consumer." The concept of reasonable reliance, however, is not always paired with a preexisting legal duty. *See, e.g.*, RESTATEMENT (SECOND) OF CONTRACTS § 90 ("A promise which the promisor should reasonably expect to induce action or forbearance on the part of the promisee or a third person and which does induce such action or forbearance is binding if injustice can be avoided only by enforcement of the promise."). It is therefore enough that a borrower's reliance that a loan servicer will act in their interest is reasonable, irrespective of whether a legal duty actually exists on the part of the loan servicer to act in the borrower's interest. Second, although Navient contends that the Complaint alleges only omissions, the Complaint alleges that Navient placed reliance inducing statements on their webpage. Thus, even assuming the truth of Navient's arguments that there must be some underlying legal duty in order for a borrower's reliance to be reasonable, the Court is satisfied that Navient's active conduct created a duty to act in accordance with their own statements.

Accordingly, the Court will deny Navient's Motion to Dismiss as it pertains to Count I of the CFPB's Complaint.

Count II

Count II of the CFPB's Complaint alleges that the same factual allegations that form the basis of Count I also violate the CFP Act's prohibition on unfair acts or practices. An act or practice is not unfair under the CFP Act unless (1) "the act or practice causes or is likely to cause substantial injury to consumers," (2) such substantial injury "is not reasonably avoidable by consumers," and (3) "such substantial injury is not outweighed by countervailing benefits to consumers or to competition." 12 U.S.C. § 5531(C)(1); *see also ITT Educ. Servs., Inc.*, 219 F. Supp. 3d at 913. Navient's only argument for dismissal of Count II is that the harm in this case was reasonably avoidable. Thus, Navient takes issue only with the second element of the unfairness standard.

"An injury is reasonably avoidable if consumers 'have reason to anticipate the impending harm and the means to avoid it,' or if consumers are aware of, and are reasonably capable of pursuing, potential avenues toward mitigating the injury after the fact." *Davis v. HSBC Bank Nev., N.A.*, 691 F.3d 1152, 1168-69 (9th Cir. 2012) (citing O*rkin Exterminating Co. v. FTC*, 849 F.2d 1354, 1365-66 (11th Cir. 1988)). Thus, "[i]n determining whether consumers' injuries were reasonably avoidable, courts look to whether the consumers had a free and informed choice." *FTC v. Neovi, Inc.*, 604 F.3d 1150, 1158 (9th Cir. 2010).

With respect to reasonable avoidability, the Bureau's Complaint alleges that Navient gave borrowers who called them incomplete or, on other occasions, no information about income-driven repayment plans and instead pushed borrowers into forbearances. The Complaint further alleges that, as a result, borrowers ended up in forbearance instead of being able to make an informed decision as to what repayment plan was best for their circumstances. These allegations, taken as true for the purpose of this Motion, are sufficient to state a claim that the injury to borrowers was not reasonably avoidable.

Navient, however, argues that because they made numerous disclosures that provided borrowers with information about income-driven repayment plans and because there was information publicly available about income-driven repayment plans, any injury was reasonably avoidable. Navient states that this Court can consider this information because federal law requires Navient to make such disclosures and there is no allegation that Navient did not make them. Even assuming the truth of Navient's contentions, dismissing Count II would require this Court to rule, as a matter of law, that borrowers understood the disclosures that were made to them so that they had "reason to anticipate the impending harm and the means to avoid it." These facts are not before the Court at the pleading stage and therefore, the Court cannot make such a ruling.

Accordingly, the Court will deny Navient's Motion to Dismiss as it pertains to Count II of the CFPB's Complaint.

Count III

Navient next seeks dismissal of Count III of the CFPB's Complaint which alleges that Navient violated the CFP Act's prohibition on unfair acts or practices by failing to adequately notify borrowers who were enrolled in income-driven repayment plans that their annual recertification notice was available. Specifically, the Complaint alleges that Navient obscured the fact that the recertification notice was available by sending borrowers—who consented to electronic notification—an email with the subject line of either "Your Sallie Mae Account Information" or "New Document Ready to view," and text in the body of the email that stated "a new education loan document is available. Please log in to your account to view it." To know that the "new education loan document" was specifically an income-driven repayment plan recertification notice, a borrower would need to click on a hyperlink in the email and go to Navient's website, where the borrower could then log in to his or her account and view the renewal notice.

As stated in the prior section, an act or practice is not unfair under the CFP Act unless (1) "the act or practice causes or is likely to cause substantial injury to consumers," (2) such substantial injury "is not reasonably avoidable by consumers," and (3) "such substantial injury is not outweighed by countervailing benefits to consumers or to competition." 12 U.S.C. § 5531(C)(1). Once again, Navient has only taken issue with the second element of the unfairness claim. Specifically, Navient argues that the harm was reasonably avoidable because borrowers could simply click on the provided link and log into their accounts to avoid the harm.

Given the allegations in the Complaint, the Court finds that, at this early stage, it cannot rule as a matter of law that the harm was reasonably avoidable. First, the allegation that the email itself does not contain any information as to what document was available or express any urgency in the matter would plausibly support a conclusion that borrowers did not "have reason to anticipate the impending harm." Second, the Complaint alleges that when Navient changed both the subject line and the body of the email to inform borrowers that the recertification notification was available, the rate at which borrowers renewed their income-driven repayment plans more than doubled. This allegation, taken as true for the purposes of this Motion, indicates that a good number of borrowers did not avoid the harm when presented with Navient's original email. The allegation that many people did not avoid the harm plausibly supports the allegation that the harm was not reasonably avoidable by borrowers.

Accordingly, the Court will deny Navient's Motion to Dismiss as it pertains to Count III of the CFPB's Complaint.

Count IV

Navient next moves to dismiss Count IV of the Bureau's Complaint. Count IV alleges that the income-driven repayment plan recertification notice that Navient sent borrowers through the postal mail between July 2011 until December of 2012 was a deceptive act or practice in violation of the CFP Act. Specifically, the Bureau's Complaint alleges that Navient's notice stated that if a borrower "provid[ed] incorrect or incomplete information the [renewal] process will be delayed," and thus implied that delay was the only consequence of submitting incorrect or incomplete information, when in truth it could have several irreversible consequences.

Unlike unfair and abusive acts or practices, the term "deceptive . . . act or practice" is not defined in the CFP Act. The same term, however, also appears in the more heavily interpreted FTC Act. Therefore, courts have construed "deceptive . . . act or practice" to have the same meaning under the CFP Act as it does under the FTC Act. *See, e.g., Gordon*, 819 F.3d at 1193 n.7; *ITT Educ. Servs.*, 219 F. Supp. 3d at 903; *CFPB v. Frederick J. Hanna & Assocs., P.C.*, 114 F. Supp. 3d 1342, 1369-70 (N.D. Ga. 2015). Thus, "[a]n act or practice is deceptive if: (1) 'there is a representation, omission, or practice that,' (2) 'is likely to mislead consumers acting reasonably under the circumstances,' and (3) 'the representation, omission, or practice is material.'" *Gordon*, 819 F.3d at 1192-93 (quoting *FTC v. Pantron I Corp.*, 33 F.3d 1088, 1095 (9th Cir. 1994)). "Deception may be found based on the net impression created by a representation." *Id.* at 1193.

Navient argues that the statement in the renewal letter was not likely to mislead a reasonable borrower because, "[w]hile the notice states that failure to submit a complete and accurate application may result in a processing delay, it does not state that no other consequences could result from such failure." Navient further argues that other parts of the letter explain the consequence of not completing the recertification, and that the statement that the CFPB cites is taken out of context. Along with their brief, Navient submitted two examples of the renewal letter they used along with the renewal forms issued by the United States. *see In re Burlington Coat Factory Sec. Litig.*, 114 F.3d 1410, 1426 (3d Cir. 1997) (holding that district courts, on a motion to dismiss, may consider a document "integral to or explicitly relied upon in the Complaint."

Upon review of the attachments, the Court cannot say, as a matter of law, that the letter was not likely to mislead a borrower acting reasonably under the circumstances. Under the plausibility standard of *Iqbal/Twombly*, neither the alleged cause of action nor the allegations of fact underlying it are capable of resolution as a matter of law on Navient's Motion to Dismiss. The Bureau has stated a plausible claim for relief that Navient's letter created a false impression that a processing delay was the only adverse consequence of filing an incomplete or inaccurate applications when, according to the Complaint, there was a host of other negative consequences. This is sufficient at the pleading stage to allege a claim for a deceptive act or practice.

Nevertheless, in their reply brief Navient argues that the CFPB's claim is still inadequate because the Bureau's claim is limited only to those borrowers making inadvertent errors or omissions. Thus, according to Navient, "[b]orrowers who . . . mistakenly submitted a defective form necessarily did so because of a mistake, not based on any alleged misrepresentation." A fair inference from the Complaint, however, is that borrowers who were misled into believing that a processing delay was the only negative consequence of submitting an incomplete or inaccurate form were not as careful when filling out the form as they would have been if they had known the true consequences of an error or omission.

Accordingly, the Court will deny Navient's Motion to Dismiss as it pertains to Count IV of the CFPB's Complaint.

. . .

****

 **6E**

Why does the CFPB have authority over Navient?

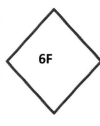 **6F**

To what extent does declaring an act or practice unlawful through enforcement action put potential violators on notice of what constitutes an unfair, deceptive or abusive act or practice? To what extent did declaring Navient's acts or practices unlawful put Navient on notice? Do you agree with the court's interpretation of the CFPB's authority? Why or why not? Do you agree with the court's conclusion regarding the role of rulemaking, litigation, and statutory interpretation? Why or why not?

 **6G**

Are the UDAAP definitions too vague to hold entities accountable for compliance?

 **6H**

Are Navient's acts or practices unfair, deceptive or abusive?

Recall that one criteria for deceptive is whether "the act or practice has been reasonably interpreted by the consumer."[468] The CFPB has provided some guidance on this criterion, namely that "whether an act or practice is deceptive depends on how a reasonable member of the target audience would interpret the representation. When representations or marketing practices target a specific audience, such as older Americans, young people, or financially distressed consumers, the communication must be reviewed from the point of view of a reasonable member of that group."[469] Recall that students, servicemembers, the elderly, and other groups are, in some respects, determined to be consumers in need of stronger consumer protections. **How might a *reasonable* student/ graduate view the information (or lack thereof) provided by Navient?** Recall *Buchanan*[470] in the context of the FDCPA violation. How might Buchanan and other members of "financial distressed consumers" reasonably view a letter referencing a settlement?

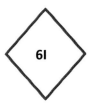

61

If the CFPB's case against Navient is successful, what enforcement powers and opportunities for relief are available under the CFPB's authority? Is UDAAP, and specifically the addition of the amorphous "abusive," a return to the old, "paternalistic" method of regulating by restricting to protect consumers from themselves rather than regulating by disclosure?[471] Why or Why Not?

---

[468] CONSUMER FIN. PROT. BUREAU, *supra* note 449, at 2.

[469] *Id.* at 6.

[470] 776 F.3d 393 (6th Cir., 2015).

[471] *See* Zywicki, *supra* note 218, at 919 (posing that "the definition seems to be a discrete break with the philosophy that has animated the regulation of consumer credit for the past several decades—namely, a disclosure-based system designed to empower rather than displace consumer choice by harnessing the power of markets for consumers. The 'abusive' standard, by contrast, appears to be a return to old-fashioned substantive regulation of earlier generations.").

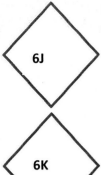

Compare *Navient*, a 2017 Middle District of Pennsylvania case, to the 2016 PHH case discussed infra in Part IX.

6J

6K

Why do you think Navient challenges the CFPB's constitutionality? Here, arguably, the CFPB is using some of its most controversial[472] powers—the CFPB is using its enforcement powers for rulemaking. **Do you think that Navient could have prevailed on its claim of the CFPB's unconstitutionality if Navient prevailed on its argument that the CFPB exceeds its authority by enforcing a law for which no corresponding regulations have been issued?**

6L

Does the President's inability to remove the CFPB Director at will interfere with the President's powers? Why or Why Not?

Consider the following legal commentary on this case:

> That the CFPB Director is somehow more accountable to the President, is a legal fiction at best. If the President has no power to remove the Director without cause, the Director is not accountable to him. Period. The President can approach the Director, ask him to implement a certain policy, and the Director can ignore the President with impunity. That is not accountability, however one may measure it. It is true that the five FTC Commissioners, the entire board of the Federal Reserve, or the SEC Commissioners could do the same. But, those interactions are more like the ones the President faces in dealing with Congress or the Judiciary, interactions that the Constitution contemplated and intended. With the CFPB Director, the President stands powerless before the unitary executive of a federal agency whose will can stand in direct contrast to his own. If that is not an affront to the Constitution's notion of the President as a unitary executive, what is?[473]

6M

Recall that since Mick Mulvaney's appointment as Acting Director in November 2017, measures have been undertaken to reduce the power of the CFPB. Specifically, Mick Mulvaney requested $0 from the Federal Reserve as the CFPB's budget, purportedly for the purpose of reducing the

---

[472] Zywicki, *supra* note 218, at 917 (describing the UDAAP regulatory power as "perhaps the most threatening.").

[473] *See* Theodore R. Flo, *Middle District of Pennsylvania Ignores Key Constitutional Questions in Navient Case*, Ballard Spahr Consumer Fin. Monitor Blog (Aug. 9, 2017), https://www.consumerfinancemonitor.com/2017/08/09/middle-district-of-pennsylvania-ignores-key-constitutional-questions-in-navient-case/.

CFPB's power.[474]   Recall that the CFPB Director is not removable at will by the President. Specifically, the CFPB Director is removable for cause, namely, inefficiency, neglect of duty, or malfeasance.[475]   **Did Director Mulvaney neglect his duties by not requesting funding for the CFPB, if his actions were aligned with the President's wishes?** Consider the following consumer complaint narrative, filed in the CFPB Consumer Complaint Database on September 16, 2015. Certain information concerning the complaint is redacted.

---

[474] *See* Stacy Cowley, *Consumer Bureau's Chief Gives Big Raises, Even as He Criticizes Spending*, N.Y. TIMES, Apr. 5, 2018), https://www.nytimes.com/2018/04/05/business/cfpb-mick-mulvaney-pay-raises.html; *see also* Stacy Cowley, *Consumer Watchdog's Latest Budget Request: $0*, N.Y. TIMES, Jan. 18, 2018, https://www.nytimes.com/2018/01/18/business/cfpb-mick-mulvaney.html?module=inline.
[475] 12 U.S.C. 5491(c)(3).

Navient is a student loan servicer. Consider that student loan debt increased by sixty-eight billon dollars in 2017.[476] Consider the following consumer complaint narrative filed with the CFPB:[477]

> *This bank is not allowing me to pay my car payment. There are many issues please see below:1 XXXX Made my first payment with a check and sent in the stub to set up automatic payment. they never set up automatic payment. And are refusing to set it up now. 2 XXXX They never contacted me to tell me my payment was late, I have to reach out to them. The first time I was on hold, I waited for at least XXXX minutes for an associate to answer. When he answered he refused to take a payment or assist in anyway. His name was XXXX. When I asked to speak to a manger he kept me on hold for an additional XXXX mins. Then said he could not waive the {$15.00} dollar pay by phone fee, when I told him I did n't want to make a payment through the automated system he said there was nothing he could do. I eventually decided he was going to do nothing for me and attempted to make a payment online3) when I attempted to make a payment online they would not let me make a payment without verifying my pay from account. I tried and the verification did not work. I think it is a bit ridiculous to make a person jump through this many hoops just to make a payment. It seems and little unfair and abusive of them to do this to customers who just want to pay and set up an automatic payment. It seemed to me like they want customers to pay late and not set up automatic payments. I always pay my bills and put them on auto pay and have not had problems with other financial institutions. I was forced by the car company to use this bank and am very dissatisfied with the service. On XXXX XXXX, 2015 I called and spoke with associate XXXX in their bill pay department. He was unable to fix the " Bill Pay " because it had locked. So he got me in contact with XXXX who works for Bank of America auto loan department. She gladly took my payment with no problem or fee, she also opened a payment dispute and request to get my automatic payments set up. However, I have no confirmation this was actually done. She said it will be investigated which could take up to 10 business days and then I will receive a letter. This would make my payment late again. I do not think it is fair I am being penalized, when the original error occurred at BOA not setting up my automatic payments. I did my due diligence in trying to make payments. Additionally, this hurts my loan amount. With the way amortization works on car loans it was taken out at varying cycles which causes interest to be paid out differently and essentially not lower my principal as much. They are costing me money in interest for the ineptitude at taking a payment from a customer wanting to make payments on time each month. Please stop these unfair and abusive practices and require them to set up automatic payments when it is an option on their billing statements. I think this is a violation of UDAAP, FCBA, and possible TILA. Since it is not disclose how difficult they make it to make a payment. Thank you for your time.*

---

[476] *See* CONSUMER FIN. PROT. BUREAU ANN. REP., *supra* note 342, at 12.

[477] CONSUMER FIN. PROT. BUREAU ONLINE CONSUMER COMPLAINT DATABASE, https://www.consumerfinance.gov/data-research/consumer-complaints/search/detail/1567561, last visited Dec. 2, 2018.

6N

The company responded timely, and the complaint was "closed with explanation" from the company. The company elected not to permit a response viewable to the public. **Does this consumer complaint amount to a UDAAP violation? Why or Why Not? What additional information would you need to decide?**

Consider the following consumer complaint narrative, filed in the CFPB Consumer Complaint Database on November 17, 2016. Certain information concerning the complaint is redacted.

Consumer complaint narrative:[478]

> *I applied for a loan through SoFi. The advertisement says that Fixed rates are as low as 3.5 % APR. I applied for the loan and they were only able to get my 5.24 %. I called and asked a rep how they determine the score. They said a variety of factors such as job industry, duration of employment and a few others. However, my credit score is XXXX, near perfect. I explained this fact. That was barely acknowledged. I then asked what percentage of people have received a 3.5 % APR rate under their current offerings. The representative then said, " I have n't seen any applications with that rate. " Under UDAAP, this may be considered a deceptive practice if no one can feasibly obtain this rate or SoFi knows that the amount is so astronomically low, that it is virtually impossible for any applicants to receive such a rate.*

6O

The company responded timely, and the complaint was "closed with explanation" from the company. The company elected not to permit a response viewable to the public. **Does this consumer complaint amount to a UDAAP violation? Why or Why Not? What additional information would you need to decide?**

Recall the reference in Part I concerning the recurring historical conflict in U.S. financial services between the agricultural United States (primarily Southern states) and the commercial United States (primarily Northern states) and more recently between "Wall Street" vs. "Main Street" following the financial crisis of 2008. Further, recall the reference in Part II regarding the reputational consequences of the CFPB's consent order with Wells Fargo following the creation of fake bank accounts that harmed consumers. The CFPB's consent order, paragraphs 18, 20, and 21, "Findings and Conclusions as to

---

[478] CONSUMER FIN. PROT. BUREAU ONLINE CONSUMER COMPLAINT DATABASE, https://www.consumerfinance.gov/data-research/consumer-complaints/search/detail/2212333, last visited Dec. 6, 2018.

Unauthorized Deposit Accounts and Simulated Funding" determined that Wells Fargo's activities were unfair and abusive, namely:

> By opening unauthorized deposit accounts and engaging in acts of simulated funding, [Wells Fargo] caused and was likely to cause substantial injury to consumers that was not reasonably avoidable, because it occurred without consumers' knowledge, and was not outweighed by countervailing benefits to consumers or to competition.
>
> . . .
>
> [Wells Fargo's] acts of opening unauthorized deposit accounts and engaging in simulated funding materially interfered with the ability of consumers to understand a term or condition of a consumer financial product or service, as they had no or limited knowledge of those terms and conditions, including associated fees.
>
> . . .
>
> Additionally, [Wells Fargo's] acts of opening unauthorized deposit accounts and engaging in simulated funding took unreasonable advantage of consumers' inability to protect their interests in selecting or using consumer financial products or services, including interests in having an account opened only after affirmative agreement, protecting themselves from security and other risks, and avoiding associated fees.[479]

Here, the CFPB has determined that Wells Fargo is in violation of UDAAP. As referenced in Part II, Wells Fargo was responsible for paying $100 million in fines[480] and also suffered reputational consequences. In the Wall Street Journal article, *Next Test for Wells Fargo: Its Reputation*, author Emily Glazer notes that Wells Fargo "positioned itself as a solid, Main Street lender that avoided the excesses of the financial crisis and other missteps on Wall Street. That image is in danger now of being challenged by disclosures of improper account and product openings by employees unveiled in an enforcement action the bank entered into. . ."[481] Consider that Morningstar named Wells Fargo CEO John Stumpf CEO of the Year in 2016, just fewer than eight months before the CFPB consent order, stating that the CEO "guided the bank through a difficult period in the industry and shunned activities that put profits ahead of customers."[482] **Do you agree or disagree?**

6P

Recall the 5Ws from Part I:

Who is regulated under UDAAP?

---

[479] In the Matter of Wells Fargo Bank, N.A., Consent Order 2016-CFPB-0015, https://files.consumerfinance.gov/f/documents/092016_cfpb_WFBconsentorder.pdf

[480] *See* Consumer Fin. Prot. Bureau, *supra* note 126.

[481] Glazer, *supra* note 132.

[482] *See* Press Release, Morningstar, Chicago, Wells Fargo's John Stumpf Receives Morningstar's 2015 CEO of the Year Award, https://corporate.morningstar.com/us/asp/popup.aspx?xmlfile=PR5566.xml.

Who is protected under UDAAP?

What is the protection? What is the appropriate law or regulation?

When is the protection applicable? (Under what circumstances does the protection apply?

Why does the protection exist? Would applying the law or rule make sense in context?

VII. CONSUMER FINANCIAL PRIVACY

A. LAWS AND RULES

Recall that the Truth in Lending Act, the Equal Credit Opportunity Act, and the Fair Debt Collection Practices Act, provisions are located within 15 U.S.C. Chapter 41: Consumer Credit Protection.[483] Specifically, TILA, ECOA, and FDCPA provisions are found within Subchapter I: Consumer Credit Cost Disclosure, Subchapter IV: Equal Credit Opportunity, and Subchapter V: Debt Collection Practices, respectively.[484] Collectively, these subchapters, among others, make up the Consumer Credit Protection Act of 1968.[485] However, requirements with respect to consumer financial privacy are located in the Gramm-Leach-Bliley Act and implementing Regulation P.[486] The CFPB has rulemaking authority with respect to the consumer financial privacy provisions of the Gramm-Leach Bliley Act, financial institutions, and those subject to the CFPB's enforcement authority.

The Gramm-Leach-Bliley Act ("GLBA") governs consumer financial privacy.[487] In contrast to laws applicable to a specific segment of financial service providers, for example "creditors" or "debt collectors," Congress intended that "financial institutions" respect customer privacy.[488] Recall that **"financial institution"** can encompass many different entity types. With some exclusions for the purposes of the consumer financial privacy law, recall from Part IC that a financial institution is generally any "institution the business of which is engaging in activities that are financial in nature."[489]

Consumer financial privacy has three important protections, for the purposes of this text: (1) prohibition against disclosure of certain information, (2) requiring notice to consumers of what information is or may be shared or collected, under what circumstances, and the financial institution's policies and practices concerning the sharing of the information, and (3) providing an opportunity for consumers to opt-out of certain information-sharing by the financial institution.[490]

The GLBA prohibits the disclosure of "nonpublic personal information" to "nonaffiliated third parties" without notice required by the law.[491] Nonpublic personal information is a defined term in both the GLBA and in Regulation P. **Nonpublic personal information** is "personally identifiable financial

---

[483] *See* 15 U.S.C. § 1601 *et seq.*; 15 U.S.C. § 1691 *et seq.*; 15 U.S.C. § 1692 *et seq.*

[484] *See* 15 U.S.C. § 1601 *et seq.*; 15 U.S.C. § 1691 *et seq.*; 15 U.S.C. § 1692 *et seq.*

[485] *See generally* 15 U.S.C. § 1601 *et seq.*

[486] See *generally* 15 U.S.C. § 6801 *et seq.* (Fastcase 2018); 12 C.F.R. § 1016 *et seq.* (Fastcase 2018).

[487] *See* generally 15 U.S.C. § 6801 *et seq.*

[488] *See* 15 U.S.C. § 6801.

[489] *See* 12 C.F.R. § 1016.3(l) (Fastcase 2018); 12 U.S.C. § 1843(k)(4) (Fastcase 2018); 15 U.S.C. § 6809(3) (Fastcase 2018) (defining financial institution as any "institution the business of which is engaging in financial activities [. . .]").

[490] *See* 12 C.F.R. § 1016.1(a) (Fastcase 2018).

[491] *See* 15 U.S.C. §6802(a) (Fastcase 2018).

information and any list, description or other grouping of consumers (and publicly available information pertaining to them) that is derived using any personally identifiable financial information that is not publicly available."[492] Personally identifiable financial information is also a defined term under Regulation P. Specifically Regulation P defines **personally identifiable financial information** as information a consumer provides to a financial institution or to an institution subject to the CFPB's rulemaking authority: (1) about a financial product or service from the institution, (2) about the consumer resulting from any transaction involving a financial product or servicer between the institution and consumer, or (3) the institution otherwise obtains about the consumer in connection with providing the financial product or service to the consumer.[493] Finally, a **nonaffiliated third party** is defined in 15 U.S.C. § 6809(5) as any entity that is not an affiliate of, or related by common ownership or affiliated by corporate control with, the financial institution, but does not include a joint employee of such institution.[494]

CONTENT

The GLBA prohibits the disclosure of nonpublic personal information to nonaffiliated third parties unless the financial institution notifies the **consumer** of three things. The financial institution must notify the consumer that the information may be disclosed to the third party.[495] This notification may be referred to, for the purposes of this text, as the "privacy notice." The financial institution must also notify the consumer that the consumer can, within a specified time, opt-out of the financial institution disclosing the information.[496] Finally, the financial institution must notify the consumer of how the consumer can opt-out.[497] Collectively, the opt-out notifications may be referred to, for the purposes of this text, as the "opt-out notice." Collectively, the "privacy notice and "opt-out notice" may be referred to, for the purposes of this text as the "Regulation P Privacy Notice."

Consumer is a defined term under Regulation P. A **consumer** is any individual who obtains or has obtained a financial product or service from a financial institution or from a person subject to the CFPB's rulemaking authority, that is to be used primarily for personal, family, or household purposes.[498] Examples of what constitutes a "consumer" are in Regulation P.[499] A financial institution does not have to provide the opt-out notice in instances where the financial institution shares nonpublic personal information to a nonaffiliate in order for the nonaffiliate to perform services for the financial institution, provided that the financial institution (1) does notify the consumer that the information is being shared, and provided that (2) the financial institution has a contractual agreement with the servicer provider to

---

[492] *See* 12 C.F.R. § 1016.3(p); *see also* 15 U.S.C. § 6809(4) defining nonpublic personal information as personally identifiable financial information provided by a consumer to a financial institution, resulting from any transaction with the consumer or any service performed for the consumer, or otherwise obtained by the financial institution.
[493] *See* 12 C.F.R. § 1016.3(q)(1).
[494] *See* 15 U.S.C. § 6809(5).
[495] *See* 15 U.S.C. § 6802(b)(1)(A).
[496] *See* 15 U.S.C. § 6802(b)(1)(B).
[497] *See* 15 U.S.C. § 6802(b)(1)(C).
[498] *See* 12 C.F.R. § 1016.3(e)(1).
[499] *See* 12 C.F.R. § 1016.3.

maintain confidentiality of the nonpublic personal information.[500] There are a number of additional consumer financial privacy requirements exceptions.[501] For example, the Regulation P Privacy Notice does not apply to disclosing nonpublic personal information with the consumer's consent, to consumer reporting agencies, in order to comply with other laws or rules, or in the event of a proposed or actual sale, merger, transfer, or exchange of all or a portion of a business or operating unit, if the disclosure concerns solely consumers of such business or unit.[502] One notable Regulation P Privacy Notice exception is for disclosure of nonpublic personal information "as necessary to effect, administer, or enforce a transaction requested or authorized by the consumer or in connection with:

> (A) servicing or processing a financial product or service requested or authorized by the consumer;
> (B) maintaining or servicing the consumer's account with the financial institution, or with another entity as part of a private label credit card program or other extension of credit on behalf of such entity; or
> (C) a proposed or actual securitization, secondary market sale (including sales of servicing rights), or similar transaction related to a transaction of the consumer."[503]

Otherwise, an institution disclosing nonpublic personal information to nonaffiliated third parties must provide an "initial privacy notice" and an "annual privacy notice" concerning the institution's policies and practices pursuant to 15 U.S.C.§6803(a).[504] A financial institution is prohibited from disclosing nonpublic personal information without providing the Regulation P Privacy Notices(s), where required.[505] The initial and annual privacy notices must disclose the financial institution's policies and practices regarding disclosing nonpublic personal information to nonaffiliated third parties and the information the financial institution discloses to the nonaffiliated third parties.[506] In addition, the financial institution must disclose the financial institution's policies and practices regarding disclosing nonpublic personal information of customers who are no longer customers of the financial institution.[507] Finally, the financial institution must disclose its policies and practices regarding how the financial institution protects the nonpublic personal information of consumers.[508] The privacy notice disclosures must inform the consumer of the institution's policies and practices of disclosing nonpublic personal information to nonaffiliated third parties, including (1) the categories of persons to whom the nonpublic personal information is or may be disclosed, (2) the categories of nonpublic personal information the financial institution collects, (3) the categories of nonpublic personal information the financial institution discloses; (4) the categories of nonpublic personal information the institution discloses about its former

---

[500] *See* 15 U.S.C. §6802(b)(2).

[501] *See* 15 U.S.C. §6802(e).

[502] *See* 15 U.S.C. §6802(e).

[503] *See* 15 U.S.C. §6802(e)(1); 12 C.F.R. 1016.1(a).

[504] *See* 15 U.S.C. § 6803(a); 12 C.F.R. 1016.4; 12 C.F.R. 1016.5.

[505] *See* 12 C.F.R. 1016.10(a)(1)(i).

[506] *See* 15 U.S.C. § 6803(a)(1).

[507] *See* 15 U.S.C. § 6803(a)(2).

[508] *See* 15 U.S.C. § 6803(a)(3).

customers and the categories of persons to whom the institution discloses; (5) if the institution shares nonpublic personal information with nonaffiliated third parties, a separate statement of the categories of information disclosed and categories of third parties with whom the institution has contracted; (6) explanation of consumer's rights to opt-out of disclosure of nonpublic personal information to nonaffiliated third parties and how to opt out, (7) policies the financial institution maintains to protect the confidentiality and security of the nonpublic financial information, and (8) the information communicated to persons related to the financial institution by common ownership or affiliated by corporate control.[509] If the institution shares nonpublic personal information with affiliates or others under common ownership, the institution must disclose to the consumer that the consumer can limit the sharing before the financial institution shares.[510] The financial institution cannot disclose nonpublic personal information to nonaffiliated third parties without notifying the consumer of the consumer's ability to opt out of the disclosure and without giving the consumer a reasonable opportunity to opt out.[511] What constitutes a reasonable opportunity to opt out is discussed *infra*. Obviously, the financial institution can only disclose such protected information to the extent that the consumer does not exercise the right to opt out of the disclosure.[512] In other words, an entity that shares nonpublic personal information pursuant to an exception, must provide a privacy notice but the consumer does not have a right to opt-out. Further, entities sharing information, even if the information-sharing is to an affiliate and not to a third party, must provide a privacy notice of their policies and practices.

TIMING

The financial institution must provide the initial privacy notice to a **customer** at the time the customer relationship is established and to a **consumer** before the financial institution shares the consumer's information.[513] In other words, the customer must receive a Regulation P Privacy Notice: an initial privacy notice and an annual privacy notice, both of which must include the opt-out notice if the financial institution will share nonpublic personal information with a nonaffiliated third party, and the sharing is not subject to an exception. The consumer must receive a privacy notice and opt-out notice only if and prior to the financial institution's sharing nonpublic personal information with a nonaffiliated third party, and the sharing is not subject to an exception. **Customer** is a defined term in Regulation P. A customer is a consumer with a continuing relationship with institution under which the institution provides one or more financial products or services to the consumer that are used primarily for personal, family or household purposes.[514] The regulation provides examples of what constitutes a continuing relationship.[515] If the financial institution does not disclose nonpublic personal information to nonaffiliated third parties, then the initial privacy notice is not required.[516] If the financial institution

---

[509] *See* 15 U.S.C. § 6803(c); 15 U.S.C. § 1681a(d)(2)(A)(iii); 12 C.F.R. 1016.6(a)(1)-(9) (Fastcase 2018).
[510] *See* 15 U.S.C. §1681a(d)(2)(A)(iii).
[511] *See* 12 C.F.R. 1016.10(a)(1)ii)-(iii).
[512] 12 C.F.R. 1016.10(a)(1)(iv).
[513] 12 C.F.R. 1016.4(a)(1)-(2); *see* 15 U.S.C. § 6803(a).
[514] *See* 12 C.F.R. 1016.3(i)-(j).
[515] *See, e.g.*, 12 C.F.R. 1016.3(j)(2)(i).
[516] *See* 12 C.F.R. 1016.4(b)(1).

does not have a customer relationship with the consumer, an initial privacy notice is not required.[517] The annual notice must be provided to the customer at least annually during the customer/financial institution relationship.[518] A financial institution is not required to provide an annual notice to a former customer.[519]

The regulation provides examples of timing for a reasonable opportunity for the consumer to opt out.[520] Specifically, Regulation P examples, and consequently, the industry standard, is to permit the consumer at least thirty days to opt out if the consumer received a mailed or electronic notice.[521] A consumer may exercise the consumer's right to opt out at any time,[522] and the financial institution must comply with the consumer's opt-out request within a reasonably practicable time after receiving the request.[523]

FORM

The privacy notices must be in writing or, if the consumer agrees, electronically.[524] Further, notices must be provided so that each consumer can reasonably expect to receive actual notice.[525] Regulation P provides examples of what may constitute a reasonable expectation of actual notice, but in no event may notice be oral.[526] The notice should be (1) a hand-delivered, printed copy to the consumer, (2) a mailed, printed copy to the consumer's last known address, or (3) posted on the institution's electronic site with acknowledgement of receipt by the consumer required in order to proceed with the transaction.[527] Notices must be clear and conspicuous.[528]

As referenced above, the financial institution cannot disclose nonpublic personal information to nonaffiliated third parties without notifying the consumer of the consumer's ability to opt out of the disclosure and without giving the consumer a reasonable opportunity to opt out.[529] The financial institution gives the consumer a reasonable ability to opt of disclosure of the consumer's nonpublic personal information to nonaffiliated third parties if the institution (1) designates check-off boxes in prominent positions on the forms with the opt-out notices, (2) includes a reply form with the notice and the address where the form may be mailed, (3) provides a toll-free number where the consumer may

---

[517] *See* 12 C.F.R. § 1016.4(b)(2).
[518] *See* 15 U.S.C. § 6803(a).
[519] *See* 12 C.F.R. § 1016.5(b)(1).
[520] *See* 12 C.F.R. § 1016.7(a)(3) (Fastcase 2018).
[521] *See* 12 C.F.R. § 1016.7(a)(3).
[522] *See* 12 C.F.R. § 1016.7(h).
[523] *See* 12 C.F.R. § 1016.7(G).
[524] *See* 12 C.F.R. § 1016.9(a) (Fastcase 2018); *see* 15 U.S.C. § 6803(a).
[525] *See* 12 C.F.R. § 1016.9(a).
[526] *See* 12 C.F.R. § 1016.9(d).
[527] *See* 12 C.F.R. § 1016.9(b).
[528] *See* 12 C.F.R. § 1016.7(a).
[529] *See* 12 C.F.R. § 1016.10(a)(1)ii)-(iii).

opt out, or (4) provides an electronic means to opt out, if the consumer has consented to electronic communications.[530]

As a reminder, institutions are not required to provide a Regulation P Privacy Notice if the nonpublic personal information is being disclosed "as necessary to effect, administer or enforce a transaction that a consumer requests or authorizes, or in connection with" specified tasks/activities as referenced *supra*.[531]

---

[530] *See* 12 C.F.R. § 1016.7(a)(2)(ii).
[531] *See* 12 C.F.R. § 1016.1(a); *see also* 15 U.S.C. § 6802(e)(1).

B. ENFORCEMENT

Consumer Financial Privacy is enforced by the CFPB over those institutions over which the CFPB has regulatory oversight.[532] The prudential regulators enforce consumer financial privacy with regard to those entities over which the prudential regulators have enforcement authority.[533] Prior to the creation of the CFPB, GLBA was enforced by the Federal Trade Commission over nondepository institutions and by the prudential regulators over depository institutions.

Recall that the Consumer Financial Protection Bureau provides a safe harbor for use of model forms issued with rules.[534] Model forms are available for compliance with the Regulation P. A financial institution that uses the Model Form for Regulation P Privacy Notice compliance is considered compliant.[535] Note that there is no private right of action for violation of consumer financial privacy.

---

[532] *See* 15 U.S.C. § 6805 (Fastcase 2018).
[533] *See* 15 U.S.C. § 6805.
[534] 12 U.S. C. § 5532(d).
[535] *See* 15 U.S.C. § 6803(4); *see also* 12 C.F.R. § 1016.2(a).

C. INTERPRETATION

Because a private right of action is not available to individuals for consumer financial privacy violations, consider the following complaint.

IN THE MATTER OF FRANKLIN'S BUDGET CAR SALES, INC. (COMPLAINT)

UNITED STATES OF AMERICA
FEDERAL TRADE COMMISSION

COMMISSIONERS: **Jon Leibowitz, Chairman**
        J. Thomas Rosch
        Edith Ramirez
        Julie Brill
        Maureen K. Ohlhausen

In the Matter of Franklin's Budget Car Sales, Inc., also dba Franklin Toyota/Scion, a corporation.	**Docket No. C-**

COMPLAINT

The Federal Trade Commission ("FTC" or "Commission"), having reason to believe that Franklin's Budget Car Sales, Inc., also dba Franklin Toyota/Scion ("Franklin Toyota" or "respondent") has violated Section 5(a) of the FTC Act, 15 U.S.C. § 45(a); the provisions of the Commission's Standards for Safeguarding Customer Information Rule ("Safeguards Rule"), 16 C.F.R. Part 314, issued pursuant to Title V, Subtitle A of the Gramm-Leach-Bliley Act ("GLB Act") (codified at 15 U.S.C. §§ 6801-6809); and the Commission's Privacy of Customer Financial Information Rule ("Privacy Rule"), 16 C.F.R. Part 313, issued pursuant to the GLB Act; and it appearing to the Commission that this proceeding is in the public interest, alleges:

1. Respondent Franklin's Budget Car Sales, Inc., also dba Franklin Toyota/Scion ("Franklin Toyota") is a Georgia corporation with its registered address as P.O. Box 648, Statesboro, Georgia 30459 and its places of business at 500 Commerce Boulevard, Statesboro, Georgia 30458; 400 Northside Drive, Statesboro, Georgia 30458; and 733 Northside Drive East, Statesboro, Georgia 30459.

2. The acts and practices of respondent as alleged in this complaint are in or affecting commerce, as "commerce" is defined in Section 4 of the Federal Trade Commission Act.

RESPONDENT'S BUSINESS PRACTICES

3. Respondent Franklin Toyota is a franchise automobile dealership that sells both new and used automobiles, leases automobiles, provides repair services for automobiles, and sells

automobile parts. In connection with its automobile sales, Franklin Toyota provides financing services to individual consumers.

4.   Since at least 2001, respondent has disseminated, or caused to be disseminated, to consumers statements concerning Franklin Toyota's privacy and data security policies and practices, including, but not limited to the following:

> We restrict access to non public personal information about you to only those employees who need to know that information to provide products and services to you. We maintain physical, electronic, and procedural safe guards that comply with federal regulations to guard non public personal information.

Franklin Toyota Privacy Policy, attached as Exhibit A.

5.   In conducting business, respondent routinely collects personal information from or about its customers, including, but not limited to names, Social Security numbers, addresses, telephone numbers, dates of birth, and drivers' license numbers (collectively, "personal information").

6.   Respondent uses computer networks to conduct its business and collect consumer information. Among other things, it uses the networks to obtain an online credit application from consumers; obtain outside lead information; maintain customer automobile and payment records; and manage customer car sales records, finance, and insurance records.

7.   Respondent did not provide its customers with annual privacy notices and did not provide a clear and conspicuous opt-out notice that accurately explains to its customers their rights to opt out of any sharing of nonpublic information with unaffiliated third parties.

RESPONDENT'S SECURITY PRACTICES

8.   Respondent has engaged in a number of practices that, taken together, failed to provide reasonable and appropriate security for personal information on its computers and networks. Among other things, respondent failed to:

a.   Assess risks to the consumer personal information it collected and stored online;

b.   Adopt policies, such as an incident response plan, to prevent, or limit the extent of, unauthorized disclosure of personal information;

c.   Use reasonable methods to prevent, detect, and investigate unauthorized access to personal information on its networks, such as inspecting outgoing transmissions to the internet to identify unauthorized disclosures of personal information;

d.   Adequately train employees about information security to prevent unauthorized disclosures of personal information; and

e.   Employ reasonable measures to respond to unauthorized access to personal information on its networks or to conduct security investigations where unauthorized access to information occurred.

9.   As a result of the failures set forth in Paragraph 8, customers' personal information was accessed and disclosed on peer-to-peer ("P2P") networks by a P2P application installed on a computer that was connected to respondent's computer network.

10.   Information for approximately 95,000 consumers, including, but not limited to, names, Social Security numbers, addresses, dates of birth, and drivers' license numbers ("customer files") was made available on a P2P network. Such information can easily be misused to commit identity theft and fraud.

11.   Files shared to a P2P network are available for viewing or downloading by anyone using a computer that operates a compatible P2P application. Generally, a file that has been shared cannot be removed from P2P networks.

VIOLATIONS OF THE FTC ACT

12.   Section 5(a) of the FTC Act, 15 U.S.C. § 45(a), prohibits unfair or deceptive acts or practices in or affecting commerce.

13.   As set forth in Paragraph 4, respondent has represented, expressly or by implication, that it implements reasonable and appropriate measures to protect consumers' personal information from unauthorized access.

14.   In truth and in fact, respondent did not implement reasonable and appropriate measures to protect consumers' personal information from unauthorized access. Therefore, the representation set forth in Paragraph 13 was, and is, false or misleading, in violation of Section 5(a) of the FTC Act, 15 U.S.C. § 45(a).

VIOLATION OF THE PRIVACY RULE

18.   The Privacy Rule, which implements Section 503 of the GLB Act, 15 U.S.C. § 6803, requires financial institutions to provide customers, no later than when a customer relationship arises and annually for the duration of that relationship, "a clear and conspicuous notice that accurately reflects [the financial institution's] privacy policies and practices," including its security policies and practices. 16 C.F.R. § 313.4(a), 313.5(a)(1), 313.6(a)(8). In addition, the Privacy Rule requires financial institutions to provide reasonable means for its customers to opt out of the institution's sharing of nonpublic customer information to nonaffiliated third parties and provide opt-out notices to consumers. 16 C.F.R. § 313.7. Violations of the Privacy Rule are enforced through the FTC Act. 15 U.S.C. § 6805(a)(7).

19.   As set forth in Paragraph 7, respondent failed to send consumers annual privacy notices and did not provide a mechanism by which consumers could opt out of information sharing with nonaffiliated third parties in violation of the Privacy Rule.

20.   The acts and practices of respondent as alleged in this complaint constitute unfair or deceptive acts or practices, in or affecting commerce, in violation of Section 5(a) of the FTC Act.

THEREFORE, the Federal Trade Commission this _____ day of _____, 2012, has issued this complaint against respondent.

By the Commission.

Donald S. Clark
Secretary

VIII. FAIR CREDIT REPORTING ACT

A. LAWS AND RULES

Recall that the Truth in Lending Act, the Equal Credit Opportunity Act, and the Fair Debt Collection Practices Act, provisions are located within 15 U.S.C. Chapter 41: Consumer Credit Protection.[536] Specifically, TILA, ECOA, and FDCPA provisions are found within Subchapter I: Consumer Credit Cost Disclosure, Subchapter IV: Equal Credit Opportunity, and Subchapter V: Debt Collection Practices, respectively.[537] Collectively, these subchapters, among others, make up the Consumer Credit Protection Act of 1968.[538] Requirements with respect to credit reporting agencies are also a part of the Consumer Credit Protection Act of 1968, namely 15 U.S.C. 1681 *et seq.*

The Fair Credit Reporting Act was passed in 1970. Prior to the CFPB, the Federal Reserve Board was tasked with rulemaking with respect to Regulation V. Regulation V, 12 C.F.R. Part 1022 *et seq.* is the implementing regulation for the Fair Credit Reporting Act. Now the CFPB is tasked with creating implementing regulations for the Fair Credit Reporting Act with respect to the requirements of users of consumer reports,[539] and the CFPB can create regulations offering guidance related to handling consumer report discrepancies/disputes.[540] The CFPB receives deference in interpretation of laws and rules over which it has rulemaking authority, including interpretation of some parts of the FCRA.[541] Note that the CFPB's rulemaking power is limited. The FCRA includes provisions regarding the use of consumer reports (as referenced above), transparency in the use of credit (in some respects, similar to ECOA), and the procedures, protections, and risks related to consumer information, including identity theft. While the CFPB has rulemaking authority regarding the use of consumer reports and transparency, the CFPB does not have rulemaking authority with respect to the procedures, protections, and risks related to consumer information. Specifically, the CFPB does not have rulemaking authority regarding the identity theft red flags and disposal of consumer information, for example. Rulemaking power in these areas is retained by the Federal Trade Commission and/or other federal agencies[542] and will not be discussed in this text.

One purpose of the Fair Credit Reporting Act was to ensure that "consumer reporting agencies adopt reasonable procedures for meeting the needs of commerce for consumer credit [...] with regard to the confidentiality, accuracy, relevancy, and proper utilization of such information."[543] This text will

---

[536] *See* 15 U.S.C. § 1601 *et seq.*; 15 U.S.C. § 1691 *et seq.*; 15 U.S.C. § 1692 *et seq.*
[537] *See* 15 U.S.C. § 1601 *et seq.*; 15 U.S.C. § 1691 *et seq.*; 15 U.S.C. § 1692 *et seq.*
[538] *See* 15 U.S.C. § 1601 *et seq.*
[539] 15 U.S.C. § 1681m(h)(6) (Fastcase 2018).
[540] *See* 15 U.S.C. § 1681s-2(a)(8) (Fastcase 2018).
[541] 15 U.S.C. § 1681s (Fastcase 2018).
[542] *See* 15 U.S.C. § 1681m(e); 15 U.S.C. § 1681(f) (Fastcase 2018).
[543] 15 U.S.C. § 1681(b).

consider three specific consumer protection provisions of the Fair Credit Reporting Act, including (1) using the consumer report, namely in the context of firm offers of credit, (2) updating the consumer report with accurate information, including in the context of consumer disputes, and (3) notifying the consumer of adverse actions, in the context of credit.

As the Fair Credit Reporting Act is a consumer protection law, and, consistent with the other consumer protection laws, **consumer** is a defined term. A consumer is an individual.[544] In addition to the consumer, there are three relevant persons discussed for FCRA purposes: (1) a user, (2) a furnisher, and a (3) consumer reporting agency. Many provisions of the FCRA apply to a "person." A **person** is defined by the Fair Credit Reporting Act to mean any individual, partnership, corporation, trust, estate, cooperative, association, government or governmental subdivision or agency, or other entity. [545] Both furnishers and users are persons, as that term is defined by the Fair Credit Reporting Act. These persons and obligations of each are discussed in more detail below, but generally, the implementing regulations apply to "persons that obtain and use information about consumers to determine the consumer's eligibility for products, services, or employment, share such information among affiliates, and furnish information to consumer reporting agencies."[546] This text focuses on the regulations applicable to those that fall within the scope of Regulation V regarding products and services and does not include information regarding employment eligibility. In addition, this text focuses on the consumer protection with which the CFPB has oversight. As a result, this text does not include a discussion of identity theft and Red Flags Rule provisions. Users and furnishers will be discussed in more detail *infra*.

A **consumer reporting agency**, also known as a credit bureau, is "any person, which, for monetary fees, dues, or on a cooperative nonprofit basis, regularly engages in whole or in part in the practice of assembling or evaluating consumer credit information or other information on consumers for the purpose of furnishing consumer reports to third parties, and which uses any means or facility of interstate commerce for the purpose of preparing or furnishing consumer reports."[547] Experian, Transunion, and Equifax are the most well-known consumer reporting agencies.

Recall Part VII, Consumer Financial Privacy. Consumer financial privacy laws and rules prohibit the disclosure of nonpublic personal information. The Fair Credit Reporting Act also limits disclosing credit report information without an authorized reason.[548] Consumer reports may be used for distinct purposes under the law.[549] Persons who use the consumer report for authorized purposes are consumer report **users**. A consumer reporting agency may provide a consumer report to a person the consumer reporting agency has reason to believe intends to use the information in connection with a credit transaction involving the consumer that the user is inquiring about and to whom the person may

---

[544] *See* 15 U.S.C. § 1681a(c).
[545] 15 U.S.C. § 1681a(b).
[546] *See* 12 C.F.R. § 1022.1(a) (Fastcase 2018).
[547] 15 U.S.C. § 1681a(f).
[548] *See generally* 15 U.S.C. § 1681b (Fastcase 2018).
[549] *See id.*

extend credit or review or collect on an account of.[550] This purpose contemplates transactions initiated by the consumer.[551] However, providing a consumer report for credit purposes is further limited. Providing consumer reports for credit purposes not initiated by the consumer is not permissible if not authorized by the consumer, unless the consumer authorizes the consumer reporting agency to provide the report or the transaction involves a firm offer of credit or insurance, among other exceptions.[552] In other words, a consumer reporting agency may provide a consumer report if it is requested for a "firm offer of credit" even if the consumer did not initiate the credit transaction and did not authorize the consumer reporting agency to provide the consumer report. [553] The permissibility of receiving credit reports by extending a "firm offer of credit" is found in 15 U.S.C. § 1681b of the Fair Credit Reporting Act.

The users of the credit report must identify themselves to the credit reporting agency, certify the purpose of use of the consumer report, and certify that the consumer report will not be used for any other purpose.[554] The consumer reporting agency may provide limited information for a firm offer of credit, namely: (1) the name and address of the consumer, (2) an identifier that is not unique to the consumer but that can be used to verify the consumer's identity, and (3) other information about the consumer that does not reveal the consumer's relationships or experience with particular creditors or other entities.[555] Consumers may elect to be removed from lists of names and addresses that consumer reporting agencies provide to persons extending firm offers of credit.[556] A **firm offer of credit** is defined in the law. Specifically, a firm offer of credit is:

> Any offer of credit to a consumer that will be honored if the consumer is determined, based on information in a consumer report on the consumer, to meet the specific criteria used to select the consumer for the offer, except that the offer may be further conditioned on one or more of the following:
> (1) The consumer being determined, based on information in the consumer's application for the credit, to meet specific criteria bearing on credit worthiness, as applicable, that are established—
> (A) before selection of the consumer for the offer; and
> (B) for the purpose of determining whether to extend credit pursuant to the offer.
>
> (2) Verification—
> (A) that the consumer continues to meet the specific criteria used to select the consumer for the offer, by using information in a consumer report on the consumer,

---

[550] *See* 15 U.S.C. § 1681b(a)(3). A consumer report may be furnished for other purposes, including for employment, for underwriting insurance, and for a determination of government granted license or benefit eligibility, among other purposes. However, for the purposes of consumer financial services in the context of credit, this chapter will focus on the law and rules related to furnishing consumer reports for credit purposes.
[551] *Cf.* 15 U.S.C. § 1681b(c).
[552] *See id.*
[553] *See id.*
[554] 15 U.S.C. § 1681e(a) (Fastcase 2018).
[555] *See* 15 U.S.C. § 1681b(c)(2).
[556] 15 U.S.C. § 1681b(f).

information in the consumer's application for the credit, or other information bearing on the credit worthiness of the consumer; or

(B) of the information in the consumer's application for the credit, to determine that the consumer meets the specific criteria bearing on credit worthiness or insurability.

(3) The consumer furnishing any collateral that is a requirement for the extension of the credit that was—

(A) established before selection of the consumer for the offer of credit or insurance; and

(B) disclosed to the consumer in the offer of credit.[557]

Persons soliciting consumers via a firm offer of credit must disclose certain information in a statement to the consumer.[558] This requirement to disclose certain information in a firm offer of credit is found in 15 U.S.C. §1681m of the Fair Credit Reporting Act. The information disclosed must be clear and conspicuous.[559] Pursuant to 15 U.S.C. §1681m(d), the statement must inform the consumer that: (1) information from the consumer's consumer report was used, (2) the consumer received the firm offer of credit because the consumer satisfied the criteria for credit-worthiness, (3) once the consumer responds to the offer, that the credit may not be extended if the consumer does not meet the criteria used to select the consumer for the offer, does not meet other credit worthiness criteria, or does not provide required collateral, where applicable; (4) the consumer may opt out of receiving such firm offers of credit in the future; and (5) how the consumer can exercise the consumer's right to opt out of receiving firm offers of credit in the future.[560] The statement must also include the address and telephone number that the consumer may use to opt out of firm offers of credit.[561]

Further guidance concerning opting out of receiving firm offers of credit is provided in Regulation V. Specifically, this disclosure is referred to as the prescreen opt-out notice.[562] The person must provide the pre-screen opt-out notice utilizing both a "short form notice" and a "long form notice."[563] Both the short form notice and the long form notice must be "clear and conspicuous" and "simple and easy to understand."[564] The short form notice must state that the consumer may opt out of receiving firm offers of credit and the telephone number to use for the consumer to exercise the opt-out right.[565] The short form notice must also direct the consumer to the long form notice and not include any other

---

[557] *See* 15 U.S.C. §1681a(l).

[558] 15 U.S.C. §1681m(d).

[559] *Id.*

[560] 15 U.S.C. § 1681m(d)(1).

[561] 15 U.S.C. § 1681m(d)(2).

[562] *See* 12 C.F.R. § 1022.54(c) (Fastcase 2018).

[563] *See id.*

[564] *See* 12 C.F.R. § 1022.54(c)(1)(2); 12 C.F.R. § 1022.54(b) (Simple and easy to understand is defined by the regulation to mean a layered format, using plain language that can be understood by ordinary consumers, clear and concise sentences, paragraphs and sections; and short explanatory sentences, definite, concrete, everyday words, use of active voice; and avoidance of double negatives; avoidance of legal and technical business terminology, avoidance of imprecise explanations subject to different interpretations, and use of language that is not misleading).

[565] *See* 12 C.F.R. 1022.54(c)(1).

information.[566] Finally, the short form notice has specific form requirements, including with respect to type size, location (on the front side of a page or otherwise in close proximity to the marketing message), and conspicuousness (including type style and distinguishing the notice from other text).[567] The long form notice must disclose the information required by 15 U.S.C. §1681m(d) discussed *supra*. The long form notice also has specific form requirements, including with respect to the type size, location, and conspicuousness.[568]

Compare and contrast the form requirements for the disclosures required by Regulation V with the disclosures required by other laws and rules. **How do the form requirements differ from the form requirements of other regulations or laws requiring consumer disclosures?**

Persons who make firm offers of credit must keep the criteria used to select the consumer and credit worthiness criteria for at least three years.[569] The CFPB provides an example of the firm offer of credit transaction and verification process:

> On January 1, a credit card lender obtains a list from a consumer reporting agency of consumers in County Y who have credit scores of 720, and no previous bankruptcy records. The lender mails solicitations offering a pre-approved credit card to everyone on the list on January 2. On January 31, a consumer responds to the offer and the lender obtains and reviews a full consumer report that shows a bankruptcy record was added on January 15. Since this consumer no longer meets the lender's predetermined criteria, the lender is not required to issue the credit card.[570]

Persons, including users of consumer reports, have additional requirements. Persons must provide an oral, written, or electronic adverse action notice to the consumer if the person takes an adverse action that is based on information in the consumer report.[571] This requirement to provide an adverse action notice is found in 15 U.S.C. §1681m. An **adverse action**, for credit purposes, is defined under the Fair Credit Reporting Act as a denial or revocation of credit, a change in terms of an existing credit arrangement, or a refusal to grant credit in substantially the amount or on substantially the terms requested.[572] The person who takes adverse action based on information in the consumer report must also disclose, in writing or electronically to the consumer, the consumer's numerical credit score (if applicable),[573] as well as the range of possible credit scores, four key factors that adversely affected the

---

[566] *See* 12 C.F.R. § 1022.54(c)(1).
[567] *See id.*
[568] *See* 12 C.F.R. § 1022.54(c)(2).
[569] 15 U.S.C. § 1681m(d)(3).
[570] *See* CONSUMER FIN. PROT. BUREAU, *Consumer Laws and Regulations: Fair Credit Reporting Act, Manual V.2*, at 24, https://s3.amazonaws.com/files.consumerfinance.gov/f/documents/102012_cfpb_fair-credit-reporting-act-fcra_procedures.pdf.
[571] 15 U.S.C. § 1681m(a)(1). Persons must also comply with requirements when adverse actions are based on information other than in a consumer report. *See generally* 15 U.S.C. §1681m(b). However, this text does not explore these adverse action types and corresponding requirements in detail.
[572] 15 U.S.C. § 1691(d)(6).
[573] 15 U.S.C. § 1681m(a).

credit score, the date the credit score was generated, and the name of the person providing the credit score.[574]   The key factors disclosed mean all relevant elements or reasons adversely affecting the credit score for the particular individual, listed in order of importance based on the effect to the credit score.[575]   The person must also disclose orally, in writing, or electronically (1) the name, address, and telephone number of the consumer reporting agency that provided the consumer report to the person,[576] (2) that the consumer reporting agency did not make the adverse decision and cannot provide specific reasons to the consumer concerning the adverse decision,[577] (3) the consumer's right to obtain a free copy of the consumer's credit report from the consumer reporting agency within 60 days of the adverse action,[578] and (4) that the consumer has the right to dispute information in a consumer report with the consumer reporting agency.[579]   The disclosures required for an adverse action notice pursuant to the Fair Credit Reporting Act are found in 15 U.S.C. §1681m.

Recall the circumstances under which an adverse action notice is required under ECOA. Recall the definition of an **adverse action** for the purposes of ECOA. **How do the ECOA and FCRA adverse action requirements differ, if at all?** Adverse action notices under the ECOA and Regulation B are intended to protect against credit discrimination by requiring creditors to explain the reasons adverse action was taken. The FCRA adverse action notice requirement is intended to make consumers aware of negative consumer report information related to the consumer's credit. Creditors often provide one notice that is compliant with both ECOA and FCRA.

The Fair Credit Reporting Act requires, among other things, that persons report accurate information, correct information, and update information furnished to consumer reporting agencies[580] A **furnisher** uses consumer credit information (consumer reports) and provides information regarding consumer accounts and relationships back to consumer reporting agencies. The term furnisher is not defined in the Fair Credit Reporting Act. However, furnisher is defined in the implementing regulation. A **furnisher** is an entity that furnishes information relating to consumers to one or more credit reporting agencies for inclusion in the consumer report.[581]

A person is prohibited from reporting inaccurate consumer information to the consumer reporting agencies if the person knows or has reasonable cause to believe the information is inaccurate.[582] The person is prohibited from providing information to a consumer reporting agency if the person has been notified by the consumer that the information is inaccurate and the information is actually inaccurate.[583] The Fair Credit Reporting Act also requires that furnishers promptly notify a consumer reporting agency,

---

[574] 15 U.S.C. § 1681g(f)(1).

[575] 15 U.S.C. § 1681g(f)(2)(B).

[576] 15 U.S.C. § 1681m(a)(3)(A).

[577] 15 U.S.C. § 1681m(a)(3)(B).

[578] 15 U.S.C. § 1681m(a)(4)(A).

[579] 15 U.S.C. § 1681m(a)(4)(B).

[580] *See* 15 U.S.C. § 1681s-2(a)(1)-(2) (Fastcase 2018).

[581] *See* 12 C.F.R. § 1022.41(c) (Fastcase 2018).

[582] 15 U.S.C. § 1681s-2(a)(1).

[583] 15 U.S.C. §1681s-2(a)(1)(B).

correct, and update information about the furnisher's transactions and experiences with the consumer that the furnisher has inaccurately furnished to the consumer reporting agency.[584]

Ultimately, the furnisher is responsible for establishing and implementing reasonable, written policies and procedures regarding the accuracy and integrity of consumer information furnished to consumer reporting agencies.[585] **Accuracy** is defined in Regulation V. **Integrity** is defined in Regulation V. These definitions in the implementing regulation provide guidance on furnishing requirements. **Accuracy** is information that the furnisher provides to a consumer reporting agency about the account or relationship with the consumer that correctly reflect the terms of and liability for the account or relationship, that reflects the consumer's performance or other conduct concerning the account or relationship, and identifies the appropriate consumer.[586] **Integrity** is information that a furnisher provides to a consumer reporting agency about the account or relationship with the consumer that (1) is substantiated by the furnisher's records at the time the information is furnished, (2) is furnished in a form and manner that is designed to minimize the likelihood that the information may be incorrectly reflected in a consumer report, and (3) includes the credit limit, if applicable and in the furnisher's possession, and (4) includes the information in the furnisher's possession about the account or other relationship that the Consumer Financial Protection Bureau has determined would be misleading in a credit-worthiness determination if not included.[587]

Pursuant to the Fair Credit Reporting Act, the consumer may dispute information in the consumer report directly with the person by sufficiently identifying the information in dispute, explaining the reason for the dispute, and providing supporting documents to the person.[588] Regulation V states that documentation for the furnisher to substantiate the dispute could include a copy of the relevant portion of the inaccurate consumer report, a police report, account statements, or a court order, for example.[589]

Once the consumer submits a direct request disputing the information to the person, the person is required to conduct an investigation of the disputed information, review the relevant information provided by the consumer, complete the investigation, and provide the results of the investigation to the consumer within 30 days of receiving notice of the dispute.[590] This initial request from the consumer is called a direct dispute. **Direct dispute** is defined in Regulation V. A direct dispute that mandates the investigation required by the statute is a dispute by the consumer submitted directly to the furnisher "concerning the accuracy of information in the consumer report and pertaining to an account or other relationship that the furnisher has or had with the consumer."[591] It is notable that a furnisher must conduct a *reasonable* investigation of a direct dispute, pursuant to Regulation V, if the dispute relates to (1) the consumer's liability for the credit account or debt, (2) the terms of the credit account or debt, (3)

---

[584] 15 U.S.C. § 1681s-2(a)(2).
[585] 12 C.F.R. § 1022.42 (Fastcase 2018).
[586] *See* 12 C.F.R. § 1022.41(a).
[587] 12 C.F.R. § 1022.41(d); 12 C.F.R. Appendix E to Part 1022 I(b)(2)(iii) (Fastcase 2018).
[588] 15 U.S.C. § 1681s-2(a)(8)(D); *see* 12 C.F.R. 1022.43(d) (Fastcase 2018).
[589] 12 C.F.R. § 1022.43(d)(3).
[590] 15 U.S.C. § 1681s-2(a)(8)E); 12 C.F.R. 1022.43(e).
[591] 12 C.F.R. § 1022.41(b).

the consumer's performance, conduct, or relationship with the furnisher, or (4) any information in the consumer report regarding the account or relationship that bears on the consumer's credit worthiness, credit standing, credit capacity, etc.[592] If a consumer disputes consumer report information, the person is required to notify the consumer reporting agency that the information is disputed,[593] and the consumer reporting agency must update the consumer report to indicate that the information is disputed.[594] The person is only required to conduct the reasonable investigation if the consumer's direct dispute is submitted to the addresses designated in the regulation, namely (1) the furnisher's address as disclosed in the consumer report, (2) the furnisher's designated address for direct disputes provided to the consumer in writing, or (3) any business address of the furnisher if the furnisher has not designated a direct dispute address or an address on the consumer report.[595] Finally, if the investigation reveals that the disputed information is inaccurate, the person is required to notify the consumer reporting agency, update and correct the disputed information.[596] In addition to guidance in the regulations, the requirements imposed upon a furnisher relating to both accurate information furnishing and direct disputes are found in 15 U.S.C. §1681s-2(a)(1)-(3) and (8).

A consumer may also dispute the consumer's consumer report information with the consumer reporting agency.[597] If the consumer disputes information with the consumer reporting agency, the consumer reporting agency will notify the furnisher of the disputed information as the consumer reporting agency must conduct a "reinvestigation."[598] To conduct the "reinvestigation," the consumer reporting agency needs to learn from the furnisher whether the information the consumer disputes is, in fact, inaccurate.[599] Upon receiving notification of the consumer dispute from the consumer reporting agency, the furnisher must conduct an investigation of the disputed information, review the relevant information that the consumer reporting agency provided, complete the investigation, and provide the results of the investigation to the consumer reporting agency within thirty days of the consumer reporting's agency's receipt of the consumer dispute.[600] If the furnisher determines that the reported information is inaccurate or incomplete, the furnisher must notify other consumer reporting agencies of the results of the furnisher's investigation.[601] Finally, if the furnisher determines that the reported information is inaccurate, incomplete, or cannot be verified, the furnisher must promptly delete, modify, or permanently block the reporting of the disputed information.[602] The requirements of furnishers regarding consumer disputes by the consumer to the consumer reporting agency, that the consumer reporting agency notifies the furnisher of, are found in 15 U.S.C. §1681s-2(b)(1)-(2).

---

[592] *See* 12 C.F.R. § 1022.43(a).

[593] 15 U.S.C. § 1681s-2(a)(3).

[594] 15 U.S.C. § 1681c(f).

[595] 12 C.F.R. § 1022.43(c).

[596] 15 U.S.C. § 1681s-2(a)(8)E); *see also* 12 C.F.R. § 1022.43(e).

[597] *See generally* 15 U.S.C. §1681i (Fastcase 2018).

[598] 15 U.S.C. § 1681i(2).

[599] 15 U.S.C. § 1681i(2).

[600] 15 U.S.C. § 1681s-2(b)(1); 15 U.S.C. § 1681i(a)(1)(A).

[601] 15 U.S.C. § 1681s-2(b)((1)(D).

[602] 15 U.S.C. § 1681s-2(b)((1)(E).

In addition to (1) reporting accurate information, (2) complying with direct dispute requirements, (3) complying with requirements related to a consumer's dispute to the consumer reporting agency, and (4) establishing and implementing written policies and procedures related to the accuracy and integrity of consumer information, the furnisher has at least one additional requirement under FCRA. If a financial institution extends credit, regularly furnishes information to a consumer reporting agency, and furnishes negative information to the consumer reporting agency regarding credit extended to a customer, the financial institution must provide written notice to the customer, within 30 days after the reporting of negative information, informing the consumer that the negative information may or has been furnished.[603] The CFPB clarifies that negative information is "any information concerning a customer's delinquencies, late payments, insolvency, or any form of default."[604] The requirements imposed upon furnishers concerning reporting negative information are found in 15 U.S.C. 1681s-2(a)(7).

---

[603] *See* 15 U.S.C. § 1681s-2(a)(7).
[604] *See* CONSUMER FIN. PROT. BUREAU, *supra* note 570, at 59.

B. ENFORCEMENT

Prior to the CFPB, the Federal Trade Commission was tasked with enforcement of the Fair Credit Reporting Act, and the Federal Reserve Board was tasked with rulemaking with respect to Regulation V. Regulation V, 12 C.F.R. Part 1022 *et seq.* is the implementing regulation for the Fair Credit Reporting Act. The CFPB is tasked with enforcement of the Fair Credit Reporting Act with respect to the institutions where the CFPB has enforcement authority. Recall that the CFPB has exclusive rulemaking, enforcement, and federal supervisory authority over nondepository institutions, including "larger participants." The CFPB has oversight over larger participants in the consumer reporting market with annual receipts in excess of seven million dollars.[605] Review 12 U.S.C. § 5565 for relief that is available for violation of rule or law enforced by the CFPB. Recall that relief by the CFPB can include:

> (A) rescission or reformation of contracts;
> (B) refund of moneys or return of real property;
> (C) restitution;
> (D) disgorgement or compensation for unjust enrichment;
> (E) payment of damages or other monetary relief;
> (F) public notification regarding the violation, including the costs of notification;
> (G) limits on the activities or functions of the person; and
> (H) civil money penalties.[606]

Civil penalties may not be imposed without due process: notice and a hearing for the person accused of the violation.[607]

The Federal Trade Commission retains enforcement authority with respect to consumer reporting agencies not under the CFPB's authority.[608] The Federal Trade Commission may initiate a civil action for a "knowing" violation of the Fair Credit Reporting Act.[609] Specifically, the Federal Trade Commission may bring an action against persons with a "pattern or practice of violations," and such liability is limited to $2,500 per violation.[610]

Recall the discussion of FDCPA compliance liability in Part V. **Why does FCRA liability extend to each violation and FDCPA liability is limited to each cause of action?[611]**

---

[605] 12 C.F.R. § 1090.104(b) (Fastcase 2018).
[606] 12 U.S.C. § 5565 (Fastcase 2018).
[607] *Id.*
[608] 15 U.S.C. § 1681s(a)(1).
[609] 15 U.S.C. § 1681s(a)(2)(A).
[610] 15 U.S.C. § 1681s(a)(2).
[611] *Cf.* 15 U.S.C. § 1681s(a)(2); *Wright*, 22 F. 3d 647 at 650-51.

The CFPB may enforce compliance with respect to larger participant consumer reporting agencies, covered persons, users, and furnishers subject to the FCRA.[612] In addition, other federal regulators, including federal banking regulators and NCUA, may also enforce FCRA compliance with respect to the institutions that those agencies regulate.[613]

Individual actions may also be initiated, in limited circumstances, under the FCRA. Specifically, an action may be maintained against a person who is negligent in the person's failure to comply with the FCRA.[614] In a negligence civil liability action, the consumer may receive actual damages that result from the person's negligent compliance.[615] In addition, an action may be maintained against a person who is willful or knowing in the person's failure to comply with the FCRA.[616] In a willful civil liability action, the consumer may receive actual damages or damages between $100 and $1,000, whichever is greater.[617] Alternatively, for a willful violation by a natural person, where the person obtains a consumer report from a consumer reporting agency "under false pretenses or knowingly without a permissible purpose," the person may be liable for actual damages or $1,000, whichever is greater.[618] For a willful violation, the consumer may receive punitive damages.[619] The statute of limitations for such individual actions is limited to the earlier of two years after the date the plaintiff discovers the violation or five years after the date of the violation itself.[620]

There are limitations to civil liability and administrative enforcement. Consumers are prohibited from initiating civil actions against consumer reporting agencies, users, and furnishers related to defamation, invasion of privacy, or negligence (except as discussed *supra*), with respect to disclosing information.[621] However, the restriction is not applicable if false information was furnished with malice or willful intent to injure the consumer.[622] Only federal regulators may enforce the provisions of 15 U.S.C. §1681m; there is no private right of action for consumers.[623] Further, no person is subject to a compliance violation of 15 U.S.C. §1681m, including for adverse action notice requirements and for firm offers of credit compliance, if the person shows by a preponderance of the evidence that the person maintained reasonable procedures to comply with 15 U.S.C. §1681m at the time of the violation.[624] No person is liable through a civil action for a negligent or willful violation of 15 U.S.C. 1681m, including for adverse action notice requirements and for noncompliance with duties required of users making firm offers of

---

[612] 15 U.S.C. § 1681s(b).

[613] *Id.*

[614] 15 U.S.C. § 1681o(a) (Fastcase 2018).

[615] 15 U.S.C. § 1681p (Fastcase 2018).

[616] 15 U.S.C. § 1681n (Fastcase 2018).

[617] 15 U.S.C. § 1681n(a)(1).

[618] *Id.*

[619] *Id.*

[620] 15 U.S.C. § 1681p.

[621] 15 U.S.C. § 1681h(e) (Fastcase 2018).

[622] *Id.*

[623] *See* 15 U.S.C. § 1681m(c), (h)(8).

[624] 15 U.S.C. § 1681m(c).

credit.[625] Therefore, although there are model notices available for compliance with prescreened firm offers of credit disclosures, a safe harbor for use of the model is inconsequential, as there is no private right of action. No financial institution is subject to a compliance violation of failure to notify the consumer of furnishing negative information, provided that the financial institution maintained reasonable policies and procedures to comply or the financial institution reasonably believed that the institution was legally prohibited from contacting the consumer.[626] A person failing to comply with notifying the consumer of negative information furnished is also not subject to a private right of action by the consumer.[627] Individual civil actions are not permissible for the failure of a person to furnish accurate information with knowledge or notice of the inaccuracy.[628] Nor are individual actions for failure to conduct a reasonable investigation of a direct dispute permissible.[629] However, civil actions may be permissible for willful, knowing, or negligent liability violations from failure to conduct the investigation and other requirements related to duties arising from the notification from the consumer reporting agency to the person for a consumer dispute.[630]

Why do you think civil actions for adverse action notice requirements are not available under FCRA? Recall that civil liability is available for failure to provide an adverse action notice under the Equal Credit Opportunity Act.[631] **Why do you think civil actions for firm offers of credit disclosures compliance are not available under FCRA?**

---

[625] 15 U.S.C. § 1681m(h)(8).
[626] 15 U.S.C. § 1681s-2(a)(7)(F).
[627] 15 U.S.C. § 1681s-2(c)(1).
[628] *See* 15 U.S.C. § 1681s-2(c).
[629] *See id.*
[630] *See* 15 U.S.C. § 1681s-2(b).
[631] *See* 15 U.S.C. § 1691e; 12 C.F.R. § 1002.16.

C. INTERPRETATION

Consider whether the Fair Credit Reporting Act utilizes a restriction consumer protection method or a disclosure consumer protection method. Does FCRA resolve the issue of access to information to create a "fair" playing field or does FCRA resolve the issue of access to financial markets by encouraging financial inclusion?

COLE V. U.S. CAPITAL[632]

RIPPLE, Circuit Judge.

Oneta S. Cole filed a complaint, and later an amended complaint, in which she alleged violations of the Fair Credit Reporting Act ("FCRA"). The defendants, U.S. Capital, Inc., AutoNation USA Corp. ("AutoNation"), and Jerry Gleason Chevrolet, Inc. ("Gleason Chevrolet"), moved to dismiss the second amended complaint. The district court granted the defendants' motion. For the reasons set forth in the following opinion, we reverse the judgment of the district court and remand the case for further proceedings consistent with this opinion.

Facts

Ms. Cole received a promotional credit flyer from U.S. Capital, Inc. and Gleason Chevrolet. The flyer, which she attached to her complaint, states that Ms. Cole is "pre-approved to participate in an exclusive offer from U.S. Capital and Jerry Gleason Chevrolet." The flyer explains that she is eligible to "receive a Visa or MasterCard with limits up to $2000 as well as up to $19,500 in AUTOMOTIVE CREDIT!" *Id.* The flyer then discusses Ms. Cole's ability to purchase a car from Gleason Chevrolet without payments until 2002. Under large, bold letters it instructs Ms. Cole how to activate her card by responding prior to December 8, 2001.

In the bottom one inch (approximately) of the page, in much smaller type, the flyer informs Ms. Cole that:

We have determined that you meet our initial criteria for inclusion in this special credit offer. Because it is an exclusive opportunity we could not offer it to every one. You were selected based on information obtained in your consumer report from Trans Union L.L.C. and the final acceptance is subject to your ability to meet our full eligibility requirements.

The text then specifies the criteria that she would have to meet to take advantage of the offer. Among the requirements, the recipient of the offer must not have a monthly car payment that exceeds 50% of her gross income, the recipient must be eighteen years of age with an annual income of at least $18,000, and all bankruptcies must be discharged. The flyer then states that:

Lender reserves the right to require consumer to pay off currently financed vehicle and may require consumer to increase down payment, which will affect equity and collateral. In any event, you are guaranteed to receive a credit line of at least three hundred dollars for the purchase of a vehicle, GRSI, Coral Springs, FL. If at the time of offer consumer no longer meets the initial criteria, offer may be revoked. We hope you are pleased with the opportunity it affords. If you prefer that your name be omitted from future offerings, please contact Trans Union, Marketing Opt Out, and PO BOX 97328, Jackson, MS 39288-7328 or call 1-888-546-8688.

---

[632] 389 F.3d 719 (7th Cir., 2004).

Finally, the flyer concludes with a "CREDIT CARD DISCLAIMER."

It states that the customer authorizes U.S. Capital Financial Services to act as an agent to obtain a credit card for the customer. It then explains that "[g]uaranteed approval is neither expressed nor implied, interest rates may vary from 2.9% to 24.9% based on individual credit worthiness and lenders credit parameters."

District Court Proceedings

After receiving the flyer, Ms. Cole brought the present action in district court seeking statutory damages and attorneys' fees for alleged violations of the FCRA. In her initial complaint, Ms. Cole alleged that she had not requested the materials that she had received from the defendants. Furthermore, she had not authorized anyone to access her credit report, and therefore, there was no legitimate reason for the defendants to access her credit information. Specifically, Ms. Cole alleged that the materials did not qualify as a firm offer of credit as used in the FCRA. She claimed that "[a]n offer of a $300 line of credit useable only to finance the purchase of an automobile is a sham." The offer was made, she averred, to obtain credit information; it was not extended with the expectation that consumers would avail themselves of the offer.

Ms. Cole also alleged that the terms of the offer were too vague to constitute an offer capable of acceptance. In support of this allegation, Ms. Cole pointed to the fact that the flyer reserves the right to set material terms. Additionally, the offer is ambiguous; the $300 line of credit is characterized first as "guaranteed," but the flyer later states that "[g]uaranteed approval is neither expressed nor implied." Finally, she claimed that the reservation of the right to require the consumer to pay off existing automobile loans "effectively constitutes an option to withdraw the $300 line of credit."

The district court dismissed Ms. Cole's first amended complaint. It held that the defendants had obtained the plaintiff's credit report for a permissible purpose under the FCRA. Specifically, the court held that the defendants obtained the report for the extension of a firm offer of credit. The court rejected Ms. Cole's contention that the $300 credit line was "too paltry a sum to be a `firm offer.'" It reasoned that "the complaint does not allege the $300 credit line to be a sham nor is any inference in the mailing." The court found the offer of "at least" $300 was consistent with the FCRA because the FCRA "permits conditioning a firm offer of credit on `the consumer being determined, based on information in the consumer's application for the credit[,]... to meet specific criteria bearing on credit worthiness'" that were established before the selection of the consumer for the offer. Accordingly, the court concluded that the complaint failed to state a claim upon which relief could be granted.

Ms. Cole then filed a second amended complaint in which she alleged that the flyer was not a firm offer of credit because (1) it was a sham to justify obtaining credit information; (2) it contained an offer that is too vague to be accepted; (3) the language of the flyer was ambiguous or mutually inconsistent; (4) the reservation of a right to require the consumer to pay off existing car loans constituted an option to withdraw the $300 offer; and (5) the disclosure did not comply with the requirements of § 1681m(d) because it is not clear and conspicuous.

Again, the defendants moved to dismiss the complaint, and the district court granted the motion. The court found that there was a guarantee of a $300 credit line and that the flyer indicated that the offer would be honored as required by the FCRA. The court explained that there was no suggestion, other than Ms. Cole's conclusory allegations, that the $300 credit amount would not have been honored. Additionally, the court reasoned, some consumers would be eligible for more than the minimum amount of credit.

The district court also rejected Ms. Cole's argument that the offer was too vague to constitute an offer under Illinois law. The court held that Illinois law did not apply to the offer because there was a presumption, unrebutted in this case, that Congress did not make the application of the federal law dependent on state law. The court believed that Congress intended the FCRA to have uniform application, and, therefore, the definition of what constitutes an offer under Illinois law was not relevant to the determination of whether the flyer constituted a firm offer of credit under § 1681. The court therefore dismissed the complaint as amended.

Ms. Cole timely appealed.

DISCUSSION

. . .

Firm Offer of Credit

As set forth above, the district court dismissed Ms. Cole's second amended complaint on the ground that the offer contained in the flyer was a "firm offer of credit" for purposes of the FCRA. In its view, because the extension of a "firm offer of credit" was a permissible reason for accessing an individual's information under the FCRA, the defendants' actions did not violate the FCRA. Our consideration of the district court's dismissal begins with the statute itself.

Applicable Provisions of the FCRA

   a.   **the statutory definition in context**

In interpreting the FCRA provisions applicable to Ms. Cole's claims, we must keep in mind the "language and design of the statute as a whole." *Milwaukee Gun Club v. Schulz*, 979 F.2d 1252, 1255 (7th Cir.1992). We must "construe statutes in the context of the entire statutory scheme and avoid rendering statutory provisions ambiguous, extraneous, or redundant; we favor the more reasonable result; and we avoid construing statutes contrary to the clear intent of the statutory scheme." *In re Merchants Grain, Inc.*, 93 F.3d 1347, 1353-54 (7th Cir.1996).

Section 1681 sets forth the congressional findings that prompted the adoption of the FCRA as well as the purpose of the Act. In this section, Congress made it clear that the FCRA is designed to preserve the consumer's privacy in the information maintained by consumer reporting agencies. *See* 15 U.S.C. § 1681(a)(4). Specifically, Congress stated: "There is a need to insure that consumer reporting agencies exercise their grave responsibilities with fairness, impartiality, and a respect for the consumer's right to privacy." *Id.; see also Trans Union Corp. v. FTC*, 81 F.3d 228, 234 (D.C.Cir.1996) ("Along with accuracy of collected information, a major purpose of the Act is the privacy of a consumer's credit-related data."); Amicus Br. at 15-16. One means by which Congress effectuated this purpose was prohibiting the release of consumer credit reports unless the release occurs for one of the permissible purposes set forth in 15 U.S.C. § 1681b(a). Section 1681b(a) in turn provides that, "[s]ubject to subsection (c) of this section, any consumer agency may furnish a consumer report under the following circumstances and no other...."

Many of the enumerated permissible purposes set forth in § 1681b are transactions initiated by the consumer; these purposes therefore do not create significant privacy concerns. The subsection does set forth, however, limited situations in which a consumer credit agency may furnish a consumer report even though the consumer has not initiated or authorized the release. One such instance is when a credit or insurance provider is extending the consumer a "firm offer of credit." § 1681b(c)(1)(B)(i). In allowing consumer agencies to release information for the purpose of a "firm offer of credit," Congress "balance[d] any privacy concerns created by pre-screening with the benefit of a firm offer of credit or insurance for all consumers identified through the screening process." *See* S.Rep. No. 103-209, 13 (1993). "In exchange for allowing credit and insurance providers to obtain lists based on more sensitive information ... the bill requires that the credit or insurance provider make a `firm offer,' as defined in section 101 of the Committee bill, of credit or insurance to all consumers on the list." *Id.* at 14. As one of our sister circuits has observed, "Congress apparently believe[d] that people are more willing to reveal personal information in return for guaranteed offers of credit than for catalogs and sales pitches." *Trans Union Corp. v. FTC*, 267 F.3d 1138, 1143 (D.C.Cir.2001).

b. the statutory definition

The term "firm offer of credit" is defined in the FCRA as "any offer of credit or insurance to a consumer that will be honored if the consumer is determined, based on information in a consumer report on the consumer, to meet the specific criteria used to select the consumer for the offer." 15 U.S.C. § 1681a(l). The statute provides that the offer may be conditioned on three specific requirements. First, the creditor may apply additional pre-selected criteria bearing on the consumer's creditworthiness. *See* § 1681a(l)(1). Second, the firm offer may be conditioned on verification "that the consumer continues to meet the specific criteria used to select the consumer for the offer." § 1681a(l)(2). Finally, the offer may be conditioned on the consumer's furnishing any collateral that was both established before the selection of the consumer for the offer and disclosed to the consumer in the offer. *See* § 1681a(l)(3).

Application

Ms. Cole maintains that the offer contained in the flyer was merely a sham to justify obtaining her credit report. She argues that, given the insignificant amount of credit, the offer was not made with the expectation that a significant number of consumers would accept the offer, and, therefore, it cannot constitute a "firm offer of credit" for purposes of the statute.

The defendants counter that the lynchpin of "firm offer of credit" is that some amount of credit — however small — is guaranteed. According to the defendants, "the FCRA does not require a minimum amount" of credit to be offered and therefore the" `preapproval could be for any amount, perhaps even as low as $1.'" [] Thus, in the defendants' view, the fact that the offer was only for $300 does not take it outside of the statutory definition.

We believe that the reading of "firm offer of credit" suggested by the defendants, and accepted by the district court, eviscerates the explicit statutory purpose of protecting consumer data and privacy. *See* 15 U.S.C. § 1681(a)(4). Indeed, such a definition would permit anyone to gain access to a sea of sensitive consumer information simply by offering some nominal amount of guaranteed credit. The statutory scheme of the FCRA makes clear that a "firm offer" must have sufficient value for the consumer to justify the absence of the statutory protection of his privacy. A definition of "firm offer of credit" that does not incorporate the concept of value to the consumer upsets the balance Congress carefully struck between a consumer's interest in privacy and the benefit of a firm offer of credit for all those chosen through the pre-screening process. From the consumer's perspective, an offer of credit without value is the equivalent of an advertisement or solicitation. It is clear that Congress did not intend to allow access to consumer credit information "for catalogs and sales pitches." *Trans Union Corp.*, 267 F.3d at 1143. Such importuning simply — and understandably — is not among the permissible reasons for which a credit agency may disclose a consumer's credit information. *See Trans Union Corp.*, 81 F.3d at 234; *see also Tucker v. Olympia Dodge of Countryside, Inc.*, 2003 WL 21230604, at *3 (N.D.Ill. May 28, 2003). Defining a firm offer of credit as merely any offer that will be honored elevates form over substance, "exalt[s] artifice above reality and ... deprive[s] the statutory provision in question of all serious purpose." *Gregory v. Helvering*, 293 U.S. 465, 470, 55 S.Ct. 266, 79 L.Ed. 596 (1935); *see also Clark v. Rent-It-Corp.*, 685 F.2d 245, 248 (8th Cir.1982) (stating that the Truth In Lending Act ("TILA") "is remedial in nature, and the substance rather than the form of credit transactions should be examined in cases arising under it" (internal quotation marks and citation omitted)).

We believe therefore that the district court's focus on whether the offer would have been honored was inappropriately narrow. Although the statute requires that an offer of credit be honored in order to qualify as a "firm offer of credit," see 15 U.S.C. § 1681a(l) ("The term `firm offer of credit or insurance' means any offer of credit or insurance to a consumer that will be honored...."), this element is not dispositive. To determine whether the offer of credit comports with the statutory definition, a court must consider the entire offer and the effect of all the material conditions that comprise the credit product in question. If, after examining the entire context, the court determines that the "offer" was a guise for solicitation rather than a legitimate credit product, the communication cannot be considered a firm offer of credit.

In making this assessment, one important term for courts to evaluate is the amount of credit to be extended. However, neither a creditor nor a debtor considers the amount of credit in a vacuum; both must know the other terms attached to that credit to determine whether it is advantageous to extend or to accept the offer. The terms of an offer, such as the rate of interest charged, the method of computing interest and the length of the repayment period, may be so onerous as to deprive the offer of any appreciable value.

Here, the pleadings reasonably support the plaintiff's claim that the offer was a sham made to justify access to the consumer credit reports. First, it is far from clear from the flyer that the offer of credit will be honored even if the consumer meets the conditions set forth in the offer. The offer initially states that, "[i]n any event you are guaranteed to receive a credit line of at least three hundred dollars for the purchase of a vehicle, GRSI, Coral Springs, FL." However, later within the offer, the following language appears: "Guaranteed approval is neither express nor implied." Therefore, the language of the flyer itself creates a question whether the offer of credit will be honored.

Additionally, the relatively small amount of credit combined with the known limitations of the offer — that it must be used to purchase a vehicle — raises a question of whether the offer has value to the consumer. Finally, several material terms are missing from the offer. Although the offer indicates that interest rates may vary from 3.0 to 24.9 percent, the precise rate of interest for a particular consumer is unknown. Furthermore, the offer does not specify the method by which interest will be compounded nor the repayment period, although these factors are essential considerations in determining whether the offer has any value. These missing terms render it impossible for a court to determine from the pleadings whether the offer has value. Because the allegations of the complaint state facts that would permit Ms. Cole to establish that the communication had no real value, the district court erred in dismissing Ms. Cole's complaint.

Clear and Conspicuous Statement

Ms. Cole also contends that, even if the flyer contains a firm offer of credit, it nonetheless violates the FCRA for failing to make required disclosures in a clear and conspicuous manner. The district court granted the defendants' Rule 12(b)(6) motion with respect to this claim without discussion. Whether the disclosures contained in the flyer are clear and conspicuous is a matter of law that we review de novo. *See Lifanda v. Elmhurst Dodge, Inc.*, 237 F.3d 803, 805-06 (7th Cir.2001); *Smith v. Check-N-Go of Illinois, Inc.*, 200 F.3d 511, 514 (7th Cir.1999).

Disclosures Required by the FCRA

The FCRA provides that any person using a consumer report to make a firm offer of credit "shall provide with each written solicitation made to the consumer regarding the transaction a clear and conspicuous statement" disclosing statutorily required information. 15 U.S.C. § 1681m(d) (emphasis added). The notice must inform the consumer that: (1) the recipient's consumer credit report was used in determining who should be sent the offer; (2) the consumer was selected because the consumer satisfied certain criteria; (3) the offer may not be extended if the consumer does not continue to meet the criteria bearing on creditworthiness or provide the required collateral; (4) the consumer has the right to opt out of future offers by prohibiting the unsolicited use of information contained in their consumer file; and (5) the consumer may exercise that right by calling a specified toll-free number or by contacting the credit agency at a given address. See id.

The FCRA does not define the term "clear and conspicuous," and, in fact, there is little case law interpreting the term as used in § 1681m. *See Sampson*, 2003 WL 21785612, at *3 (commenting on the lack of case law defining "clear and conspicuous" in the FCRA). However, the term "clear and conspicuous" is a staple in commercial law. *See Channell v. Citicorp Nat'l Servs., Inc.*, 89 F.3d 379, 382 (7th Cir.1996) (noting that neither the Consumer Leasing Act nor regulations defined the term but that the "words were staples of commercial law"). Accordingly, courts that have addressed the term in the FCRA often have turned to cases involving the Uniform Commercial Code ("UCC") and TILA for guidance. *See Stevenson v. TRW Inc.*, 987 F.2d 288, 295 (5th Cir.1993) (defining "clear and conspicuous" language used in 15 U.S.C. § 1681i(d) with reference to TILA and UCC cases); *Tucker v. New Rogers Pontiac, Inc.*, 2003 WL 22078297, at *4 (N.D.Ill. Sept.9, 2003) (addressing the phrase in 15 U.S.C. § 1681m(d)(1) by relying on a TILA decision); *Sampson*, 2003 WL 21785612, at *3-4 (relying on cases from the Fair Debt Collection Practices Act, TILA and other sections of the FCRA to interpret the term in § 1681m).

For example, in *Stevenson*, 987 F.2d 288, the only federal court of appeals case to consider the meaning of "clear and conspicuous" in the context of the FCRA, the Fifth Circuit looked to how the term had been interpreted for purposes of the UCC. That court stated:

The term "conspicuous" has been construed most frequently with the Uniform Commercial Code § 2-316(2), which requires that any exclusion or modification of the implied warranty of merchantability be conspicuous, and that any exclusion or modification of the implied warranty of fitness for a particular purpose be made in a conspicuous writing. A contract's warranty disclaimer satisfies the conspicuous requirement when it is printed in all capital letters, when it appears in a larger type than the terms around it, or when it is in a larger and boldface type. Likewise, a disclaimer in boldface type, printed in all capitals on the face of the warranty above the buyer's signature meets the definition of conspicuousness. A disclaimer is not conspicuous, however, when it is printed in small print on the back of the document, when it is the same size and typeface as the terms around it, or when it is not in boldface or capital lettering. *Stevenson*, 987 F.2d at 296 (internal citations omitted). After reviewing these standards, the court evaluated the notice at issue to determine whether it was conspicuous:

TRW's notice of the consumer's right to have corrected reports sent to creditors was printed in the same size type as the other terms in the same paragraph. The paragraphs around the notice appeared in larger, boldface type. Even if Stevenson read the back of his first credit report, there was nothing to draw his attention particularly to the statutory notice. We conclude that the district court did not err in finding that TRW negligently violated the notice requirement of § 1681i(d).

Like the Fifth Circuit, we believe it is appropriate to draw upon the wealth of UCC and TILA case law in determining the meaning of "clear and conspicuous" under the FCRA. The UCC defines conspicuous as "so written, displayed, or presented that a reasonable person against which it is to operate ought to have noticed it." U.C.C. § 1-201(10). When evaluating a disclaimer of warranty against this standard, we have looked to how many times a customer was made aware of the notice, whether the notice was on the front or back of the document in question, whether the language of the notice was emphasized in some way (such as by bolding the text or by employing all capitals) and whether the notice was set off from the rest of the document so as to draw attention to it. *See H.B. Fuller Co. v. Kinetic Sys., Inc.*, 932 F.2d 681, 689 (7th Cir.1991).

We also have considered the definitions of "clear" and "conspicuous" with respect to TILA. At issue in *Lifanda*, 237 F.3d at 805-06, was whether a disclosure of the term of insurance and the amount of the premium was clear and conspicuous. We stated:

The term of the insurance is set forth in the Auto Theft Registration form, but is set forth in the smallest type on the form, which is so minuscule as to be barely legible. Although the district court notes that TILA does not mandate any minimum type size, it simply does not follow that type size is irrelevant to a determination of whether a disclosure is "conspicuous." If the term "conspicuous" is to retain any meaning at all, it cannot be met as a matter of law by type disproportionately small to that in the rest of the document, and which is itself barely legible. Far from being conspicuous, the "disclosure" here is quite the opposite. *Id.* at 808 (internal citation omitted).

The above cases make it clear that there is not one aspect of a notice that necessarily will render it "clear and conspicuous" for purposes of the FCRA. We must consider the location of the notice within the document, the type size used within the notice as well as the type size in comparison to the rest of the document. We also must consider whether the notice is set off in any other way — spacing, font style, all capitals, etc. In short, there must be something about the way that the notice is presented in the document such that the consumer's attention will be drawn to it.

Application

Turning to the flyer, the required disclosures are condensed into a single paragraph at the very bottom of the flyer. The paragraph consists of nine lines of text that occupy, generously speaking, one inch of space. The font size is no larger than six-point and is the smallest font on the page by several sizes. The notice is not distinct in any way (except in how small it is) — either through color, emphasis or font style. The remainder of the flyer, however, utilizes all caps, bold, italics and various font sizes to emphasize other information being communicated.

 Under any test of conspicuousness, the notice must fail. The type in this disclaimer fairly can be described as disproportionately small compared to the surrounding text; indeed, its size approaches that which cannot be read with the naked eye. The text is the smallest text on a page that is filled with larger type, as well as type that is bolded and italicized. The notice does nothing to draw the reader's attention to this material; to the contrary, the flyer appears to be designed to ensure minimal attention by the reader. Consequently, we must conclude that the district court erred in holding that the defendants' disclosures were clear and conspicuous as a matter of law; indeed, the opposite appears to be the case.

Conclusion

For the foregoing reasons, we reverse the judgment of the district court and remand the case for further proceedings consistent with this opinion. Ms. Cole may recover her costs in this court.   REVERSED and REMANDED

****

8A   **Why does the court consider Cole's "clear and conspicuousness" argument if there is no private right of action for section 1681m claims?** Some federal courts have determined that no

private right of action exists for violations of section 1681m.[633] In addition, interpretation in this area of law is still being formed.

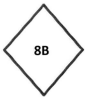

8B

Return to Figure 2C. **What are the interests of the owners'/investors of U.S. Capital, AutoNation, and Gleason Chevrolet in the outcome of the *Cole*[634] case? In what way does the court's decision potentially impact U.S. Capital, AutoNation, and Gleason Chevrolet? How does the court's decision impact U.S. Capital's marketing vendors or other supplier/partner stakeholders?**

8C

Is the value of credit relative?

---

[633] *See, e.g., Perry v. First Nat'l Bank*, 459 F.3d 816, 823 (7th Cir. 2006); *see also Pearson v. Security Finance Corporation of Alabama Inc.*, No. 1:17-cv-522-WKW-TFM (M.D. Ala. Nov. 6, 2017).
[634] 389 F.3d 719 (7th Cir., 2004).

SULLIVAN V. GREENWOOD CREDIT UNION[635]

LYNCH, Circuit Judge.

This putative class action challenges the legality, under the Fair Credit Reporting Act ("FCRA" or "the Act"), 15 U.S.C. § 1681 *et seq.*, of an unsolicited letter to a consumer about the offering of credit for a home loan. Defendant Greenwood Credit Union sent the letter to plaintiff, Anthony Sullivan, and others based on a list of individuals meeting certain minimal credit requirements that Greenwood had purchased from a credit reporting agency, a process called pre-screening. This unsolicited letter to Sullivan and others triggered the requirements of the FCRA, which permits the unconsented-to use of credit information only for specific purposes, one of which is the extending of a "firm offer of credit" as defined by the Act. If Greenwood has willfully used credit information for an unpermitted purpose, Greenwood would have to pay actual damages or a statutory penalty between $100 and $1,000 per person. This case is about plaintiff's efforts to collect that statutory penalty for a class of consumers; there is no claim Sullivan was wrongfully denied credit.

This case does not involve a claim that the letter was a sham and merely a marketing device for a consumer purchase. There is also no claim that Greenwood would have used the same criteria by which it selected Sullivan to receive the letter to deny him credit. Rather, the plaintiff's argument is that the letter was based on such minimal criteria and the actual extension of credit was so contingent on other conditions that the letter could not be a firm offer of credit.

After allowing some discovery, the district court granted summary judgment to the defendant, finding that Greenwood's letter to the proposed plaintiff class constituted a "firm offer of credit" as that term is defined by the FCRA. Construction of the FCRA's term "firm offer of credit" is a matter of first impression for this circuit. We affirm.

In 2006, Greenwood purchased from TransUnion Credit Bureau a list of names and addresses of homeowners who met certain financial criteria, including having at least $10,000 in revolving debt and a credit score of 500 or greater. The plaintiff met those criteria and was on this list. Greenwood obtained only a consumer report containing contact information; it did not receive any homeowner's full credit report nor any homeowner's particular credit score.

Greenwood used this list to send unsolicited copies of a form letter to each of the pre-qualified homeowners, including Sullivan. The body of the letter stated, among other things, that:

Because of your excellent credit, you have been pre-approved* * for a home loan, up to 100% of the value of your home. . . . . If you have not yet taken advantage of some of the lowest rates in decades, you still have time to secure a great program by contacting one of our knowledgeable mortgage originators today! This is your opportunity for a no cost, no obligation telephone consultation

---

[635] 520 F.3d 70 (1st Cir., 2008).

. . . !   * * Limited time offer to customers who qualify based on equity, income, debts, and satisfactory credit. Rates and terms subject to change without notice. Most loan programs require both a satisfactory property appraisal and title exam for final approval. . . . If at time of offer you no longer meet initial criteria, offer may be revoked.

In addition, the letter contained the following italicized notices in a different typeface from the rest of the letter:

You can choose to stop receiving "prescreened" offers of credit from this and other companies by calling toll-free [telephone number]. See PRESCREEN & OPT-OUT NOTICE on the other side for more information about prescreened offers.   . . . .

PRESCREEN & OPT OUT NOTICE — This "prescreened" offer of credit is based on information in your credit report indicating that you meet certain criteria. This offer is not guaranteed if you do not meet our criteria including providing acceptable property as collateral. If you do not want to receive prescreened offers of credit from this and other companies, call TransUnion at . . . or visit the website . . .; or write. . . .

The letter did not contain specific loan terms, such as an interest rate or the duration of the loan. Sullivan had never consented to the disclosure of any of his credit information to Greenwood. Upon receiving the letter, Sullivan made no attempt to respond to the letter or contact Greenwood.

Instead, on August 8, 2006, Sullivan filed a putative class action, on behalf of a class of the approximately two million consumers who received the letter, in federal district court in Massachusetts, alleging that Greenwood was in violation of the FCRA. Sullivan argues that because he never consented to the disclosure of his credit information to Greenwood, Greenwood could only legally have obtained information that he met the pre-screening criteria if it was for the purpose of granting a "firm offer of credit." He contends that the letter he received is not a "firm offer of credit" because it "is lacking crucial terms for it to be an offer" and "is so vague and lacking in terms as not to constitute an `offer capable of acceptance'." He seeks statutory damages of $1,000 per person in the class, punitive damages, and attorneys' fees and expenses. *See* 15 U.S.C. § 1681n(a).

The district court allowed the plaintiff limited discovery. The plaintiff moved for class certification and, after discovery concluded, the defendant moved for summary judgment. On August 13, 2007, the district court granted summary judgment to the defendant, holding that Greenwood's letter constituted a "firm offer of credit" under the FCRA. It dismissed the class certification motion as moot. This appeal followed.

We review the district court's entry of summary judgment *de novo. Mellen v. Trs. of Boston Univ.*, 504 F.3d 21, 24 (1st Cir.2007). There are no material disputes of fact; the issues are ones of law.

The Role of the FCRA Within the Consumer Credit Protection Act's Statutory Scheme

The Consumer Credit Protection Act, Chapter 41 of Title 15, U.S.C., initially enacted in 1968, is a comprehensive consumer protection statute that accomplishes its purpose through a number of subchapters, each of which regulates a different aspect of or actor in the credit industry. The FCRA is only one of these subchapters.

Subchapter I of the Consumer Credit Protection Act is the Truth in Lending Act ("TILA"), 15 U.S.C. § 1601 *et seq.*, which imposes disclosure requirements on creditors. Subchapter II places restrictions on garnishment of compensation, 15 U.S.C. § 1671 *et seq.* Subchapter II-A is the Credit Repair Organizations Act, 15 U.S.C. § 1679 et seq., which protects consumers from unfair trade practices by credit repair organizations. Subchapter III is the FCRA, 15 U.S.C. § 1681 *et seq.*, which primarily regulates credit reporting agencies but also places requirements on users of credit information from these agencies. Subchapter IV is the Equal Credit Opportunity Act, 15 U.S.C. § 1691 *et seq.*, which prohibits discrimination in the extension of credit. Subchapter V is the Fair Debt Collection Practices Act, 15 U.S.C. § 1692 *et seq.* Subchapter VI is the Electronic Fund Transfer Act, 15 U.S.C. § 1693 *et seq.*, which regulates the participants in electronic fund transfer systems. We turn to certain of the subchapters.

The Fair Credit Reporting Act

Congress enacted the FCRA in 1970 as part of the Consumer Credit Protection Act "to ensure fair and accurate credit reporting, promote efficiency in the banking system, and protect consumer privacy." *Safeco Ins. Co. of Am. v. Burr*, ___ U.S. ___, 127 S.Ct. 2201 2205, 167 L.Ed.2d 1045 (2007); *see TRW Inc. v. Andrews*, 534 U.S. 19, 23, 122 S.Ct. 441, 151 L.Ed.2d 339 (2001); *see also* 15 U.S.C. § 1681. Congress adopted a variety of measures designed to ensure that credit reporting agencies report only appropriate information. Some measures are imposed on agencies directly, others on users of credit information, such as Greenwood. As to users of credit information, the Act sets out a statutory scheme which, among other things, allows the purchase of various forms of information compiled in consumers' credit reports from consumer credit reporting agencies for certain specified business purposes. 15 U.S.C. § 1681b. One of these purposes is to extend credit or insurance to a consumer. *Id.* § 1681b(a)(3)(A), (a)(3)(C).

In 1996, Congress amended the FCRA to allow creditors or insurers to purchase pre-screened lists of names and addresses of consumers who met certain criteria without each consumer's consent as long as they plan to extend to the consumer a "firm offer of credit or insurance." *Id.* § 1681b(c)(1); Pub.L. No. 104-208, § 2404, 110 Stat. 3009, 3009-430 (1996). That provision is at issue in this case. Once a creditor planning to extend firm offers of credit provides a consumer reporting agency with a set of financial criteria, the consumer reporting agency can provide the creditor the contact information, and no more, for consumers who meet those criteria. *See* 15 U.S.C. § 1681b(c). As a result, the purported extender of credit, here Greenwood, does not receive any consumer's full credit report. Greenwood cannot receive the full credit report without the consumer's permission. Here, Greenwood never received the full credit report.

In addition, the Act imposes disclosure requirements on creditors who use pre-screened lists. *Id.* § 1681m. There is no claim Greenwood failed to comply with these disclosure requirements.

The Act provides a private right of action and imposes civil liability on users of credit information and consumer reporting agencies for noncompliance with the requirements of the Act, so long as the person acted willfully, *id.* § 1681n(a), knowingly, *id.* § 1681n(b), or negligently, *id.* § 1681o. In the case of a corporation that willfully fails to comply with any requirement of the Act, a court has discretion to award actual damages or statutory damages between $100 and $1,000 per consumer, in addition to punitive damages and attorneys' fees. *See id.* § 1681n(a).

The Truth in Lending Act

This case is not brought under TILA and there is no claim that Greenwood violated TILA. We discuss TILA to put into context the limited purposes of the FCRA.

Congress focused on creditors, not credit reporting agencies, when it enacted the TILA in 1968 to "assure a meaningful disclosure of credit terms so that the consumer will be able to compare more readily the various credit terms available to him and avoid the uninformed use of credit," which would enhance "economic stabilization . . . and the competition among the various financial institutions." 15 U.S.C. § 1601(a); *see also Koons Buick Pontiac GMC, Inc. v. Nigh*, 543 U.S. 50, 53-54, 125 S.Ct. 460, 160 L.Ed.2d 389 (2004). "The Act requires a creditor to disclose information relating to such things as finance charges, annual percentage rates of interest, and borrowers' rights, *see* [15 U.S.C.] §§ 1631-1632, 1635, 1637-1639, and it prescribes civil liability for any creditor who fails to do so, *see* [15 U.S.C.] § 1640." *Koons*, 543 U.S. at 54, 125 S.Ct. 460. TILA's remedial scheme provides a right of action for both individual and class plaintiffs. *See* 15 U.S.C. § 1640. If a creditor violates TILA's requirements, a consumer is entitled to the sum of actual damages and statutory damages. The sum varies based on whether the action was maintained on a class or an individual basis and the type of credit transaction involved. *See id.* Unlike the FCRA, there is no scienter requirement for creditor liability. *See id.* § 1640(c).

Pertinent to our case, the TILA's requirement of disclosure of specific credit terms kicks in at a point in the credit transaction subsequent to a FCRA firm offer of credit. That is, TILA applies "at the time an application is provided to the consumer" for home equity loans, 12 C.F.R. § 226.5b(b), or "before consummation of the transaction" for mortgages, *id.* § 226.17(b). *See Soroka v. JP Morgan Chase & Co.*, 500 F.Supp.2d 217, 222 (S.D.N.Y.2007). Before then, the firm offer of credit is governed by the FCRA disclosure requirements. Here, Sullivan made no further communication after the FCRA firm offer, so the TILA is not implicated.

Was Greenwood's Letter a "Firm Offer of Credit"?

Sullivan brings his action under the FCRA. He may prevail only if he establishes that the letter he received was not a "firm offer of credit" under the FCRA.

Each side relies on a canon of statutory interpretation to support its argument. The plaintiff invokes the Supreme Court's use of "the general rule that a common law term in a statute comes with a common law meaning, absent anything pointing another way," in its recent *Safeco* decision. 127 S.Ct. at 2209. The Court used this canon to interpret the term "willfully" in the FCRA, 15 U.S.C. § 1681(n)(a), when the statute did not otherwise define the term. *Id.* Sullivan argues that the common law meaning of the term "firm offer of credit" would require the disclosure of specific credit terms to the plaintiff.

The defendant rightly points out, however, that the term "firm offer of credit" is not subject to that canon because the term is explicitly defined in the FCRA. The statutory definition imposes no requirement that a "firm offer of credit" must provide terms for credit such as interest rate and duration. Invoking the canon of expressio unius est exclusio alterius, Greenwood argues that if Congress had wanted to require that more specific credit terms be included in a "firm offer of credit," it would have said so.

Plaintiff replies that the statutory definition only applies to the term "firm" and that we should resort to the common law to define what is an "offer" of credit. He points out that the statute states: "The term `firm offer of credit or insurance' means any offer of credit or insurance to a consumer that will be honored . . . ." 15 U.S.C. § 1681a(l) (emphasis added). He concludes that the term "offer" still has independent meaning, undefined by the statute. We disagree.

We start with the language of the statute and its grammar. Congress chose in its definition to put into quotes for the term it was defining "firm offer of credit or insurance," and not just "firm."

Next, we look to the more complete language of the statute, and conclude plaintiff's reading is inconsistent with the rest of the statute. The Act defines a "firm offer of credit or insurance" as:

any offer of credit or insurance to a consumer that will be honored if the consumer is determined, based on information in a consumer report on the consumer, to meet the specific criteria used to select the consumer for the offer, except that the offer may be further conditioned on one or more of the following:

(1) The consumer being determined, based on information in the consumer's application for the credit or insurance, to meet specific criteria bearing on credit worthiness or insurability, as applicable, that are established—   (A) before selection of the consumer for the offer; and

(B) for the purpose of determining whether to extend credit or insurance pursuant to the offer.

(2) Verification

(A) that the consumer continues to meet the specific criteria used to select the consumer for the offer, by using information in a consumer report on the consumer, information in the consumer's application for the credit or insurance, or other information bearing on the credit worthiness or insurability of the consumer; or

(B) of the information in the consumer's application for the credit or insurance, to determine that the consumer meets the specific criteria bearing on credit worthiness or insurability.

(3) The consumer furnishing any collateral that is a requirement for the extension of the credit or insurance that was—

(A) established before selection of the consumer for the offer of credit or insurance; and

(B) disclosed to the consumer in the offer of credit or insurance.   15 U.S.C. § 1681a(l).

Under this language, an offer of credit meets the statutory definition so long as the creditor will not deny credit to the consumer if the consumer meets the creditor's pre-selection criteria. The term "firm offer of credit" does not require the offeror include additional terms other than the pre-selection criteria. As one court has colloquially put it, "a firm offer of credit under the Act really means `a firm offer if you meet certain criteria.'" *Kennedy v. Chase Manhattan Bank USA, NA*, 369 F.3d 833, 841 (5th Cir.2004).

The statutory scheme imposes disclosure requirements on a "firm offer of credit" in a variety of ways. The creditor must disclose that "information contained in the consumer's consumer report was used," 15 U.S.C. § 1681m(d)(1)(A). It requires disclosure that the consumer received the offer because he satisfied the criteria used to select the customer for the offer, *id.* § 1681m(d)(1)(B), but does not purport to require the creditor to include more criteria than used here. And the statute requires disclosure that the offer can be conditioned on collateral or other pre-determined criteria, *id.* § 1681m(d)(1)(c), that the consumer has the right to opt out of pre-screened offers, *id.* § 1681m(d)(1)(d), and of how the consumer can exercise that right, *id.* § 1681m(d)(1)(e).

Further, the statute contemplates that there will be subsequent stages of communications beyond the "firm offer of credit," if the consumer is interested, during which additional terms will be offered. The statute expressly provides that "the [firm] offer may be conditioned on one or more of the following. . . ." In 15 U.S.C. § 1681a(l)(1), the statute refers to information which the customer will later supply in an "application for credit." It also refers to a later decision to "extend credit." *Id.* Thus, the statute is clear that the fact that the initial letter to the consumer does not yet resolve those additional conditions does not mean the letter fails to be a firm offer of credit.

The Fifth Circuit's decision in *Kennedy*, 369 F.3d 833, provides an example. *Kennedy* involved a situation in which two consumers' joint application for a credit card was rejected after they had received a letter from a bank stating that they were pre-approved for a credit card account. *Id.* at 837. The court nonetheless found that the letter met the statutory definition of a "firm offer of credit," and that the rejection was proper because the consumers could not meet the bank's additional pre-determined creditworthiness criteria. *Id.* at 841-42. The plaintiff's preferred definition is inconsistent with the Fifth Circuit's approach. We have found no circuit precedent which reads the statute as plaintiff does.

The plaintiff reads a Seventh Circuit case, *Cole v. U.S. Capital*, 389 F.3d 719 (7th Cir.2004), to support his interpretation of "firm offer of credit." We disagree. In that case, that court found a mailing not to constitute a firm offer of credit when the mailing purportedly offered a $300 credit line towards the purchase of an automobile but did not include specific credit terms. The court held that "the offer was a sham made to justify access to the consumer credit reports," and because it "was a guise for solicitation rather than a legitimate credit product, the communication cannot be considered a firm offer of credit." Id. at 728.

The problem before us is different from the problem in Cole. As the Seventh Circuit clarified in a later case, "Cole's objective was to separate bona fide offers of credit from advertisements for products and services, determining from `all the material conditions that comprise the credit product in question . . .

[whether it] was a guise for solicitation rather than a legitimate credit product.'" *Murray v. GMAC Mortgage Corp.*, 434 F.3d 948, 955-56 (7th Cir.2006) (quoting *Cole*, 389 F.3d at 728) (alteration in original). The purpose of the Cole mailing was "to identify potential auto buyers," *id.* at 955, and so the issue in Cole was whether the mailing was a "firm offer of credit," as opposed to a "firm offer of credit," *see id. See also Dixon v. Shamrock Fin. Corp.*, 482 F.Supp.2d 172, 177 (D.Mass.2007) (noting that in Cole "the `offer of credit' was in fact a sales pitch for a car dealership"). The problem here is not whether this is a bona fide offer of credit.

The problem here is also not a bait-and-switch problem. In other statutes, such as the TILA, Congress mandated truth in the descriptions of other credit terms. There is no claim here of untruthful disclosures.

Plaintiff argues that Congress intended for individuals whose private credit information is accessed in any form by a creditor to be given something of value in the exchange. The "value" of the offer made by Greenwood, plaintiff argues, is zero, and so the congressional intent is thwarted. Even if that were the intent, and it were permissible to substitute assumptions about intent for the plain language of the statute, we disagree that the value of the letter to the consumer is zero.

There was some value in the letter. Greenwood's letter informed the plaintiff that, based on certain credit information, he had been pre-selected as meeting certain eligibility requirements for the extension of credit. The letter informed him that if he were interested he could contact Greenwood and determine, based on other information, whether he would meet certain conditions. The letter did not guarantee him a loan, but did guarantee that he would not be disqualified from a loan on the basis of the pre-selection criteria. In turn, there was little invasion of consumer privacy. Greenwood never received his full credit report. It received only the plaintiff's contact information and that he met certain pre-selection criteria. This is a minimal invasion of privacy, offset by the value of the information in the letter to the plaintiff.

We affirm the entry of judgment for defendant.

****

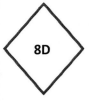 **Why is Sullivan able to bring this action against Greenwood, considering that civil actions are not permissible for violation of duties of consumer report users extending a firm offer of credit?**

 **May a consumer reporting agency provide a pre-screened consumer report for a user bank that wants to market to certain consumers to open bank accounts?**

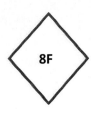

8F

How can a firm offer of credit be distinguished from other sales or marketing materials?

Compare *Sullivan v. Greenwood* to the next case, *Murray v. New Cingular Wireless*, a 2008 Seventh Circuit Court of Appeals case, which, similarly, considers the value of a firm offer of credit.

EASTERBROOK, Chief Judge.

We have grouped for decision three appeals under the Fair Credit Reporting Act presenting issues that have arisen in numerous suits throughout the circuit. Each of the appeals presents at least two issues, several of which recur in multiple appeals. We therefore organize the opinion around these issues rather than the facts of the cases, which we use to illustrate the problems.

Must an offer of credit be valuable to all or most recipients? A company usually may access a consumer's credit information only if the consumer initiates the transaction. The statute makes an exception, however: Firms may obtain lists of names and addresses that credit bureaus generate from their databases according to the stated criteria. For example, a bank might ask for a list of everyone in Illinois who purchased a home, with a mortgage loan, during the last three years and is current on payment. That list may be used to make an offer of refinancing, or of a loan against the equity in the residence. The statute allows this only if the person requesting the information uses it to make "a firm offer of credit or insurance". 15 U.S.C. § 1681b(c)(1)(B)(i).

Suppose someone wants to use credit information to promote merchandise. One way to do this might be to make an offer of the product (say, a television set or a suite of furniture) together with a token line of credit (say, $100 toward $10,000 worth of furniture). We held in *Cole v. U.S. Capital, Inc.*, 389 F.3d 719 (7th Cir. 2004), that this gimmick does not work — that the offer must have value if viewed as one of credit alone. "A definition of `firm offer of credit' that does not incorporate the concept of value to the consumer upsets the balance Congress carefully struck between a consumer's interest in privacy and the benefit of a firm offer of credit for all those chosen through the pre-screening process. From the consumer's perspective, an offer of credit without value is the equivalent of an advertisement or solicitation [for the product rather than the loan]." *Id.* at 726-27.

Ever since *Cole* plaintiffs have contended that this approach must be applied, not only to distinguish between offers of merchandise and offers of credit, but also to decide whether even a simple offer of credit is valuable enough to justify the use of consumers' credit files. Two of the cases before us present arguments of this kind. Darrell Bruce contends that KeyBank did not make a "firm offer of credit" because its offer of home-equity financing did not include all material terms, and without knowing every term (such as whether interest was to be simple or compound) the consumer could not assess the offer's value. Ilene Price and other plaintiffs contend that Capital One Bank did not make a "firm offer of credit" because the flyer offering them Visa cards did not state the minimum line of credit each would receive, and without this knowledge the offer's worth was uncertain. Both Bruce and Price rely heavily on Cole.

---

[636] 523 F.3d 719 (7th Cir., 2008)

As we have said, these are just the latest attempts to apply *Cole* to pure offers of credit. None has succeeded. *See, e.g., Forrest v. Universal Savings Bank, F.A.*, 507 F.3d 540 (7th Cir.2007); *Perry v. First National Bank*, 459 F.3d 816 (7th Cir. 2006). Some of our decisions have analyzed the offer to see whether it would be attractive to a substantial fraction of recipients. But the principal reason why none of these claims has prevailed, and why none of them can prevail, is that § 1681b(c)(1)(B)(i) calls for a firm offer of credit but not a valuable firm offer of credit. A firm offer of credit suffices. *Cole* did not doubt this. The problem in *Cole* was how to disentangle an offer of merchandise from an offer of credit when they are made jointly (in *Cole*, the merchant was selling cars and offered to extend credit for a small fraction of the price). We asked whether the offer of credit would be valuable standing alone in order to see whether the non-consensual check of a person's credit history had been used to make an offer of merchandise, something the statute does not allow.

Murray v. GMAC Mortgage Corp., 434 F.3d 948 (7th Cir.2006), remarked that "Cole's objective was to separate bona fide offers of credit from advertisements for products and services, determining from `all the material conditions that comprise the credit product in question . . . [whether it] was a guise for solicitation rather than a legitimate credit product'." 434 F.3d at 955-56 (emphasis in *Cole*; internal citation omitted). What was an observation in *Murray* is now a holding. *Cole* is beside the point for pure offers of credit. When credit histories are used to offer credit (or insurance) and nothing but, the right question is whether the offer is "firm" rather than whether it is "valuable." That the interest rate is said to be "too high" or the line of credit "too low" or the rule for compounding interest unstated is not relevant to the question posed by § 1681b(c)(1)(B)(i).

Does a promise of "free" merchandise mean that an offer is not one "of credit"? Thomas Murray contends that a telephone company violated FCRA by obtaining from a credit bureau a list of persons to receive a circular that touts a "free phone." This phone is available only to someone who signs up for a year or more of service, but as Murray sees things the lure of a phone makes it hard for the consumer to understand that the point of the offer is the service. True, phone service is neither "credit" nor "insurance," but the circular offers phone service on credit, because the service is provided before payment is due. Deferred payment is "credit" as the statute uses that word. 15 U.S.C. § 1681a(r)(5), incorporating § 1691a(d). A "free" phone is anything but free, as it can't be had apart from the service plan; payments for service include the cost of the phone, which is amortized over the length of the contract. So payment for the phone is deferred no less than payment for the phone service; the entire offer therefore is one of credit, whether or not a given consumer gets the point.

Now it is true that the credit can't be used to buy someone else's product. Verizon does not extend credit to users of AT & T's service, or the reverse. Nor will Ford lend money to buy an Audi. This does not detract from the fact that an offer of a Ford with deferred payment is an offer of credit. The offer need not be fully portable to be "credit" within the statutory definition: "The term `credit' means the right granted by a creditor to a debtor to defer payment of debt or to incur debts and defer its payment or to purchase property or services and defer payment therefor." 15 U.S.C. § 1691a(d).

Must the initial flyer contain all material terms? KeyBank's offer of home-equity credit stated that the interest rate would be "based on" the prime rate according to the Wall Street Journal at the time the loan was made and could vary "by district, product and credit qualification." It did not mention terms such as the loan's duration and did not specify all fees. Capital One Bank's offer of a Visa card did not state the minimum amount of credit that each card would have. Plaintiffs say that these omissions negate the existence of a "firm offer of credit." To the extent this argument rests on *Cole* and the proposition that an offer with omitted terms lacks value, it is wrong for the reason given already. To the extent that these arguments reflect a belief that there can be no offer of any kind without all material items, it is wrong because "firm offer" is a defined phrase.

The term "firm offer of credit or insurance" means any offer of credit or insurance to a consumer that will be honored if the consumer is determined, based on information in a consumer report on the consumer, to meet the specific criteria used to select the consumer for the offer, except that the offer may be further conditioned on one or more of the following:

(1) The consumer being determined, based on information in the consumer's application for the credit or insurance, to meet specific criteria bearing on credit worthiness or insurability, as applicable, that are established—

(A) before selection of the consumer for the offer; and

(B) for the purpose of determining whether to extend credit or insurance pursuant to the offer.　　(2) Verification—

(A) that the consumer continues to meet the specific criteria used to select the consumer for the offer, by using information in a consumer report on the consumer, information in the consumer's application for the credit or insurance, or other information bearing on the credit worthiness or insurability of the consumer; or

(B) of the information in the consumer's application for the credit or insurance, to determine that the consumer meets the specific criteria bearing on credit worthiness or insurability.

(3) The consumer furnishing any collateral that is a requirement for the extension of the credit or insurance that was—

(A) established before selection of the consumer for the offer of credit or insurance; and

(B) disclosed to the consumer in the offer of credit or insurance.

15 U.S.C. § 1681a(l). The question posed by this definition is whether the offer will be honored (if the verification checks out), not whether all terms appear in an initial mailing. Anyone who has read a disclosure statement under the Real Estate Settlement Practices Act knows that the number of terms for a home-equity loan is formidable, and even the list under the Truth in Lending Act (which would apply to the credit card) is nothing to sneeze at. Neither § 1681a(l) nor anything else in FCRA says that the initial communication to a consumer must contain all of the important terms that must be agreed on before credit is extended. Trying to disclose everything in the first contact would make the document turgid and, paradoxically, uninformative, because it would be harder to read and grasp. Consumers would lose

some of the benefit of competition among lenders—which is facilitated by the sort of offers these plaintiffs received.

Does a power to vary the deal's terms make the offer not "firm"? KeyBank's letter informed readers that the rate of interest would vary by "product and credit qualification" and that closing costs could run between $1,000 and $2,000. Tiny type added: "Actual rates, fees and terms are based on those offered as of the date of application and are subject to change without notice." It is possible to read these caveats to make the offer illusory. Then there might be nothing on the table that a consumer could accept, and the statutory definition of a "firm offer" would not be satisfied.

We say that it is possible to read the caveats this way, but that reading is not inevitable. Caveats such as the one in this letter may reflect nothing more than the statutory privilege to verify a consumer's qualifications and raise the rate of interest (or required security) if it turns out that the consumer is less credit-worthy than it appeared from the preliminary screening. Or perhaps the reference means that routine terms such as late fees (are they $25 or only $15?) may change between when a brochure is printed and the time any given consumer signs on the dotted line, and that the terms will be those generally applicable when the contract comes into force. That would not make an offer less than firm, as the statute defines that phrase.

So has KeyBank reserved a right to walk away by naming onerous terms any time it does not want to lend money to a particular customer, or has it just made clear the power to charge more if, after verification, the consumer is not as good a credit risk as things seemed initially? It would be possible to inquire, through discovery, how KeyBank has used the powers reserved in its letter. Bruce did not seek discovery on this issue, however. His position, in the district court and here, is that the letter's language is all that matters. Because the letter is ambiguous, that position is untenable. Plaintiff has the burden of persuasion, so his decision to forego discovery means that the language in KeyBank's letter cannot be used to defeat the existence of a "firm offer of credit".

Capital One Bank's letter does not contain as bald a reservation of a power to set terms later, but the omission of a minimum line of credit and maximum interest rate comes to the same thing. Here too the lender is doing no more than the statute permits. It isn't possible to give definitive credit limits and rates without knowing the consumer's full credit history and other particulars, such as income. Only very simple screening precedes these offers. Anyone who passes the screen is assured of credit, but people who on a follow-up check have higher-than-minimum credit scores will get better rates and higher limits, while those who have (since the screening) fallen below the minimum will have to pay higher interest rates for less credit. Capital One Bank could not reveal all of the details in the space allowed by an initial offer—and the full algorithm that relates credit information to credit terms may be a trade secret. The statute does not require the revelation of these details as part of a "firm offer"; but unless the algorithm in all its complexity is to be laid out, any honest offer will leave some matters for future determination. *Accord, Sullivan v. Greenwood Credit Union*, 520 F.3d 70 (1st Cir.2008).

Is six-point type "conspicuous"? Anyone who uses consumer credit information in a transaction that was not initiated by the consumer must "provide with each written solicitation made to the consumer" a statement that

(A) information contained in the consumer's consumer report was used in connection with the transaction;

(B) the consumer received the offer of credit or insurance because the consumer satisfied the criteria for credit worthiness or insurability under which the consumer was selected for the offer;   (C) if applicable, the credit or insurance may not be extended if, after the consumer responds to the offer, the consumer does not meet the criteria used to select the consumer for the offer or any applicable criteria bearing on credit worthiness or insurability or does not furnish any required collateral; [523 F.3d 725]

(D) the consumer has a right to prohibit information contained in the consumer's file with any consumer reporting agency from being used in connection with any credit or insurance transaction that is not initiated by the consumer; and

(E) the consumer may exercise the right referred to in subparagraph (D) by notifying a notification system established under section 1681b(e) of this title.

15 U.S.C. § 1681m(d). This statement must be "clear and conspicuous". The word "clear" presumably means "in easy to understand language." But what is "conspicuous"? The statute does not offer a definition—which means, alas, that the demand for "conspicuous" notice is not "clear."

The Federal Trade Commission issued in 2005 a regulation defining "conspicuous" to mean at least 8-point type for the full notice, plus a short notice in 12-point type on the brochure's first page. 16 C.F.R. § 642.3. The Commission can't adopt substantive rules for private litigation; this regulation concerns only its enforcement activities. *See* 15 U.S.C. § 1681s(a)(1), (e). Still, it offers a useful guidepost that was unavailable to Cingular, which sent its offer to Murray. (We call the defendant "Cingular" even though it now operates under the name AT & T. Counsel assured us that the entity "New Cingular Wireless Services, Inc." still exists.) Cingular used 6-point type. The first word is all capitals. But 6-point type is tiny. A printer's point is 0.01384 of an inch, so 6-point type is about 1/12 inch tall, and a glyph in 6-point type has 1/4 the area of the same glyph in 12-point type. This is what Cingular's disclosure, at the bottom of a page dominated by a color picture of a Nokia cell phone and largetype (14 to 24 point) promotional language, looked like:

DISCLOSURE: We'd like you to know about the terms of this pre-approved offer. You were selected to receive this special offer because you satisfied certain criteria for creditworthiness, which we have previously established. We used information obtained from a consumer-reporting agency. We may choose to withdraw this offer if we determine you do not meet the criteria used to select you for the offer or any other applicable criteria bearing on creditworthiness. You have the right to prohibit information contained in your credit files with this or any consumer-reporting agency from being used with any credit transaction that is not initiated by you by notifying Equifax, Inc., c/o Equifax Options, P.O. Box 740123, Atlanta, GA 30374-0123, or by calling 1(888) 567-8688.

Cingular concedes that this disclosure flunks not only the FTC's approach but also the standard we devised in *Cole*, which held that a statement much smaller than the principal type on the page cannot be "conspicuous." 389 F.3d at 731. But the brochure was mailed before Cole issued, and Cingular did not have its benefit.

Six-point type in black ink is not "conspicuous" when the bulk of the page contains much larger type. Whether 6-point type in color might suffice is a question we need not address, since Cingular used color only for the picture and its promotional text.

Is the use of 6-point type a "willful" violation of FCRA? Cingular's violation of the statute entitles Murray to actual damages, but he has not tried to prove any. Instead he seeks statutory damages, which may range from $100 to $1,000 per violation whether or not the consumer was injured. 15 U.S.C. § 1681n(a). But statutory damages are available only for willful violations of the Act, and the Supreme Court held in *Safeco Insurance Co. v. Burr*, ___ U.S. ___, 127 S.Ct. 2201, 167 L.Ed.2d 1045 (2007), that this means recklessness — something more than negligence but less than knowledge of the law's requirements.

"Recklessness" is a protean term, one that might flunk the statutory requirement of clarity if included in a disclosure statement. But it is the Supreme Court's understanding of the statute. The Court did not stop with the word "reckless." It added that

a company subject to FCRA does not act in reckless disregard of it unless the action is not only a violation under a reasonable reading of the statute's terms, but shows that the company ran a risk of violating the law substantially greater than the risk associated with a reading that was merely careless. 127 S.Ct. at 2215. This standard, the Court stated, is objective.

Cingular's reading of the Act was mistaken, but if the error was careless it did not create a risk substantially above the risk usually associated with careless readings. Because the statute does not define "conspicuous", and the FTC had not issued its guidance, where was a company to turn? Appellate decisions are a logical place, but they did not help much. When Cingular mailed its brochure, two courts of appeals had interpreted that term. *Stevenson v. TRW Inc.*, 987 F.2d 288 (5th Cir. 1993), read it the way we later did in Cole. But *Guimond v. Credit Bureau Inc.*, 1992 WL 33144, 1992 U.S.App. LEXIS 2640 (4th Cir. Feb. 25, 1992), concluded that a disclosure in "small but clear and readable type" is "conspicuous" as far as FCRA is concerned. Although *Guimond* is non-precedential, the fourth circuit (like other federal appellate courts) uses that designation only for decisions that follow well-understood rules that need no elaboration. That *Guimond* thought obvious in 1992 a position that Stevenson held obviously wrong in 1993 shows something of the problem facing Cingular.

If federal appellate decisions under FCRA don't solve this problem (at least had not solved it before Cingular acted), the most natural alternative is state law. And the logical place to turn is the Uniform Commercial Code, which uses the phrase "clear and conspicuous" in several sections. It is hard to avoid thinking that whoever drafted § 1681m(d) must have assumed that "clear and conspicuous" is a term of art in commercial law and therefore needs no federal definition. Unfortunately, that assumption is wrong, because, although the UCC supplies a definition, it is internally contradictory.

"Conspicuous", with reference to a term, means so written, displayed, or presented that a reasonable person against which it is to operate ought to have noticed it. Whether a term is "conspicuous" or not is a decision for the court. Conspicuous terms include the following:

(A) a heading in capitals equal to or greater in size than the surrounding text, or in contrasting type, font, or color to the surrounding text of the same or lesser size; and

(B) language in the body of a record or display in larger type than the surrounding text, or in contrasting type, font, or color to the surrounding text of the same size, or set off from surrounding text of the same size by symbols or other marks that call attention to the language.   UCC § 1-201(b)(10) (2001 revised ed.). Every state has a statute modeled on this language. Cingular found § 1-201(b)(10)(A) and concluded that capitalizing the word "DISCLOSURE" brought the paragraph within the definition, because the immediately preceding paragraph also was in 6-point type. But the main part of § 1-201(b)(10), which defines "conspicuous" as something that the person affected "ought to have noticed", implies that some type can be so small that a capitalized heading "equal to or greater in size than the surrounding text" will not be enough. It is of course possible to read (A) and (B) as safe harbors, working even if the affected person assuredly would not have noticed the statement; then 1-point type in light grey would do, even though it would be invisible to normal readers, provided only that it followed a throwaway paragraph in 1-point light-grey type. That would be an implausible reading of § 1-201(b)(10).

We do not think it reckless, however, for Cingular to have read § 1-201(b)(10)(A) as authorizing its approach, when the actual paragraph was in 6-point type that is readable despite its small size. The problem is not that people can't read black sans-serif type at that size, but that the eye is not drawn to it. Even if it was careless to conclude from § 1-201(b)(10)(A) that capitalizing the first word was enough, Cingular did not take a risk "substantially greater" than is associated with ordinary carelessness. It would be reckless today to use the same notice, given *Cole* and such assistance as 16 C.F.R. § 642.3 provides, but it was not reckless to act as Cingular did in 2003.

To sum up:

In Murray, the offer of a free phone in connection with a service plan is an offer of credit. Although the disclosure required by 15 U.S.C. § 1681m(d) was not conspicuous, Cingular did not wilfully violate FCRA because it was not reckless. The district court did not anticipate *Safeco*'s adoption of a recklessness standard but came to the same ultimate conclusion on each issue, 432 F.Supp.2d 788 (N.D.Ill. 2006), and its judgment is affirmed.

In *Bruce v. Keybank Nat. Ass'n*, the circular made a "firm offer of credit" despite the omission of some material terms and the reservation of a power to change terms. The district court erroneously held otherwise, see 2006 WL 3743749, 2006 U.S. Dist. LEXIS 91371 (N.D.Ind. Dec. 15, 2006), but went on to conclude that the violation was not willful because KeyBank did not know that it was violating the Act. That approach, too, is erroneous in light of *Safeco* (which was released after the district court's opinion). Neither of the district court's missteps calls for a remand. Because we hold that there was no violation, the judgment is affirmed.

In *Price*, the district court held that the omission of a minimum line of credit is compatible with a "firm offer of credit" and entered judgment for Capital One Bank. 2007 WL 1521525, 2007 U.S. Dist. LEXIS 37796 (E.D.Wis. May 22, 2007). We agree with this conclusion and affirm.

****

Are the cell-phone products or services offered credit? Recall Part V, Fair Debt Collection Practices Act. Financial services debt represents one-third of collection revenue and telecommunications debt represents one-fifth of debt collection revenue.[637] The telecommunications companies typically neglect reporting to the credit reporting agencies until the account is in collections, and "the median telecom collection balance is $408."[638] **Given these figures, what are the long-term potential effects of marketing traps for products and services?**

Consider the life cycle of potential credit, beginning with a minimal invasion of privacy via a use of the consumer report to advertise a firm offer of credit. If the extension of credit is accepted by the consumer, the required material terms are disclosed prior to consummation pursuant to TILA. Compliance requirements shift from the user to the creditor, who is the same "person." If the consumer defaults, the credit extension goes into debt collection, and the compliance requirements shift from the creditor to the debt collector.

Telecom services are typically paid on a monthly basis.[639] Recall the court's determination in *Laramore*[640] in Part IVC that a lease, paid monthly, did not amount to an extension of credit for ECOA purposes. Compare this determination with telecommunications marketing amounting to credit for the purposes of the Fair Credit Reporting Act firm offer of credit and monthly telecommunications payments amounting to debts for the purposes of the Fair Debt Collection Practices Act. **Is it possible to have a debt without an extension of credit under the various consumer protection laws? If Laramore obtained a lease and failed to pay the monthly rent, would the management company be subject to the FDCPA if attempting to communicate with Laramore on the defaulted payments? Why or Why not? What additional information would you need to know in order to decide, if any?** Recall the definitions under each relevant law.

---

[637] *See* CONSUMER FIN. PROT. BUREAU ANN. REP., *supra* note 342, at 9.

[638] *See* CONSUMER FIN. PROT. BLOG, More than 1-in-5 Consumers Had Telecommunications-Related Collections on Their Consumer Report in the Past 5 Years, (Aug. 22, 2018), https://www.consumerfinance.gov/about-us/blog/more-1-5-consumers-had-telecommunications-related-collections-their-consumer-report-past-5-years/.

[639] *See id.*

[640] 397 F.3d 544 (7th Cir., 2005).

HOWARD V. DIRECTV GRP., INC.[641]

ORDER

Presently pending before the Court is Defendant DirectTV, Inc. ("DirecTV") and MasTec North America, Inc.'s ("MasTec") Opposition to Plaintiff's Motion to Amend, or in the Alternative, Motion to Dismiss Plaintiff's Second Amended Complaint. Upon due consideration, Defendants' motion to dismiss Plaintiff's Second Amended Complaint is GRANTED.

This action arises from the unauthorized installation and billing of satellite television services and bundled communication packages. Plaintiff contends that the installation of these services detrimentally affected his credit. The relevant facts are set forth below.

Factual Background

Claims Relating to the AT&T Account

On November 14, 2006, unbeknownst to Plaintiff, Defendant AT&T Mobility, LLC ("AT&T") used Plaintiff's personal credit information to install and activate a bundled communication package at the property owned by Richard R. Weiber, Jr. ("Weiber"). Several months later, BellSouth Telecommunications ("BellSouth") contacted Plaintiff and informed him of a delinquent account registered at Weiber's address. The phone number associated with this account was 706-798-1722. Suspecting that the delinquent account was the result of identity theft, Plaintiff filed an incident report with the Richmond County Sheriff's Department.

Plaintiff subsequently received and completed a fraud package and identity theft affidavit from the BellSouth Risk Management Center. On March 12, 2007, BellSouth informed Plaintiff that the 706-798-1722 phone number was established without his authorization. As a result, BellSouth employees told Plaintiff that the delinquent report would not be referred to a collection agency and would not appear on Plaintiff's credit report.

However, on June 6, 2008, Plaintiff received a collection letter from Nationwide Recovery System informing him that they had been retained by AT&T to collect a debt of $447.00. Plaintiff disputed the debt and called the AT&T fraud department, which stated that the suspected fraud would be investigated. After a subsequent investigation, AT&T informed Plaintiff that the account was in fact fraudulent and that he would not be responsible for any charges.

Claims Relating to the DirecTV Account

On July 6, 2008, Plaintiff received a letter from the law office of Mitchell N. Kay, P.C., informing him that the firm had been retained by DirecTV to collect a debt of $233.60. The letter stated that Plaintiff owed this amount as a result of services provided in connection with a DirecTV account identified as #62898476-A. Plaintiff contacted the law office and explained that the billing must have been the result

---

[641] *Howard v. Directv Grp., Inc.* No. CV 109-156 (S.D. Ga. May 21, 2012).

of a mistake. He stated he never requested or received any services from DirecTV and had no idea how his name and personal information became affiliated with any of its accounts. Upon verifying Plaintiff's address and social security number, the representative concluded that Plaintiff had opened the account and was therefore responsible for the resulting debt.

After learning of the pending claim against him, Plaintiff contacted Experian, a credit reporting agency, and asked that Experian place a security alert on his account. He also requested a copy of his credit report. Experian represented that it would notify the other two major reporting agencies, Transunion and Equifax, and would advise them to place fraud alerts on Plaintiff's accounts.

On July 14, 2008, Plaintiff received a credit report that did not contain any references to pending collection actions or accounts connected to DirecTV. However, on October 20, 2008, Plaintiff requested and received a follow-up report. The follow-up report showed a pending collection action, identified DirecTV as the creditor, and listed the relevant account number as #62898476. Upon receiving this report, Plaintiff contacted DirecTV. DirecTV informed Plaintiff that although an account had been opened using his personal information, the account had since been closed. DirecTV personnel connected Plaintiff to its fraud department, which agreed to investigate the matter. On November 5, 2008, Plaintiff received a letter from DirecTV regarding the results of its investigation and informing Plaintiff that it had concluded that he was not responsible or liable for any debts associated with account #62898476.

. . .

Fair Credit Reporting Act, 15 U.S.C. § 1681 *et seq.*

In his Second Amended Complaint, Plaintiff alleges various violations of the FCRA. The FCRA protects consumers from having inaccurate information about their credit status circulated to credit reporting agencies. *Pickney v. SLM Fin. Corp.*, 433 F. Supp. 2d 1316, 1318 (N.D. Ga. 2005) (internal citations omitted). Under this Act, furnishers of information to credit reporting agencies have a duty to, among other things, investigate disputed information and report the results of these investigations to credit reporting agencies. *Id.* Plaintiff alleges that Defendants negligently initiated a collection action against him without verifying the accuracy of the information and without notifying him. He claims that this conduct violates §§ 1681s-2(a), 1681m(d)(1) and 1681m(e)(1)(A) of the FCRA. Defendants, however, assert that these claims should be dismissed as no private right of action exists under §§ 1681s-2(a) and 1681m.

15 U.S.C. § 1681s-2(a)

Plaintiff alleges that Defendants negligently submitted negative or adverse information to a credit reporting agency without notifying him in violation of 15 U.S.C. § 1681s-2(a) (7) (A). Section 1281s-2 (a) of the FCRA requires furnishers of information to submit accurate information to credit reporting agencies. *Green v. RBS Nat'l Bank*, 288 Fed. Appx. 641, 642 (11th Cir. 2009). However, the FCRA does not provide a private right of action to redress such a violation. *See* 15 U.S.C. § 1681s-2(d); *Blackwell v. Capital One Bank*, No. 6:06-cv-066, 2008 WL 793476, at *2 (S.D. Ga. Mar. 25, 2008) ("[C]laim[s] for failure to provide accurate information under § 1681s-2(a) must be dismissed because there is no private right of action to enforce that duty."); *Neal v. Equifax Credit Info. Servs., Inc.*, No. l:03-cv-761, 2004 WL 5238126, at *4 (N.D. Ga. Mar. 11, 2004) ("[E]very court that has addressed the issue in a reported decision has concluded that private plaintiffs have no cause of action under 15 U.S.C. § 1681s-2(a)."). Thus, Plaintiff's claim under subsection (a) must be dismissed.

15 U.S.C. § 1681s-2(b)

Although not specifically alleged in the Second Amended Complaint, Plaintiff appears to also raise a claim pursuant 15 U.S.C. § 1681s-2(b). Section 1681s-2(b) provides that once a furnisher of information receives notice of a dispute from a consumer reporting agency, it must conduct an investigation into the disputed information and report any inaccuracies. Unlike § 1681s-2(a), § 1681s-2(b) creates a private right of action, but only if the furnisher received notice of the consumer's dispute from a consumer reporting agency. *Green*, 288 Fed. Appx. at 642. Thus, to support an FCRA claim against a furnisher of information, a private plaintiff must allege that the furnisher, after receiving proper written notice of a dispute regarding the completeness or accuracy of information provided by a person to a consumer reporting agency, did one of the following: (1) failed to conduct an investigation with respect to the disputed information; (2) failed to review all relevant information provided by the consumer reporting agency pursuant to § 1681i(a)(2) of the FCRA; (3) failed to report the results of the investigation to the consumer reporting agency; or, (4) if an item of information disputed by a consumer is found to be inaccurate, incomplete, or cannot be verified after any reinvestigation, failed to modify, delete, or permanently block the reporting of that item of information. *See* 15 U.S.C. § 1681S-2(b).

The Court allowed Plaintiff to amend his Amended Complaint because it did not contain any factual allegations supporting a claim under § 1681s-2(b). However, the Second Amended Complaint does not cure the deficiencies of the Amended Complaint. Plaintiff has not alleged that any credit reporting agency sent Defendants a dispute notice, triggering a duty to investigate. Moreover, Plaintiff does not allege that Defendants failed to conduct a reasonable investigation or failed in any other way outlined above. Accordingly, to the extent Plaintiff may be asserting a claim under § 1681s-2(b), that claim fails and is dismissed.

15 U.S.C. §§ 1681m(d)(l)& 1681m(e)(1)(A)

Plaintiff further claims that Defendants negligently completed a credit transaction not initiated by Plaintiff in violation of § 1681m(d)(1) and failed to maintain reasonable procedures to avoid identity theft in violation of § 1681m(e)(1)(A). Defendants, however, contend that there is no private cause of action under § 1681m and that those claims should therefore be dismissed.

Section 1681m provides that civil liability for willful or negligent non-compliance "shall not apply to any failure by any person to comply with this section." 15 U.S.C. § 1681m(h) (8) (A). The FCRA further provides that § 1681m "shall be enforced exclusively under § 1681s of this title by the Federal agencies and officials identified in that section." 15 U.S.C. § 1681m(h) (8) (B). Thus, there is no private right of action to enforce § 1681m. *See, e.g. , Perry v. First Nat' 1 Bank*, 459 F.3d 816, 823 (7th Cir. 2006) (holding [t]he unambiguous language of § 1681m(h)(8) demonstrates that Congress intended to preempt private causes of action to enforce § 1681m"); *Floyd-Keith v. Homecomings Fin.*, LLC, 2:09-cv-

769, 2010 WL 3927596, at *8 (M.D. Ala. Sept. 17, 2010); *Crowder v. PMI Mortgage Ins. Co.*, No. 2:06-cv-114, 2006 WL 1528608, at *2 (M.D. Ala. May 26, 2006). As such, Plaintiff's claims under § 1681m must be dismissed.

. . .

CONCLUSION

Upon the foregoing, Defendants' motion to dismiss Plaintiff's Second Amended Complaint is GRANTED.

****

What private rights of action are available to consumers under the FCRA?

81

MEMORANDUM AND ORDER

This case is based on the denial of a residential home loan for property in Omaha, Nebraska. The plaintiffs, Justin and Erin Riddle, were the prospective borrowers, and CharterWest Bank was the prospective lender. Generally, the Riddles allege they tried to withdraw their application to switch to another lender, and that CharterWest wrongfully retaliated against them by quickly denying their application and falsely reporting the denial to the Federal Housing Administration (FHA) as "denied due to unpaid child support."

Before the Court are motions to dismiss filed by CharterWest and the Federal Reserve Bank of Kansas City. CharterWest's motion will be granted in part and denied in part, and the Federal Reserve's motion will be granted in its entirety.

BACKGROUND

As of April and May 2016, the Riddles and CharterWest were engaged in the process of gathering the documentation necessary for an FHA home loan. But an issue arose out of Justin's child support obligation. Pursuant to a child custody order, Justin's ex-wife legally had sole custody of their daughter. But due to circumstances that prevented Justin's ex-wife from exercising custody, the two had come to an informal arrangement whereby their daughter lived with Justin, and his ex-wife arranged every few months to clear his accrued child support arrearage.

The Riddles' mortgage loan officer, Grant Whitehead, explained in a May 12, 2016 email to Justin that because child support liens have priority over new liens, including mortgages, "this needs to be addressed prior to closing or paid at closing." Justin replied, explaining the situation and offering further evidence if required. In an email the next day, Justin told Whitehead that his ex-wife would provide a notarized statement waiving his child support obligation, and clear his balance.

At the same time, Justin was generally frustrated with CharterWest, believing that Whitehead had been rude to him and that CharterWest was being deliberately difficult. So, on May 12, he sent an email explaining his dissatisfaction and advising CharterWest that if they could get their deal closed by May 18, then the Riddles would work with CharterWest; otherwise, the Riddles would "take [their] approval to a different lender" and expect a refund of CharterWest's fees. Later that day, Justin emailed asking for a copy of the Riddles' file. Whitehead promised to email the documents.

On May 13, the Riddles contacted Whitehead's manager, Gary Walters, and said they no longer wanted to deal with Whitehead. The Riddles contacted another lender and provided their file. On May 16, at 4:13 p.m., Justin emailed CharterWest asking for his FHA case number so he could transfer to the other lender. At 4:17 p.m., Gary Walters at CharterWest sent Justin a letter informing him that CharterWest

---

[642] *Riddle v. Charterwest Bank*, No. 8:18-CV-17 (D. Neb. May 8, 2018).

would "not be able to approve" the Riddles' loan. The letter advised that the loan was a "higher risk" according to the FHA underwriting system, and that Child Support is not paid as agreed. The decree we have states you are to pay monthly $417. We noted the payment history but it does not match the decree and therefore translates into delinquent payments. We would need something from the court documenting the agreement you have to pay accordingly to the history. We CANNOT just take your word for it. It does not work that way on FHA loans. If we cannot get anything then we can submit it without it but it will hurt your chances for approval. The letter further advised that the Riddles would need at least 2 months of house payments in reserve in their checking account, and that 2015 tax transcripts would be required. These requirements appear to be contrary to earlier representations from Whitehead that only a 1 month reserve would be necessary.

The Riddles proceeded with their new lender, but were informed by the new lender that there was a problem: their loan could not be approved because on May 17, CharterWest had "put a credit reject code in the comments section in the system" indicating that their loan application had been denied because of unpaid child support. On June 16, the Riddles contacted Walters and asked that the credit reject code be removed because (1) CharterWest should not have denied their loan after they withdrew their application and (2) they had provided all the child support documentation CharterWest had asked for. They also provided Walters with documentation that child support had been waived and no support was owed. Walters replied refusing the Riddles' request. Justin asked Walters to explain how CharterWest's decision to deny the loan had been made without the information that had been requested, and Walters again stated that only a court order waiving Justin's child support obligation would have been satisfactory. Justin asked Walters to show when a court order was requested of them. Walters did not respond.

The Riddles emailed Walters and the bank branch manager indicating their intent to appear at the branch in the morning with their documentation. They were met by sheriff's deputies who said that CharterWest had reported a threat, and were directed to leave the property. The Riddles lodged complaints with the FHA and Consumer Financial Protection Bureau, which were referred to the Federal Reserve's consumer affairs department. The Federal Reserve rejected the Riddles' complaint.

The Riddles sued CharterWest in Douglas County District Court, on September 13, 2017, asserting claims for breach of fiduciary duty, tortious interference with a business relationship, and fraud. CharterWest moved to dismiss pursuant to Neb. Ct. R. Pldg. § 6-1112(b)(6), and the district court entered an "Order of Dismissal Without Prejudice" on November 8, dismissing the Riddles' complaint without prejudice and granting leave to file an amended complaint within 14 days.

The Riddles did not file an amended complaint within 14 days. Instead, on December 13, they filed a new complaint asserting the same claims and some new ones, including the Federal Reserve as a new defendant. On January 16, 2018, the Federal Reserve removed the complaint to this Court. On January 30, CharterWest filed its motion to dismiss. On February 2, the Douglas County District Court entered a "Nunc Pro Tunc Order of Dismissal Without Prejudice" which again dismissed the complaint without prejudice, but omitted the language allowing leave to file an amended complaint.

. . .

DISCUSSION

The Riddles' complaint asserts [. . .] (4) violation of the Fair Credit Reporting Act (FCRA), 15 U.S.C. § 1681 *et seq.*; (5) "willful noncompliance"; and (6) conspiracy. CharterWest and the Federal Reserve each move to dismiss the complaint. the Court will consider their arguments separately.

. . . .

Fair Credit Reporting Act

Next, the Riddles assert a claim under the FCRA. Their theory is a little difficult to parse—the complaint primarily refers to an alleged failure to send an "adverse action letter" upon denial of their loan application. They also allege that CharterWest violated the FCRA by "fraudulently denying and improperly coding an application that had been withdrawn before any decision was made." And they refer to "Regulation B," which the Court assumes is referring to 12 C.F.R. § 1002.2(c), which defines an "adverse action" for purposes of credit reporting.

CharterWest's primary argument is that, while furnishers of credit information have a duty to provide accurate information to a credit reporting agency, § 1681s-2(a), Congress did not create a private right of action to enforce that duty, § 1681s-2(d). That's true—in fact, Congress expressly precluded such actions. *See* § 1681s-2(d). So, the Riddles cannot sue CharterWest under the FCRA for, allegedly, making a false statement in credit reporting.

There are other provisions of the FCRA that may permit private enforcement. For instance, the theory the Riddles seem to be relying on is the private right of action against businesses that use consumer credit reports but do not provide the "adverse action" notice required by § 1681m(a). *See* §§ 1681n(a) and 1681o(a); *Safeco Ins. Co. of Am. v. Burr*, 551 U.S. 47, 52-53 (2007). But that requirement is in play when a lender denies an application in reliance on a consumer credit report, and here, no such reliance is alleged: CharterWest did not deny the Riddles' loan application based on information from a consumer credit report. There is also a disclosure requirement for adverse action based on information from third parties, but that simply requires that the lender "disclose the nature of the information to the consumer" upon written request from the consumer. There seems to be little dispute here that CharterWest disclosed the nature of the information supporting denial of the Riddles' loan when the denial was made.

There may also be a private right of action against entities like CharterWest that provide information to credit reporting agencies, if the provider of information has been given notice of a dispute and failed to investigate the accuracy of the reported information. *See Ilodianya v. Capitol One Bank USA NA*, 853 F. Supp. 2d 772, 774 (E.D. Ark. 2012) (collecting cases). But the requirement that a provider of information investigate a dispute depends on the provider receiving notice of the dispute from the credit reporting agency. *See* § 1681s-2(b); *see also* § 1681i(a)(2). In other words, the FCRA sets up a process: a lender that denies credit to a consumer based on a credit report must notify the consumer why credit was denied, and tell the consumer how to contact the credit reporting agency. § 1681m(a). The consumer may then dispute any information contained in his or her file with the credit reporting agency. § 1681i(a)(1). The credit reporting agency must then reinvestigate the information, notifying the information provider about the dispute. § 1681i(a)(2). And the information provider then has a duty to investigate the dispute. § 1681s-2(b). But there is no allegation here that the information provider, i.e. CharterWest, had its duty to investigate triggered by notice of a dispute from a credit reporting agency.

In sum, to the extent that the Court can parse the Riddles' FCRA claim, the Court is aware of no private right of enforcement supporting a civil claim under the FCRA on the facts they allege. Accordingly, the Court will dismiss their FCRA claim.

"Willful Noncompliance"

The Riddles' next claim is for "willful noncompliance": they allege that CharterWest was told it had erred in denying the Riddles' loan based on "child support" but had "refused to correct the illegal denial, despite having evidence proving that the denial was in fact inaccurate." It is not obvious at first glance what the Riddles' "willful noncompliance" claim is alleging noncompliance with. But the Court's best guess is that the Riddles are referring to § 1681n of the FCRA, which provides civil liability for "willful noncompliance" with any requirement imposed under § 1681 *et seq.*

That said, as explained above, the Court can find no requirement of the FCRA that is privately enforceable and fits the facts. Accordingly, this claim will be dismissed as well.

. . .

CONCLUSION

As explained above, the Court will dismiss all the Riddles claims [. . .] against CharterWest [. . .] CharterWest's motion to dismiss is granted . . .

****

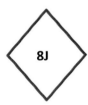

8J   **Why didn't the court simply determine that no private right of action exists for a violation of 15 U.S.C. 1681m rather than stating that the denial was not on the basis of information in a consumer report?** Some federal courts have determined that no private right of action exists for violations of section 1681m.[643] In addition, interpretation in this area of law is still being formed.

---

[643] *See, e.g., Perry v. First Nat'l Bank*, 459 F.3d 816, 823 (7th Cir. 2006); *see also Pearson v. Security Finance Corporation of Alabama Inc.*, No. 1:17-cv-522-WKW-TFM (M.D. Ala. Nov. 6, 2017).

8K

Under what circumstances is the FCRA adverse action notice required? Under what circumstances is the ECOA adverse action notice required?

BRUNSON V. PROVIDENT FUNDING ASSOCS.[644]

ORDER AND JUDGMENT Before LUCERO, O'BRIEN, and GORSUCH, Circuit Judges.

If nothing else, this case illustrates the necessity of judicial restraint. Assuming Bruce Brunson's allegations and his supporting evidence accurately state the facts and fairly capture all relevant circumstances, it appears Provident Funding Associates (Provident) did not treat him, its customer, well. In fact, the Provident team seems much like The Gang That Couldn't Shoot Straight. But it is not our place to pass judgment on Provident's business practices. Courts have no roving commission to "do good." They are, quite properly, constrained to applying the law in deciding the issues presented and nothing more, unsettling as that may sometimes be. So guided, we set emotion aside and decide the issues here presented.

Provident initiated foreclosure proceedings on Brunson's home because he was seven months behind on his mortgage payments. That was a different case, but it precipitated this one. In this case Brunson seeks damages, claiming Provident negligently led him to believe he could avoid foreclosure if he continued to make monthly payments, but that did not happen. He also argues Provident violated the Fair Credit Reporting Act (FCRA), 15 U.S.C. §§ 1681-1681x [. . .] He appeals from a summary judgment entered in favor of Provident. We affirm.

Factual Background

The parties are well familiar with the facts, so we touch on them only briefly. In November 2004, Brunson borrowed $98,000 from Provident and used his home in Salt Lake City, Utah, as collateral for the thirty-year loan, which called for a fixed interest rate for three years and an adjustable rate thereafter. From January through July 2008, Brunson failed to make the required monthly payments ($1,148.22). Provident began foreclosure proceedings and scheduled the sale of the home for July 30, 2008. The day before the sale and after an unsuccessful attempt to modify the loan, Brunson filed a Chapter 13 bankruptcy petition resulting in an automatic stay, *see* 11 U.S.C. § 362, and preventing the foreclosure. Provident updated Brunson's account to reflect the bankruptcy filing by placing it in its "bankruptcy module."

Brunson's proposed bankruptcy plan acknowledged arrearages ($12,116.90) on the debt he owed to Provident (approximately $109,000). It called for him to make his regular monthly payments to Provident and, in addition, remit $201.95 a month to the bankruptcy trustee to be applied to the arrearages. The bankruptcy case was dismissed in October 2008 because Brunson's lawyer failed to file a required form. Although the bankruptcy court notified Provident of the dismissal and Provident's

---

[644] *Brunson v. Provident Funding Assocs.*, No. 13-4029 (10th Cir. Apr. 20, 2015

bankruptcy specialists have access to PACER, Provident did not remove Brunson's account from its bankruptcy module.

After the dismissal of his bankruptcy case, Brunson enlisted the assistance of Michael Blackburn, Chief Operations Officer of Perfect Home Living, a nonprofit organization affiliated with the United States Department of Treasury's Homeownership Preservation Task Force. Its purpose is to help homeowners avoid foreclosure. Brunson and Blackburn made numerous calls to Provident in late 2008 seeking a loan modification. They were repeatedly informed by Provident that its records showed Brunson to still be in bankruptcy. Brunson and Blackburn told Provident the bankruptcy had been dismissed but Provident did not remove the account from its bankruptcy module. Nevertheless, it directed Brunson to continue making payments.

Brunson did so, making monthly payments to Provident from August 2008 to November 2009. Although an interest rate adjustment lowered his monthly payment from $1,148.22 to $1,102.20 in January 2009, he continued to make the higher payment. Provident applied these payments to the defaulted amount. For example, Provident applied the August 2008 payment to the January 2008 payment, the September 2008 payment to the March 2008 payment, the October 2008 payment to the February 2008 payment, the November 2008 payment to the April 2008 payment and so forth; his last payment, in November 2009, was applied to the April 2009 payment.8 Thus, even while making payments, Brunson continued to remain seven months in arrears.

On December 1, 2009, Provident sent Brunson a letter giving notice of another interest rate adjustment. The letter stated the payment due on January 1, 2010, would decrease from $1,102.20 to $990.06, and the loan balance was $95,088.94 "assuming [Brunson had] made all payments when due." Inexplicably, three weeks later, Brunson received a letter from Provident rejecting his December 2009 payment as "short." The letter instructed him to call Provident. On December 28, 2009, Brunson spoke with James Karanfiloglu, Provident's service compliance manager, who told him Provident had mistakenly maintained his account in its bankruptcy module even after the bankruptcy case had been dismissed and did not discover its mistake until December 2009.9 Karanfiloglu told Brunson his payments had been applied to the arrearages and he remained seven months behind in his payments.

Brunson responded the next day (December 29) with a "Qualified Written Request" (QWR)11 seeking documentation from Provident pursuant to RESPA. Brunson also ceased making payments because Provident told him the monthly payments would not be accepted unless he brought his account to no more than one month delinquent. Despite this dispute, on December 31, 2009, Provident's Annual Tax and Interest Statement to Brunson did not indicate his payments were past due.

Brunson hired an attorney who sent another QWR on January 20, 2010. Five days later, Provident sent Brunson a notice of default stating he must pay $10,066.92 plus his monthly payment within thirty days to bring his loan current and prevent foreclosure. On January 28, Provident responded to the January 20 QWR. Although it questioned the propriety of the QWR, Provident provided Brunson the loan documents, his payment history, and an assistance package to be completed if he sought a loan modification. On March 24, 2010, Provident sent a more detailed response to the QWR. It explained its failure to remove his account from the bankruptcy module and gave him thirty days to bring the account current and avoid foreclosure. At this point, Provident notified Brunson he must pay $19,619.58 to cure the default; this amount included not only the missed payments but also other fees including over $7,000 in legal fees. In May 2010, when Brunson did not cure the default, Provident transferred his account to its foreclosure department.

Discussion

. . .

FCRA

From February 2008 to January 2010, Provident continuously reported Brunson's account as delinquent to credit reporting agencies (CRAs). It stopped reporting the delinquency from February 2010 to April 2010 while it investigated and responded to the January 20 QWR but resumed its reporting in May 2010. Brunson claims Provident, as a "user of credit," violated FCRA when it failed to send him deficiency notices prior to reporting his delinquency to the CRAs. He claims this negative reporting prevented him from securing alternative financing to prevent the foreclosure.

15 U.S.C. § 1681m applies to "users" of consumer credit reports. It requires "any person tak[ing] any adverse action with respect to any consumer that is based in whole or in part on any information contained in a consumer report" to provide, inter alia, "notice of the adverse action to the consumer." 15 U.S.C. § 1681m(a)(1). While Provident may have been a "user" of a consumer credit report when it decided to provide financing to Brunson, his allegations relate to Provident's reporting of Brunson's account as delinquent to CRAs. These allegations refer to Provident's status as a "furnisher," not a "user", of information under FCRA. Thus, § 1681m does not apply.

Under 15 U.S.C. § 1681s-2, "furnishers" of information to CRAs are prohibited from, among other things, knowingly providing inaccurate information to a CRA. 15 U.S.C. § 1681s-2(a)(1). If such furnisher is a "financial institution that extends credit and regularly and in the ordinary course of business furnishes information to a [CRA]," it must provide written notice to its customer when it provides negative information about that customer to a CRA. 15 U.S.C. § 1681s-2(a)(7)(A)(i). Once it gives "such notice, the financial institution may submit additional negative information to a [CRA] . . . with respect to the same transaction, extension of credit, account, or customer without providing additional notice to the customer." 15 U.S.C. § 1681s-2(a)(7)(A)(ii). But, while FCRA allows federal agencies and state officials to enforce these obligations, it does not allow consumers, like Brunson, a private right of action to do so. 15 U.S.C. § 1681s-2(c), (d); *see also Sanders v. Mountain Am. Fed. Credit Union*, 689 F.3d 1138, 1147 (10th Cir. 2012); *Nelson v. Chase Manhattan Mortg. Corp.*, 282 F.3d 1057, 1059 (9th Cir. 2002). Thus, even assuming Provident failed to provide the required notice, Brunson is without recourse.

. . .

AFFIRMED.

****

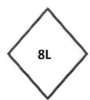

8L

Does FCRA apply to the credit information on businesses, i.e. business credit reports? Does FCRA apply to an individual's credit report used for a business loan? Why or Why not?

8M

What is the difference between a user and a furnisher for FCRA purposes?

As of December 2, 2018, the CFPB Consumer Complaint Database housed more than 1,170,000 consumer complaints.[645] Note that, as of December 2, 2018, 173,796 complaints were identified by the "Credit Reporting, credit repair services, or other personal consumer reports" product/sub-product category.[646] "Problem with a credit reporting company's investigation into an existing problem" represented 38,898 complaints as the complaint issue or sub-issue in the CFPB Consumer Complaint Database as of December 2, 2018.[647] This subcategory includes but is not limited to a dispute investigation that fails to fix the consumer report error, investigations that take in excess of thirty days to complete, and the consumer not being notified of the results of the consumer's dispute.[648] "Credit reporting company's investigation" represented 16,883 complaints as the complaint issue or sub-issue in the CFPB Consumer Complaint Database as of December 2, 2018.[649] In addition, "incorrect information on the credit report," including but not limited to the account status and account terms represented 102, 686 complaints as the complaint issue or sub-issue in the CFPB Consumer Complaint Database as of December 2, 2018.[650] "Improper use of your credit report" represented 28,278 complaints as the complaint issue or sub-issue in the CFPB Consumer Complaint Database as of December 2, 2018.[651] This subcategory includes but is not limited to receiving unsolicited financial products or offers after opting out.[652] "Advertising and marketing, including promotional offers" accounts for 2,315 consumer complaints as the complaint issue or sub-issue in the CFPB Consumer Complaint Database as of December 2, 2018.[653] This subcategory includes but is not limited to consumers who believe that they did not receive the terms advertised or promoted.[654]

---

[645] *See* CONSUMER FIN. PROT. BUREAU ONLINE CONSUMER COMPLAINT DATABASE, https://www.consumerfinance.gov/data-research/consumer-complaints/search/?from=0&searchField=all&searchText=&size=25&sort=created_date_desc, last visited December 2, 2018.
[646] *See id.*
[647] *See id.*
[648] *See id.*
[649] *See id.*
[650] *See id.*
[651] *See id.*
[652] *See id.*
[653] *See id.*
[654] *See id.*

8N

Does the establishment of an unbiased means of scoring credit help or hurt consumers? Consider consumers who are deemed as "credit invisible": "they do not have a credit record maintained by one of the three nationwide consumer reporting agencies."[655] Credit invisibility is more prominent in "credit deserts" where there is less access to traditional financial institutions to extend credit.[656] These credit deserts occur most often in rural and low-income urban areas.[657]

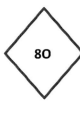

8O

(1) **Who** is regulated under FCRA and Regulation V?

(2) **Who** is protected under FCRA and Regulation V?

(3) **What** is the protection? What is the appropriate law or regulation?

(4) **When** is the protection applicable? (Under what circumstances does the protection apply?

(5) **Why** does the protection exist? Would applying the law or rule make sense in context?

****

Compare and contrast the form, timing, and content requirements for the Truth in Lending Act, the Equal Credit Opportunity Act, the Fair Debt Collection Practices Act, the Fair Credit Reporting Act, and the Gramm-Leach-Bliley Act consumer privacy provisions.

Compare and contrast the definition(s) of creditor in the Truth in Lending Act, Equal Credit Opportunity Act, and the Fair Debt Collection Practices Act. Is creditor defined in the Gramm-Leach-Bliley Act for the purposes of consumer financial privacy? Why or Why not?

---

[655] *See* CONSUMER FIN. PROT. BUREAU, *Data Point: The Geography of Credit Invisibility*, at 4, *available at* https://s3.amazonaws.com/files.consumerfinance.gov/f/documents/bcfp_data-point_the-geography-of-credit-invisibility.pdf.

[656] *See* CONSUMER FIN. PROT. BUREAU, Data Point: The Geography of Credit Invisibility, at 15, *available at* https://s3.amazonaws.com/files.consumerfinance.gov/f/documents/bcfp_data-point_the-geography-of-credit-invisibility.pdf.

[657] *See id.* at 13.

Compare and contrast the definition(s) of consumer in the Truth in Lending Act/Regulation Z, the Fair Debt Collection Practices Act, the Consumer Financial Privacy laws and regulations, and the Fair Credit Reporting Act.

Compare and contrast the violations that permit a private right of action and those violations that do not permit a private right of action? Is the consumer adequately protected without a private right of action for certain laws and regulations? Why or Why Not?

Compare the Fair Debt Collection Practices Act to the Fair Credit Reporting Act. How can restrictions against "self-help" tactics used by debt collectors and creditors be balanced with the need for debt collectors and creditors to collect payments owed?[658]

Compare the Equal Credit Opportunity Act with the Fair Credit Reporting Act. The credit (consumer) report may be used as both a shield for consumers (to establish an unprejudiced method to determine credit-worthiness) and a sword for lenders (to encourage repayment of amounts owed by consumers to avoid damage to the consumer's credit reputation).

Consider who is regulated under each law and who is exempt from compliance. Are the exemptions express or otherwise intended or are the exemptions developed via caselaw interpretation or other loophole?

Compare consequences of violations, including whether a private right of action is available and the statute of limitations.

---

[658] *See* Hynes, *supra* note 20, at 15 ("Federal and state laws restrict many of the tools that creditors have traditionally used to force repayment, including the reporting of past consumer behavior and nonlegal mechanisms such as contacting the debtor and third parties to request repayment. Self-help can be effective; debtors repay loans in order to avoid unpleasant phone calls, threatening letters, humiliation in front of friends, employers, and family members, and damage to their credit reputation.").

IX. THE FINANCIAL CRISIS AND THE FUTURE OF FINANCIAL SERVICES

A. THE FINANCIAL CRISIS

The creation of the Consumer Financial Protection Bureau was intended to centralize the protection of consumers as a regulatory objective but also to reduce risky, unchecked behaviors of some financial institutions, which ultimately impacted the U.S. market as well as consumers. In many respects the indirect consequences that led to the 2008 Financial Crisis may be compared and contrasted with the sweeping regulatory reforms that followed the Great Depression. Recall the discussion in Part I concerning the historical context for financial services regulation as well as the relationship between consumer protections and buttressing the financial system.

There are a number of theories concerning the reason for the 2008 financial crisis. This text considers the dichotomy between access to financial services/choice and consumer protection. More specifically, this text will consider the mortgage crisis, deregulation, and expanded access to financial services as a factual case study related to the financial crisis.

As discussed in Part I, banks traditionally provided many different services. In the last fifty years, services across providing residential mortgage products became segmented and offered by other entities. For example, traditionally, a bank may originate, fund, and service a loan. In the last fifty years, the shift in consumer financial services has resulted in the origination, funding, and servicing of a residential mortgage loan potentially occurring across three different financial institutions. Segmenting these services allowed for expertise and efficiencies in each service, but the segmentation also permitted a separation across the lifecycle of the loan. This segmentation, particularly among home mortgages, became significant for at least two reasons. First, access to home-ownership expanded exponentially in the years leading up to the financial crisis. Second, the segmentation created a lack of ownership and accountability for the asset. Both of these factors, namely the large number of mortgages (due to access expansion) and the lack of direct responsibility for the mortgage asset (due to segmentation), indirectly reduced the quality of the asset.

Why were there so many mortgages? Of all the consumer products and services discussed, why did mortgages create such a large portion of the consumer debt pie? It is important to be aware of the shift in financial services and the context of consumer financial protection laws:

> [T]he drivers of home mortgage growth were not just economic but also regulatory. An explicit national goal of greater homeownership generated bipartisan support for mortgage subsidies. Throughout most of the postwar period, consumer interest

payments on all forms of debt gave rise to tax deductions. Under the Tax Reform Act of 1986, most of these deductions were removed, leaving only mortgage interest deductions on federal income taxes. These policies, combined with low interest rates, contributed to a rise in homeownership levels from 51 percent in 1949 to 69 percent in 2007.[659]

The traditional mortgage product, in contrast to the creative mortgage products that, some argue, led up to the 2008 Financial Crisis, were **fixed rate** 30-year term mortgages. In other words, the interest rate charged on the principal stayed fixed over the life of the loan. A fixed rate mortgage allows a borrower to predict the borrower's installment payment (usually monthly) over the life of the loan. If interest rates rise or lower during the life of the loan, the borrower's mortgage payment, consisting of principal and interest, remains unaffected.

Over time less traditional mortgage products, that allowed for creative means to finance home purchases, gained in popularity, including the **adjustable rate** mortgage. Adjustable rate mortgages, in contrast to fixed rate mortgages, adjust to variations in market interest rates. As a result, the borrower's installment payment may change over time as it reacts to changes in market interest rates. The initial interest rate on an adjustable rate mortgage is typically lower than the interest rate available on a fixed rate mortgage. As a result, adjustable rates allowed for greater access to financing and home ownership.

9A **Are there any risks to the lender in offering fixed rate mortgages?**

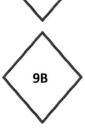

9B **Why would a consumer choose an adjustable rate mortgage if it is disclosed that the interest rate (and payment) may increase?**

Why is the initial interest rate on an adjustable rate mortgage typically lower than the interest rate on a fixed mortgage?[660]

Is it helpful to the consumer that the creditor disclose whether the interest rate is for an adjustable rate mortgage (variable interest rate) or a fixed interest rate mortgage? Recall the discussion of the Truth In Lending Act and accompanying rules. **Would disclosure of the interest alone be meaningful if the consumer is unable to compare across different products?** Consider that "financial service providers can exacerbate the information asymmetry by [. . .]

---

[659] RYAN ET AL., *supra* note 2, at 493.

[660] John Y. Campbell, Howell E. Jackson, Brigitte C. Madrian, and Peter Tufano explain that "an adjustable-rate mortgage normally has a lower interest rate than fixed-rate options, since lenders need not charge homeowners the cost of a one-sided bet on inflation." Campbell et al., *supra* note 26, at 97.

obscuring key product characteristics through advertising/marketing or product differentiation. Such steps make it more difficult for consumers to compare products."[661]

As a result of policies intended to encourage home mortgage growth and greater access to home ownership, underwriting became less strict. Return to Figure 1C. What part of the loan transaction occurs at underwriting? Borrowers were able to qualify with a larger variety of mortgage products available to fit the borrower's unique circumstance. This included, in addition to adjustable rate mortgages, interest-only loans, "no-doc" loans, and 80/20 loans.This social benefit may have proved short-term, however, when borrowers were no longer able to timely repay their debts. In other words, borrowers defaulted on their loans. Because a large number of borrowers defaulted on home loans, which are both a common form of debt and often the highest amount of consumer debt, the impact was pervasive. However, this pervasiveness, arguably, was exasperated by a lack of accountability for the asset, discussed *infra*.

Following the financial crisis, parts of the Truth in Lending Act were amended to increase the likelihood that borrowers had the "**Ability to Repay**" credit transactions secured by a dwelling.[662] Specifically, a creditor may not make such a loan unless the creditor makes a reasonable and good faith determination at or before consummation that the consumer will have a reasonable ability to repay the loan according to its terms.[663] The regulation defines what constitutes a reasonable determination.[664] Specifically, the regulation requires that the creditor consider the consumer's:

(1) Current or reasonably expected income or assets
(2) Employment status, if income from employment is a credit-worthiness determination
(3) Monthly payment on the loan at issue
(4) Monthly payment on other loans that the creditor has knowledge of or has reason to have knowledge of
(5) Monthly payment on other mortgage-related obligations (taxes and insurance, for example)
(6) Current debt obligations, alimony, and child support
(7) Debt-to-income ratio
(8) Credit history.[665]

Further, the regulation requires verification, via third-party records, of information, income, and assets that the creditor relies upon for credit-worthiness determinations.[666] Third-party records that the creditor may rely upon include tax returns filed with the Internal Revenue Service ("IRS"), IRS Form W-2s, payroll statements, and financial institution records, for example.[667] The Ability to Repay rule

---

[661] Lumpkin, *supra* note 27, at 125.

[662] 12 C.F.R. § 1026.43 (Fastcase 2018).

[663] 12 C.F.R. § 1026.43(c)(1).

[664] 12 C.F.R. § 1026.43(c)(2).

[665] *Id.*

[666] 12 C.F.R. § 1026.43(c)(3)-(4).

[667] 12 C.F.R. § 1026.43(c)(4).

provides a safe harbor for creditors. Specifically, a "qualified mortgage" is presumed to comply with the Ability to Repay rule.[668] A **qualified mortgage** is a mortgage with (1) regular, periodic payments that are substantially equal, (2) a loan term that does not exceed thirty years, (3) points and fees that do not exceed an amount specified in the regulation based on loan amount; (4) the creditor underwriting the loan considering the monthly payment for mortgage related obligations; (5) the creditor considering before the income, assets, debt obligations, child support and alimony prior to consummation; (6) and the debt to income ratio does not exceed forty-three percent.[669] If the loan meets the requirements of a "qualified mortgage," it is eligible for purchase by the Federal National Mortgage Association or the Federal Home Loan Mortgage Corporation.[670] Further, qualified mortgages are eligible to be insured by the U.S. Department of Housing and Urban Development or the Rural Housing Service and eligible to be guaranteed by the U.S. Department of Veterans Affairs or the U.S. Department of Agriculture.[671]

 9C   **Is the ability to repay rule a restrictive consumer protection method or a disclosure consumer protection method?**

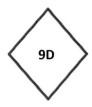 **9D**   **Is it appropriate for private financial institutions to be prohibited from making loans that do not follow specific criteria, set by regulation? Why or Why Not? Would a financial institution have any interest in extending credit to a consumer that the financial institution either knows or should know will not have the ability to repay? Why or Why Not?** Consider, for example, to what extent the financial institution will suffer limited financial harm or repercussions due to nonpayment. Recall the discussion of "safety and soundness" in Part I. Safety and soundness includes both (1) the quality of a bank's Assets as well as (2) the quality and adequacy of the bank's Capital under the CAMELS System.[672]

In the two decades prior to the Financial Crisis of 2008, mortgages began to be securitized. In other words, the risk of nonpayment of the mortgage was spread among investors. As discussed *supra*, the shift in consumer financial services has resulted in the origination, funding, and servicing of residential mortgage loans potentially occurring across three different financial institutions.

A bank may originate the mortgage loan and hold the mortgage loan on the bank's books until the mortgage loan reaches maturity, for example, in 30 years, on a 30-year mortgage loan term. However,

---

[668] 12 C.F.R. § 1026.43(e).

[669] 12 C.F.R. § 1026.43(e)(2). Note, however, that additional types of qualified mortgages exist under the rule, including for small creditors portfolio loans under 12 C.F.R. 1026.43(e)(5) and for temporary balloon-payment qualified mortgages under 12 C.F.R. 1026.43(e)(6) (2018).

[670] 12 C.F.R. § 1026.43(e)(4)(ii) (2018).

[671] *Id.*

[672] *See* St. Louis Fed. *supra* note 10.

consider the question posed earlier: Are there any risks to the lender in offering fixed rate mortgages? Keeping the loan on the bank's balance sheet at a fixed rate for thirty years may create a mismatch in the asset (the loan) versus the bank's liabilities and may increase risk for the bank. There is incentive for the bank to remove this asset (the mortgage loan) from its balance sheet both to reduce its risks and to free up additional capital to increase profitability. By removing the mortgage loan[673] from the institution's balance sheet, the risk of nonpayment (default by the borrower) is reduced and the risk of loss due to rising interest rates is reduced. By removing the loan from the institution's balance sheet, the bank recoups the money loaned faster to be able to use for another profit-generating purpose. A financial institution may achieve these goals by selling this asset.

How might the financial institution sell this asset and/or otherwise convince a third party that the risks that the financial institution is seeking to forego are worthwhile to the investor/purchaser? The financial institution may sell the asset to the investor at a discount. This, however, may not be desirable. Alternatively, the mortgage loans may be securitized, transforming an illiquid asset into a liquid asset, and reducing risk. In other words the mortgage loans may be pooled together and sold as securities to investors. Prior to the financial crisis, interest rates remained low to encourage home ownership. The securities were backed by the mortgage loan asset. With credit more easily-accessible and reduced underwriting standards, the quality of pooled mortgages was likely poor. Matthew Sherman, research assistant at the Center for Economic and Policy Research, explains that, "as housing prices started to decline and adjustable rate mortgages reset to higher levels, many borrowers felt squeezed and defaulted on their loans. The mortgage-backed securities linked to these mortgage loans, spread across nearly all financial institutions, began to lose value."[674] Recall the discussion of "bank runs" in Part I, namely the description of this issue as a "liquidity" issue for a bank. In contrast, in some respects, the challenge presented by the Financial Crisis may be described as an asset quality issue.

Once the borrower defaults on the loan, the creditor may initiate foreclosure proceedings. Foreclosure can occur once the borrower defaults, receives notification of the default, and fails to cure the default. Recall from Part, the Fair Debt Collection Practices Act protections apply to consumers with defaulted debts.

9E   **Was the 2008 financial crisis a public policy failure?**

---

[673] The following explanation is a simplified example for the purposes of illustration. Additional sources should be reviewed to gain a more complete understanding of the nuances of a bank's financial statement, including balance sheet, in comparison to a company financial statement, for example.

[674] Matthew Sherman, *A Short History of Financial Deregulation in the United States*, Ctr. for Econ. & Policy Research (July 2009) at 13.

9F Were institutions responsible for engaging in risky activities in which they had limited experience and did not understand? Were consumers responsible for taking advantage of new products and services offered to them, that they had limited experience and capacity to understand?

Whatever the (hotly-contested) cause of the financial crisis, the result was the creation of the CFPB and emphasis on consumer protection. Following the 2008 recession, "customers have gone from disliking banks in general but liking their own bank to hating the banks and being just okay with their own banker."[675] Were banks the cause of the financial crisis? Do banks need to be regulated more to protect consumers? However, note that Yale Law School Professor Roberta Romano opines that post-financial crisis legislation imposed "considerable costs on non-financial companies, which could well be in a multiple of billions of dollars, due to time-consuming disclosure requirements whose regulatory objectives have no connection to the financial crisis."[676] Others too have criticized that the CFPB was conceptualized prior to the financial crisis, not in reaction to the financial crisis, and played no role in addressing the causes of the financial crisis.[677]

Considering the proposed impact of mortgage debt to the financial crisis, in what other ways may public policy impact consumers and the financial system? In *A Brief Postwar History of U.S. Consumer Finance*, the authors state that:

> Other forms of household borrowing also were encouraged. Loans for higher education were promoted through government-sponsored insurance, and these left students with high balances to repay upon graduation. In 1996, 58 percent of bachelor's degree recipients graduated with an average of $18,000 in student loan debt (inflation adjusted); by 2008, nearly two-thirds of bachelor's degree graduates had debt, averaging $23,000.[678]

9G Return to the definitions in Part IC: Types of Financial Services. **Are student loans secured or unsecured loans?**

---

[675] McGregor, *supra* note 135.

[676] Romano, *supra* note 4, at 7.

[677] Zywicki, *supra* note 218, at 861 (stating "There is absolutely no evidence that failures in consumer protection actually contributed in a major way to the crisis.").

[678] RYAN ET AL., *supra* note 2, at 493-494.

9H Can similarities be drawn between policies expanding access to home ownership and policies expanding access to a college education? Can similarities be drawn between the Financial Crisis of 2008 and the warned student debt crisis?[679]

As of December 2, 2018, the CFPB Consumer Complaint Database housed more than 1,170,000 consumer complaints.[680] Note that, as of December 2, 2018, 47,810 complaints were identified by the "Student Loan" product/sub-product category.[681] However, note that "the CFPB is limited in how it can address student loans since it has no jurisdiction over public-sector lending in education. That authority instead belongs to the Department of Education."[682]

Considering the most recent historical context for consumer financial services regulation and the creation of the CFPB, what is the future of consumer financial services and for regulation?

The CFPB warned in the Project Catalyst Report: Promoting Consumer-Friendly Innovation that "some of the mast creative products in the history of consumer finance were exotic mortgage products that led to the financial crisis and economic collapse of 2007-2008 that devastated the lives of millions of Americans. Similarly, the very same technology that can empower consumers in their decision-making can equally be adapted to steer consumers toward products that may not be in their best interests."[683] Consider the future of consumer financial services and regulation in the next chapter whether you agree or disagree.

---

[679] *See* Consumer Fin. Prot. Bureau, *50 State Snapshot of Student Debt: A Nationwide Look at Complaints about Student Loans*, https://s3.amazonaws.com/files.consumerfinance.gov/f/documents/cfpb_student-loans_50-state-snapshot_complaints.pdf ("Student loan borrowers collectively owe more than $1.4 trillion in student loan debt."); *see also* Seth Frotman & Christa Gibbs, *Too Many Student Loan Borrowers Struggling, Not Enough Benefitting from Affordable Repayment Options*, CONSUMER FIN. PROTECTION BLOG (Aug. 16, 2017), https://www.consumerfinance.gov/about-us/blog/too-many-student-loan-borrowers-struggling-not-enough-benefiting-affordable-repayment-options/.

[680] *See* CONSUMER FIN. PROT. BUREAU ONLINE CONSUMER COMPLAINT DATABASE, https://www.consumerfinance.gov/data-research/consumer-complaints/search/?from=0&searchField=all&searchText=&size=25&sort=created_date_desc, last visited Dec. 2, 2018.

[681] *See* CONSUMER FIN. PROT. BUREAU ONLINE CONSUMER COMPLAINT DATABASE, https://www.consumerfinance.gov/data-research/consumer-complaints/search/?from=0&searchField=all&searchText=&size=25&sort=created_date_desc, last visited Dec. 2, 2018.

[682] *See* Adam Christopher Smith & Todd J. Zywicki, *Behavior, Paternalism, and Policy: Evaluating Consumer Financial Protection* 24 (Geo. Mason L. & Econ. Research Paper No. 14-05, Mar. 12, 2014), *available at* https://ssrn.com/abstract=2408083.

[683] *See* Consumer Fin. Prot. Bureau, Project Catalyst Report: Promoting Consumer-Friendly Innovation, (Oct. 2016), at 10, https://s3.amazonaws.com/files.consumerfinance.gov/f/documents/102016_cfpb_Project_Catalyst_Report.pdf.

B. THE FUTURE OF FINANCIAL SERVICES

The future of financial services may be considered in this section in two ways: (1) what is the future of consumer financial services and (2) what is the future of consumer financial services regulation?

What is the future of consumer financial services?

Many of the consumer financial services laws and rules included in this text may be described as "reactive." Policies, laws, and rules formed in reaction to social, economic, and political goals. Further, policies, laws, and rules are often created in reaction to major shifts, including following financial crises. Is it possible for government to instead behave proactively in attempting to prevent social and economic issues and/or to prevent financial crises? Are there benefits to limiting the scope of innovation in financial services until any unintended negative consequences may be discerned? Do individual consumers need protecting? Consumers as a group? The financial system as whole? If innovation occurs due to a need to compete in the market, do financial institutions need protection from themselves, to slow the speed of innovation? In *Consumer Protection and Financial Innovation: A Few Basic Propositions*, Stephen Lumpkin, Principal Administrator in the Financial Affairs Division of the OECD Directorate for Financial and Enterprise Affairs, poses the question: "Whose fault is it when product choices turn out to be poor ones or inappropriate ones for retail financial consumers? Where is the line to be drawn between *caveat emptor* versus *caveat vendor*?"[684] Lumpkin concludes that "system stability is enhanced when risks are properly identified and properly allocated. [. . .] In most cases, those most capable of absorbing risk will not be retail consumers."[685]

Innovation in products and services is not unique to the financial services industry,[686] but how to address innovation in financial services and consumer protection can present a distinctive risk. In other words, there are unique challenges that come with innovation in financial services, including unanticipated risks.[687] There are several different ways to approach innovation in financial services. Often it boils down to whether to regulate or not to regulate. Consider first why a traditional financial services institution and a financial services "disruptor" may innovate. At first glance, a financial service

---

[684] Lumpkin, *supra* note 27, at 131.

[685] *Id*. at 132.

[686] *See* Zywicki, *supra* note 218, at 901 (arguing "Analogously, simply because credit cards today are more complicated than credit cards were forty years ago, it does not follow that the increased complexity was intended solely to confuse consumers. Thus, while simplification is a useful goal, it cannot be a transcendent goal in itself— at least not without considering functionality and the role of consumer choice.").

[687] *See* Lane, *supra* note 5 ("It is inevitable that consumer protection issues will arise that could not have reasonably been foreseen or may be the result of fraud, criminal conduct or human error. What is important is that where these issues arise, we take corrective action swiftly and work to redress the detriment to consumers.").

or product is straightforward. There are no cognizable differences between, for example, a loan offered by a bank vs. a loan offered by a fintech company. A consumer may consider price and may consider with whom the consumer already has an established relationship.[688] All things being equal, how can financial institutions compete against each other and lure customers to utilizing their products or services? Lumpkin explains that:

> Product innovators have various options to attempt to stay ahead of their competitors. They can, for example, add bells and whistles to existing products to differentiate them in markets characterised by relatively homogeneous products or into which perceived close substitutes have been introduced; tweak products developed for a different clientele to adapt them for the mass market; use marketing and advertising to convince consumers that their particular product is special when, in fact, no fundamental difference exists; or they can increase product complexity, thereby obscuring key characteristics.[689]

How can governments protect individual consumers, protect consumers as a whole, and protect potentially negative impacts to the financial system that cannot yet be perceived? How do regulation and other potential barriers to entry into a market impact the innovative companies, the existing traditional financial services institutions, and consumers?

In the Forbes article, *Lessons from Uber: Why Innovation and Regulation Don't Mix*, contributor Larry Downes uses Uber as an example of the conflict between innovation and regulation. Specifically, Downes argues:

> [I]t's no wonder that in the bizarre world of licensed taxicabs and limousines, incumbents faced with the sudden arrival of disruptive technologies that could vastly improve their quality, efficiency, and profitability but which also introduce new competitors and new supply chain partners, respond as if their very existence is threatened. It is, of course. Enter Uber.[690]

Downes highlights the burden faced by Uber in fighting regulatory challenges to the company's ability to operate in certain markets without "required" licenses rather than being embraced for "new approaches to old businesses."[691]

Some argue that new products or services should be regulated. In other words, the regulator tasked with overseeing similar products and services must authorize or approve the new product or service. However, as Downes argues, the regulation of such products, which current laws and rules do not consider, may slow the benefits of innovation. For example, if the innovation creates efficiency, reduces

---

[688] *See* Lumpkin, *supra* note 27, at 128-30.

[689] *Id.* at 133.

[690] *See* Larry Downes, *Lessons from Uber: Why Innovation And Regulation Don't Mix*, FORBES, (Feb. 6, 2013), https://www.forbes.com/sites/larrydownes/2013/02/06/lessons-from-uber-why-innovation-and-regulation-dont-mix/#6f1f221dde94.

[691] *See id.*

costs, or expands access, government intervention may hinder these benefits if the financial service provider is burdened by cumbersome regulations that slow production, increase costs, and dictate who can access the product or service.[692] In addition, regulation may reduce competition.[693]

9I

Does limited financial services regulation foster modernization and innovation? Why or Why Not?

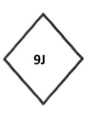

9J

Recall the definition of "abusive" under UDAAP. In the article, *The Consumer Financial Protection Bureau: Savior or Menace?*, author Todd Zywicki warns that "the 'abusive' standard could impose a sort of 'suitability' standard on lenders, forcing them to determine whether certain products are appropriate for certain consumers or categories of consumers, [. . .] [and could result in] chilling innovation of new products."[694] **Does the "abusive" standard require financial services providers to act in the consumer's best interests?[695] If so, could such a requirement impede innovation? Why or Why Not? Recall the *Buchanan* FDCPA case.[696] Does the decision in that case require that the debt collector have a fiduciary-like relationship with the debtor in advising the borrower that the debt is no longer collectible? Why or Why Not?**

9K

Consider Gorsuch's opinion in *Santander* that "it's hardly unknown for new business models to emerge in response to regulation, and for the regulation in turn to address new business models."[697] **Are there some ways that innovation, such as the emergence of debt buyers who**

---

[692] *See* Merle, *supra* note 49 ("Rolling back regulations has been a cornerstone of the Trump administration, which argues that excessive rulemaking strangles economic growth.") (quoting Representative Jeb Hensarling (R-Tex) and then chairman of the House Financial Services Committee, " 'The extreme overregulation it imposes on our economy leads to higher costs and less access to financial products and services, particularly for Americans with lower and middle incomes.' ").

[693] Llewellyn, *supra* note 7, at 8; Downes, *supra* note 690 (stating "Taxi and limousine services operate in a non-market economy because cities and states long-ago determined that the benefits of eliminating competition outweighed the costs. So it's worth asking again what those costs and benefits are, and whether the balance, thanks to the availability of disruptive new technologies, has changed [. . .]. The costs of removing competitive pressures from industries are also significant. Chief among them: in the absence of market dynamics, there are few if any incentives to innovate. Why should the driver of my last cab ride spruce up his vehicle, when every taxi at the cab stand charges the same fare and goes whenever its turn comes up? When price is controlled and new entrants are prohibited, only a fool would spend money to differentiate their product or service.").

[694] Zywicki, *supra* note 218, at 920.

[695] *Id.*

[696] 776 F.3d 393 (6th Cir., 2015).

[697] 173 S.Ct. 1718 at 1725.

are arguably not contemplated by the FDCPA[698] for example, can be harmful to consumers? Fintech disruptors have permitted revised expectations regarding the type and delivery of financial services and products. Fintech companies may expand financial services access and reduce costs. **Is it possible to have both innovative products *and* clearer disclosures? Or does innovation imply complexity and reduce the likelihood of clearer disclosures? How will new products and services comply with existing regulations? How can the risks of new products be assessed and mitigated?[699] What risks can the market tolerate? Are existing regulations appropriate for application to new products and services?**

The shift in financial services and providers is not new. Financial services products, institutions, and services may expand or constrict over time. It is the task of the financial regulator to ready itself for these shifts. The Consumer Financial Protection Bureau established "Project Catalyst" to benefit innovation in consumer financial services.[700] The CFPB has also proposed the creation of a "disclosure sandbox."[701] In addition, the Office of the Comptroller of the Currency has taken measures to bring fintech within its regulatory purview.[702] Recall that the Office of the Comptroller of the Currency typically regulated banks with national charters. Recall that banks can be distinguished from other types of financial institutions. Consider the following article reprinted with permission from The Banking Law Journal, entitled *The OCC's Proposed Fintech Charter: If it Walks Like a Bank and Quacks Like a Bank, It's a Bank.*

This article was first published in the April 2017 issue of the Banking Law Journal. © Matthew Bender & Co., Inc. All Rights Reserved.

**Footnotes in the following reprinted article are independent of footnotes in the full text of this work.

---

[698] *See id.* at 1724 ("on petitioners' account, Congress never had the chance to consider what should be done about those in the business of purchasing defaulted debt. That's because, petitioners tell us, the 'advent' of the market for defaulted debt represents " 'one of the most significant changes' " to the debt market generally since the Act's passage in 1977.").

[699] *See* Downes, *supra* note 690 (opining that some regulations are needed, including for safety, price-predictability and insurance. Downes provides a worst-case scenario example to illustrate stating, "Uber and its start-up peers are the darlings today of consumers and innovation-minded politicians alike, but watch what happens the first time a passenger is assaulted by an inadequately-screen driver, or when a shared-ride vehicle gets into a serious accident without adequate insurance.").

[700] *See* Press Release, Consumer Fin. Prot. Bureau, CFPB Finalizes Policy to Facilitate Consumer-Friendly Innovation (Feb. 18, 2016), available at https://www.consumerfinance.gov/about-us/newsroom/cfpb-finalizes-policy-to-facilitate-consumer-friendly-innovation/; *cf.* Zywicki, *supra* note 218, at 858 (stating that "the creation of the CFPB squandered this historical opportunity for innovative and effective consumer protection reform.").

[701] *See* CONSUMER FIN. PROT. BUREAU BLOG, *BCFP Office of Innovation Proposes 'Disclosure Sandbox' for Fintech Companies to Test New Ways to Inform Consumers*, (Sep. 13, 2018), https://www.consumerfinance.gov/about-us/blog/bcfp-office-innovation-proposes-disclosure-sandbox-fintech-companies-test-new-ways-inform-consumers/.

[702] *See generally* OFFICE OF THE COMPTROLLER OF THE CURRENCY, *Recommendations and Decisions for Implementing a Responsible Innovation Framework* (Oct. 26, 2016).

The OCC's Proposed Fintech Charter: If It Walks Like a Bank and Quacks Like a Bank, It's a Bank

*Lawrence D. Kaplan, Chris Daniel, Thomas P. Brown, Gerald S. Sachs, and Lauren Kelly D. Greenbacker**

The authors of this article explain a recent whitepaper, "Exploring Special Purpose National Bank Charters for Fintech Companies," in which the Office of the Comptroller of the Currency announces that it may charter a new type of special purpose national bank to facilitate the provision of core banking activities—receiving deposits, paying checks, or lending money—through financial technology.

The Office of the Comptroller of the Currency ("OCC") has announced that it may charter a new type of special purpose national bank to facilitate the provision of core banking activities—receiving deposits, paying checks, or lending money—through financial technology ("Fintech"). The OCC's announcement of a new form of special purpose national bank charter intended for Fintech (the "Fintech Bank Charter") came in the form of a whitepaper entitled *Exploring Special Purpose National Bank Charters for Fintech Companies*, which was released on December 2, 2016 (the "Whitepaper").[1] Through its willingness to consider applications for a Fintech Bank Charter, the OCC is acknowledging that the financial services industry is evolving, and recognizing that technology makes financial products and services more accessible and easier to use. Notwithstanding the foregoing, Fintech special purpose national banks ("Fintech Banks") will be subject to the same rigorous standards of safety and soundness, fair access and fair treatment that apply to all national banks and federal savings associations under its jurisdiction.

---

* Lawrence D. Kaplan (lawrencekaplan@paulhastings.com) is of counsel in the Global Banking and Payments Systems practice of Paul Hastings LLP. Chris Daniel (chrisdaniel@paulhastings.com) serves as co-chair of the firm's Payment Systems practice and is a partner in the Corporate Department. Thomas P. Brown (tombrown@paulhastings.com) is a partner in the firm's Antitrust and Competition and the Global Banking and Payment Systems practices. Gerald S. Sachs (geraldsachs@paulhastings.com) is of counsel and Lauren Kelly D. Greenbacker (laurenkellygreenbacker@paulhastings.com) is an associate in the firm's Global Banking and Payment Systems practice.

[1] *See* OCC, *Exploring Special Purpose National Bank Charters*, (Dec. 2016) *available at* https://occ.gov/topics/bank-operations/innovation/special-purpose-national-bank-charters-for-fintech.pdf; *see also, Remarks by Thomas J. Curry Regarding Special Purpose National Charters for Fintech Companies* (Dec. 2, 2016), *available at* https://occ.gov/news-issuances/speeches/2016/pub-speech-2016-152.pdf.

The OCC recognizes that the demographics of the financial marketplace also are changing with 85 million millennials becoming consumers of financial services—a demographic that has come of age using and relying on technology. As the Whitepaper notes, these market forces have resulted in technology-driven nonbank companies seeking new ways to deliver financial products and services. While frequently viewed as competition to traditional banks, given the challenges of bank regulation, technology companies frequently consider whether to become banks themselves. The Fintech Bank Charter may be a vehicle to do so. Whether the Fintech Bank Charter would carry with it all of the obligations of being a full-service bank, including the application for and receipt of FDIC insurance, and the significant regulation of bank holding companies under the Bank Holding Company Act ("BHCA")[2] remains uncertain.[3] To be clear, and we think this thought has been lost by some commentators on the Whitepaper, this entity will be a bank and will be regulated as a bank with all of the requisite burdens and obligations of being a bank.

Notwithstanding the limited nature of the Fintech Bank Charter, as discussed below, the OCC has noted its intention to impose conditions on approval of a Fintech Bank Charter; accordingly, even when available, it will not be the right mechanism for every Fintech company. While half a loaf is better than none, the limitations and obligations imposed on an entity with a Fintech Bank Charter are a sobering reminder to the Fintech community that bank regulators regulate, and that the price of admission to become even a special purpose bank with a limited focus will likely be high. Marketplace forces and careful consideration of the broader legal landscape will determine whether such steep price is worth it.

OCC'S CHARTERING AUTHORITY AND APPLICABLE LAW

The Whitepaper is significant for its reaffirmation that the OCC has the authority to grant special purpose charters for national banks and federal savings associations under the National Bank Act and the Home Owners' Loan Act ("HOLA"), respectively.[4] Existing OCC regulations define a "special

---

[2] 12 U.S.C. §§ 1841 et seq.

[3] See Letter of the Conference of State Bank Supervisors to OCC, *Receiverships for Uninsured National Banks* (Nov. 14, 2016), *available at* https://www.csbs.org/regulatory/policy/Documents/2016/CSBS%20Comment%20Letter%20on%20OCC%20Receiverships%20for%20Uninsured%20National%20Banks%20NPRM.pdf.(hereinafter, "CSBS Letter").

[4] See 12 U.S.C. §§ 1 et seq. and 1461 et seq. The OCC also has authority, under the International Banking Act, 12 U.S.C. § 3102, to license a foreign bank to operate a federal

purpose national bank" as a bank that conducts activities other than fiduciary activities that engages in at least one of the following three core banking functions: receiving deposits; paying checks; or lending money.[5] The OCC previously has used such authority to charter other types of national banks including credit card banks. Because the OCC views the provision of financial services through Fintech as merely an extension of its existing chartering authority, this reaffirmation of its chartering authority was not effectuated through a formal rulemaking under the Administrative Procedure Act (the "APA").[6]

A national bank is a type of corporate organization authorized under the National Bank Act and the laws of the United States[7] that engages only in activities deemed to be permissible as identified in statutes, OCC regulations, and guidance issued by the OCC.[8] Specifically, the National Bank Act affirmatively permits national banks to engage in lending.[9] The Whitepaper further notes that issuing debit cards or engaging in other means of facilitating payments electronically is the modern equivalent of "paying checks," which is identified as another core activity of national banks.

A significant benefit to Fintech entities operating under a Fintech Bank Charter would be that a Fintech Bank would have the same status and attributes under federal law as a full-service national bank, and thus would be able to operate with the benefit of federal law preemption of inconsistent state laws, subject, of course, to limitations imposed by the Dodd-Frank Wall Street Reform and Consumer Protection Act (the "Dodd-Frank Act").[10] Limitations on state examination or visitorial authority would also apply.[11]

---

branch or agency in the United States. Given that all federal savings associations chartered under the HOLA must have deposit insurance issued by the Federal Deposit Insurance Corporation (the "FDIC"), the Whitepaper focuses only on chartering national banks, which are only required to obtain deposit insurance if they accept deposits. Whether the OCC may grant a charter for a national bank that does not accept deposits is an issue that will be subject to significant debate. *See, e.g.,* CSBS Letter.

[5] *See* 12 C.F.R. § 5.20(e)(1).

[6] 5 U.S.C. § 551-9. However, challenges to this regulatory interpretation could be forthcoming. For instance, a challenge pursuant to the federal APA may be leveled at the OCC following the granting of the first such Fintech Bank Charter.

[7] 12 U.S.C. §§ 21 *et seq.*

[8] 12 U.S.C. §§ 24 *et seq.* and 12 C.F.R. Parts 1-199.

[9] 12 U.S.C. § 24 (seventh).

[10] 12 U.S.C. §§ 5301 *et seq.*

[11] 12 C.F.R. § 7.4010.

Under the current standard for federal preemption, specific state laws do not apply if they would require a national bank to be licensed in order to engage in certain types of activity or business (e.g., making loans). However, state laws that would generally apply to national banks include state laws on anti-discrimination, fair lending, debt collection, taxation, zoning, criminal laws, and torts.[12] Moreover, the OCC has taken the position that state laws aimed at unfair or deceptive treatment of customers apply to national banks. Finally, any other state laws that only incidentally affect national banks' exercise of their federally authorized powers to lend, take deposits and engage in other federally authorized activities would not be preempted and thus would be applicable to a Fintech Bank Charter.

As noted in the Whitepaper, Fintech Banks will be subject to the same laws, regulations, examination, reporting requirements, and ongoing supervision as other national banks. Statutes and regulations that by their terms apply to national banks would apply to all special purpose national banks, even uninsured national banks, include legal lending limits, as well as restrictions on transactions with affiliates and insider lending requirements.[13] Other laws that apply to all entities engaged in financial services include:

- the Bank Secrecy Act ("BSA");[14]

- other anti-money laundering ("AML") laws[15] and the economic sanctions administered by the U.S. Department of the Treasury's Office of Foreign Assets Control;[16]

- Electronic Funds Transfer Act;[17]

- Truth in Lending Act;[18]

- Real Estate Settlement Procedures Act;[19]

---

[12] *See* 12 C.F.R. §§ 7.4001, 7.4007, 7.4008.

[13] 12 U.S.C. § 84 and 12 C.F.R. Part 32; 12 U.S.C. §§ 371c and 371c-1 and 12 C.F.R. Part 223; and 12 U.S.C. §§ 375a(a) and (b) and 12 C.F.R. Part 215.

[14] 31 U.S.C. §§ 5311–5330; 12 U.S.C. §§ 1818(s), 1829(b), and 1951–1959; 31 C.F.R. Part 103; 31 C.F.R. Chapter X.

[15] 18 U.S.C. §§ 1956–57; 31 U.S.C. §§ 5301, 5340–5342, 5351–5355; Pub. L. 102-550, 106 Stat. 4044; Pub. L. 104-132, 114 Stat. 1214; and Pub. L. 108-458, 118 Stat. 3638 (codified as amended in scattered sections of the U.S. Code).

[16] 31 C.F.R. Chapter V.

[17] 15 U.S.C. § 1693b and 12 C.F.R. Part 205.

[18] 15 U.S.C. §§ 1601 *et seq.* and 12 C.F.R. Part 1026.

[19] 12 U.S.C. §§ 2601–2617 and 12 C.F.R. Parts 1024 and 1026.

- Home Mortgage Disclosure Act;[20]
- Equal Credit Opportunity Act;[21]
- Fair Credit Reporting Act;[22]
- Fair Housing Act;[23]
- Service Members Civil Relief Act;[24] and
- Military Lending Act[25] and each law's respective implementing regulations.

A special purpose national bank also would be subject to the prohibitions on engaging in unfair or deceptive acts or practices under Section 5 of the Federal Trade Commission Act[26] and unfair, deceptive or abusive acts or practices under Section 1036 of the Dodd-Frank Act.[27]

While not discussed in the Whitepaper, special purpose national banks are subject to the Change in Bank Control Act, which would require that any person acquiring control of a Fintech Bank obtain prior OCC approval after at least a 60-day public notice and comment period.[28] As a result, prior agency approval would be required for a Fintech Bank to engage in an exit transaction or a material capital raising transaction. In addition, if a Fintech Bank is deemed to have insured deposits, a transfer of such deposit liabilities or an assumption of another bank's deposit liabilities would be subject to the Bank Merger Act[29] and change in control transactions could involve approval by the Board of Governors of the Federal Reserve System.[30] In addition, changes in a national bank's permanent capital could require notice to or an application for prior approval to the OCC,[31] which also could impact the timing of capital raising transactions.

---

[20] 12 U.S.C. §§ 2801 *et seq.* and 12 C.F.R. Part 1003.

[21] 15 U.S.C. §§ 1691 *et seq.* and 12 C.F.R. Part 1002.

[22] 15 U.S.C. §§ 1681 and 12 C.F.R. Part 222.

[23] 42 U.S.C. §§ 3601-3619 and 24 C.F.R. Part 100.

[24] 50 U.S.C. app. §§ 501 *et seq.*

[25] 10 U.S.C. § 987; 32 CFR Part 232.

[26] 15 U.S.C. § 45.

[27] 12 U.S. C. § 5531.

[28] *See* 12 U.S.C. § 1817(j); 12 C.F.R. § 5.50. If the Fintech Charter is owned by a bank holding company, a change in control of such bank holding company would be subject to the BHCA.

[29] 12 C.F.R. § 1828(c) and 12 C.F.R. § 5.33.

[30] 12 U.S.C. § 1842.

[31] 12 C.F.R. § 5.46.

Fintech Banks also would be subject to limitations on their ability to pay dividends, which are restricted to undivided profits during the current year, with a one- or two-year look back as a limitation.[32] In addition, Fintech Banks would be subject to restrictions on certain incentive compensation arrangements that are deemed to pose inappropriate risks to the bank.[33]

Furthermore, a Fintech Bank that makes a material change to its approved business plan would also need prior OCC approval, which could impact the ability of a Fintech company to quickly change its focus.[34]

It is important to reiterate that there is a question about whether the OCC can grant a Fintech Bank Charter that does not include the power to take deposits. Deposit-taking is a defining attribute of a bank, and if the OCC charters a Fintech Bank that does not have deposit-taking powers, the question is whether that entity could actually be deemed to be a "bank" (i.e., has the OCC exceeded its statutory chartering authority?). If the Fintech Bank accepts deposits (other than trust deposits), it must apply to the FDIC for deposit insurance, and the Fintech Bank would, therefore, be a "bank" for purposes of the BHCA, necessitating the regulation of the Fintech Bank's corporate parent(s) to regulation as a bank holding company, including restrictions on its nonbanking activities.

REGULATION OF FINTECH BANKS

While the OCC would be the primary prudential regulator and supervisor of a special purpose national bank, depending on the structure of the bank and the activities it conducts, other federal regulators may have oversight roles over its ownership structure and/or the operations of the bank.

While the OCC contemplates in the Whitepaper that issuers of debit cards could obtain a Fintech Bank Charter, the structure of the underlying accounts accessible through the debit card will be critical, unless the underlying accounts are de-coupled and held as deposits at a separate depository institution. While it is possible to structure a payment transmission through a fiduciary relationship, thereby avoiding the need for FDIC deposit insurance,[35] such

---

[32] 12 U.S.C. § 60 and 12 C.F.R. § 5.64.

[33] *See* Section 965 of the Dodd-Frank Act and proposed regulations promulgated by the OCC at 81 *Fed Reg.* 37670 (June 10, 2016), *available at* https://www.gpo.gov/fdsys/pkg/FR-2016-06-10/pdf/2016-11788.pdf.

[34] *See* 12 C.F.R. § 5.53; *see also* OCC, *OCC Significant Deviation Policy* (Aug. 21, 2003), *available at* https://www.occ.gov/static/licensing/form-deviation-policy-v2.pdf.

[35] 12 U.S.C. § 1815(a). "Trust funds" for purposes of the FDI Act means "funds held by an

structure could raise issues from a consumer protection perspective, leaving consumers with little if the bank were to fail and subjecting the bank's management to claims of breaches of their fiduciary duty to protect funds in transit. This structure also could be implemented today through a national trust bank.

As the concept of what is or is not a deposit as defined under Section 3(l) of the Federal Deposit Insurance Act ("FDI Act"),[36] the FDIC would appear to have significant input into the efficacy of a Fintech Bank Charter for entities engaged in payments. In its capacity as an insurer, the FDIC is risk-adverse, and if it determines that funds accepted by a Fintech Bank should be classified as "deposits," the Fintech Bank would be required to obtain deposit insurance issued by the FDIC, subjecting such bank to FDIC jurisdiction and backup enforcement authority. The OCC's push for a Fintech Bank Charter has historical precedent, as at the inception of internet banking it was the FDIC that raised red flags to internet companies seeking to form banks, even though the OCC was willing to charter such entities.[37] Accordingly, industry interest and the OCC's willingness to charter special purpose national banks could be tempered if the FDIC deems a Fintech Bank to be accepting deposits.

Moreover, if a Fintech Bank accepts deposits, its corporate shareholders would be subject to the BHCA and rules and regulations of the Board of Governors of the Federal Reserve System thereunder.[38] If the bank is deemed (i) an insured depository institution or (ii) accepts demand depositors and is engaged in the business of making commercial loans, provided that the entity does not qualify for any of the exceptions from the definition of "bank" in the BHCA, such as trust banks, credit card banks, credit unions and industrial loan companies. If subject to the BHCA, a corporate shareholder would be subject to Federal Reserve oversight and supervision, including significant limitations on its nonbank activities.

Corporate shareholders of a Fintech Bank that only engages in lending, and is funded without deposits, would not be a "bank" for purposes of the BHCA. However, corporate shareholders of entities "receiving deposits" and some entities "paying checks" could be subject to the BHCA as well depending upon the structure of the funds held by the bank paying such checks. If structured in

---

insured depository institution in a fiduciary capacity and includes, without being limited to, funds held as trustee, executor, administrator, guardian, or agent."

[36] 12 U.S.C. § 1813(l).

[37] *See, e.g.,* OCC Conditional Approval 312 (May 1999) and subsequent OCC Corporate Decision 99-30 (Sept. 1999).

[38] 12 U.S.C. § 1841.

a fiduciary capacity, the shareholder would not be subject to the BHCA; however, if the underlying funds of the payments transaction are deemed as deposits, then the shareholder is subject to the BHCA and the bank would also be subject to FDIC supervision.

Compliance with laws and regulations promulgated by the Consumer Financial Protection Bureau ("CFPB") would be regulated by the OCC, unless the Fintech Bank is over $10 billion in assets, which would cause its compliance with consumer laws to be regulated by the CFPB.[39] The CFPB also maintains jurisdiction over certain nonbank financial services providers such as mortgage originators or servicers and entities the CFPB designates as "larger market participants" through rulemaking.[40] Nonetheless, establishment of a Fintech Bank Charter could benefit nonbanks engaged in mortgage origination or servicing, if such entities maintain less than $10 billion in assets.

CHARTERING PROCESS

The chartering process for a Fintech Bank would be the same as for a full-service national bank, applying supervisory standards involving safety and soundness, as well as requirements to provide fair access to financial services, treat customers fairly, and comply with all applicable laws and regulations. The OCC traditionally tailors these standards based on a bank's size, complexity, and risk profile.

Initially, formation of all national banks involves three key components—a well-developed business plan, sufficient capital, and qualified management. Each of the following factors will be critical in an OCC determination to charter a Fintech Bank:

(1) *Business Plan.* The business plan of a bank is the key component of any charter proposal, as it articulates a bank's activities and how the bank will use its resources to meet its goals and objectives and will set forth metrics of progress. As in the formation of a full service bank, the OCC expects a three-year comprehensive plan for a Fintech Bank Charter applicant to discuss:

- Markets to be served;
- Products and services;
- Assessments of risks inherent with the proposed products and services, including BSA/AML, consumer protection, and fair

---

[39] 12 U.S.C. § 5515.

[40] Given the current political climate, such rulemakings are unlikely.

lending;

- Risk controls and management information systems;
- Capital and metrics to monitor appropriate capital levels, as discussed below;
- Financial inclusion, as discussed below; and
- Recovery and exit strategies, as discussed below.

(2) *Capital.* As set forth in the Whitepaper, the OCC is not setting specific capital requirements for Fintech Banks, but will require that applicants identify minimum and ongoing capital levels need to be commensurate with the risk and complexity of the proposed activities (including on- and off-balance sheet activities). This is similar to how the OCC evaluates capital at national trust banks.[41]

The OCC's evaluation of capital adequacy (initial and ongoing) will then consider the risks and complexities of the proposed products, services, and operating characteristics, taking into account both quantitative and qualitative factors.[42] In addition to assessing the quality and source of capital, the OCC also considers on- and off-balance sheet composition, credit risk, concentration, and market risks. Moreover, Fintech Bank Charter applicants whose business activities include off-balance sheet would be subject to the OCC's minimum regulatory capital requirements; however, the minimum capital levels required may not adequately reflect the risks associated with off-balance sheet activities. Accordingly, Fintech Bank Charter applicants will be expected to propose a minimum level of capital that the proposed bank would meet or exceed at all times. This requirement parallels an existing requirement imposed on national trust banks, which typically have few assets on the balance sheet than other institutions, and are typically required to hold a specific minimum amount of capital, which often exceeds the capital requirements for other types of banks. Similarly, the OCC would consider adapting capital requirements applicable to a Fintech Bank Charter applicant

---

[41] *See* OCC Bulletin 2007-21: Revised Guidance: Capital and Liquidity (June 2007), *available at* https://www.federalreserve.gov/newsevents/speech/brainard20161202a.htmhttps://www.occ.gov/news-issuances/bulletins/2007/bulletin-2007-21.html.

[42] Qualitative elements that influence the determination of capital adequacy include the scope and nature of the bank's proposed activities, quality of management, funds management, ownership, operating procedures and controls, asset quality, earnings and their retention, risk diversification, and strategic planning.

as necessary to adequately reflect its risks and to the extent consistent with applicable law.

(3) *Liquidity.* Similarly, the OCC will focus on a Fintech Bank Charter applicant's liquidity management and capacity to readily and efficiently meet expected and unexpected cash flows and collateral needs at a reasonable cost, without adversely affecting either daily operations or the financial condition of the bank. Liquidity will be evaluated commensurate with the risk and complexity of the proposed activities. In assessing the liquidity position of a Fintech Bank Charter applicant, the OCC considers a proposed bank's access to funds as well as its cost of funding.[43]

(4) *Fair Lending and Financial Inclusion.* While not formally subjecting non-depository Fintech-Chartered banks to the Community Reinvestment Act ("CRA"),[44] the Whitepaper notes that the OCC's statutory mission includes ensuring that national banks treat customers fairly and provide fair access to financial services, factors typically addressed through CRA compliance by full service banks. Nonetheless, in an attempt to placate community groups that fear a transfer of banking services from entities subject to the CRA to entities exempt from the CRA, the OCC will require an applicant seeking a Fintech Bank Charter that engages in lending activities to demonstrate a commitment to financial inclusion that supports fair access to financial services and fair treatment of customers. The nature of the commitment would depend on the entity's business model and the types of loan products or services it intends to provide. For example, Fintech Bank Charter applicants seeking to engage in lending will need to address the following elements:

- an identification of, and method for defining, the relevant market, customer base, or community;

- a description of the nature of the products or services the company intends to offer (consistent with its business plan), the

---

[43] Key areas of consideration identified by the OCC include projected funding sources, needs, and costs; net cash flow and liquid asset positions; projected borrowing capacity; highly liquid asset and collateral positions (including the eligibility and marketability of such assets under a variety of market environments); requirements for unfunded commitments; and the adequacy of contingency funding plans. All aspects of liquidity should address the impact to earnings and capital, and incorporate planned and unplanned balance sheet changes, as well as varying interest rate scenarios, time horizons, and market conditions.

[44] 12 U.S.C. §§ 2901 *et seq.*

marketing and outreach plans, and the intended delivery mechanisms for these products or services;

- an explanation of how such products and services, marketing plans, and delivery mechanisms would promote financial inclusion (e.g., provide access to underserved consumers or small businesses); and

- full information regarding how the proposed bank's policies, procedures, and practices are designed to ensure products and services are offered on a fair and non-discriminatory basis. For example, the OCC may ask an applicant that plans to extend credit to provide the terms on which it plans to lend, including a description of the protections it plans to provide to individuals and small business borrowers.

(5) *Alternative Business Strategies and Recovery.* Like the OCC requires of full service banks subject to a business plan requirement, Fintech Banks will be required to propose alternative business and recovery strategies to address various best-case and worst-case scenarios and identify specific financial or other risk triggers that would prompt the board and management's determination to unwind the operation in an organized manner. These strategies must provide a comprehensive framework for evaluating the financial effects of severe stress that may affect an entity and options to remain viable under such stress. The business plan must address material changes in the institution's size, risk profile, activities, complexity, and external threats, and be integrated into the entity's overall risk governance framework. Plans must be specific to that entity, aligned with the entity's other plans, and coordinated with any applicable parent or affiliate planning. A plan should include triggers alerting the entity to the risk or presence of severe stress, a wide range of credible options an entity could take to restore its financial strength and viability, and escalation and notification procedures. While the objective of these business and recovery strategies is to remain a viable entity, the OCC may also require a company to have a clear exit strategy.

The OCC's formal licensing process will involve four stages:[45]

(1) *The prefiling stage*, in which potential applicants engage with the

---

[45] *See* OCC's Licensing Manual OCC, "Charters," *Comptroller's Licensing Manual* (Sept. 2016), *available at* https://www.occ.gov/publications/publications-by-type/licensing-manuals/charters.pdf, applies to both full service and special purpose national banks.

OCC in formal and informal meetings to discuss their proposal, the chartering process, and application requirements.

(2) *The filing stage*, in which the organizers prepare and submit the application, including a three-year business plan. Organizers also must publish notice of the charter application as soon as possible before or after the date of the filing. An applicant's senior management and management of controlling shareholders also must submit biographical information, personal financial information, and be fingerprinted.

(3) *The review and evaluation stage*, in which the OCC conducts background and field investigations, and reviews and analyzes the application to determine whether the proposed bank: has a reasonable chance of success; will be operated in a safe and sound manner; will provide fair access to financial services; will ensure compliance with laws and regulations; will promote fair treatment of customers; and will foster healthy competition.

(4) *The decision stage*, which includes three phases:

- the *preliminary conditional approval phase*, during which the OCC decides whether to grant preliminary conditional approval of the proposed special purpose charter;

- the *organization phase*, during which the bank in organization raises capital, prepares for opening, and the OCC conducts a preopening examination; and

- the *final approval phase*, during which the OCC decides whether the bank has met the conditions for opening.

Like with full service charter proposals, the OCC has noted that it will impose a number of standard conditions on a Fintech Bank when it grants preliminary conditional approval, such as the establishment of appropriate policies and procedures and the adoption of an internal audit system appropriate to the size, nature, and scope of the bank's activities. Moreover, the OCC may impose additional conditions for a variety of reasons, including, for example, to ensure the newly chartered bank does not change its business model from that proposed in the application without prior OCC approval,[46] to mandate higher capital and liquidity requirements, or to require the bank to have a resolution plan to sell itself or wind down if necessary. In addition, in the

---

[46] *See also* OCC, *OCC Significant Deviation Policy* (Aug. 21, 2003), *available at* https://www.occ.gov/static/licensing/form-deviation-policy-v2.pdf.

case of an uninsured bank, the OCC may impose requirements by way of conditions similar to those that apply by statute to an insured bank, to the extent appropriate given the business model and risk profile of a particular applicant. The OCC likely would impose additional conditions in connection with granting a Fintech Bank Charter based on the Fintech applicant's business model and risk profile.

INITIAL VIEWS OF WINNERS AND LOSERS

A special purpose national bank clearly will benefit:

- Fintech companies seeking to operate under one national license rather than on a state-by-state regime (e.g., lenders, mortgage lenders, mortgage services, and money transmitters);

- Nonbank lenders, mortgage originators, and servicers with less than $10 billion in assets, which can avoid CFPB supervision;

- Payment processors or prepaid card program managers, which can control their own operations without being subjugated to a bank partner; and

- Full service banks, which no longer will have to compete with nonbank Fintech companies, which they perceive are operating on an uneven playing field, as the laws and regulations applicable to all banks will apply to Fintech Banks.

However, as discussed above, special purpose national banks will impose a host of requirements that nonbank Fintech companies currently are not subject to, including:

- Higher capital and liquidity requirements than a full-service bank;

- Compliance with obligations to ensure financial inclusion;

- Ongoing monitoring of business activities;

- Rigorous examinations by the OCC (and perhaps the FDIC and Federal Reserve);

- FDIC and possibly Federal Reserve oversight if the Fintech Bank accepts deposits; and

- Regulation of significant corporate transactions under the Change in Bank Control Act and, perhaps, the Bank Merger Act and/or the BHCA.

In addition, Fintech Banks could adversely impact:

- State banking departments, which depend on licensing and examina-

335

tion revenue; and

- Full service banks, which franchise their charters for programs managed by nonbank Fintech companies.

ACTION PLAN

Considerations in Applying for a Fintech Bank Charter

While the Whitepaper confirms that the OCC will consider charter applications by companies engaged in financial technology that are engaged in core banking activities such as receiving deposits, paying checks or lending money, such entities must explore whether or not a special purpose national bank charter would enhance their operations. Principally, such analysis must consider whether cost of federal regulation and the benefit of federal preemption outweigh the cost of state-by-state system licensure or partnering with an existing bank.[47] Similarly, such analysis clearly must focus on whether converting to a national charter would cause a change in operations, such as from a licensed money transmitter to an entity that could be deemed to be receiving deposits, which would cause a cavalcade of additional regulatory obligations.

OCC Solicitation of Comments

Moreover, in addition to evaluating the consequences of converting to a Fintech Bank Charter companies had the opportunity to comment on types of activities and expectations that the OCC should require for entities seeking a Fintech Bank Charter. Specifically, the OCC sought input on these 13 questions before January 15, 2017, and the forthcoming regulation is expected to reflect the public comments:

(1) What are the public policy benefits of approving Fintech companies to operate under a National bank charter? What are the risks?

(2) What elements should the OCC consider in establishing the capital and liquidity requirements for an uninsured special purpose national bank that limits the type of assets it holds?

---

[47] While the OCC has long allowed banks to franchise their charters, subject to appropriate risk-management, the Whitepaper reaffirms that national banks and federal savings banks are authorized to engage in relationships with nonbank third parties. *See, e.g.,* OCC Bulletin 2001-47, *Third Party Relationships* (Nov. 1, 2001), *available at* http://ithandbook.ffiec.gov/media/27914/occ-bul_2001_47_third_party_relationships.pdf, which was then superseded by OCC Bulletin 2013-29, *Risk Management Guidance, available at* https://www.occ.gov/news-issuances/bulletins/2013/bulletin-2013-29.html.

(3)   What information should a special purpose national bank provide to the OCC to demonstrate its commitment to financial inclusion to individuals, businesses, and communities? For instance, what new or alternative means (e.g., products, services) might a special purpose national bank establish in furtherance of its support for financial inclusion? How could an uninsured special purpose bank that uses innovative methods to develop or deliver financial products or services in a virtual or physical community demonstrate its commitment to financial inclusion?

(4)   Should the OCC seek a financial inclusion commitment from an uninsured special purpose national bank that would not engage in lending, and if so, how could such a bank demonstrate a commitment to financial inclusion?

(5)   How could a special purpose national bank that is not engaged in providing banking services to the public support financial inclusion?

(6)   Should the OCC use its chartering authority as an opportunity to address the gaps in protections afforded individuals versus small business borrowers, and if so, how?

(7)   What are potential challenges in executing or adapting a Fintech business model to meet regulatory expectations, and what specific conditions governing the activities of special purpose national banks should the OCC consider?

(8)   What actions should the OCC take to ensure special purpose national banks operate in a safe and sound manner and in the public interest?

(9)   Would a Fintech special purpose national bank have any competitive advantages over full-service banks the OCC should address? Are there risks to full-service banks from Fintech companies that do not have bank charters?

(10)   Are there particular products or services offered by Fintech companies, such as digital currencies, that may require different approaches to supervision to mitigate risk for both the institution and the broader financial system?

(11)   How can the OCC enhance its coordination and communication with other regulators that have jurisdiction over a proposed special purpose national bank, its parent company, or its activities?

(12)   Certain risks may be increased in a special purpose national bank because of its concentration in a limited number of business

activities. How can the OCC ensure that a special purpose national bank sufficiently mitigates these risks?

(13) What additional information, materials, and technical assistance from the OCC would a prospective Fintech applicant find useful in the application process?

 Should a fintech company be regulated like a bank, including safety and soundness regulatory burdens, capital requirements and other rules and requirements, if the fintech company does not accept deposits? Why or Why Not?

 Should a fintech company be regulated by the Office of the Comptroller of the Currency or is another regulator more appropriate? Recall the different types of regulatory methods in Part I, including by entity, service, and objective.

 Why would banks be in favor of fintechs having a national charter?

As of July 31, 2018, the Office of the Comptroller of the Currency issued a press release indicating that it would begin accepting national bank charters from financial technology companies, after "extensive outreach with many stakeholders over a two-year period, and after reviewing public comments solicited. . ."[703]

If history serves as a predictor, the variety of financial products and services will continue to evolve. In addition, consumer demographics and what constitutes acceptable behavior in the provision of financial services continues to change and develop. Finally, the financial institutions themselves change as fintech companies continue to emerge in the traditional financial services market to offer a multitude of different services using differing methods. For example, in 2013 the Federal Financial Institutions Examination Council issued guidance on social media financial services compliance. The guidance states that:

> The Equal Credit Opportunity Act, as implemented by Regulation B, prohibits creditors from making any oral or written statement, in advertising or other marketing techniques, to applicants or prospective applicants that would discourage on a prohibited basis a reasonable person from making or pursuing an application. However, a creditor may affirmatively solicit or encourage members of traditionally disadvantaged groups to apply for credit, especially groups that might not normally seek credit from that creditor.[704]

---

[703] *See* Press Release, Office of the Comptroller of the Currency, OCC Begins Accepting National Bank Charter Applications From Financial Technology Companies, (July 31, 2018), available at https://www.occ.gov/news-issuances/news-releases/2018/nr-occ-2018-74.html.

[704] *See* FED. FIN. INSTITUTIONS EXAMINATION COUNCIL, *Social Media: Consumer Compliance Risk Management Guidance* (Sept. 2013), at 9, available at https://files.consumerfinance.gov/f/201309_cfpb_social_media_guidance.pdf.

90 **Are creditors who advertise primarily through social media discouraging older Americans from applying for credit if older Americans disproportionately use social media less?[705] Why or Why Not?**

The Federal Financial Institutions Examination Council provides an FDCPA example, stating:

> Communicating via social media in a manner that discloses the existence of a debt or to harass or embarrass consumers about their debts (e.g., a debt collector writing about a debt on a Facebook wall) or making false or misleading representations may violate the FDCPA.[706]

Innovation in financial services cannot be discussed without considering regulatory arbitrage in context. Typically, one benefit of innovation may be that current law does not contemplate the novel product or service. Therefore, arguably, the new product or service remains unregulated until such time as a potential regulator makes an example of an industry participant, laws are amended, or guidance is issued definitively addressing the topic. The benefits of an unregulated product or service can be numerous. Regulatory oversight can increase initial costs for new companies, including with respect to capital requirements and/or licensing or chartering fees imposed by the regulatory body. Regulatory oversight can also increase ongoing costs, including as a result of license renewals, supervisory examination fees, and/or fines. Further, being regulated can create challenges for investment. Recall that, generally speaking, banks' activities are funded by deposits. However, other nondepository institutions are capitalized, typically, through investment or corporate debt. Financial tech companies, among other industry disruptors, for example, have "pressure to quickly get into market, realize revenue and prove acquisition and risk models to investors [that] could lead to products being brought forth prematurely in order to hit tight deadlines and avoid hurdles to future investments."[707] Therefore, increased regulatory costs can deter initial investment as well as deter future investment if the costs prevent the company from reaching financial goals needed to lure investors.

Because of the potential burdens imposed by regulatory oversight, a new company may seek to limit or avoid regulation through **regulatory arbitrage**. An entity may seek to limit its regulation by "choosing" its regulator. Recall from Part I, the different types of financial institutions. To the extent that regulation is imposed based on entity type, a new company may make an informed decision regarding

---

[705] *See* Monica Anderson & Andrew Perrin, PEW RESEARCH CTR. INTERNET & TECHNOLOGY, *Tech Adoption Climbs Among Older Adults* (May 17, 2017), http://www.pewinternet.org/2017/05/17/technology-use-among-seniors/ ("A majority of seniors do not use social media, and the share that do is considerably smaller than that of the general population.").

[706] *See* FED. FIN. INSTITUTIONS EXAMINATION COUNCIL, *supra* note 704, at 11.

[707] *See* John Wirth, *Pros and Cons: Seven Common Characteristics of FinTech Startups*, TRANSUNION BLOG (Mar. 30, 2017), https://www.transunion.com/blog/pros-cons-seven-common-characteristics-of-fintech-startups.

its entity type/how it is initially organized thereby "choosing" the regulator that may be the least burdensome. A regulator that has a limited enforcement budget, that is less likely to impose fines, or that conducts infrequent supervisory examinations, may be the most appealing. As a result, a company may determine whether it will apply for a specific charter, license, or other authorization that is available to the company. In fact, regulators may even quarrel and disagree over regulating an entity, service, or product.[708] Without the ability to regulate, some state or federal agencies may lose fee and fine revenue needed to operate the agency. Regulatory arbitrage may take on a multitude of forms but is essentially taking advantage of differences or similarities in regulation to yield distinctly beneficial outcomes. Adam Levitin, Professor of Law at Georgetown University Law Center, describes regulatory arbitrage in the context of bank chartering and consumer protection:

> Maintaining chartering business is crucial for bank regulatory agencies both because their primary authority is largely coextensive with chartering and because some regulators receive the majority of their budgets from chartering fees, rather than Congressional appropriations. A bank regulator that sought more vigorous consumer-protection regulations or enforcement would put the entities it regulated at a disadvantage relative to those regulated by others, which might trigger charter-flight to other regulators. Likewise, a bank regulator might be able to attract more chartering business and a greater budget through with a laxer approach to consumer protection regulation.[709]

In addition to lost revenue, regulators must contend with (1) political pressures, (2) the fear of strained relationships with the regulated companies , and (3) the effects of imposing fines or revoking licenses, including the loss of that institution to consumers who need the service provided as well as the potential loss of local jobs that the institution provides.[710]

Will the proposed charter, offered by the Office of the Comptroller of the Currency, for fintech companies, which were previously exclusively licensed by individual states, create an opportunity for regulatory arbitrage? Why or Why Not? If both an OCC charter and individual state licenses are available for companies potentially performing the same services or activities, what considerations will help determine which route the company will pursue?

The co-dependent relationship between the regulator and the regulated that forms over time may be described as **regulatory capture**. In the article, *Lessons From Uber: Why Innovation And Regulation Don't Mix*, Forbes contributor Larry Downes explains that:

---

[708] *See* Statement by DFS Superintendent Maria T. Vullo on Treasury's Endorsement of Regulatory Sandboxes for Fintech Companies and the OCC's Decision to Accept Fintech Charter Applications, (July 31, 2018), https://www.dfs.ny.gov/about/statements/st1807311.htm, (stating "a national fintech charter will impose an entirely unjustified federal regulatory scheme on an already fully functional and deeply rooted state regulatory landscape.").

[709] *See* Levitin, *supra* note 6, at 333.

[710] *See* John Cheves, *Payday Lenders Cited Hundreds of Times, Face Few Consequences in Kentucky*, LEXINGTON HERALD LEADER, (July 8, 2016), https://www.kentucky.com/news/politics-government/article88451342.html.

Since regulators and the industries they oversee deal almost exclusively only with each other, they tend over time to develop a customer-provider relationship, in which both have a vested interest in continuing the regulatory system long after the public interest benefits have been vastly outweighed by the anti-innovation costs.

The regulator becomes the industry's cheerleader, and regulations shift subtly from protecting the public interest to protecting the status quo. [711]

Regulatory capture occurs when "bureaucrats often become entangled with the firms they attempt to control,"[712] including the "revolving door between private firms and public bureaus, with individuals cycling between the two as their careers progress."[713] In the article *Behavior, Paternalism, and Policy: Evaluating Consumer Financial Protection* the authors use an example of a former CFPB employee, stating that with the employee's "unique knowledge of the decision-making process within the CFPB, surely [the employee] has an advantage in determining how to skirt the boundaries set forth by the very bureau for which he used to work."[714] Regulatory capture is one reason that can account for the "subordination of consumer protection to bank profitability"[715] as the regulator begins to act "in the interests of the industry it regulates, rather than in the public interest."[716]

In addition to limiting the burden of regulatory oversight, regulatory arbitrage may also attempt to avoid regulation altogether. Specifically, avoiding regulation can be accomplished by restructuring transactions, known as categorical arbitrage, or by geographic relocation, known as jurisdictional arbitrage. Recall the distinction between a safe harbor expressed exemption vs. a loophole. Through categorical arbitrage, a financial services provider may take advantage of a loophole in a law or rule to ensure that the activities fall squarely within the unanticipated loophole. Further, through jurisdictional arbitrage, a company may establish its presence, or headquarters in an area with rules or laws that are more favorable to the company. For example, a company may form under the laws of a state with generous interest rates rather than a state with low interest rate limits. Regulatory arbitrage is often referred to as a race to the bottom.[717] Specifically, entities are seeking to comply with as few regulations as possible to reduce the cost of compliance. This race to the bottom yields a race to the top: the company that has lower compliance costs may have a competitive advantage over industry peers.

How can instances for regulatory arbitrage be reduced?

Who are the stakeholders in the determination of to what extent a new product, service, or activity will be regulated?

---

[711] Downes, *supra* note 690.

[712] Smith &Zywicki, *supra* note 682, at 30.

[713] *Id.*

[714] *See id.* at 30.

[715] Levitin, *supra* note 6, at 331.

[716] *Id.*

[717] Levitin, *supra* note 6, at 329.

In determining whether to regulate a service or product or not to regulate a service or product, it may be helpful to consider an amended version of the 5Ws within this text. It may also be helpful to consider what powers constitute regulation, including supervision, enforcement, and rulemaking powers.

(1) WHO is regulated?: Who is attempting to be exempt from compliance or avoid oversight? If the regulator regulates by entity, how does the **<u>entity</u>** differ from **WHO is currently regulated**? Would the entity enjoy a competitive advantage if not regulated? Does the regulator want to preserve the established institutions' foothold in the market if the established institutions' products are tested and understood?

(2) WHO is protected? Does the entity provide financial services or products to **<u>consumers</u>**? Does the entity provide financial services or products to businesses? Is providing this service or product beneficial? If there is a market for the financial product or service, should it be allowed, even if it is potentially harmful to consumers, or should the regulator protect the consumer from himself?

(3) WHAT needs regulating? Does the entity provide a **<u>financial service</u>**? If the regulator regulates by **<u>service</u>**, is this financial service different from the services that the regulator would typically regulate? Can the existing regulatory framework be applied to the new product or service?

(4) WHEN: (Under what circumstances does the law serve its purpose/objective?)

(5) WHY: What objective is the law intended to meet? If the regulator regulates by objective, would the **<u>objective</u>** of consumer protection be met if the new company is not regulated?

Consider Figure 9B on the following page.

Is the idea regulated?

☐ **What?**

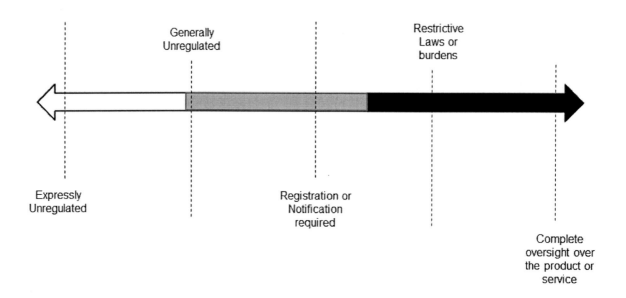

Figure 9B

When considering whether or not an idea is "regulated," in addition to enforcement, supervision, and rulemaking powers, to what extent a new idea is regulated or not regulated falls upon a spectrum that can be difficult to discern for new companies. The least regulated product or service is a product or service that is "expressly unregulated." An expressly unregulated product or service means that the law or regulatory guidance specifically indicates that the proposed activity is exempt from regulation. Expressly unregulated may, alternatively, mean that the company has a "no-action" letter in hand for that company specifically, narrowly tailored for that company's business activities at the time the letter is provided. The "no-action" letter advises the recipient that the regulator will not take action against the company for its proposed activities. An activity, product, or entity that is expressly unregulated has the lowest regulatory burden.

The next potential category of regulation for a new company that may be uncertain of whether its activities, products or services are regulated is the "generally unregulated" category. Generally unregulated describes when the relevant law does not specifically state that the proposed activity is exempt, and the company does not have a no-action letter from the regulator to their company. However, the company has an unofficial impression that their proposed activities, products or services will not be regulated. The company may have this impression because it is relying upon a no-action letter issued to another company, because the regulator unofficially or informally indicated that the activities, products or services will not be regulated, and/or the law does not specifically describe or contemplate the proposed activities. Generally unregulated activities, products, or services can be risky for the institution because a no-action letter issued to another company is not reliable as to the new company's activities, products or services. Further, an informal communication from a regulator is also not as reliable as formal guidance issued, a no-action letter, or an express law exempting the activity, product or service. While the institution may, initially, save on the costs of regulation, it may expend time and other resources in an attempt to maintain this unofficial status and avoid regulation.

The next potential category for a new company is the requirement to register or notify a regulator of certain activities. Often times in this instance, there are no ongoing regulatory burdens. However, the regulator wants to be aware of the company and its activities.

The fourth potential category for a new company is restrictive laws or burdens. Specifically, as discussed in this text, there are laws and rules that are applicable to the company that may impose certain burdens on the company or restrict certain activities. However, the power to enforce these laws or rules is limited as there is little or no supervisory or enforcement oversight.

The last category of potential regulatory burden for a new company is "complete oversight." Complete oversight means that there is license, charter, or other authorization required that may serve as a barrier to entry into the market, there are laws that restrict the service, activity or product, and there are ongoing compliance requirements including, for example, license renewals and examinations. Complete oversight includes the ability to enforce the relevant laws and rules, as well as to supervise compliance with the relevant laws and rules.

Finally, consider the benefits of financial services regulation for future actors. Historically, financial services regulation has attempted to protect consumers and to buttress the financial system. Further, depending on the economic theories at work, the financial regulators may end up solidifying the dominance of current players, including traditional banking institutions. However, regulation can be beneficial, to new services and products. Regulation can bring legitimacy to the financial product or service so that the market for the product or service can expand. This comparison can be applied to regulatory landscapes in general, including, for example in investing, where, generally speaking, regulation and the sophistication of the investor are inversely related. The benefits of legitimacy may be applied to online banking, for example. In the early stages of online banking, it is not surprising that there could be concern for the protection of the consumer's private information and concern regarding transmitting sensitive information through the internet. Early adopters of this new, convenient means of allowing consumers access to the consumers' account information had to convince regulators of how the institutions were going to continue to operate within existing regulations through the new medium. Once a consumer knows that there is oversight, the consumer may feel more comfortable to utilize the service or try the new product. In other words, once the product is legitimized, it can be utilized by more people. In addition, recall the reputational consequences Wells Fargo faced following the fake account scandal, discussed *supra*. Regulatory compliance can benefit new companies attempting to establish a foothold in a crowded market. Specifically, companies can promote a "culture of compliance" as a part of the company's marketing strategy. Consider for example, the outrage expressed in the press by community banks reacting to the Wells Fargo scandal. These banks were taking advantage of an opportunity to distinguish themselves as good actors in a field of bad actors.

What is the future of consumer financial services regulation?

Next, consider the future of financial services regulation. First consider whether the CFPB is sufficient to serve its intended purpose. For example, **are consumer protection regulations, particularly regulations restricting or requiring behavior, needed? Or can the market catch up to consumer desires without government intervention?**[718] Since the CFPB's creation, the CFPB purports to have obtained $12.4 billion in relief to consumers from enforcement action for more than thirty-one million consumers.[719]

How can consumer financial services regulation continue to meet the needs of consumers considering the dynamic state of financial services innovation and the shifts in consumer wants and needs? Recall the discussion of serving consumers for whom English is a second language. Consider that "one out of 12 people over the age of 5 in the U.S. are limited English proficient (LEP), meaning that they speak English less than very well. [. . .] LEP consumers may find it difficult to access financial products and services."[720] **In what ways may LEP consumers encounter challenges to accessing financial products and services?**

Second, consider the diverging views on the CFPB, namely, whether the CFPB serves consumers or whether the CFPB has been clouded in fulfilling political whims with no cognizable basis for support.[721] Specifically, what may become of the Consumer Financial Protection Bureau based on constitutionality challenges and ongoing shifts in political power and ideology? Georgetown University Law Center Professor Adam Levitin surmises the following:

> Even without political pressure, the CFPB faces a constant challenge in terms of measuring and then balancing the consumer protection benefits from regulation with the costs of regulation and the potential impact of those costs on the availability and pricing of consumer financial products and services. What remains to be seen, however, is whether the CFPB will back away from more controversial rulemaking and enforcement activity because of the political threat it faces or whether the agency will pursue the policies it believes to be substantively right irrespective of the political situation. In other words, will the agency's own interests affect and guide its behavior?

---

[718] *See* Hynes, *supra* note 20, at 32 ("a proper defense of consumer credit regulation must explain why the market would not supply these benefits if consumers are willing to pay for them. [. . .] the market does respond to some degree to consumer demand for credit protections.").

[719] *As of June 4, 2018. CFPB figures are updated quarterly on the bureau's website homepage, available at https://www.consumerfinance.gov/.

[720] *See* Alice Chang, Dubus Correal, & Holly Zaharchuk, CONSUMER FIN. PROT. BUREAU BLOG, *Five Ways Banks and Lenders Work with People who Speak or Understand Limited English*, (Nov. 22, 2017), https://www.consumerfinance.gov/about-us/blog/five-ways-banks-and-lenders-work-people-who-speak-or-understand-limited-english/.

[721] Zywicki, *supra* note 218, at 917 (arguing that "Dodd-Frank instead creates a structure that virtually guarantees the full manifestation of standard bureaucratic pathologies [and] fails to account for the real driving force behind the breakdown of consumer finance—a runaway expansion of litigation and regulation—and instead promises more of the same.").

Furthermore, are those interests best served by compromising and living to fight another day or by taking a principled stand and hoping to rally political support on that basis? The CFPB is a powerful new agency, but it is also one very much aware of its vulnerability and likely to proceed carefully and soberly in the face of its political situation.[722]

What about the future of the CFPB and its regulatory powers? Consider the following client memorandum, "What's Next for PHH v. CFPB?," written in 2016.

This memorandum was authored by Charles S. Duggan, Randall D. Guynn, Neil H. MacBride; Fiona R. Moran; Edmund Polubinski III; and Margaret E. Tahyar. It is reprinted with the express permission of Davis Polk & Wardwell LLP.

**Footnotes in the following reprinted article are independent of footnotes in the full text of this work.

---

[722] *See* Levitin, *supra* note 6, at 369.

What's Next for PHH v. CFPB?

October 15, 2016

Introduction

Not surprisingly, the many media and political reactions to the *PHH Corp. v. CFPB* decision have reflected the competing stakeholder interests around every aspect of the CFPB.[1] In this memorandum, we step back a bit and make some observations about the strategic choices facing the CFPB, the Obama Administration, the next President, and the next Congress in light of the decision. We begin with a short review of the tension between the two contradictory Supreme Court cases upon which the federal administrative state is built and explain how they informed the D.C. Circuit's invalidation of the CFPB's independent structure. We then discuss the D.C. Circuit's statutory interpretation, which we believe will have wide implications across a range of regulatory enforcement actions, both in the financial sector and beyond. We also discuss the extent to which the D.C. Circuit's ruling may raise questions as to the validity of past or pending CFPB rulemaking and enforcement actions. Finally, we end with an exploration of the considerations behind the possible next steps by the CFPB and other stakeholders.

Background

The case stems from a 2014 administrative proceeding in which the CFPB and PHH Corporation ("PHH") appealed to Director Richard Cordray an Administrative Law Judge's ("ALJ") recommended finding that PHH violated the Real Estate Settlement Procedures Act ("RESPA"). The ALJ had recommended disgorgement of $6.44 million based, in part, on a ruling that alleged violations before July 21, 2008 were not actionable because they fell outside the applicable 3-year statute of limitations.

Upholding the decision in part and reversing in part, Director Cordray expressly rejected the then-existing written guidance on RESPA's application to captive reinsurance on which PHH had relied. That guidance had been issued by the Department of Housing and Urban Development ("HUD"), which was the agency responsible for interpreting RESPA before the creation of the CFPB. Director Cordray determined that PHH violated RESPA with each payment by mortgage insurers rather than, as the ALJ recommended, when each reinsured loan closed. Finally, Director Cordray determined that RESPA's 3-year statute of limitations applies only to court actions and not to administrative proceedings. On these bases, he increased the disgorgement penalty from $6.44 million to $109 million.

PHH appealed the decision to the United States Court of Appeals for the District of Columbia Circuit. PHH argued that Director Cordray's interpretation of RESPA was inconsistent with its plain language and longstanding precedent and therefore not entitled to *Chevron* deference and that the Director's retroactive reinterpretation of the statute violated the Due Process Clause of the Fifth Amendment.[2] PHH also argued that Director Cordray incorrectly determined that statutes of limitations were inapplicable to an administrative proceeding. Finally, it argued that the agency's decision was invalid for the independent reason that the CFPB's structure violates the Constitution. Before oral argument, the D.C. Circuit asked the parties to address the historical precedents for independent agencies led by a single director and any proposed remedies for structures that did not pass constitutional muster.

---

[1] No. 15-1177 (D.C. Cir. Oct. 11, 2016). The full opinion is available here.

[2] *Chevron U.S.A., Inc. v. Natural Res. Def. Council, Inc.*, 467 U.S. 837 (1984).

The PHH Corp. v. CFPB Decision

The Constitutional Ruling

The D.C. Circuit held, in a majority decision written by Judge Kavanaugh, that in light of the Supreme Court's separation of powers precedents, the CFPB is unconstitutionally structured because it is headed by a single director who can be removed by the President only for cause rather than at will. The court then severed the unconstitutional for-cause removal provision from the rest of the Dodd-Frank Act, making it clear that henceforth the Director is removable by the President at will. If the court's ruling stands, the CFPB will continue to operate but will now do so as an agency within the executive branch, rather than as an independent agency.[3]

The constitutional tension is created by two contradictory Supreme Court cases. The first, *Myers v. United States*, was decided in 1926 and held that executive power is typically exercised by the President or by removable-at-will subordinate officers subject to the supervision and command of the President.[4] The second case, *Humphrey's Executor v. United States*, decided in 1935, over the objections of President Franklin D. Roosevelt, held that Congress could create an independent agency subject to less control by the President.[5] In *PHH Corp. v. CFPB*, the D.C. Circuit expressed the view that the Supreme Court had permitted the creation of independent agencies because, among other things, the agency at issue in *Humphrey's Executor* was designed to be non-partisan, to act with impartiality, and most importantly, to be led by a "body of experts" rather than a single director.[6] As noted by the panel, independent agencies now "possess authority over vast swaths of American economic and social life."[7] The tension between *Myers* and *Humphrey's Executor* has been apparent in virtually every separation of powers case involving agencies.[8]

Following *Humphrey's Executor*, the vast majority of independent agencies have been led by multi-member boards.[9] The CFPB is an exception. Established under the Dodd-Frank Act, the CFPB is headed by a single director who is authorized to enforce 19 distinct consumer protection laws and removable only for cause, i.e., for "inefficiency, neglect of duty, or malfeasance in office."[10] The D.C. Circuit opined that the Director "is the single most powerful official" in the government, other than the President, at least within the Director's narrower sphere of authority. This concentration of power, in the view of the panel, is a departure from historical practice, is exceptional in our constitutional structure, and makes the CFPB a "historical anomaly."[11] This, the panel said, "strongly counsels caution with respect to single-Director independent agencies" like the CFPB.[12]

---

[3] *PHH Corp.*, No. 15-1177 at *28 n.4.

[4] 272 U.S. 52 (1926).

[5] 295 U.S. 602 (1935).

[6] *PHH Corp.*, No. 15-1177 at *21.

[7] *Id.* at *22.

[8] The existence of independent agencies contradicts the theory of a "unitary" executive, or one where executive power resides solely in the President.

[9] The court lists over 20 examples.

[10] *PHH Corp.*, No. 15-1177, at * 23 (citing 12 U.S.C. § 5491(c)(3) and *Humphrey's Executor*, 295 U.S. at 620).

[11] *Id.* at *27.

[12] *Id.* at *33.

In explaining why the CFPB's "departure from historical practice matters," the D.C. Circuit reasoned that, where the constitutional text does not resolve the separation of powers issue, longstanding practices should inform a court's decision as to what the law is. For example, the Supreme Court in a very recent 9-0 opinion written by Justice Breyer, *NLRB v. Noel Canning*, interpreted a 200-year old practice regarding Senate recess appointments as a constitutional standard.[13] In *Free Enterprise Fund v. Public Company Accounting Oversight Board*, a divided 5-4 Supreme Court drew a line between one level and two levels of for-cause removal in part because historical practice had settled on one level of for-cause removal.[14]

The Constitution, as interpreted by the *Humphrey's Executor* Court, does not answer *how* independent agencies should be structured, just that they can be constitutional. In an in-depth analysis, the panel examined the historical purpose behind the multi-member boards that govern agencies such as the SEC or NLRB—a concern for safeguarding individual liberty. The panel focused on the CFPB's lack of the sort of "critical check" on abuse applicable to traditional independent agencies: majority, deliberative, and diverse decision-making.[15] According to the panel, a single director is more prone to extreme, idiosyncratic, and influenced decision-making and is thus more likely to infringe on individual liberties. The single director structure was particularly concerning to the panel in light of the CFPB's quasi-judicial and quasi-investigative authority.[16]

Furthermore, the *PHH* court held that the CFPB's structure—having a single director with for-cause removal only—contradicts the Constitution's bedrock principle of dividing power among and within multiple entities (e.g., two houses in the legislative branch, equal votes among the Chief and Associate Justices of the Supreme Court, etc.). The panel emphasized that, apart from the executive branch, which has power concentrated in one person but subject to national election and accountability, the Constitution reflects the notion that multi-member bodies are less likely to engage in arbitrary decision-making and abuses of power. In fact, the panel asserted that the multi-member agency form has "become synonymous with independence."[17] Since the CFPB represents a "sharp break" from that historical practice, lacks the internal checks of other agencies, and poses a great threat to individual liberty, the panel held that its structure raises grave constitutional doubt.[18] According to the panel, "*Humphrey's Executor* does not mean that anything goes."[19]

The *PHH* panel's 52-page analysis of the history and structure of independent agencies, with its copious citations to public statements and recent Supreme Court opinions written by Justices both liberal and conservative, was clearly intended to signal the depth and seriousness of the panel's analysis. Judge Kavanaugh is well acquainted with cases regarding the President's executive power. In 2008, Judge Kavanaugh dissented from the D.C. Circuit's opinion in *Free Enterprise Fund* upholding the structure of the Public Company Accounting Oversight Board ("PCAOB"); the D.C. Circuit's opinion was later invalidated by the Supreme Court.[20] Here, Judge Kavanaugh hinted in a footnote that *Humphrey's*

---

[13] 134 S. Ct. 2550, 2657 (2014).

[14] 561 U.S. 477, 484, 505 (2010).

[15] *PHH Corp.*, No. 15-1177, at *44-45.

[16] *Id.* at *48-49.

[17] *Id.* at *52 (internal quotation marks and citations omitted).

[18] *Id.* at *53.

[19] *Id.* at *58.

[20] *Free Enterprise Fund v. Public Co. Accounting Oversight Bd.*, 537 F.3d 667, 685-715 (D.C. Cir. 2008) (Kavanaugh, J., dissenting).

Executor and the reasoning of *Free Enterprise Fund* are in tension with one another but noted that it was not the D.C. Circuit's place to overrule *Humphrey's Executor*.[21] It is noteworthy that Judge Henderson did not join this portion of the opinion but also did not address or criticize it substantively.

While carefully not calling *Morrison v. Olson* itself into question, the majority opinion copiously cites Justice Scalia's dissent from that case, notes that the dissent has been complimented by Justice Kagan and also points to a number of other separation of powers statements, in opinions or otherwise, by Justice Breyer.[22] The D.C. Circuit noted the "nearly universal consensus" that the independent counsel law upheld in *Morrison v. Olson* was a mistake.[23] In our view (shared by the three authors of this memorandum who are former Supreme Court law clerks), the press and instant pundits have been mistaken to the extent they have characterized the potential views of the Supreme Court on this separation of powers issue as clearly falling along classic conservative/liberal lines. While it seems likely that Justices Roberts, Alito, and Thomas would uphold the ruling, given the 9-0 decision in *Noel Canning* and other statements by Justices Breyer and Kagan, it is far from clear the other Justices would vote to reverse the D.C. Circuit.

The Court's Remedy: Severing the For-Cause Removal Provision

PHH argued that if the for-cause removal provision was unconstitutional, the panel must strike down the CFPB and prevent its continued operation. The D.C. Circuit declined to go that far. Instead, the panel noted that partial invalidation is the favored course, so long as (1) Congress would have preferred a law with the offending provision severed over no law at all, and (2) the law with the offending provision severed would otherwise remain fully operative.[24]

The court concluded that there was no evidence that Congress would have preferred no CFPB at all to a CFPB whose director is removable by the President at will. As the court pointed out, the Dodd-Frank Act itself states that if any provision is found to be unconstitutional, the remainder "shall not be affected thereby."[25] The court stressed that the restructured CFPB would still be able to "regulate the offering and provision of consumer financial productions or services under the federal consumer laws," as Congress had intended.[26]

The approach by the *PHH* court followed the one taken by the Supreme Court in *Free Enterprise Fund*. In *Free Enterprise Fund*, the petitioners claimed that the Sarbanes-Oxley Act violated the separation of powers by creating a five-member PCAOB board not subject to Presidential removal. There, the Supreme Court agreed, but it did not strike down the entire law. Instead, the Supreme Court followed the "normal rule" and invalidated only the offending provision.[27] We believe that the D.C. Circuit is on solid ground in *PHH* in deciding to sever the for-cause removal provision it found to be unconstitutional. If the constitutional ruling stands, the portion of the court's ruling on severability is unlikely to be overturned.

---

[21] *PHH Corp.*, No 15-1177 at *59 n.15.

[22] *Id.* at *3-4, 8-9, 29, 30-31, 33-34, 36-37, 40, 43, 52, 54, 59; *see also Morrison v. Olson*, 487 U.S. 654 (1988).

[23] *Id.* at *33. A three judge panel of the D.C. Circuit originally invalidated the independent counsel statute. That panel was composed of Judge Silberman, Judge Williams and then Judge Ruth Bader Ginsburg. Judge Ginsburg dissented. *In re Sealed Case*, 838 F.2d 476 (D.C. Cir. 1988). In *Morrison v. Olson*, 487 U.S. 654 (1988), the Supreme Court reversed 7-1 with Justice Scalia dissenting. Judge Randolph, who joined Judge Kavanaugh in the constitutional ruling in *PHH*, was on the D.C. Circuit at the time that it decided *In re Sealed Case*.

[24] *PHH Corp.*, No. 15-1177 at *66 (citing *Free Enterprise Fund*, 561 U.S. at 508-09).

[25] 12 U.S.C. § 5302.

[26] *PHH Corp.*, No. 15-1177 at *67-68 (quoting 12 U.S.C. § 5491(a)).

[27] *PHH Corp.* No 15-1177 at *66 (quoting *Free Enterprise Fund*, 561 U.S. at 508).

The Statutory Rulings

The D.C. Circuit also reached PHH's statutory interpretation challenges: that the CFPB misinterpreted RESPA, that it violated the Due Process Clause by applying its interpretations retroactively, and that it failed to observe a statute of limitations in penalizing PHH's conduct. The three-judge panel unanimously ruled in PHH's favor on each of these points.

The entire panel held that the CFPB's interpretation of RESPA "flout[ed] not only the text of the statute but also decades of carefully and repeatedly considered official government interpretations."[28] The court rejected the CFPB's calls for *Chevron* deference, concluding that there was no statutory ambiguity. The D.C. Circuit also held that CFPB's retroactive application of its new interpretation of RESPA to PHH's conduct contravened the foundational due process principle of fair notice. The court stated that the CFPB violated "Rule of Law 101" and characterized its retroactive imposition of penalties as "gamesmanship."[29] The court remanded to permit the CFPB to determine whether the reinsurance payments exceeded reasonable market value under RESPA.

By rejecting the CFPB's interpretation of RESPA, the D.C. Circuit aligned with the "longstanding interpretation" of the statute by HUD. The D.C. Circuit's ruling that an agency cannot change the course of a long-standing interpretation in the midst of an enforcement action reaffirms an important principle of administrative law which applies across a range of agencies.

The panel also rejected the CFPB's arguments that Dodd-Frank imposes no statute of limitations on agency administrative enforcement actions. It held that the statutes of limitations for all 19 federal consumer protection laws enforced by the CFPB apply to administrative actions. As the CFPB has often taken the position that statutes of limitations do not apply to investigations or administrative proceedings, we view this interpretation as highly significant, and it will be a welcome relief to many.

Impact of the Decision on Other Agencies

In an attempt to defend its structure, the CFPB had pointed to four other agencies: the Social Security Administration ("SSA"), the Office of Special Counsel ("OSC"), the Office of the Comptroller of the Currency ("OCC"), and the Federal Housing Finance Agency ("FHFA"). The CFPB argued that because these other agencies, like the CFPB, each have a single director, there was no constitutional issue. The D.C. Circuit did not find the comparisons persuasive.

With respect to the SSA and OSC, the panel noted that these agencies, unlike the CFPB, do not unilaterally bring law enforcement actions or impose fines and penalties against private citizens for violations of statutes or agency rules. With respect to the OCC, its head, unlike the Director, is removable at will by the President. This analysis suggests that these agencies are on solid ground.

In contrast, the panel did not contest the CFPB's comparison to the FHFA, which, like the CFPB, has a single director that can be removed only for cause. Rather, the panel noted that the two agencies are contemporaries and said that the FHFA's structure "raises the same [constitutional] question" as the structure of the CFPB.[30] If the court's decision stands, it seems likely the FHFA will face challenges. The statute creating the FHFA does not have a severability clause.

---

[28] *Id.* at *76.

[29] *Id.* at *86, 88.

[30] *Id.* at *33.

Impact of the Decision on Past or Pending CFPB Actions

The D.C. Circuit's ruling raises questions as to the validity of past or pending CFPB rulemaking and enforcement actions. The panel expressly declined to consider the ramifications of the constitutional portion of its decision on this issue.[31] The panel noted that the constitutional defects of the NLRB and the PCAOB were remedied without "major tumult." If the cases that restructured those decision-making bodies serve as a guide, the effects of the *PHH* decision on past or pending actions may be limited. Following *Noel Canning*, the NLRB, then properly constituted, essentially readopted its earlier order, and the D.C. Circuit held this action was a proper approach. After *Free Enterprise Fund*, the SEC took the position that *Free Enterprise Fund* did not invalidate pending PCAOB actions, which the SEC observed could be ratified by a properly constituted PCAOB.[32]

The CFPB has grappled with this issue before. The Supreme Court's ruling in *Noel Canning* was widely understood to also invalidate the President's 2012 recess appointment of Director Cordray. After Director Cordray was re-nominated and confirmed by the Senate, he issued a "Notice of Ratification" that "affirm[ed] and ratif[ied] any and all actions" taken while serving as a recess appointee. The Ninth Circuit thereafter held that so long as Congress had properly granted the CFPB the authority to bring the enforcement action in question, the Notice of Ratification was sufficient to validate an ongoing enforcement action.[33] Similarly, in the context of rulemaking, the U.S. District Court for the District of Columbia held that Director Cordray's Notice of Ratification was sufficient to ratify prior rulemakings.[34]

In light of these precedents, challenges to the CFPB's rulemakings and enforcement actions based on the separation of powers issue found by the D.C. Circuit are likely to face significant hurdles. In contrast, the issues the D.C. Circuit found with the CFPB's abuse of power may make the CFPB vulnerable in challenges to some enforcement actions if the challengers are able to show similar types of Due Process or statutory interpretation issues. As noted above, the D.C. Circuit was sharply critical of the CFPB's interpretation of the statute and found that the CFPB's order had violated "bedrock principles of due process."[35] This strong language suggests that a limited set of challengers to CFPB enforcement actions may find success at the D.C. Circuit.

What's Next?

There are multiple possibilities for next steps with an added degree of uncertainty in light of the election. Without making any predictions in a volatile and changing environment, here are some considerations that we expect are in the minds of politicians and policymakers.

- The deadline for seeking *en banc* review is 45 days after a final order. For a *cert* petition, the parties will have 90 days, with a 60-day possible extension. Both dates fall after the election on November 8th.

- Using an *en banc* petition to play out the time may appeal to the Administration, in that it gives the next President a chance to take a view.

---

[31] *Id.* at *69 ("We need not here consider the legal ramifications of our decision for past CFPB rules or for past agency actions.").

[32] SEC Release No. 34-78764, In the Matter of Laccetti.

[33] *CFPB v. Gordon*, 819 F.3d 1179 (9th Cir. 2016). Gordon's petition for rehearing *en banc* before the Ninth Circuit was denied. Justice Kennedy has extended the deadline to file a *cert* petition with the Supreme Court to November 17, 2016.

[34] *State Nat'l Bank of Big Spring v. Lew*, Civil Action No. 12-1032 (ESH), 2016 WL 3812637 (D.D.C. July 12, 2016). The *Big Spring* court declined to rule on Big Spring's separation of powers argument, noting that *PHH* was currently before the D.C. Circuit.

[35] *PHH Corp.*, No. 15-1177 at *12.

- After losing 3-0 on the statutory points, the CFPB may see limited downside to seeking an *en banc* ruling. At the least, the CFPB might get a forceful and substantive dissent, something that is lacking in the current opinion.

- The cloud placed over the FHFA would likely also be considered in deciding whether to grant *en banc* rehearing.

- It seems highly unlikely that the current Congress will enact new legislation to create a multi-person commission for either the CFPB or FHFA. What the next Congress might do is unknowable before the election.

- PHH, whose business purpose aligned with advocates for the unitary executive theory, has now won and thus has no incentive to seek *en banc* or Supreme Court review.

- The decision increases Presidential power and a new Administration may not object to that result.

- An 8-person Supreme Court may or may not want to grant *cert* in *PHH* in light of the limited nature of the impact on other agencies. The Supreme Court will most certainly receive any *Gordon* petition first, but it does not follow that the decision to grant or deny a *cert* petition in *Gordon* will impact that same decision in *PHH*.

- Were the Supreme Court to grant *cert*, it is not at all clear that its decision would break down on conventional conservative/liberal lines.

- The Supreme Court need not resolve the longstanding *Myers/Humphrey's Executor* tension should it take this case. It could, like the D.C. Circuit panel, decide it on the narrower ground that "*Humphrey's Executor* does not mean that anything goes."

These considerations and variables make it impossible to determine whether the courts, the executive branch, or the legislature will be the ultimate decision maker. Of course, some might say that is entirely fitting for a separation of powers topic.

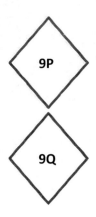

In the *PHH* case,[723] partly at issue was that the CFPB rejected former HUD guidance. **If HUD was previously responsible for interpretation of the law (RESPA) as to companies like PHH, did the CFPB err in not abiding by HUD guidance? Does accepting former guidance/interpretations defeat the purpose of the CFPB?**

Note that the 2016 opinion in the *PHH* case was authored by Judge Brett Kavanaugh.[724] Kavanaugh was appointed and confirmed to the Supreme Court of the United States in 2018. **What could Kavanaugh's placement on the U.S. Supreme Court mean for the future of the CFPB?**

Note that the CFPB has the authority to enforce nineteen consumer protection laws as of 2017. This text has covered limited portions of six such laws. **With so many industries as stakeholders, is independence or checked power more ideal for the CFPB?** Davis Polk & Wardwell notes that the D.C. Circuit's decision "increases presidential power and a new administration may not object to that result."[725] **Is this 2016 prediction accurate? Why or Why Not?**

Recall Navient's challenge to the CFPB's authority in Part VI C. **What will be the long-lasting legacy of the CFPB, its powers, and the associated regulations?** Note that the Economic Growth, Regulatory Relief and Consumer Protection Act was signed into law on May 24, 2018. The law relieves some regulatory burdens on smaller institutions:

> At a signing ceremony at the White House, Trump said the legislation "rolls back the crippling Dodd-Frank regulations that are crushing community banks and credit unions nationwide. They were in such trouble. One size fits all — those rules just don't work."[726]

Further, Acting CFPB Director Mulvaney stated, in support of the legislation, that it "will improve consumers' access to credit and reduce regulatory burdens," and " 'These changes will allow community

---

[723] *PHH Corp. v. CFPB*, 839 F.3d 1 (D.C. Cir. 2016).

[724] *Id.*

[725] Charles S. Duggan, et al., Davis Polk & Wardwell Client Memorandum, What's Next for PHH v. CFPB, (Oct. 15, 2016), at 7.

[726] Erica Werner, *Trump Signs Law Rolling Back Post-Financial Crisis Banking Rules*, Wash. Post, May 24, 2018, https://www.washingtonpost.com/business/economy/trump-signs-law-rolling-back-post-financial-crisis-banking-rules/2018/05/24/077e3aa8-5f6c-11e8-a4a4-c070ef53f315_story.html?utm_term=.e5f8342a926b.

banks and credit unions to focus on making prudent loans to prospective homebuyers without being tied up in expensive and excessive red tape.' "[727]

9T   The restrictive nature of consumer financial protection laws have been criticized as "mak[ing] it harder and more expensive for consumers to borrow," "creat[ing] a 'supernanny agency' that is designed to substitute the choice of bureaucrats for those of consumers," and "jeopardiz[ing] financial recovery by reducing credit during a severe economic recession."[728] Such laws are also criticized for increasing the cost of doing business for financial institutions, increasing the costs of compliance, and increasing litigation costs, all of which are ultimately passed on to consumers.[729] **Do you agree or disagree?**

---

[727] *See* Kelsey Ramìrez, *President Trump Signs Dodd-Frank Rollback into Law*, Housing Wire, May 24, 2018, https://www.housingwire.com/articles/43464-president-trump-signs-dodd-frank-rollback-into-law.

[728] *See* David S. Evans & Joshua D. Wright, *The Effect of the Consumer Financial Protection Agency Act of 2009 on Consumer Credit*, 22 Loy. Consumer L. Rev. 277, 280.

[729] *See id.* at 281; *see also* Zywicki, *supra* note 218, at 928 (stating "excessive and unresponsive regulation raises the price of, and reduces access to, high-quality credit, while also harming precisely those that the regulations were purportedly to help. The most vulnerable consumers will be deprived of credit choices, resulting in those consumers turning even more desperately to alternatives.").

X. FACT PATTERNS

FACT PATTERN INSTRUCTIONS

The fact patterns enclosed are intended to serve as an opportunity to test your understanding of the materials for this course.

You may find that there are additional facts that are missing in order for you to make a determination. For example, it may be helpful to note what laws, rules or theories you considered and what additional information you need to advise properly or what follow up questions you would have for your client.

MAN'S BEST FRIEND

The city of Oakhurst has experienced a boom of restaurants with outdoor space that permit animals on the patios, balconies, or other spaces for outdoor eating. The restaurants want to keep their cool, laid-back feel and bohemian atmosphere by allowing owners to bring their pets. Specifically, the restaurants are most profitable during the summer because people like to take advantage of outdoor seating and a pet-friendly atmosphere. However, recently there have been several incidences of unsupervised pets attacking restaurant patrons and/or other pets at multiple restaurants. Several of these attacks have resulted in small claims suits against pet owners for payment of vet bills and/or human emergency room bills. The lawsuits have created a back log at the local court. Other, unrestrained pets have displayed aggressive behavior and have been responsible for stealing food off the plates of some restaurant patrons while the patrons were eating. Further, individuals who walk in the neighborhood have commented that they are unable to gauge which unleashed animals have become separated from nearby owners at the patio and which animals are strays. Nevertheless, many Oakhurst residents have enjoyed the move of commercial businesses into the neighborhood and the benefit that their pets can join them for Sunday brunch.

The restaurant coalition is considering a vote next month on whether to move coalition member restaurants to the neighboring city of Decatur when the restaurant leases in Oakhurst expire at the end of the year. The city of Decatur currently has no leash laws and has deemed itself the "Pet Oasis," with generally pet-friendly laws, including for pets in public places. Oakhurst city council would like to keep the restaurants in Oakurst because having the restaurants has increased the attractiveness of the neighborhood by giving it a more walkable feel. In addition, the demand for property in the walkable neighborhood has increased property values, which has increased the base for property taxes to the city of Oakhurst. The city would like to balance the need to protect citizens with the opportunity for fun dining options that benefit the same citizens as well as the community as a whole.

You are an aide to a city council member who has asked that you draft a leash law that protects the interests of the citizens of Oakhurst.

<u>Your draft law should be no more than 2 paragraphs.</u> *Make sure your draft includes the following key elements:*

Who *needs to be regulated?* ***Who*** *should be exempt from compliance?*

Who *needs to be protected?*

What *needs regulating?*

When: *(Under what circumstances does the law serve its purpose/objective?)*

Why: *What objective is the law intended to meet?*

Upon completing your sample law, draft context that explains what you contemplated in order to complete your sample law, namely:

1. Purpose: How the law meets the goals of the stakeholders, including the city, current residents, restaurant owners, potential future residents, and potential future restaurants. Identify any other stakeholders that your law contemplates and how those stakeholders may be impacted (benefits or burdens).

*2. Loopholes and Safe Harbors: Please explain what persons, circumstances, prohibitions or requirements you ultimately decided **not** to include in your law and why. Do you anticipate the development of any loopholes?*

THE RADLEYS: PART I

Edgar Radley and his wife, Judy Radley (the "Radleys") wish to bring a private cause of action against Universal Financial ("Universal") alleging that Universal has engaged in abusive debt collection practices in violation of the Fair Debt Collection Practices Act ("FDCPA") and is routinely engaged in reporting false credit information to credit reporting agencies in violation of the Fair Credit Reporting Act.

Mr. Radley is the owner and only employee of "Radley's Builders." Radley's Builders is licensed as a general contractor to perform carpentry work in New Mexico. Mr. Radley is also employed part-time at a home improvement store.

The Sale

On October 5, 2014, Radley purchased a backhoe from New Mexico Equipment Center, LLC. A backhoe is a piece of machinery used for large digging jobs. Specifically, backhoes are useful for demolitions, breaking ground, and general construction. Mr. Radley contends that he purchased the backhoe for personal use—to build his family home and driveway. It is undisputed that the backhoe was used by Mr. Radley for personal use and not used by his business. Mr. Radley sold the backhoe immediately after he was done using it. The backhoe was never used by Radley's Builders.

The invoice from New Mexico Equipment Center documenting the sale ("Invoice") lists "Radley's Bldrs" as the purchaser. In the state of New Mexico, businesses pay a lower sales tax on goods purchased than the sales tax that individuals pay on goods purchased. The Invoice shows that the Radley's Builders business paid the lower sales tax applicable to business purchases, rather than the higher sales tax charged to individuals for purchases.

In an application for a city building permit for the construction of his home and driveway Mr. Radley identified the building contractor as the company "Radley's Bldrs." As previously mentioned, the Radley's Builders business is licensed as a general contractor to perform carpentry work in New Mexico. By listing the business for the permit, Mr. Radley was able to avoid cumbersome procedures that are required of individuals who do not have a contractor's license.

The Loan

One month before purchasing the backhoe, Mr. Radley obtained a loan from the Albuquerque Community and Savings Bank to finance the purchase of the backhoe. ("Bank Loan"). The loan agreement was signed by Mr. Radley as an individual, rather than as Radley's Builders, and identified the intended use for the loan as the purchase of "equipment [and] other personal goods."

Mr. Radley initially made payments on the Bank Loan to the Albuquerque Community and Savings Bank for four months. Thereafter, Mr. Radley failed to repay the Bank Loan, and the loan went into default. Once the Bank Loan went into default, Albuquerque Community and Savings Bank sent the Bank Loan account to Universal, a national collection agency. At the time of the default, $4,000 had been paid toward the backhoe, but an outstanding balance of $97,000 remained. Over a six-month period, Universal sent seven collection letters to Mr. Radley in his capacity as an individual. Over the same period, Universal called Mr. Radley and Mr. Radley's wife at home on numerous occasions.

Collection

A Universal employee called the home improvement store ("Store") that Mr. Radley worked at part-time. The Universal employee wanted to verify Mr. Radley's employment status but was told that the verification request had to be in writing. Thereafter, the Universal employee faxed to the Store a standard employment verification form which included Universal's name, address, logo, and phone number. It also included spaces to state the individual's name, employment status, date of hire, corporate payroll address, and position, and to note whether the individual works full time or part time. The form noted that the document was for employment verification and made no reference to debt collection.

Eventually Mr. Radley sent multiple letters. Mr. Radley sent one letter to Albuquerque Community and Savings Bank, where the Bank Loan was obtained. Mr. Radley sent one letter to Dunn & Bradstreet, which provides credit reports on businesses. Mr. Radley sent one letter to TransUnion. TransUnion provides credit reports on individuals. Mr. Radley sent one letter to Universal. As previously stated, Universal is a national collection agency. Mr. Radley's letters disputed the information being reported on his individual credit report and on the business credit report for Radley's Builders. Specifically, Mr. Radley's individual credit report with TransUnion showed Mr. Radley as owing $101,000—the original purchase price/loan amount for the backhoe. Radley contends that this information is inaccurate, as the correct balance is $97,000. Universal contends, after a reasonable investigation of the dispute, that the correct balance, as a result of late fees and other penalties, is now $101,000. Universal concluded, after an internal investigation, that the account information was only reported on Mr. Radley's individual credit report as a result of Mr. Radley personally guaranteeing a business loan for Radley's Builders. Mr. Radley's requested resolution was that his personal credit report shows a true balance of $97,000

Mr. Radley further disputed in his letter to Dunn & Bradstreet that the account was incorrectly reported on the business credit report with Dunn & Bradstreet for Radley's Builders. Mr. Radley's requested resolution was that the past due account be removed from Dunn & Bradstreet's business credit report for Radley's Builders.

Radley's Builders just contracted to complete a large construction project. However, Mr. Radley believes that the backhoe debt on his business credit report is preventing him from getting a loan for raw materials.

Mr. Radley contends that Universal has reported inaccurate credit information on his individual credit report and has failed, as a furnisher, to correct the information to the credit reporting agencies. Further, Radley contends that Universal has falsely reported an account on Radley's Builders credit report that does not belong to the business. Finally, Radley's suit also alleges that Universal's collection practices violate the FDCPA.

Please be prepared to discuss points of support that demonstrate knowledge of the law and its applicability. Students should not rely on outside case law or other source materials that cannot be referenced from assigned readings or in class discussion.

Answer the following questions in the order outlined below. If you find that you need more information to draw a conclusion, please describe what additional information you would need and why you need the information/the relevance of the missing information.

Has Universal, a national collection agency, committed any Fair Debt Collection Practices Act violations? Toward this end, please answer the questions below in the following order:

a. Is Universal a debt collector under the FDCPA? Why or Why not?

b. Is this Bank Loan a business loan or a consumer loan? Why or Why not?

c. Is there a "debt" as that term is defined?/Is FDCPA applicable to the Bank Loan here? Why or Why not?

d. Has Universal 1. engaged in harassment or abuse, 2. made false or misleading representations, or 3. communicated with third parties about a debt, or otherwise violated the Fair Debt Collection Practices Act? Why or Why not?

e. If you have determined that there are FDCCPA violations committed, are there any financial or regulatory consequences to these violations?
   i.   Namely, is there a private right of action for FDCPA violations?

      1. If so, is this private right of action available to Mr. Radley?

      2. Is this private right of action available to Mr. Radley's spouse?

      3. Is this private right of action available to Radley's Builders?

ii.   *Does a regulatory body exercise regulatory power over Universal? Explain.*

          1. *If Universal is regulated as a collection agency, who regulates Universal?*

          2. *Which regulatory powers, and under what circumstances, might such regulatory powers be exercised over Universal?*

f. *Has Albuquerque Community and Savings Bank committed any Fair Debt Collection Practices Act violations? Why or why not?*

THE RADLEYS: PART II

Edgar Radley and his wife, Judy Radley (the "Radleys") wish to bring a private cause of action against Universal Financial ("Universal") alleging that Universal has engaged in abusive debt collection practices in violation of the Fair Debt Collection Practices Act ("FDCPA") and is routinely engaged in reporting false credit information to credit reporting agencies in violation of the Fair Credit Reporting Act.

Mr. Radley is the owner and only employee of "Radley's Builders." Radley's Builders is licensed as a general contractor to perform carpentry work in New Mexico. Mr. Radley is also employed part-time at a home improvement store.

The Sale

On October 5, 2014, Radley purchased a backhoe from New Mexico Equipment Center, LLC. A backhoe is a piece of machinery used for large digging jobs. Specifically, backhoes are useful for demolitions, breaking ground, and general construction. Mr. Radley contends that he purchased the backhoe for personal use—to build his family home and driveway. It is undisputed that the backhoe was used by Mr. Radley for personal use and not used by his business. Mr. Radley sold the backhoe immediately after he was done using it. The backhoe was never used by Radley's Builders.

The invoice from New Mexico Equipment Center documenting the sale ("Invoice") lists "Radley's Bldrs" as the purchaser. In the state of New Mexico, businesses pay a lower sales tax on goods purchased than the sales tax that individuals pay on goods purchased. The Invoice shows that the Radley's Builders business paid the lower sales tax applicable to business purchases, rather than the higher sales tax charged to individuals for purchases.

In an application for a city building permit for the construction of his home and driveway Mr. Radley identified the building contractor as the company "Radley's Bldrs." As previously mentioned, the Radley's Builders business is licensed as a general contractor to perform carpentry work in New Mexico. By listing the business for the permit, Mr. Radley was able to avoid cumbersome procedures that are required of individuals who do not have a contractor's license.

The Loan

One month before purchasing the backhoe, Mr. Radley obtained a loan from the Albuquerque Community and Savings Bank to finance the purchase of the backhoe. ("Bank Loan"). The loan agreement was signed by Mr. Radley as an individual, rather than as Radley's Builders, and identified the intended use for the loan as the purchase of "equipment [and] other personal goods."

Mr. Radley initially made payments on the Bank Loan to the Albuquerque Community and Savings Bank for four months. Thereafter, Mr. Radley failed to repay the Bank Loan, and the loan went into default. Once the Bank Loan went into default, Albuquerque Community and Savings Bank sent the Bank Loan account to Universal, a national collection agency. At the time of the default, $4,000 had been paid toward the backhoe, but an outstanding balance of $97,000 remained. Over a six-month period, Universal sent seven collection letters to Mr. Radley in his capacity as an individual. Over the same period, Universal called Mr. Radley and Mr. Radley's wife at home on numerous occasions.

Collection

A Universal employee called the home improvement store ("Store") that Mr. Radley worked at part-time. The Universal employee wanted to verify Mr. Radley's employment status but was told that the verification request had to be in writing. Thereafter, the Universal employee faxed to the Store a standard employment verification form which included Universal's name, address, logo, and phone number. It also included spaces to state the individual's name, employment status, date of hire, corporate payroll address, and position, and to note whether the individual works full time or part time. The form noted that the document was for employment verification and made no reference to debt collection.

Eventually Mr. Radley sent multiple letters. Mr. Radley sent one letter to Albuquerque Community and Savings Bank, where the Bank Loan was obtained. Mr. Radley sent one letter to Dunn & Bradstreet, which provides credit reports on businesses. Mr. Radley sent one letter to TransUnion. TransUnion provides credit reports on individuals. Mr. Radley sent one letter to Universal. As previously stated, Universal is a national collection agency. Mr. Radley's letters disputed the information being reported on his individual credit report and on the business credit report for Radley's Builders. Specifically, Mr. Radley's individual credit report with TransUnion showed Mr. Radley as owing $101,000—the original purchase price/loan amount for the backhoe. Radley contends that this information is inaccurate, as the correct balance is $97,000. Universal contends, after a reasonable investigation of the dispute, that the correct balance, as a result of late fees and other penalties, is now $101,000. Universal concluded, after an internal investigation, that the account information was only reported on Mr. Radley's individual credit report as a result of Mr. Radley personally guaranteeing a business loan for Radley's Builders. Mr. Radley's requested resolution was that his personal credit report shows a true balance of $97,000

Mr. Radley further disputed in his letter to Dunn & Bradstreet that the account was incorrectly reported on the business credit report with Dunn & Bradstreet for Radley's Builders. Mr. Radley's requested resolution was that the past due account be removed from Dunn & Bradstreet's business credit report for Radley's Builders.

Radley's Builders just contracted to complete a large construction project. However, Mr. Radley believes that the backhoe debt on his business credit report is preventing him from getting a loan for raw materials.

Mr. Radley contends that Universal has reported inaccurate credit information on his individual credit report and has failed, as a furnisher, to correct the information to the credit reporting agencies. Further, Radley contends that Universal has falsely reported an account on Radley's Builders credit report that does not belong to the business. Finally, Radley's suit also alleges that Universal's collection practices violate the FDCPA.

Please be prepared to discuss points of support that demonstrate knowledge of the law and its applicability. Students should not rely on outside case law or other source materials that cannot be referenced from assigned readings or in class discussion.

Answer the following questions in the order outlined below. If you find that you need more information to draw a conclusion, please describe what additional information you would need and why you need the information/the relevance of the missing information.

1. *Has Universal committed any Fair Credit Reporting Act violations against Mr. Radley? Toward this end, please answer the questions below in the following order:*

   a. *Is Universal a furnisher, as that term is defined? Why or Why not?*
   b. *Is Universal a credit report user? Why or Why Not?*
   c. *Has there been a direct dispute as that term is defined? Why or Why not?*
   d. *Is Universal required to conduct an investigation? Why or Why not?*
   e. *Has Universal reported erroneous information? Please explain.*
   f. *Has Universal failed to report updated information regarding transactions? Please explain.*
   g. *What additional duties does Universal have under the Fair Credit Reporting Act, if any?*
   h. *Is there a private right of action available to Mr. Radley for any Fair Credit Reporting Act violations by Universal? Explain.*

2. *Has Albuquerque Community and Savings Bank committed any Fair Credit Reporting Act violations against Mr. Radley? Toward this end, please answer the questions below in the following order.*

   a. *Is Albuquerque Community and Savings Bank a furnisher, as that term is defined? Why or Why not?*
   b. *Is Albuquerque Community and Savings Bank a credit report user? Why or Why Not?*

c. Has there been a direct dispute as that term is defined? Why or Why not?

d. Is Albuquerque Community and Savings Bank required to conduct an investigation? Why or Why not?

e. Has Albuquerque Community and Savings Bank reported erroneous information? Please explain.

f. Has Albuquerque Community and Savings Bank failed to report updated information regarding transactions? Please explain.

g. Is there a private right of action available to Mr. Radley for any Fair Credit Reporting Act violations by Albuquerque Community and Savings Bank? Explain.

MORTGAGE DREAMS

Mortgage Dreams Inc. is a mortgage lender that offers loans to self-employed individuals to help them realize their dreams of homeownership. In some instances, the income of self-employed individuals can be difficult to verify, and such individuals may prove to be a higher credit risk and/or more likely to default on their mortgage loan. Mortgage Dreams' underwriting team relies on various credit studies released by Harvard University that determined that, on average, legal permanent residents are less likely to default on mortgage loans than are U.S. citizens born in the United States. Therefore, Mortgage Dreams' business model relies on tapping into an underserved part of the consumer market—immigrant business owners—and providing loans for the purchase of individual residences where other lenders might consider such a loan too risky a venture. During the loan application process, Mortgage Dreams asks for the individual's immigrant status. Based on the information provided, Mortgage Dreams makes an inference regarding the individual's national origin and offers lower interest rates to certain individuals based on their nationality. Mortgage Dreams funds the mortgage loans and uses a wholly-owned subsidiary, Home Money Solutions, to service the loans and collect on any defaulted mortgage loans owned and originated by Mortgage Dreams. Home Money Solutions does not engage in any other activities.

Because of the nature of the business, Home Money Solutions has taken an aggressive stance on collecting on past due mortgage payments so that Mortgage Dreams can continue to fund new loans. Both Mortgage Dreams Inc. and Home Money Solutions are licensed by the Georgia Department of Banking and Finance, which licenses mortgage lenders and mortgage servicers and charters state banks. Both Mortgage Dreams and Home Money Solutions are based in Atlanta and serve customers in Atlanta primarily. Mortgage Dreams Inc. has been in business for fifteen months in Georgia and is not licensed in any other state. The Department of Banking and Finance has notified Mortgage Dreams and Home Money Solutions that the Department will conduct a periodic exam as of today and asks the companies to produce the loan agreement for loan files that have closed in the last week, copies of advertisements, policies and procedures, scripts, etc.

Mortgage Dreams and Home Money Solutions have retained the law firm of Johnson Allen Mahoney to review its current practices prior to producing the documents for the periodic exam, for the purpose of general advising. You are an attorney with the law firm, and Mortgage Dreams and Money Solutions have sent for your review the attachments listed below. Prior to retaining Johnson Allen Mahoney, neither Mortgage Dreams nor Home Money Solutions utilized inside or outside counsel because they had few, if any legal issues, since they were relatively new companies. In addition, since they are new companies, neither has a history of previous violations. Mortgage Dreams has thrived in Georgia and currently has a pending license application with the state of South Carolina to obtain a mortgage lender license. So far, Mortgage Dreams has only had one CFPB complaint that it is aware of.

Since Mortgage Dreams is a small, unknown lender, it keeps most of the loans it originates and funds on its own balance sheet. Mortgage Dreams keeps and collects on performing loans. Mortgage Dreams keeps defaulted loans on its balance sheet but, for efficiency purposes, uses Home Mortgage Solutions to service the loans. With an intended expansion into South Carolina, Mortgage Dreams hopes to begin selling some of its performing loans (loans that are current and in good standing) to investors.

Mortgage Dreams plans to sell these loans to free up more money for Mortgage Dreams to lend in South Carolina. Loan Buyer LLC is interested in purchasing these loans, and Loan Buyer LLC and Mortgage Dreams are currently in negotiations for the purchase of the loan pool. Loan Buyer LLC is conducting due diligence of Mortgage Dreams, Home Money Solutions, and the loan pool to determine value. Loan Buyer LLC has warned Mortgage Dreams that Loan Buyer will reduce its offer price for the loan pool if the loan pool has a high volume of account discrepancies, disputes, and/or probable violations that will subject the loans to private rights of action or otherwise reduce the likelihood of Receivable Buyer's ability to collect on the loans after the purchase from Mortgage Dreams.

Plaintiffany Litigiouso is a fired-up plaintiff's attorney intent on working for the little guy. She has built a successful solo practice bringing class-action lawsuits against financial institutions for compliance violations. She often enlists the help of her paralegal in perusing the public CFPB Complaint Database for wronged consumers. Plaintiffany and her paralegal read the complaint narratives, using them as a source for potential clients and then Plaintiffany hires a private investigator to track down the consumer. Many of her cases are frivolous and without merit, but she often locates sympathetic plaintiffs, including veterans, students, and the elderly. While her cases are frivolous, she has been successful in obtaining many undisclosed settlements for clients by threatening to reveal company transgressions on a local, but highly-rated, consumer report weekly television program. Plaintiffany Litigiouso has successfully resolved numerous bar complaints against her, in her favor and continues to fight another day for "consumer financial justice."

FunTrust Bank is a South Carolina state-chartered bank headquartered in Charleston with assets of $9 billion. FunTrust has hit a stride in the past three years due to the restaurant boom in the destination city. Specifically, FunTrust Bank has funded many business purpose loans and commercial real estate loans to help jump start businesses of immigrants who have transplanted to Charleston wanting to open thriving restaurants along the coast.

MoonTrust Bank has the exact same business model as Mortgage Dreams, Inc., (relying on the same business practices and Harvard study) namely providing residential mortgage loans to self-employed, immigrant business owners. MoonTrust Bank is located in and serves consumers in Valdosta, a city in South Georgia. MoonTrust bank has been in operation for three years and is a small, Georgia-chartered community bank with $16 Billion in assets.

Exhibit 1: Call Center Script used by employees of Home Money Solutions, Inc. to collect on defaulted loans. The script has been in use for five months.

Exhibit. 2: CFPB Consumer Complaint filed in portal and response

Exhibit. 3: Mortgage Dreams Loan Agreement

Group 1: Identify any potential law violations committed by Mortgage Dreams, Inc. *Your responses to these questions will serve as the basis for the discussion/advice to your client. Specifically, you need to be prepared to present (1) What are the potential law violations? Rank in order of causing the highest level of risk to lowest level of risk. What other information, if any, do you need in order to advise your client?*

Group 2: You represent Loan Buyer LLC in the purchase of loans from Mortgage Dreams, Inc.

Please advise your client of any instances in which Loan Buyer may wish to reduce its "price" for the Mortgage Dreams loan pool based on whether the loan pool has a high volume of account discrepancies, disputes, and/or probable violations that will subject the loans to private rights of action or otherwise reduce Loan Buyer's ability to collect on the loans after the purchase from Mortgage Dreams. Mortgage Dreams has offered Loan Buyer a discount on the loan pool purchase if Loan Buyer continues to use Home Mortgage Solutions to service the loans. Advise your client, Loan Buyer LLC, of whether it should accept this discount and continue to use Home Mortgage Solutions OR if Loan Buyer should select another servicer, if Loan Buyer purchases the loans from Mortgage Dreams.

Group 3: Identify any potential law violations committed by Home Money Solutions. *Your responses to these questions will serve as the basis for the discussion/advice to your client. Specifically, you need to be prepared to present (1) What are the potential law violations? Rank in order of causing the highest level of risk to lowest level of risk. What other information, if any, do you need in order to advise your client?*

Group 4: You represent both FunTrust Bank and MoonTrust Bank. *Both institutions' employees met employees of Mortgage Dreams at a lending conference last month. After a few too many drinks, Mortgage Dreams' employees began to share with FunTrust and MoonTrust employees the information disclosed above about the company's practices. FunTrust and MoonTrust have hired your firm to advise on whether they should be concerned with the outcome of any consequences that Mortgage Dreams may face as a result of any compliance violations.*

Exhibit 1: Home Money Solutions Call Center Script for Collection Calls

(1) Ask to speak to borrower

(2) Identify who you are

(3) Once you are able to speak to borrower, indicate that you are calling in reference to past due mortgage loan

(4) Verify the accuracy of the account information

(5) If borrower is unwilling to pay on mortgage, offer them an incentive by telling them that they can make half of their monthly mortgage payment now and the other half at the end of the month, and the company will apply the full amount without considering the loan in default or charging a default fee. If the consumer selects this option, be sure to contact accounting/billing to add a "midmonth" transactional fee for submitting payments in the middle of the month

(6) Try to make contact with the borrower at least once per day during the week to try to help them remember to pay the debt. No need to make weekend calls.

(7) Before ending the call, inform consumers that they can set up automatic monthly debits to pay their mortgage for no additional cost

(8) Any employee who has a success rate of 75% or more of getting partial payments on defaulted loans will receive monthly bonuses equal to 1% percent of payments (in dollar amounts) collected that month.

Direct any questions regarding this script to your immediate supervisor.

Steven Gellar

President,
Home Money Solutions

Exhibit 2 CFPB Complaint

Received 12/19/2017

Case Number: 123456

Product: Mortgage

Issue: Improper Contact or Sharing of Info, Cont'd Attempts to Collect Debt Not Owed

Describe What Happened: I own my own lawn business and got a loan from Mortgage Dreams Inc. to buy a house. I have been living in the house for five months. My new girlfriend, who is staying with me, says that "Home Money Solutions" keeps calling the house once a week at 6 am and told her that I am in default on my loan and to send them a check for the past due amount. I am usually at work by 6 am because I like to start cutting the grass before it gets too hot outside, but my girlfriend is kinda mad that they keep waking her up. I have never spoken to them myself because I don't know who they are. I don't know why they keep calling me because I don't have a loan with Home Money Solutions, and I refuse to pay anyone until this is cleared up. I never gave Mortgage Dreams my permission to share my personal information with whoever this Home Money Solutions is, and I don't think it's cool to be giving out my name, telephone number, and account number all willy nilly. I don't even know them!

Desired Resolution: I want Mortgage Dreams to stop sharing my information with other companies. I'll pay my mortgage when Mortgage Dreams explains to me who Home Money Solutions is and why they are giving away my secret info.

Consumer Information:

First Name: Floyd Last Name: Radley

Street: 123 Elsewhere Lane City: Ellijay State: Georgia

Product Information: Mortgage

Company Name: Mortgage Dreams Inc.

Mortgage Dreams Response CFPB Complaint Response:

This response is filed on behalf of Mortgage Dreams, Inc. to CFPB Consumer Complaint No. 123456. Mortgage Dreams originated a loan with borrower. Mortgage Dreams subsequently entered into an agreement with Home Money Solutions whereby Home Money Solutions would act as the servicer on borrower's loan. Notification was made to borrower via letter addressed to borrower's primary residence, that Home Money Solutions would be servicing this loan. Thereafter, Home Money Solutions received information from Mortgage Dreams about borrower and information regarding borrower's loan, including borrower's payment history, in order to service the loan. Mortgage Dreams is permitted to share consumer's personal financial information without consumer limiting that information-sharing. As such, Mortgage Dreams believes it acted appropriately, as authorized by contract or by law, in sharing borrower's information with Home Money Solutions.

LOAN AGREEMENT

Date: Effective Date: (you may get funds prior to this date)	No.: Final Maturity Date:
Mortgage Dreams, Inc. info@mortgagedreams.com (888) 555-5555	Borrower's Name: Borrower's Address: Phone: Cell Phone: Email address:

DISCLOSURES

ANNUAL PERCENTAGE RATE The cost of your credit as a yearly rate.	Amount Financed The amount of credit provided to you or on your behalf.	Total of Payments The amount you will have paid after you have made all payments as scheduled.	

Your Payment Schedule will be:

Number of Payments	Amount of Payment	When Payments Are Due

Security: MORTGAGE DREAMS does have a security interest in the loan.

Prepayment: If you pay all or part of the loan early you will not have to pay a penalty.

See the terms of this Agreement for any additional information about nonpayment, default, any required repayment in full before the scheduled due date, and prepayment refunds and penalties.

1. PARTIES. In this Consumer Loan Agreement ("Agreement") the words "you", "your" and "I" mean the borrower listed above who has electronically signed this Agreement. The words "we", "us," and "our" mean   MORTGAGE   DREAMS."

2. SUPPORTING MATERIALS. You agree to provide to us all information we require, including but not limited to bank statements and proof of income. If you identify as Muslim, you must also provide photo identification and a voided check, and/or any other materials requested by us to process your loan. We may require additional information from you during the term of this Agreement to combat fraud, accommodate changes to your personal information, or otherwise service your account. You agree to provide such information upon request.

3. LOAN LIMITATIONS. We are not permitted to extend credit to individuals under the age of 18. Further, we do not accept applications in Texas, Arizona, New Mexico, and California from individuals from Mexico.

4. INTEREST AND PAYMENTS. We use the simple interest method to calculate the interest. Interest is not compounded. Payments will be applied first to interest, then to any outstanding fees or charges, and then to any outstanding Principal. Early payments or paying more than scheduled may decrease the amount of interest that accrues. Late payments may increase the amount of interest that accrues. For more information you may contact us by email at info@Mortgage Dreams.com or by phone at (888)-555-5555.

5. PREPAYMENT. You may pay in advance in any amount at any time and you will not incur an additional charge, fee, or penalty. Prepayment may reduce the total amount of interest that accrues.

6. VERIFICATION. You certify and warrant that the information you have given in connection with this Agreement is true and correct. You acknowledge and agree that we rely on the information you provide to us in order to decide whether to approve this Agreement. You also give us consent to obtain information about   you   from   consumer   reporting   agencies   and/or   other   sources.

7. DEFAULT: Except as limited by applicable law, we may declare you to be in default under this Agreement if: (a) you provide us false or misleading information about yourself, your financial condition, Your Bank Account, or any other matter, (b) you omit or fail to provide any information required by us, (c) you fail to make the entire payment due by a scheduled Due Date or if your payment is dishonored or returned to us unpaid for any reason, or (d) you agree to make alternative payment arrangements and fail to make those payment(s) on time as agreed.

8. CONSUMER REPORTS & THIRD PARTY INFORMATION. You authorize us to obtain consumer reports and other information about you from consumer reporting agencies and other third parties in connection with your loan and at any time that you owe us money under this or any Agreement. You give us permission to access your credit report in connection with any transaction or extension of credit and on an ongoing basis to review this Agreement, taking collection action on this Agreement, monitoring your financial and credit status, or for any other permissible purpose. Upon your request, you will be informed of whether a consumer credit report was ordered, and if it was, you will be given the name and address of the   consumer   reporting   agency   that   furnished   the   report.

9. PRIVACY NOTICE AND TERMS OF USE. By signing this Agreement, you acknowledge and agree to MORTGAGE DREAMS's Privacy Notice as stated on MORTGAGE DREAMS's website and further agree that you have reviewed and are in possession of a copy of the Privacy Notice.

10. SERVICE MEMBERS. Federal law provides important protections to members of the Armed Forces and their dependents relating to extensions of consumer credit. In general, the cost of consumer credit to a member of the Armed Forces and his or her dependent may not exceed an annual percentage rate of 36%.

BY SIGNING THE BOX BELOW AND CLICKING THE "I AGREE" BUTTON, YOU ARE ELECTRONICALLY SIGNING THIS AGREEMENT. YOU AGREE THAT YOU HAVE THE FINANCIAL ABILITY TO REPAY IN ACCORDANCE WITH THIS AGREEMENT. YOU ACKNOWLEDGE THAT: (A) YOU HAVE READ THE TERMS AND CONDITIONS OF THIS AGREEMENT, (B) UNDERSTAND THE AGREEMENT IN ITS CURRENT LANGUAGE PROVIDED, AND (C) AGREE TO ALL OF THE TERMS AND CONDITIONS OF THIS AGREEMENT.

Borrower:

[I AGREE]

Abbie Jones sought financing to buy a used car from Harper's Chevrolet. After reviewing her credit report, Harper's Chevrolet decided that it would be useless to send her loan application to any lender. Instead of notifying Abbie of this, Harper's notified Abbie that it could get her financing if she obtained a co-borrower. Abbie produced her grandmother as a co-borrower of the loan. Abbie filed a lawsuit against Harper's Chevrolet under the Equal Credit Opportunity Act, stating that Harper's Chevrolet denied her credit, without providing an adverse action notice to her. She contends that Harper's Chevrolet effectively denied her credit when it failed to notify Abbie that it did not send her application to any lender. Harper's Chevrolet has retained Johnson Allen Mahoney to assist with the litigation and to advise on whether the company is in violation of the Equal Credit Opportunity Act.

Abbie Jones, a recently-divorced mother of two children, received a direct mail solicitation from Harper's Chevrolet, a small-town seller of new and used automobiles, indicating that she was pre-approved for the financing of the purchase of a car. Harper's obtained Abbie's name (in order to send the direct-mail solicitation) from a credit reporting agency. The scope of the list of names that the credit reporting agency provided was of people who had recently filed for bankruptcy and who had credit scores between 590 and 630.

Abbie was interested in purchasing a used car. She called the number listed on the mailing. She answered a few questions about her income and employment status and gave Harper's her social security number so that it could access her full credit report. Harper's itself does not provide financing for the cars it sells. Instead, it attempts to arrange for financing through banks or finance companies. Harper's obtained a copy of Abbie's credit report, with Abbie's consent, and, based on the credit report, knew that Abbie would not be eligible for financing/would not be approved by any of the institutions through which Harper's typically arranges auto-financing on behalf of its customers. Specifically, Abbie's credit score was now 550 and no longer met the original criteria for the credit offer. Shortly after Abbie's call, she received a return call from Harpers inviting her to come to the dealership. When she arrived at the dealership, Harper's did not indicate that they did not seek credit from a bank or finance company on her behalf. Instead, the Harper's salesperson told Abbie that they found a bank but that it would only finance the purchase of a new car and not a used car and would only finance if there was a co-borrower for the auto loan. Harper's Chevrolet used Northern Community Bank, a state-chartered bank in a large metropolitan area with assets amounting to six billion dollars, for the loan at issue.

Abbie wondered at the time whether Harper's Chevrolet made her obtain a co-borrower because she was unmarried. Specifically, the Harper's salesperson engaged in small talk with her about her interest in a used car. Abbie indicated that, following her divorce, her husband kept the family minivan and joint custody of their two children. She recalled that the salesperson, an older gentleman, gave her a "disapproving look" at the mention of the divorce. Because she felt uncomfortable, she went on to explain to the salesperson that, as a result of the divorce, she needed a vehicle that she could use when the children were staying with her. Later, when filling out paperwork on Abbie's behalf, an administrative person asked Abbie whether she was receiving child support or alimony. Abbie again felt uncomfortable about the focus on her ex-husband and did not disclose child support or alimony to Harper's.

While Abbie was interested in a used 2011 Honda Odyssey, which had good reviews for safety and child locks, she ultimately ended up with a new 2018 Chrysler Pacifica minivan. The older salesman remarked endearingly "I'll bet your husband used to handle these types of things for you. Picking out a car can be tough when you don't have a man to help you out, but trust me; the 2018 Pacifica is better for you and your kids. I know what's under the hood, and I wouldn't steer a pretty lady wrong." Abbie later wondered whether Harper's Chevrolet talked her into getting a loan for a new car, rather than the used car that she wanted, because she was a woman.

Abbie and her grandmother submitted new information to Harper's that included both Abbie and her grandmother's credit scores and their incomes. Harper's submitted this information to Northern Community Bank, and Northern Community Bank funded an auto loan for the 2018 Pacifica with Abbie and her grandmother as co-borrowers. As co-borrowers, both Abbie and her grandmother were obligated to repay the car loan. Abbie's grandmother signed the co-borrower documents, which listed Northern Community Bank as the lender, but Abbie's grandmother did not read the papers she signed, and did not understand that she would also be liable for the car loan. At the time her grandmother signed the documents, Abbie wondered whether her grandmother's old age had anything to do with the high interest rate attached to the car loan. Soon after the purchase, Abbie defaulted on the loan. Abbie's grandmother refused to make payments on the loan, and Northern Community Bank continues to demand payment on the loan. Northern Community Bank calls Abbie and her grandmother one time per week each to request payment on the loan. In the last call to Abbie, the Northern Community Bank employee asked Abbie, "how would you feel as a mother if your kids have to start walking to school? The bank may have no choice but to take back the vehicle." In the last call to Abbie's grandmother, the Northern Community Bank employee left a voicemail message on Abbie's grandmother cell phone stating: "Clock's ticking." Abbie's grandmother has recently contacted the credit reporting agency requesting that the loan be removed from her credit report as she does not believe that she owes money to Northern Community Bank.

Harper's general counsel maintains that Harper's does not have the authority to deny credit because, as the dealership, it does not have the authority to grant credit. It only arranges financing through banks and finance company partners. Therefore, the general counsel concludes that Harper's cannot be in violation of ECOA'S requirement that an adverse action be provided when credit is denied. In addition, Harper's general counsel suggests that, because Abbie never submitted an application to a lender or finance company, that she did not submit an application for the purposes of ECOA.

Group 1:

You are outside counsel for Harper's and are aware of the ECOA adverse action notice requirements, the purpose behind the notice requirements, and that discrimination is discouraged by requiring creditors to explain credit decisions. Harper's general counsel has asked you to join a call and advise on whether Harper's unilateral decision not to submit a credit application to any lender constitutes an adverse action for purposes of ECOA, thereby triggering the requirement that Harper's provide a notice. The general counsel is expecting, in advance of the call, that you will have had an opportunity to review and interpret any relevant statutes or regulations, relying on definitions, legal requirements, etc. as well as any public policy considerations related to consumer protection. Harper's general counsel will be reporting your advice to the company's owners and wants your input on any consequences, if any, that the company would have to contend with if Abbie were successful in her adverse action claim.

Group 2:

You represent Abbie and her grandmother and they have asked you to determine whether Harper's may have committed any other consumer financial services violations unrelated to the adverse action notice potential violation. Please advise whether you will consider Abbie and her grandmother separately or together. Please advise whether there are any other potential consumer financial services violations, and, if so:

a. What are the methods of pursuing such violations eg. via lawsuit, via regulatory agency consumer complaint, etc.?

b. Against whom, if at all, does Abbie and/or her grandmother have claims or consumer complaints?

One partner at your law firm has a call scheduled with Abbie, and another partner at your law firm has a call scheduled with Abbie's grandmother. Each partner/client is expecting that, in advance of the call, you will have had an opportunity to review and interpret any relevant statutes or regulations, relying on definitions, legal requirements, etc. as well as any public policy considerations related to consumer protection.

Group 3:

You are outside counsel for Northern Community Bank. Northern Community Bank has informed you that there is a pending lawsuit on a defaulted loan for which Northern Community Bank has been attempting to collect payment. Northern Community Bank has provided to you the information above and has requested that you advise on whether Northern Community Bank has committed any violations. Further, Northern Community Bank has requested that you advise on whether it can continue to attempt to collect payments on the loan at issue using its current method and/or whether any of its own violations, if any, or violations by Harper's, prevent further collection of payment on the loan. Northern Community Bank will be reporting your advice to the bank's board of directors and executive officers and wants your input on any regulatory consequences, if any, that the bank may have to contend with if Harper's or Northern Community is held responsible for any consumer financial services violations. You should be specific in your response as to the consequences of each potential violation, if any.

Group 4:

You are outside counsel for Harper's. Harper's General Counsel has interviewed Harper's employees who corroborated the facts and statements referenced above. As a result, Harper's has asked that you advise whether Harper's should be concerned with any other potential consumer financial services violations, under ECOA or otherwise. You have an upcoming call scheduled with the General Counsel. The General Counsel has indicated to you that another law firm is looking into the adverse action notice issue; you are expected to advise on any legal/compliance issues outside of the adverse action notice claim only. The General counsel is expecting, in advance of the call, that you will have had an opportunity to review and interpret any relevant statutes or regulations, relying on definitions, legal requirements, etc. as well as any public policy considerations related to consumer protection. Harper's General Counsel will be reporting your advice to the company's owners and wants your input on any regulatory consequences, if any, that the company would have to contend with if Abbie has any other claims and/or is successful in bringing any other claims.

Elliot Financial is a national consumer lender with locations in all fifty states. Elliot Financial makes personal loans of less than $10,000 to low-income consumers with credit scores between 461 and 554. In 2015 Elliot Financial had more than 600,000 outstanding consumer loans and originated 5700 loans nationwide that year. The average APR on the loans was 27% and the FICO score 520. As of January 1 2017, thirty seven percent of Elliot Financial's outstanding loans were past due. As of January 2017, eighteen percent of the outstanding loans were more than thirty days past due. The CFPB has enforcement, rulemaking, and supervisory authority over Elliot Financial as a "covered person" providing financial services to consumers. A recent exam has been performed by the CFPB Supervision Team, and the following findings were included in the exam report:

(1) Elliot Financial required consumers to provide four to eight names and phone numbers as references when they applied for financing. When consumers fell behind in payments, Elliot Financial called these references in an attempt to get the consumers to call Elliot Financial to discuss the consumers' past-due accounts. The references have filed more than 200 complaints about these calls in the CFPB consumer complaint database. Specifically, the resolution desired by these references was for Elliot Financial to stop calling them about the consumer, their friend or family member's debt.

(2) In December 2013, Elliot Financial started using a third-party loan servicing platform to compile information to be furnished to credit reporting agencies. By April 2014, Elliot Financial outsourced its furnishing completely. The conversion to a third-party servicing platform was a massive transition that led to inaccuracies in Elliot Financial's furnished information. Following the December 2013 conversion, Elliot Financial furnished duplicate account information for at least 3,500 accounts. The CFPB examiners cite as an example that one consumer had a loan of $5,000 that was reported four times on her credit report thereby making her appear that she had sought multiple extensions of credit at the same time and was indebted $20,000 rather than $5,000. Elliot Financial did not detect these furnishing inaccuracies until November 2014, and it corrected the inaccuracies in April 2015. In 2014, Elliot Financial furnished inaccurate balances for consumers on 3,839 past due accounts, largely due to problems with the conversion. The CFPB examiners cite as an example that one consumer's credit report showed an outstanding past due balance of $1,796 even though he had been making payments on the past due amount for six months and in fact had a past due balance of only $375. While Elliot Financial accepted his payments and applied them to his outstanding balance, this information was not conveyed to the third party responsible for furnishing information to credit reporting agencies. Elliot Financial did not detect these furnishing inaccuracies until July 2015, and it suspended furnishing until the cause of the inaccuracy was corrected in December 2015.

(3) Elliot Financial received approximately 2,000 disputes per year related to its credit information furnishing practices. Elliot Financial had two employees who processed the credit information disputes that were received. Due to the limited number of resources, the company issued an automatic response to consumers disputing account information provided to consumer reporting agencies. Namely the automated response was issued within 24 hours and indicated that the company had conducted a thorough investigation and determined that there were no inaccuracies found in the account information. CFPB examiners found that this response was sent to most consumers even if a reasonable investigation would have revealed that the account information reported was inaccurate. The company utilized a software program that searched for buzz words among the disputes, namely "CFPB," "Commissioner," and "Department," and the employees were instructed to escalate and investigate only credit report disputes that had some indication that the consumer had reported the complaint to a third party regulator.

(4) Elliot Financial conducted an internal compliance audit in 2016 that included a review of accounts. The company was aware that it had a problem with the furnishing of information and that the conversion to a third-party platform for furnishing had led to widespread inaccuracies in the furnished information. Elliot Financial also concluded that the credit reporting inaccuracies led to an increase in the number of consumer debt disputes. While Elliot Financial identified numerous issues following its internal compliance audit, it did not amend its current policy or procedure regarding responding to credit report disputes, did not increase staff to handle disputes, nor otherwise make any changes to resolve any issues identified. Elliot Financial has not updated its credit dispute policies since before it transitioned the credit reporting task to the third party in 2013.

You are employed as an enforcement attorney with the CFPB. It is your job to review the facts provided by the examiners and identify any law/regulatory violations by Elliot Financial. Draft a clear recommendation to your immediate boss of what law violations, (limited to the laws covered in this course), you believe the CFPB may pursue against Elliot Financial. Your draft should be in the format of a legal memo, organized as follows:

I.   Identify the potential law violations, clearly connecting the law violation to the text of the law.

II.   Identify strengths and weaknesses in the facts the supervisory examiners have provided that support your conclusions regarding the law violations. Be sure to include what information, if any, may be more helpful to know or obtain if the CFPB pursues the violations.

III.   Finally, identify any mitigating or aggravating factors that your boss should consider when determining whether a lenient or punitive approach should be taken with respect to the imposition of any fines, if any.

RED NOTE MONEY

You are an attorney working at the law firm of Johnson Allen Mahoney LLC. Red Note Money is a start-up consumer lender offering loans between $1,000 and $10,000 in twelve states, including Texas. Red Note Money is a client of Johnson Allen Mahoney and is requesting counsel on a matter as described below.

Recently, Red Note Money learned that some of the advertisements that its marketing vendor utilized may be in violation of the advertising disclosure laws. The advertisement was an announcement on the radio as well as a direct mailer. Mailer 1 was sent to 100 residents in Dallas, Texas and Mailer 2 was sent to 2,500 residents in El Paso, Texas, which borders Mexico. See mailers attached as Exhibit 1. The radio advertisement was aired on a local morning show that boasts a (primarily Spanish-speaking) listener audience of 60,000 and on an English radio show with the same number of listeners. The radio advertisement on the English radio show included English information and English disclosures of the same content as in Mailer 1. The radio advertisement on the Spanish radio show included Spanish information of the same content as Mailer 2, but with English disclosures. The radio advertisement aired 100 times on the Spanish morning show and 100 times on the English radio show.

Since its inception, Red Note Money has been funded by a group of investors called Wealthy Students, Inc. that has extended a line of credit to Red Note Money of up to fifty-five million dollars. Wealthy Students, Inc. has an interest in Red Note Money's loan receivables. In other words, the fifty-five million dollar extension of credit is secured by the payments that Red Note Money receives from borrowers. Red Note Money has almost exhausted this funding source and has utilized forty-five million dollars from Wealthy Students, Inc. to make forty-five million dollars in loans in the twelve states where it is licensed. As a part of its agreement with Wealthy Students, Inc. Red Note Money is prohibited from having any regulatory action issued against it. If Red Note Money receives a regulatory action, any remaining funding, from Wealthy Students, Inc., not yet used will be rescinded.

Red Note Money is currently in its second round of capital-raising and has two interested companies. Red Note Money is currently in talks to close a deal with potential investors—Fancy Entrepreneurs, LLC for $25 million. Fancy Entrepreneurs, LLC will sign on the dotted line for a new stream of funding, via a capital injection, provided that Red Note Money hits the fifty million dollar benchmark in accounts/loans originated to demonstrate the health and viability of the company. The capital injection would be reflected on the balance sheet as paid in capital/owner's equity. Red Note Money will hit the benchmark of $50M by quarter end (March 31, 2018), provided that it draws from the remaining line of credit with Wealthy Students, Inc. and continues to make loans in Texas—it's largest market out of the twelve states. If Red Note Money lost its license in Texas or had to otherwise cease operations, it would still be profitable provided that it was able to continue making loans in the other eleven states. However, Red Note Money, would, of course, be required to let go of its employees that originate loans for Texas consumers.

Loan Shark Investments is also interested in Red Note Money and is offering a loan of $25 million at a 27% interest rate. If Red Note Money accepts funding from Loan Shark Investments, it will be reflected as debt on Red Note Money's balance sheet, which could harm its potential to lure investors in the future as debt will count against the health and viability of the company. There are no conditions to accepting a loan from Loan Shark Investments, other than the interest rate on the loan. However, Loan Shark Investments was founded by Natalia Suárez Díaz, a savvy business woman from Uruguay, who only invests in companies providing services to a portion of the population that is underserved. Loan Shark's brand is synonymous with supporting the expansion of financial services for the U.S. immigrant population and extends funding to companies that promote this ideal.

As a part of its loan application, Red Note Money has applicants identify in a drop down menu how they became aware of Red Note Money—by mail advertisement, radio advertisement, etc., so that its marketing team can determine which promotional tools are successful at obtaining new consumer applicants.

Consumer Carla, a native Spanish speaker, received mailer 2 in the mail and sought a loan with Red Note Money by calling the telephone number on the mailer. Consumer Carla spoke to a call center representative who took her application over the phone. Consumer Carla was approved for a loan with an APR of 29% and eighteen monthly payments of $465. Consumer Carla spoke to the call center representative in English and electronically signed her loan agreement, the terms of which were written in English. Required disclosures related to her loan terms were also in English. Consumer Carla used the money to pay for a family vacation to her native country of Argentina, where she was able to visit many places and introduce her children to members of her extended family. The month after returning from her vacation, Carla received her first bill for payment on her loan. It was at this time that she noticed, that the interest rate she received when closing on her loan (twenty-nine percent) was on the higher end of the rates advertised in the mailer (between eighteen and thirty-six percent). She began to think she received a bad deal and that she never would have agreed to the terms if the disclosures had been in Spanish and she fully understood them in order to make an informed decision.

Consumer Carla told her story to TEXAS SCAMS, SHAMS, AND COMPLIANCE WHAMM(IES), a monthly online consumer blog. The publisher of the blog requests comment from Red Note Money before the blog post is published at the end of the month (February 28, 2018), detailing Consumer Carla's account and deeming Red Note Money a scam that preys on immigrants. Consumer Carla has made no direct complaint with Red Note Money, and the request for comment was the first time Red Note Money became aware of Consumer Carla's dissatisfaction.

As a result of current circumstances, Red Note Money has forwarded to you their advertisements for review to double check that they are not in violation the law.

At this time, Red Note Money does not currently have an exam scheduled in Texas, but the state typically conducts risk-based exams.

Please be prepared to answer the following questions. Your responses to these questions will serve as the basis to the discussion/advice to your client. Specifically, you need to be prepared to present (a) the *risks to your client, (b) options available to your client, (c) why one option would be more favorable to your client than the alternative (be prepared to explain your cost/benefit analysis)*

1. *What are the potential law violations? Rank in order of causing the highest level of risk to lowest level of risk.*
2. *What are the financial consequences to consider? How would you advise your client and why?*
3. *What are the reputational consequences to consider? How would you advise your client and why?*
4. *What are the regulatory consequences to consider? How would you advise your client and why?*
5. *What other information, if any, do you need in order to advise your client?*
6. *Who are the stakeholders?*
7. *What are the stakeholders' interests?*
8. *What outcome would most benefit each of the stakeholders? What outcome would least benefit each of the stakeholders?*

Exhibit 1:

Mailer 1

APPROVED!
Getting a Loan should be easy! Call us today at (404) 555-6862 or
get started at www.RedNoteMoney.com

Up to $10,000 fast for home improvement projects, medical bills, holiday shopping, or the next family vacation!
Interest rates between 18 and 36 percent

Your loan amount and APR are determined after submitting your application. We offer eighteen-month terms. A loan of $XXXX, with a fixed interest rate of XX% and an origination fee of X% would require eighteen monthly payments of $XXX with an APR of XX% for the life of the loan.

This "prescreened" offer of credit is based on information in your credit report indicating that you meet certain criteria. This offer is not guaranteed if you do not meet our criteria. If you do not want to receive prescreened offers of credit from this and other companies, call the consumer reporting agencies toll-free, 1.888.567.8688; or write: Experian Direct Marketing, PO Box 919, Allen, TX 75013; Equifax Information Service Center, PO Box 740123, Atlanta, GA 30374-0123; or TransUnion Name Removal Option, PO Box 505, Woodlyn, PA 19094-0505.

APPROVED!

Conseguir un préstamo debe ser fácil! ¡Llámenos hoy al 404 555-6862 o comenzar a www.RedNoteMoney.com

¡Hasta $ 10,000 rápido para los proyectos de la mejora casera, cuentas médicas, compras del día de fiesta, o las vacaciones próximas de la familia!

Tasas de interés entre 18 y 36 por ciento

La cantidad de su préstamo y APR se determinan después de presentar su solicitud. Ofrecemos términos de dieciocho meses. Un préstamo de $ XXXX, con una tasa de interés fija de XX% y un cargo de originación de X% requeriría dieciocho pagos mensuales de $ XXX con una APR del XX% para la vida del préstamo.

Esta oferta de crédito "preseleccionada" se basa en información de su informe de crédito que indica que cumple ciertos criterios. Esta oferta no está garantizada si no cumple con nuestros criterios. Si no desea recibir ofertas de crédito preseleccionadas de esta y otras compañías, llame sin costo a las agencias de informes al consumidor, 1.888.567.8688; O escribir: Experian Direct Marketing, PO Box 919, Allen, TX 75013; Centro de Servicios de Información Equifax, PO Box 740123, Atlanta, GA 30374-0123; O TransUnion Name Removal Option, PO Box 505, Woodlyn, PA 19094-0505.

The Washington Post reported in a 2018 article that under President Donald Trump's 2019 budget plan "the CFPB would be funded through Congress rather than the Federal Reserve, giving lawmakers more influence over the agency's priorities."[730] Further, the article quotes Karl Frisch, the executive director of the group Allied Progress, as stating that the move "reflects Trump's 'unequivocal contempt for consumers and his unwavering loyalty to the big banks, predatory lenders, and Wall Street special interests.' Mulvaney is 'clearly working from the outside and the inside to destroy the CFPB and cripple its ability to protect consumers from financial predators.' "[731]

If your last name begins with A-J: *You represent the interests of a local nonprofit legal service that represents aggrieved consumers who are victims of federal consumer financial services law violations. Submit a reply to this discussion of no more than four sentences/one paragraph in support of the existing CFPB funding and powers.*

If your last name begins with K-P: *You represent the interests of the Mortgage Bankers Alliance, a national organization whose members are composed of mortgage lenders. Submit a reply to this discussion of no more than four sentences/one paragraph in support of the proposed changes to the CFPB's funding and powers.*

If your last name begins with Q-Z: *You represent the interests of the State Bankers Association, an organization whose members are composed of small depository institutions with less than $10 billion in assets. Submit a reply to this discussion of no more than four sentences/one paragraph, advising the State Bankers Association of how the State Bankers Association should respond to these proposed changes to the CFPB's budget and enforcement powers. You must choose either to support the status quo or to support the proposed changes to the CFPB, but you must offer reasons to your membership that persuades them of which option to support.*

---

[730] Renae Merle, *White House Budget Plan Proposes Cutting CFPB Budget, Restricting Enforcement Powers*, WASH. POST, (Feb. 12, 2018), https://www.washingtonpost.com/news/business/wp/2018/02/12/white-house-budget-plan-proposes-cutting-cfpb-budget-restricting-enforcement-powers/?noredirect=on&utm_term=.7794ef26ff42
[731] *Id.*

ACKNOWLEDGMENTS

Portia M. Jones

Agnes M. Jones

Donell Jones, Sr.

Judy Newberry

Paperback Book Printing

Dury Consulting LLC